T0329719

JOURNALISM IN CRISIS

Bridging Theory and Practice for Democratic Media Strategies in Canada

Journalism in Crisis addresses the concerns of scholars, activists, and journalists committed to Canadian journalism as a democratic institution and as a set of democratic practices. The authors look within Canada and abroad for solutions for balancing the Canadian media ecology.

Public policies have been central to the creation and shaping of Canada's media system and, rather than wait for new technologies or economic models, the contributors offer concrete recommendations for designing public policies that will foster journalism that supports democratic life in twenty-first century Canada. Their work, which includes new theoretical perspectives and valuable discussions of journalism practices in public, private, and community media, should be read by professional and citizen journalists, academics, media activists, policy makers, and media audiences concerned about the future of democratic news coverage in Canada.

MIKE GASHER is a former journalist and professor in the Department of Journalism and director of the Centre for Broadcasting and Journalism Studies at Concordia University.

COLETTE BRIN is a professor in the Département d'information et de communication and director of the Centre d'études sur les médias at Laval University.

CHRISTINE CROWTHER is a PhD candidate at McGill University. She worked as a journalist with the CBC for fifteen years at the regional, national, and international levels.

GRETCHEN KING is a PhD candidate at McGill University. She was news director at Montreal's community radio station CKUT 90.3 FM for ten years.

ERROL SALAMON is a PhD candidate in communication at McGill University and former member of the Community News Collective of CKUT 90.3 FM in Montreal.

SIMON THIBAULT is an assistant professor in the Department of Political Science at the Université de Montréal.

Journalism in Crisis

Bridging Theory and Practice for Democratic Media Strategies in Canada

Edited by
MIKE GASHER, COLETTE BRIN, CHRISTINE
CROWTHER, GRETCHEN KING, ERROL
SALAMON, and SIMON THIBAULT

UNIVERSITY OF TORONTO PRESS
Toronto Buffalo London

© University of Toronto Press 2016
Toronto Buffalo London
www.utppublishing.com

ISBN 978-1-4426-3736-8 (cloth)   ISBN 978-1-4426-2888-5 (paper)

Library and Archives Canada Cataloguing in Publication

Journalism in crisis : bridging theory and practice for democratic media strategies in Canada / edited by Mike Gasher, Colette Brin, Christine Crowther, Gretchen King, Errol Salamon, and Simon Thibault.

Includes bibliographical references and index.
ISBN 978-1-4426-3736-8 (cloth)   ISBN 978-1-4426-2888-5 (paper)

1. Journalism – Canada.   2. Journalism – Social aspects – Canada.
3. Journalism – Political aspects – Canada.   4. Mass media – Canada.
5. Mass media policy – Canada.   6. Democracy – Canada.   I. Gasher, Mike,
1954–, editor   II. Brin, Colette, editor   III. Crowther, Christine (Journalist),
editor   IV. King, Gretchen, editor   V. Salamon, Errol, editor   VI. Thibault, Simon,
1974–, editor

PN4909.J69 2016   302.230971   C2016-902228-5

This book has been published with the assistance of the Social Sciences and Humanities Research Council of Canada's Aid to Research Workshops and Conferences Program and the Aid to Research-related Events program from Concordia University's Office of the Vice-President of Research and Graduate Studies.

University of Toronto Press acknowledges the financial assistance to its publishing program of the Canada Council for the Arts and the Ontario Arts Council, an agency of the Government of Ontario.

Canada Council
for the Arts
Conseil des Arts
du Canada

ONTARIO ARTS COUNCIL
CONSEIL DES ARTS DE L'ONTARIO
an Ontario government agency
un organisme du gouvernement de l'Ontario

Funded by the
Government
of Canada
Financé par le
gouvernement
du Canada

Canada

Remember that freedom of the press is basic to all our freedoms, and that the greatest danger to press freedom is public apathy. So if the media bore you or bother you, don't just sit there. React ... Telephone the owner. Write to the editor. Call in on the hot line. Speak to the advertiser. Praise the performer. Some newspapers and magazines are beginning to open their pages to the people. They call it "participatory journalism." So participate.

Special Senate Committee on
the Mass Media, 1970

Contents

Part Three: New Journalism Practices

Acknowledgments

This collection began with the germ of an idea in Marc Raboy's graduate course in Global Media Governance at McGill University in the spring of 2009. It was incubated in Roberta Lentz's graduate course in Discourse and Policy Activism, and has been nurtured by acquaintances, colleagues, friends, and mentors in academia, activism, and journalism. We are grateful for the enthusiasm and the efforts of everyone who took part in the Journalism Strategies Conference at Concordia and McGill universities in April, 2012, and to the contributors to this collection who agreed to rework substantially their ideas for this book. Thanks to Ilana Hanukov for verifying the references and rendering the citations in their proper style, and thanks to Danielle Gasher for her translation work.

We are also grateful for the financial support of the following: the Social Sciences and Humanities Research Council of Canada's Aid to Research Workshops and Conferences program; the Aid to Research Related Events from Concordia University's Office of the Vice-President of Research and Graduate Studies; Media@McGill; the Centre for the Study of Democratic Citizenship / le Centre pour l'étude de la citoyenneté démocratique; le Centre d'études sur les médias, Université Laval; le Ministère de la Culture, des Communications et de la Condition féminine (Québec); Darin Barney, Canada Research Chair in Technology and Citizenship, McGill University; the Dean of Arts Development Fund, McGill University; Canadian Media Guild / la Guilde canadienne des médias; McGill Institute for the Study of Canada; Art History and Communication Studies Graduate Students Association, McGill University; Department of Journalism, Concordia University.

We would like to thank the reviewers for their comments on earlier drafts of our manuscript and especially our editor at the University of Toronto Press, Siobhan McMenemy. Her guidance and patience were much appreciated.

Finally, we would like to thank those in our personal lives whose daily support makes our work possible.

Journalism – Where to from Here?

A CONVERSATION WITH MARC RABOY
AND FLORIAN SAUVAGEAU

Marc Raboy and Florian Sauvageau have spent their lives in journalism, media analysis, and communication research. For years, they have been considered among the most attentive media observers in Canada. Shaped by different experiences, however, their conception of the ideal journalism is not the same. Sauvageau worked for a long time in mainstream media and occupied editorial management positions. Raboy also worked for some years in mainstream media, but became more involved in alternative, community media and with civil society issues.

Each in his own way has been critical of the media, the one focusing more on reform, the other favouring the development of new structures. They agree on the necessity of a public service mandate for media activities, but they have differing views on the directions and public policy initiatives required to realize such a mandate. They both believe that the state has an important role to play in the media sector, and they have collaborated numerous times on committees and working groups responsible for studying and recommending policy options. Both expect a lot from public broadcasting and are disappointed by the commercial shift of the CBC/Radio-Canada. The explosion of social media and of citizen journalism fills one of them with hope. The other is more sceptical and worries, above all, about the impact of the financial problems of newspapers on newsrooms and the future of mainstream news providers.

In this Foreword, Marc Raboy and Florian Sauvageau exchange thoughts on the Canadian media and public service experience of the past few decades, describe their expectations and disappointments, and consider journalism's future at a time of great disruption and concern.

Florian Sauvageau: This book poses questions about the relationship between journalism and democracy, the future of journalism as an institution, and considers public policy strategies that could contribute to a promising future. I might as well say it now, I am rather pessimistic about the willingness of governments to put in place the necessary public policies. The realities of the past decades seem to justify this pessimism. I will get back to this.

That being said, don't count on me to consult my crystal ball or read the tea leaves and proclaim what the future of journalism will be. I think we need to be wary of those who think they know what journalism will be like tomorrow; they are too often merely charlatans. I know what I want journalism to become, but I do not know what it will be.

The conception of journalism each of us has stems largely from personal experience. Tell me which journalism you follow, and I will tell you who you are. My journalism roots stem from, not only the Quiet Revolution period, which some say was the golden age of journalism in Quebec, but back to the 1950s and the first years of television. Marc being younger than me, our conceptions of journalism are not, in my view, quite the same, even though we can still easily reconcile our differences, considering how many years we have been working together.

My journalism stems from what we call in Quebec *La grande noirceur*, the time of Maurice Duplessis. And in the struggle against *La grande noirceur* I was a teenager, and it was at that time, unconsciously no doubt, that I decided I was going to be a journalist, seeing constantly journalists and intellectuals speaking on television. Gérard Pelletier, who became a Cabinet minister under Pierre Trudeau, André Laurendeau of *Le Devoir*, who afterwards became chair of the Royal Commission on Bilingualism and Biculturalism, René Lévesque, Jean-Louis Gagnon, who created *Le Nouveau Journal* in 1961, a newspaper that, despite its short existence, played an essential role in the transformation of journalism in Quebec. They were all highly visible on Radio-Canada, and I remember them not only because of their assault on Duplessis, but mainly because they made us discover the world, its conflicts, its "*pays et merveilles*," after the title of a program Laurendeau hosted. I admired their comfortable manner and their candid speech; they were role models. Let's remember that Radio-Canada television played, in the years preceding the Quiet Revolution, a vital role in creating an openness to the world and its issues, in helping a modern Quebec evolve, and in forming a Quebec identity.

The journalism of that time was also an intellectual pursuit, illustrated best by Claude Ryan, whose editorials in *Le Devoir* a few years later often set the tone for political debates. It is that kind of journalism that I first got to know, the kind of journalism that helps us better understand the world around us, the kind that I wanted to practise some fifteen years later, when I became the news editor and then the managing editor of Quebec City's daily newspaper *Le Soleil*.

That is also why today, when I am told that journalism must become conversational, in this era of the Internet, that I seem to have trouble adapting. My conception of journalism was formed in another world, where many journalists were, as some would deplore, great pontificators.

Marc Raboy: Indeed, it is good to be reminded that there once was a golden age of journalism in Quebec. It is significant that Florian and I are just slightly of different generations, and that may have made a difference in how we evolved and how we perceive things. I literally fell in love with journalism in the mid-1960s, when I entered McGill University at the age of sixteen and discovered the *McGill Daily*. Anything seemed possible in those days, and journalism to me was a way of participating in the great events of the time. We believed that a student newspaper was an agent of social change, and I would like to think that a newspaper, or any journalistic platform, should see itself as an agent of social change. Looking back, that was perhaps my happiest time as a journalist, and maybe it spoiled me for professional work.

When I finished school, I was immediately offered two jobs in Toronto, at the *Toronto Star* and the *Toronto Telegram*, and I went there. But after six months in Toronto, I was itching to come back to Montreal. I had the opportunity to come back and join the *Montreal Star*, and I was really eager to get back home because there was so much happening. Actually, much like today. I was put on the education beat, which meant covering student demonstrations, language debates, the education reforms of the Quiet Revolution, and most important, the newspaper at that particular moment saw itself as a progressive force in Quebec, or as a force that could at least cover what was going on in a way that contributed to public understanding. The staff of the *Montreal Star* at the time included some of the great francophone Quebec journalists of their generation, many of whom were actually unemployable in the French-language mainstream press of the late 1960s and early 1970s. But something happened almost overnight in 1970 with the outbreak of the October Crisis.

A chill set into the newsroom; happily for me, I was also involved in a small alternative magazine called *Last Post*, which ended up being the journal of record, in English at least, of that period in Quebec. And what I learned during those years, and through practising journalism in a variety of media – although they were all print media – was the importance of the institutional setting in which journalism is practised. I mean, one can be a journalist, one can try to do the best one can, but where one is actually practising journalism ends up being an important part of what one is able to accomplish. At that time, most newspapers in Canada and Quebec were still family-owned – which was better than the chains that succeeded them – but those families were part of the elites and could be expected to behave predictably, in defence of their interests.

The alternative media were often a more important and more interesting source of news and analysis – and for those working in them, conviviality and a sense of purpose. And what one sees when one actually goes back and looks at the different media of the period is how many innovative ideas, political practices, and analyses worked their way into the mainstream from the marginal media of the time. And I think that is very much still the case today. There is one institution which I think bears looking at in a distinct way, and Florian referred to the role of Radio-Canada during the period preceding the Quiet Revolution. I think the public broadcaster, the CBC, has always presented its own particular challenges and opportunities.

Sauvageau: I come back to Radio-Canada, because the role of the state is at the heart of the questions this book poses. It is clear that Radio-Canada has, for many years now, played a crucial role in Quebec's evolution. However, this was not achieved without conflicts, between political authorities and Radio-Canada, but also within Radio-Canada itself, between the management and journalists. In his exceptional book, *Missed Opportunities* (1990), Marc described these battles, demonstrating very well, whether for CBC or Radio-Canada, how difficult it was to reconcile the federal government's desire to have a public broadcaster favouring national unity, the management's classical conception of journalism, and many journalists' desire to be agents of change. I worked at Radio-Canada for a number of years and experienced these tensions first-hand.

Since the 1980s another affliction, probably more pernicious, has affected CBC/Radio-Canada, television in particular: its increasing dependency on advertising revenues to compensate for cuts to its

parliamentary appropriation, by Liberal and Conservative governments alike. The outcome is increasing competition with the private
television networks, and the resultant pursuit of audience ratings too
often compromises the public broadcaster's public service mandate.

Let's return to the larger question of public policy. We cannot consider
future policies without paying close attention to past efforts. The state
has always been interested in the media, originally to be able to control
them. Although there is an important distinction between public broadcasting and state broadcasting, the question of control remains pertinent. But we must give to Caesar what is rightfully his. Public broadcasting, independent of state or corporate power, was created in Great
Britain with the BBC, and this model served a number of countries,
including Canada. Unfortunately, opponents to public broadcasting
seem, in Canada today at least, more vocal than its supporters, many
of whom have abandoned the public broadcaster, disappointed by its
commercial turn. Public broadcasting remains, nonetheless, indispensable. I am speaking here of a real public service.

Nor can we forget the question of media concentration. When media
concentration became a significant issue at the end of the 1960s, well
before Conrad Black and Pierre Karl Péladeau, governments began to
be concerned, as much in Quebec City as in Ottawa. Beginning in the
late 1960s and early 1970s, studies were commissioned and government committees formed, producing numerous reports to gather dust
on library shelves, including the most recent, that of Dominique Payette
(Québec 2010). To return to the title of Marc's book, there were numerous missed opportunities, as many of those reports were plentiful with
interesting suggestions. My favourite is the 1981 report of the Royal
Commission on Newspapers, chaired by Tom Kent. I remember the
first words of the first chapter: "Freedom of the press is not a property
right of owners. It is a right of the people" (Canada 1981, 1). The text
continues by stating that an "undue concentration" of the daily papers
restrains those rights. The newspaper owners clearly didn't appreciate
the Kent Report. There has been no follow-up. And the concentration of
media ownership has not ceased to intensify.

The Kent Report was, in a number of respects, visionary. Already in
1981, long before the Internet, Kent and his colleagues were wary of
what is happening right now. The report hinted at the fact that new
technologies – what was then called telematics – represented an enormous danger for daily newspapers. Readers, felt the members of the
commission, could abandon newspapers for new electronic media, as

could advertisers. This is the predicament we have been experiencing for a few years now with the rise of the Internet and mobile platforms, producing the financial crisis facing the newspaper industry. The dailies, because of the importance of their newsrooms and the number of journalists they employ, still constitute an essential part of the information system because so many other news media rely on the original reporting they produce. Unfortunately, their resources have been eroded and their future remains uncertain.

Raboy: I'm glad that Florian quoted that opening line from the Kent Commission report because, in fact – and we can't say this often enough – freedom of the press and, more broadly, freedom of expression, not only in Canada, but in democratic countries worldwide, really does operate at different levels, depending on whether one actually has the means of communication in one's hands or not. A few years ago, I published with some colleagues, a book that we called *Media Divides* (Raboy and Shtern 2010), which was a kind of democratic audit of the state of communications in Canada, in which we argued that freedom of expression in Canada is a two-tiered freedom because everyone has the formal right of freedom of expression, but it is exercised differentially, depending on one's place in society. And, for a royal commission like the Kent Commission to underscore this fact in its report is really quite impressive.

There was another Canadian government report from a slightly earlier period, which did not focus on journalism per se, but on communications more broadly: *Instant World* (Canada 1971). This report was actually focused on telecommunications, and the authors – interestingly, mostly senior Department of Communication mandarins – called for a right to communicate, or more broadly speaking, a set of communication rights. So, it's interesting that there has been no shortage of interesting proposals coming from public bodies, high-level public bodies, as well as grassroots organizations, non-governmental associations, the different areas of civil society, and of course, from journalists and journalists' associations themselves. And I think if we look back as a way of informing the debate on where we're headed, the problems facing journalism in Canada and Quebec have not really changed in the past century. They've basically come down to a question of the relationship between commerce and public service. We can't put it any more succinctly than that, and we can't get away from this reality. In fact, I would go so far as to suggest that the need to pursue corporate profits in news media has been the Achilles heel of public service journalism.

Among the important efforts to use public policy that Florian mentions, one must certainly include the report that he co-authored with Gerald Caplan in 1986 on federal broadcasting policy (Canada 1986). These efforts all have in common that they situate journalism, and media more broadly, as something that should be looked at outside, or at best alongside, the sphere of commerce and business, although they recognize the place of private commercial enterprise in the media. But media essentially have a public role to play, and this can best be guaranteed by a concerted public policy approach, and a mix of independent public institutions like the CBC and the National Film Board, an independent regulatory authority which has a mandate by law to operate under broad policy guidelines – and we have such an authority in Canada, the Canadian Radio-television and Telecommunications Commission (CRTC) – and public support through funding as well as structural regulation of a range of media institutions, including independent, not-for-profit, non-commercial, community-based media.

If you go through the policy documents, you'll find that all of these mechanisms are mentioned there, and yet our governments have never followed through on most of the proposals. So, our history is littered with excellent proposals, but a remarkable lack of political will to carry them through. This has got to change or we are going to face a serious environmental crisis in the media. I think we're already in the phase of global warming with respect to mainstream media.

Sauvageau: We are indeed already living the crisis that Marc fears. There is the financial crisis that I have already mentioned. But there is more. There is the loss of credibility of the mainstream media, particularly among the younger generations, who perceive the media as serving the financial interests of their owners, and who consider, most often wrongly, journalists as valets in the service of these same interests. The increasing concentration of the media companies accentuates that perception.

There is, finally, some uncertainty regarding the future of journalism and the role of journalists in the universe of citizen journalism. The title of a book published in France some time ago by Éric Scherer (2011), addresses this question quite directly, even brutally: "Do we still need journalists?" in a world where each of us, one could say, can produce his or her own journalism and assure its publication.

Personally, I think that professional journalists are more essential than ever to help us situate ourselves in the sea of information we are drowning in. We live each day in a context of information overload, and we need someone to conduct the triage, to distinguish the essential from the accessory, to establish priorities, to help us better understand our world. Scherer sees the journalist as the "filter of the global informational tsunami," the one who selects and verifies (2011, 23). Isn't this the role journalism has always played? We need only to develop new ways to practise journalism, to better suit this era of interactivity and conversation, by forgetting some of the sermonizing of the past, but without abandoning the ideal of public service that we have discussed.

I will stop here. As I stated in the beginning, no one really knows what the future of journalism will bring. Nor on which platform, fixed or mobile, it will develop. But the platform is not so important; it is the role of journalism and the mission it undertakes that matter most.

Raboy: I am actually upbeat about the future of journalism, which I think has much more to promise than the future of many of the mainstream media institutions that we've been talking about, given the problems they face. The reason I say that is that people want news and information, and they will find ways to make it, and they will find it when it's out there and available. And I'm encouraged by the presence and the rise of a new generation of young journalists as well as new and renewed institutions. It is interesting to note the important investments in quality journalism by some of the new Internet moguls like Jeff Bezos (Amazon), who is resurrecting the *Washington Post* and Pierre Omidyar (eBay) who is starting an ambitious new news organization (First Look Media). I'm confident that new forms of journalistic expression will continue to emerge. The Internet is a new technological frontier, and I think the focus for both citizens and journalists needs to be on keeping the Internet open and accessible, as a space for public discourse. There will be good and bad information on the Internet, just like there were and are good and bad newspapers, magazines, radio, and television.

But if the platform remains open and accessible, the rest will fall into place. And in order to be sure that happens, we need to remain vigilant. In the *Guardian* some time ago, there appeared a seven-part series called "Battle for the Internet" (April, 2012) in which a whole range of gurus, including the founder of Google, Sergey Brin, scholar Jonathan Zittrain, and the creator of the World Wide Web, Sir Tim Berners-Lee, all warned that the principles by which the Internet has evolved are under threat by a combination of governments interested in controlling citizens' communication, the entertainment industry's use of patents, copyright, and intellectual property protection in its attempts to crack down on so-called piracy, and the rise of Internet silos, walled gardens, and appliances, rather than applications under the proprietary control of huge corporate empires like Apple, Facebook, and Google itself. I think the question of digital journalism is at the heart of the future of journalism, and the politics of Internet policy will have a lot to say about that future.

There are also some tremendously important issues that encompass both conventional and new forms of journalism. Deadly attacks on journalists continue in many parts of the world (71 journalists killed in 2014, according to Reporters Without Borders), the role of whistle-blowers from WikiLeaks to Edward Snowden remains to be clarified in press law and jurisprudence, and the aggressive efforts of supposedly liberal governments to prosecute journalists who reveal leaked information they find unsavoury reminds us just how fragile are the freedoms we take for granted.

These are the kinds of issues that we need to be concerned about and thinking of ways to address, and this volume is an excellent contribution to that conversation.

JOURNALISM IN CRISIS

Bridging Theory and Practice for
Democratic Media Strategies in Canada

Introduction: Whose Crisis? Journalism Is Not Just for Journalists and Policy Is Not Just for Wonks

CHRISTINE CROWTHER, SIMON THIBAULT,
ERROL SALAMON, AND GRETCHEN KING

"Crisis" in Context

In everyday language a "crisis" is understood to be an enormous problem that needs to be dealt with immediately. It suggests an element of accident; the problem has dropped on us, out of nowhere, and now we need to scramble to fix it. Take, for example, some of the discussions around the 2008 "global financial crisis" or the "crisis in journalism" – two crises that have been closely linked. Those of us behind this book began our reflections in response to some of the ways in which these discussions were being framed: "Oh no, our readers aren't subscribing to us anymore"; "Oh no, we're losing advertisers"; "Oh no, the Web is wreaking havoc with our business model"; "Oh no, we can't afford to spend money on public broadcasting anymore."

We are, of course, not alone in recognizing and trying to understand this moment in journalism's history, as a growing list of titles can attest (Aamidor et al. 2013; Anderson et al. 2014; Brock 2013; Charles 2014; Jones 2009; McChesney 2012; McChesney and Pickard 2011; Pickard 2011; Sauvageau 2012; Siles and Boczkowski 2012). Pickard (2011) notes, "Although consensus has been reached that journalism is in crisis, few agree on the nature of its decline or the means of resolving it" (73). This is not surprising, given the complex and contested nature of journalism. Simply defining journalism and explaining why it is worth caring about has long occupied those who study journalism (Christians et al. 2009; Scammell and Semetko 2000). These questions have now taken on particular urgency, though, and have become a key part of the project for many researchers investigating the crisis. Aamidor et al. (2013), for example, argue in favour of shoring up what they call quality journalism, which follows the watchdog tradition and aspires to objectivity as an ideal (even as it recognizes its unachievability). "Good journalism," they write, "should provide the information necessary for people to better understand their communities, their states, their country, and the world" (189). Charles (2014), on the other hand, ends the collection he has edited by asking if it is only when journalism "abandons such impossible pretensions" – such as objectivity – "that it may begin to become the popular, pluralist, and openly subjective – and radically inclusive and unpriviledged – mode of storytelling that society at large has always needed it to be" (234).

Siles and Boczkowski's (2012) analysis of the literature around "the newspaper crisis" shows that researchers are employing a broad range of entry points, methods, and theoretical approaches. Some focus on business models (Giles 2010; Kaye and Quinn 2010). Others look more closely at relationships between workforce changes and content (Besley and Roberts 2010; Compton and Benedetti 2010). Still others consider the implications for democratic life (Jones 2009; Nielsen and Levy 2010). Our own approach to the crisis of journalism is rooted in the traditions of political theory, political economy of the news media, cultural studies of journalism, and critical policy studies. We frame the crisis not as the product of chance, but rather of long-standing structural contradictions that have been revealed (Grossberg 2010, 68). Similar to McChesney and Pickard (2011) and Siles and Boczkowski (2012), we believe this crisis is best understood as a moment of decision making.

As we will discuss at greater length later in this chapter, there is clear normative intent in our decision to undertake this project. We believe that what Blumler and Cushion (2014) call "civically relevant" journalism faces enormous problems in Canada and around the world – problems that need to be dealt with immediately. We argue that we all have a choice: we can work to protect forms of journalism that help sustain democratic life, or we can wait and hope new technologies and economic models will deliver what we need. In assembling this book, we are choosing the former. In doing so, though, we also recognize that there are important, nuanced, and even emotional arguments to be had about what that means. This book is meant for readers who believe that journalism has a role to play in democratic life, and who are willing to engage in those arguments on a theoretical and on a practical level.

Because this book was undertaken in this particular historical moment, there are some obvious overlaps with other work being done in this area – particularly that by researchers who have worked closely with the US media reform organization Free Press. As with McChesney and Pickard (2011), we combine theory and practice, drawing on contributions from academics as well as journalists and media activists. As with a number of researchers (see McChesney and Pickard 2011; Pickard et al. 2009), we advocate public policy supports for journalism, a position we will discuss at length later in this chapter.

An important difference, of course, is that the focus of this book is the Canadian, not the US, media system. Another important difference is that while we are attempting to foster conversations about journalism in Canada, we recognize that much can be learned from experiences in other media systems. We have, therefore, decided to incorporate case studies from outside Canada as well – from Australia, Iceland, the United Kingdom, and the United States. As Siles and Boczkowski (2012) note, this approach is not common in the work around the newspaper crisis, where researchers have tended to focus on a single national context. Finally, while a number of works discuss the crisis in the context of particular sectors (such as newspapers), or particular funding models (such as advertising), we adopt the metaphor of the media ecosystem. We believe it is currently out of balance in Canada. We recognize that it comprises a complex mix of print, broadcast, and digital formats, as well as private, public, and community forms of ownership. We have decided that, if we are going to suggest means for rebalancing this ecosystem, we need to include contributors whose work addresses different parts of the whole.

Our own reflections about the crisis stem from what Siles and Boczkowski (2012) call a process-oriented approach; we consider not just how things are, but also how they came to be. Although much of the initial panic has subsided, problems that many have known and talked about in journalistic, activist, and academic circles for decades have now become part of common conversations about journalism thanks to the crisis (Blumler and Gurevitch 1995; Christians et al. 2009; Curran 2000; Habermas 1996; Raboy 1990). There is no doubt the economic and technological shocks of the mid-2000s were responsible for making it impossible to ignore these problems anymore. Yes, viewers, readers, and listeners who didn't feel well-served by legacy news organizations began exploring new alternatives the moment they became available. No, losing audiences is never good news, and, yes, it is even worse when advertisers are suddenly forced to look for ways to cut back themselves. We believe, though, that failure is a more apt way to describe what is happening in journalism than unfortunate coincidence.

We see in the crisis of journalism systemic failures in news organizations themselves and in the governments that helped create the media system they operate in. As Siles and Boczkowski (2012) show, there are any number of lenses through which these failures could be examined – among them, management theory, audience and reception studies, and sociological and cultural theory. We look at them through the lens of journalism and democracy. We decided to come together in this project because we believed that the salience of the crisis in journalism made it possible to consider a national conversation about roles journalism can play in democratic life in Canada in the twenty-first century, and how practices that fulfil those roles can be sustained (Fischer 2003; Soroka 2007; Nerone 2009). In our view, a significant part of the problem facing professional journalism is credibility. At least part of the reason journalism practised by legacy institutions has lost credibility is that many of these institutions have lost sight of their civic function. As Florian Sauvageau suggests in the Foreword he has written with Marc Raboy, the freedoms journalism is given in Canada are not there to protect journalists or journalism organizations; they are there to protect the rights of citizens to share information. Journalism, from our perspective, is therefore a democratic means, not an end in itself.

It is absolutely true that, on a personal scale, this historical moment has brought some very real pain. Good people have lost their jobs through no fault of their own. According to the Pew Research Center's *State of the Media Report*, newspapers in the United States lost more than sixteen thousand full-time jobs between 2003 and 2012 – a 30 per cent drop (Pew Research Center 2014). The report notes that the growth in digital reporting is clearly reshaping "the journalism landscape" in the United States, and it also notes that, so far, "purely in terms of bodies, the growth in digital full-time journalism jobs seems to have compensated for only a modest percentage of lost legacy jobs" (Pew Research Center 2014). Reliable data for Canada are difficult to find, but the general trends appear to be similar. The Canadian Media Guild conducted a review of layoff announcements for the period 2008 to 2013, and came up with a preliminary number of ten thousand job cuts, primarily in the print sector (Canadian Media Guild 2013). Declining revenues are usually cited as the reason for the cuts in the newspaper industry (Bradshaw 2015; Ladurantaye 2013a, 2013b). While the industry remains profitable, revenues are expected to continue falling, leading to ongoing questions about the viability of professional journalism (Edge 2014; Ladurantaye 2013c).

As devastating as the crisis in journalism is to careers and livelihoods, we believe that these personal tragedies would be compounded if we were to waste the opportunities this moment presents. This book is an effort to make the most of these opportunities. We are convinced that we all need a journalism that can help us understand and negotiate the complexity of what it means to be a citizen in the twenty-first century. We are equally convinced that we currently lack the means to ensure that this need can be met.

We are foregrounding strategies because we want to move beyond laments. At the same time, though, we believe we need to consider how much of this crisis in journalism is in fact related to questions we have been wrestling with here in Canada for some time. As the work of media historian Lisa Gitelman reminds us, many of the problems and challenges we think are new are not; they have simply taken on the hues of the times we live in (Gitelman 2006). Raboy and Sauvageau refer in their Foreword to numerous royal commissions and task forces (including the 1981 Royal Commission on Newspapers and the 1986 Task Force on Broadcasting Policy) that have already suggested public policies for addressing questions related to journalism and democracy in Canada. Raboy's book *Missed Opportunities* (Raboy 1990) nicely sums up the challenges many of these bodies have faced in moving from recommendation to implementation. While it is necessary to remember that each of the reports was addressing discrete concerns, many of their recommendations were brought about in response to changing economic and technological conditions. This book is, in part, a means for considering how many of their concerns and how much of their work remain relevant for us in this moment of economic and technological change.

From our perspective, it is in fact possible to see in this previous policy work an evolving conception of Canadian democracy and the role of news media (Crowther 2010). The historical moment we are working in offers not only the opportunity to democratize news media in Canada, but also the tools to make it happen. A great deal has been made of the democratizing power of social media and the Web. They have been popularly credited with helping elect the first black president of the United States, the leaking of hidden truths, and amplifying the 2011 Arab uprisings. While there are serious dangers in giving technology more credit than it is due, the rapid sharing of information does make it possible to seize the moment in ways that have not before been possible. This book is an attempt, therefore, to make the most of this crisis.

Deliberation, Diversity, and Dollars

We like to imagine this book as a means for bringing critically engaged publics together (Fraser 1992; Habermas 1996). We recognize that many different kinds of Canadians are concerned and are having conversations about how to deal with the crisis in journalism, including professional journalists, citizen journalists, academics, audience members, and media activists. We also recognize, though, that many of these conversations occur in isolation. We want to bring together those who believe journalism has a fundamental role to play in the health of our democracy, and who also believe that public policy has a role to play in the health of journalism. Our goal is that these concerned Canadians find ways to work together to conceptualize and advocate for public policies that will support forms of journalism that foster public deliberations. There are, of course, some basic theoretical assumptions underlying our position that we should make clear, the first being that citizens' voices need to be expressed and heard on a continual basis, and not just at election time.

We begin from a normative position that reflects the "strong deliberative turn" that political theory took in the 1990s (Dryzek 2000). It can be summarized as follows: autonomous individuals in a polity come together in a spirit of reciprocity; they do so in spaces where they can expect to hear ideas fundamentally different from their own; and they use their own critical analyses to form judgments that become public opinions that in turn have the potential to influence government decision making on an ongoing basis (Bohman 1996; Habermas 1996; Mouffe 2005; Rancière 1999; Young 2000). While journalism may not be a formal part of public deliberation – because it has neither the authority of the citizen, nor the ability of government representatives to enact laws – it can encourage an orientation towards deliberation and spaces that inform it (Held 2006; Thompson 1995). Habermas's ideal public sphere is, of course, easily recognizable here. A healthy democracy requires a healthy public sphere, a healthy public sphere requires deliberation, and effective deliberation requires diverse actors who have equal opportunities to listen and be heard (Habermas 1996). We argue that journalism can and should provide these opportunities; the problem is that the situation we currently find ourselves in reflects distortions of the public sphere, rather than the ideal (Bohman 1999; Calhoun 1992; Habermas 1996). The private sector can, of course, provide opportunities for the inclusion of diverse voices in the public sphere, and indeed it is to this sector that some are turning to address the crisis in journalism (Anderson et al. 2014; Benkler 2006). The problem of market failure, though, reminds us that we also need public policies (Bohman 1996; Carey 1995; Habermas 1996; Raboy 1990).

In making this argument we are clearly stepping outside traditions of objectivity in both academia and journalism, adopting paths from critical theory (Calhoun 1995; Christians et al. 2009). We are also taking up the challenge of trying to overcome the divide between theory and practice (Napoli and Aslama 2011). Those of us responsible for assembling this book are academics with experience in either community or professional journalism. The research each of us does touches on public policy issues. We recognize the opportunities and responsibilities that come with our scholarly work, and we see in this historical moment possibilities for transforming our reflections into actions. It does not make sense to us to sit comfortably in an analytical capacity when our objects of study are transforming in front of us. This book is, therefore, rooted in our critiques of both professional journalism and public policy-making.

We should note, though, that we all come from different journalism cultures – cultures that reflect the language (English and French), the medium (print, radio, television), and the ownership type (community, private, public) of the different newsrooms in which we have worked (Hanitzsch 2007). We also have different sets of personal experiences and interests that shape our politics. Our ideas about what journalism is and how it should be practised are therefore different as well.

Academically, our approach in bringing this collection together is broadly constructionist (Holstein and Gubrium 2008). We each recognize "that things could be otherwise and that we might make them so" (Weinberg 2008, 35). We apply this approach to democratic life in Canada, practices of journalism, and the relationship between these. We have drawn on our own experiences as practitioners, as well as on academic traditions of political economy, political theory, critical policy studies, and journalism studies to arrive at our mutual starting point; we want to connect the crisis of journalism with journalistic practices, public policies and citizen engagement, and suggest ways for supporting a "virtuous circle" (Norris 2000) of democratic practices in Canada.

We are working within an already-existing framework of scholarly media policy critique inside and outside Canada (Curran and Seaton 2003; Freedman 2008, 2014; Hackett and Zhao 2005; Livingstone and Lunt 2012; Raboy 1990; Raboy and Shtern 2010; Skinner et al. 2005; Taras 2001).

Other reform-minded media scholars around the world are also suggesting public policy solutions to what they identify as inadequate diversity and pluralism in their own media systems (Freedman 2008; Freedman et al. forthcoming; McChesney 2007). While this book is one of the few within this framework to focus on journalism, there is in fact a long history in Canada, the United States, and in other countries of using public policies to support journalism (Nielsen and Linnebank 2011; Pickard 2011; Pickard et al. 2009; Raboy 1990; Skinner et al. in this volume).

As Nielsen and Linnebank (2011) point out, there is a range of cultural, historical, and social reasons for this support. In Canada, of course, the country's immense geography and relatively small population have provided a rationale for subsidies and regulation in the communications sector (Gasher et al. 2016). In the particular case of journalism, there is a long-standing concern over the implications of ownership concentration in Canada. As mentioned earlier, a series of parliamentary reports has raised significant questions and made specific policy recommendations. In addition to the 1981 Royal Commission on Newspapers and the 1986 Task Force on Broadcasting Policy cited by Raboy and Sauvageau, these also include the 1970 Special Senate Committee on Mass Media (the Davey Committee) and the 2006 Standing Senate Committee on Transportation and Communication. As David Skinner, Kathleen Cross, and Robert Hackett note in their chapter, many of the key recommendations of these reports and commissions were not implemented. They were, however, prescient, and help us make the argument that meeting the information needs of a diverse Canadian population requires policy intervention.

The 2000s have seen a period of rapid and ongoing shifts in who owns which pieces of the Canadian media system (Skinner et al. 2005; Winseck 2014). Even as we write, another massive shift may be taking place (Bradshaw 2014b; Evans 2014; Quebecor 2014). One thing that has remained consistent is that a few players control the majority of news organizations in the country. Data from the associations representing daily, weekly, and community newspapers show that five ownership groups control 73 per cent of the daily titles in the country, and that nine ownership groups control 59 per cent of the community titles (Newspapers Canada 2015). According to Winseck (2014), that trend is even more pronounced in the television sector. "In 2013," he writes, "the top four television providers controlled 80 percent of all television revenues." Winseck's research shows, in fact, that four "giant" vertically integrated conglomerates (Bell, Rogers, Shaw, and Québecor), with holdings in telecoms, media, and Internet, control 57 per cent of the revenue for what he calls the "network media ecology" in Canada (Winseck 2014).

The private sector is, of course, only one component of the Canadian media ecosystem. The Broadcasting Act specifies that the Canadian broadcasting system is comprised of "public, private, and community elements" (Canada 1991). As a number of the chapters in this book discuss, though, there are serious questions about the ability of community and public broadcasters to bear responsibility for effectively representing the country's diversity (King et al.; Skinner et al.; Wirsig and Edwards). In their chapter, Wirsig and Edwards note that there are only nine community-owned and -administered television channels in the country; the rest, they write, are run by cable companies. While there are considerably more community radio stations, King et al. write that it is proving difficult for them to develop news departments. In both cases, the authors point to the absence of sustainable funding as a key problem. As Skinner, Cross, and Hackett note in their chapter, it is also a problem for the Canadian Broadcasting Corporation/Société Radio-Canada (CBC/SRC). In addition to being Canada's national public service broadcaster, CBC/SRC is the country's largest news organization. Its funding is based on a hybrid model of public and private sources. CBC management has responded to declining revenues from both sources by cutting jobs and services (CBC 2014; Radio-Canada 2014; Wong 2014). We argue that this all combines to present serious challenges to diversity that cannot simply be offset by changes in technology that offer possibilities for wider citizen participation (Fenton 2010).

We propose that, in looking to the future of journalism in Canada, it is necessary to acknowledge an ongoing evolution of journalism norms, away from its libertarian roots – to which scholars such as Merrill (1974, 2006) suggest it is important to stay firmly attached – through the pluralism of the social responsibility paradigm and, now, towards more participatory models (Christians et al. 2009; Jenkins 2006a). While these more participatory models lend themselves to practices that can be seen as a reaction to the organizational and financing models that have been associated with professional journalism (Atton and Hamilton 2008; Forde 2011; Witschge 2013), they are not necessarily antithetical to long-held ideals of professional journalists (Ward 2004). We, in fact, argue that there are many ways in which journalism that serves the broad goals of citizen participation and deliberation can be delivered (Romano 2010; Forde 2011). We believe the crisis in journalism provides an opportunity to move beyond discussions about citizen versus mainstream journalism, new versus old media, private versus public versus community media, and international versus national versus local news. The challenge we undertook in putting this collection together was to identify existing and emerging practices that meet the goals of citizen participation and deliberation, as well as strategies for sustaining them. It is an approach very much in keeping with what Blumler and Cushion (2014) suggest is necessary for advancing the field of journalism studies.

What are we working towards? In short, we seek mobilization within Canada's political public sphere, something made imaginable by this moment of crisis. In his reconceptualization of the public sphere, Habermas (1996) includes a more sophisticated approach to civil society than was present in his earlier work, one in which its latent power is significant. He writes that in times of crisis, "the structures that actually support the authority of a critically engaged public begin to vibrate. The balance of power between civil society and the political system then shifts" (379). We would like both to take advantage of the power of civil society and to strengthen it. We see in this historical moment opportunities to create and implement public policies that will sustain forms of journalism that will themselves help put the latent power of civil society into action on an ongoing basis.

Contributors

Who are the authors in this book? We think it is fitting – and are in fact grateful – that Marc Raboy and Florian Sauvageau agreed to write the Foreword. Both have devoted much of their working lives to the intersection of journalism and public policy. Both have played leading roles in discussions about the need for public policies that support a healthy media system in Canada for close to thirty years now. Each has been a journalist, an academic, and an adviser on government policy. Among their contributions are two of the Canadian government's policy reports alluded to earlier: *The Report of the Task Force on Broadcasting Policy* (1986; also known as the Caplan-Sauvageau Report) and *Our Cultural Sovereignty: The Second Century of Canadian Broadcasting* (2003; also known as the Lincoln Report.) Their Foreword puts the work of the other contributors here into context, reflecting in a very personal way on the pressures, obligations, and opportunities facing journalists who wish to serve public interests.

The other authors are members of publics we are attempting to engage. A challenge for a book like this is that the policy community we are addressing is extremely diverse. There are many publics, each with its own ways of understanding and describing problems (Fischer 2003). The French-English linguistic divide in Canada is perhaps the most obvious example, but scholars, policy-makers, activists, journalists, executives in journalism organizations, and members of audiences also have their own languages and starting points. Since one of our goals is to bring these different actors into conversation with each other, we have tried as much as possible to incorporate different kinds of voices in this collection – hence the variations in style and experience.

Two of the chapters are written by contributors who have worked as journalists, in the private sector and in the community sector. Sneha Kulkarni has worked as a reporter for CTV News and as a daytime news anchor with Sun News Network. Gretchen King, Chris Albinati, Anabel Khoo, Candace Mooers, and Jacky Tuinstra Harrison have been contributors to *GroundWire: Community Radio News*, a bi-weekly community radio news magazine that is co-produced and aired by community radio stations across the country. Another chapter is written by two media activists: Karen Wirsig does outreach for the Canadian Media Guild (CMG) and Catherine Edwards is the co-founder of the Canadian Association of Community Television Users and Stations (CACTUS). The remaining chapters are written by academics, some whose scholarly reputations are emerging and others who have long-established publishing records. We are particularly pleased these senior scholars have contributed to this project.

The newcomers include Chantal Francoeur, a former Radio-Canada journalist and communication scholar who is now a professor at the Université du Québec à Montréal, and Christopher Ali, an assistant professor in the Department of Media Studies at the University of Virginia. They also include Robert Washburn and Vincent Raynauld, who have collaborated on their chapter. Washburn is a print journalist who teaches in the journalism program at Loyalist College in Belleville, Ontario. Raynauld is an assistant professor in the Department of Communication Studies at Emerson College in Boston. He is also serving as a research fellow in the Engagement Lab at Emerson College, and as a research associate with Groupe de recherche en communication politique (GRCP) based at Université Laval.

Two other chapters are also collaborations. Senior scholar David Skinner, a professor in the Department of Communication Studies at

York University in Toronto, has teamed up with two other senior scholars, Kathleen Cross and Robert Hackett, both of whom are professors in the School of Communication at Simon Fraser University in Vancouver. Hackett has also collaborated on a chapter with Pinar Gurleyen, a doctoral candidate in his department. Senior scholars with their own chapters are Greg Nielsen, chair of the Department of Sociology and Anthropology at Concordia University in Montreal and co-director of the Concordia Centre for Broadcasting and Journalism Studies; Michael Meadows, a former journalist and adjunct professor of journalism in the School of Humanities at Griffith University in Brisbane, Australia; and Arne Hintz, a lecturer at the School of Journalism, Media and Cultural Studies at Cardiff University, Wales, and director of the School's MA in Digital Media and Society. Hintz is also chair of the Community Communication Section, and vice-chair of the Global Media Policy Working Group of the International Association for Media and Communication Research (IAMCR).

Contributions: Public Strategies for Journalism in the Canadian Media Ecosystem

The terms *public* and *media ecosystem* can be extremely slippery. The strategies discussed here are intended as contributions to public opinion about media policies and practices in Canada (Arendt 2005; Dewey 1927; Habermas 1996; Raboy 2006). As discussed earlier, we contend the media system created by these policies and practices is analogous to an ecosystem that is currently out of balance. We have asked the authors to reimagine the role of journalism in Canada and the ways different actors in the Canadian media ecosystem could complement each other. Their contributions reflect our perception that in Canada, as elsewhere, we are facing fundamental questions about the role of professional journalism in our democratic lives. Canadian society and the Canadian mediascape are structured very differently now than they were a century ago, when many of the current ideas about journalism as a practice were being consolidated. New, decentred, journalism practices are increasingly reforming and providing alternatives to professional journalism's conventional normative, organizational, and funding models. We believe it is necessary to ask what remains relevant, and what might need to be reconsidered.

We have also asked the authors to go a step further, to recommend policies that could sustain practices that might help rebalance the

Canadian media ecosystem. While most of the contributions to this book focus solely on policies and practices in Canada, three help broaden our perspective, providing insights into experiences in Australia, Iceland, the United Kingdom, and the United States. We have sought out experiences beyond Canada's borders because the crisis of journalism is not Canada's alone. We believe discussions about the future of journalism in our own media system will be made richer if we also reflect on strategies being pursued in other national contexts. So, who do we imagine taking part in these discussions? Our next section will explain who this book is for, and how the various chapters speak to the active audiences with whom we wish to engage (Livingstone 2005).

Journalists are sometimes too busy meeting deadlines or too sceptical to think a collection like this is relevant reading; nevertheless, we are certainly writing with them in mind. Of course, "Who is a journalist?" is a question frequently asked in the context of the new technological environment, one in which work produced by people hired by newspapers, radio stations, TV stations, and magazines shares space with blogs, tweets, and postings on Facebook. It is also a question that became the focus of intense debates in Canada thanks to a report produced for the Government of Quebec in 2010. The report, *L'information au Québec: Un intérêt public*, is often referred to as the Payette Report, after its lead author, Dominique Payette, a former Radio-Canada journalist who is now a professor in the Département d'information et de communication at Université Laval. Payette's mandate was to study the impact new technologies and the general crisis of the media were having on the ability of Quebecers to access the quality information that was seen to be fundamental to their participation in democratic life (Québec 2010). One of her working group's key recommendations was the adoption of a law that would provide a formal status for professional journalists. The argument was that this would make it possible to encourage journalism that followed strict norms (78). Perhaps predictably, some welcomed the recommendation as a means for journalists to push back against employers more focused on profits than public life, while others cringed at the thought of what this might mean for freedom of expression. We think this debate opens up important avenues of discussion, and the way we use the term *journalist* is deliberately broad – including, for instance, freelancers, staffers at legacy news organizations, and citizens producing news reports and commentary on their own time. Our position is that, though they may do it in different contexts, they all do the work of informing their audiences about current affairs.

The chapters in this book are in part an acknowledgment and exploration of the challenges of doing that work at this moment in history. It is a job journalists are doing while basic principles, such as objectivity, are being questioned and adapted, if not changed. Some might wonder if evolving notions of editorial independence might provide more fruitful discussions than a highly contested value such as objectivity. We agree that editorial independence is indeed important. We also believe, though, that it is necessary to consider how objectivity, as a traditional keystone to professional journalistic practice, relates to questions of editorial independence, both historically and in the contemporary context (Hackett and Zhao 1998; Ward 2004).

It is for that reason that we start the book with Pinar Gurleyen and Robert Hackett's contribution. They argue that "multiple and intersecting crises" such as climate change, financial instability, and globalized inequalities make now the time to reimagine the role of journalism. Their work continues Hackett and Zhao's (1998) argument that "the regime of objectivity" that has long guided North American journalism actually limits possibilities for public deliberation. Rather than arguing that journalistic objectivity should be abandoned, though, they suggest a shift. Gurleyen and Hackett recommend journalism redefine itself as a crisis discipline and "discard some of the ossified practices of objectivity that stifle political understanding and engagement, while maintaining a commitment to the truth."

Greg Nielsen also addresses traditional notions of objectivity in his chapter, arguing that the impersonal "view from nowhere" creates a frame that can limit the power of journalistic subjects who are not part of implied audiences, such as undocumented migrants and religious and cultural minorities. Nielsen suggests journalists replace objectivity with a "commitment to the story," using their research skills and their power within the public sphere to "provide fairness in dialogue rather than neutral and passive detachment."

One of the reasons questions about objectivity are particularly resonant right now is the introduction of new technologies that, as discussed earlier, make it possible for more people to share information quickly and widely. These technologies represent both opportunities and challenges for professional journalists, who often find themselves having to use tools that are either becoming outdated, or are still in the experimental stages. Two chapters consider the impact these technologies are having on day-to-day practices in newsrooms. Sneha Kulkarni presents a case study of the G20 Summit that took place in Toronto. She analyses Twitter updates on the #G20 hashtag during the afternoon of 26 June 2010 – significant, she writes, because "it represents an evolving breaking news story, during which time a peaceful protest turned chaotic." Kulkarni tracks tweets sent by professionals and non-professionals in an effort to understand their relationship. She observes that what unfolds suggests partnership, rather than competition; Twitter followers certainly contributed information themselves, but they often chose to re-tweet posts from journalists working for legacy news organizations instead of those from other eyewitnesses. Kulkarni suggests the lesson for newsrooms is that members of online communities can actually reinforce the authority of professionals, providing a means for "improving the message itself and its reach."

Chantal Francoeur's contribution also speaks to newsroom leaders. Her case study focuses on Radio-Canada's efforts to integrate journalism on all its platforms: radio, television, and the Web. In 2010, Radio-Canada attempted to create a cultural shift within the organization, wherein journalists would consider themselves "part of the same tribe," rather than being split between the different media platforms. Ethnographic research Francoeur conducted in the newsroom during this period indicates the attempt resulted in a loss of identity and a "sens dessus-dessous" for the journalists: a state of turmoil. Follow-up interviews Francoeur conducted eighteen months later indicated the integration had, for the most part, not resulted in journalists working across platforms; instead, most had returned to their traditional methods of working and their traditional media. Recognizing the opportunities presented by integration, though, Francoeur asks the question: is there another way it could be managed, one that would preserve the cultural distinctions of journalists who work in radio or television, and at the same time use their expertise in a multiplatform universe? She offers a small-scale experiment Radio-Canada conducted in the suburbs of Montreal as a possible model to follow. *Projet 450* brought together a team of ten people, each with his or her own speciality. Its primary medium was the Web, but this was used to bring together text, audio, and video. Francoeur concludes that allowing journalists to work in teams that build on their medium-specific strengths can give them the confidence, and perhaps even desire, to discover new ways of interacting with their audiences in the formats that are evolving, offering the promise of turning the topsy-turvy world of newsroom integration "right side up."

Three chapters in the collection shift questions from professional practices and norms to the needs of particular communities that are not necessarily included in mainstream news media. The authors define the boundaries of their communities differently, with Michael Meadows choosing culture, Robert Washburn and Vincent Raynauld choosing geography, and Gretchen King and colleagues choosing interests. Each of these chapters includes a case study that explores how a different model can produce forms of journalism that make it possible for community members to speak to each other.

Meadows also reflects on how this could lead to more effective conversations between members of subaltern and mainstream publics. His chapter focuses on roles of Indigenous media. He describes the strong similarities between the Australian and Canadian Aboriginal broadcasting sectors, and suggests that "at a time when trust of mainstream media in Canada, Australia, the United Kingdom, the United States, Ireland, and Northern Ireland are at an all-time low (Hanitzsch 2013), it is worthwhile exploring the modus operandi of a sector that is perhaps too often overlooked because of its perceived peripheral nature." Meadows delves deeply into a case study of Indigenous radio and television in Australia, employing Fraser's (1992) rethinking of the public sphere to help him frame his argument. He outlines ways in which media by and for Aboriginal and Torres Straight Islander communities act in parallel with mainstream media, arguing that these media both enhance the Indigenous public sphere and provide a cultural bridge to non-Indigenous public spheres: "They enable Indigenous people to deliberate together, to develop their own counter-discourses, and to interpret their own identities and experiences." In the process, "they provide sites for public opinion formation; sites where citizens can engage in collective efforts to bring their issues to the dominant public sphere; and sites where Indigenous people can attempt to influence the policies of various governments through the pressures of public opinion." Meadows suggests one way that non-Indigenous journalists could work to address the exclusion of Indigenous voices from the mainstream would be to pay more attention to both Aboriginal media processes and products.

Washburn and Raynauld focus on journalism in small-town Canada. Similar to Meadows, they argue that community journalism not only serves informational needs for its residents, but also helps sustain a community's identity and enhances "the development of social capital." They point to a worrying trend in Ontario. While the number of community newspaper titles is growing, they argue it is not indicative of an increase in community journalism; instead, they argue, it reflects "corporate owners expanding to accommodate advertisers who look to newspaper chains for convenient distribution networks." Washburn and Raynauld write that, as chain publishers find themselves under the same financial pressures felt elsewhere, there is actually a trend away from local content and towards regionalization. The result is that content carried in the community papers "is often created outside the community and has little direct reference to the audiences being served." They suggest the digital environment makes it possible to counter this trend, providing low-cost production platforms for community news media in "geographically narrow locations across Canada." They discuss at length an experiment conducted over the course of one year. Online technologies were used to create hyperlocal coverage for the town of Cobourg in south-central Ontario. *Consider This* was run by Washburn in cooperation with citizen journalists and was intended to fill gaps in local news coverage. Washburn and Raynauld argue that the contributions of citizen journalists were essential, allowing in-depth coverage of local elections, issues, and events that wasn't being offered by corporate media. They point out that sustainability was a significant problem, but suggest that, with adequate support, a model of this kind could be used to revitalize journalism in underserved communities.

King et al. adopt a national perspective in their chapter. They write that while there is a growing body of academic work related to alternative media and community radio, "there is a lack of focus on the challenges that national community-based journalism poses to traditional journalism practices, whether public or commercial, national or local." They explore the case of *GroundWire*, a biweekly community news magazine produced by journalists working in campus and community radio stations across the country. One of the goals of *GroundWire* is "to create national connections between local communities and social movements, no matter how small." King et al. write that *GroundWire* provides both training and a platform for people whose voices and interests are often left out by professional journalists who work for organizations seeking wide audiences. Like Washburn and Raynauld, they also address the problem of sustainability. They suggest a solution lies in the Broadcasting Act, which recognizes the community broadcasting sector as an element of the Canadian broadcasting system, alongside the public and private sectors.

A number of the chapters in this book make specific recommendations for public policies that affect the enabling environment, structural conditions in the media system that can influence the way journalists do their jobs (Price and Krug 2000). Among these recommendations are the following: appointing a representative from the community sector to the Canadian Radio-television and Telecommunications Commission (CRTC); expanding regional development programs to include media-based businesses; stabilizing funding for the CBC; establishing a national digital strategy; and creating tax deductions for donations from individuals and corporations who wish to support particular journalism organizations. Historically, journalists have guarded jealously – and with good reason – their independence. As alluded to in the title of this Introduction, though, journalism is not just for journalists. It is for this reason that this book is also aimed at policy-makers, policy activists, and policy recipients. In essence, everyone who lives or works in Canada.

The contribution from David Skinner, Kathleen Cross, and Robert Hackett explains in detail that the development and practice of journalism in Canada has long been shaped by public policies, from a 1917 decision by the federal government to provide an annual subsidy to Canadian Press, to federal policy positions in the 1990s that paved the way for cross-media ownership deals that "radically altered the Canadian mediascape." One of the premises underlying this book is, of course, that policy is not just for wonks. It does not descend from on high in the form of stone tablets, decipherable only by politicians and analysts. It is, rather, the product of a chain of decision making, and our goal is to broaden the number and type of actors in this chain (Fischer 2003). As Skinner et al. point out, though, democratization of media policy in Canada faces enormous challenges. Among them, the divided strategies and goals of reform advocates; the "political quiescence of journalists themselves"; and the need for stable funding for campaigns. However, the authors aren't entirely pessimistic and thus provide three brief case studies of what they call promising initiatives: Media Democracy Day, OpenMedia, and Reimagine CBC. "Such citizen-led mobilization," they write, "combined with journalistic support for policy change, is the kind of energy needed to reinvigorate Canadian journalism."

Three additional chapters focus primarily on public policies, but they do so in different national contexts. Karen Wirsig and Catherine Edwards look exclusively at Canada; Christopher Ali suggests research lessons from the United Kingdom and the United States could be applied here; and Arne Hintz draws together examples of policy innovation and advocacy from Canada and around the world. Wirsig and Edwards recommend that members of the community and public sectors of the Canadian broadcasting system form strategic partnerships in underserved communities. In making this recommendation they are considering communities of interest as well as communities that are geographically defined. They observe that both the community and public sectors have a public service mandate, but "can barely keep up with what they are doing today." In proposing their alternative, Wirsig and Edwards outline examples of how the two sectors have in the past, and could once again, work together to "improve local media infrastructure in Canadian cities, towns, and rural areas." They suggest sharing transmission infrastructure, production facilities, and even content, personnel, or production methodologies. Once again, of course, questions of motivation and sustainability arise. Wirsig and Edwards suggest one way to encourage such cooperation would be to establish a fund that would be available to both the CBC and to local community media organizations.

Ali problematizes what it means to be "local" and how, if at all, that level of the media system can be protected in a "digital, neo-liberal, and global age." He points out that broadcast regulators in both the United Kingdom and the United States have already undertaken research projects to "gauge the status" of what they respectively refer to as the "local media ecology" or "local news ecosystem." He discusses this research in the context of recent Canadian regulation that applies to providers of local news and information, arguing that Canadian efforts have been piecemeal. He recommends a comprehensive review of local news and information ecologies in Canada that would include consideration of the definitions of local and regional; consideration of all platforms and institutional models; and finally, identification of key actors, a task, he writes, that is "unrealizable without an understanding of the system as a whole."

Hintz's chapter focuses on protecting "future journalisms" whose practices are emerging as new technologies are developing. He begins by carefully outlining "shifts, dynamics and transformations" at play in media landscapes around the world. He argues these processes could lead to what Yochai Benkler has referred to as the "networked 4th estate," which includes layers of traditional news media, platforms like Wikileaks, and other information-sharing innovations discussed throughout this book. Among the policy challenges Hintz says this new fourth estate is facing in Canada and elsewhere are information control, technical infrastructure, and of course, surveillance. In the second part of his chapter, Hintz turns his attention to initiatives advocates are undertaking in an effort to meet those challenges. He uses examples from Canada, the United States, Argentina, and Europe. He also presents a case study of Icelandic Modern Media Initiative, since 2011 renamed the International Modern Media Institute (IMMI), to illustrate how policy can be used to protect the networked fourth estate and "modern freedom of expression." The goal of the IMMI is to "make Iceland a 'safe haven' for freedom of expression and investigative journalism" by putting in place new laws that will apply to all information originating from, or routed through, Iceland. Hintz calls the IMMI "an exemplary case of a civil society campaign that seeks to circumvent restrictions to journalism and free expression by transforming a national policy environment." He writes that the initiative resulted from the "post-crisis policy window" opened in the wake of Iceland's economic collapse in 2008. Activists used an approach he calls policy hacking, with "cherry-picked laws and regulations from other countries." Hintz notes that part of the success of the campaign was that it moved beyond simply advocating for change, and instead undertook to construct a new policy environment. This is, of course, the spirit in which this book is written.

As the numerous contributions from scholars might suggest, this book is also for academics – from the social sciences, from public administration, and from the humanities. It is particularly aimed at those interested in negotiating the divide between theory and practice. Academics are uniquely placed to support the work of journalists and policy-makers. A challenge, of course, is overcoming ontological and epistemological differences between their working worlds. The chapters included here reflect very different traditions of scholarship, including political economy and cultural studies. Part of the reason for including the range of voices we have in this collection is to help researchers recognize common concerns, and perhaps discover new insights by looking at their objects of study from new vantage points.

Conclusion

Our hope in bringing these chapters together is not to present readers with a final word on where journalism and public policy should be at this moment in time. Our hope, rather, is to open up spaces for discussion among Canadians who share concerns about the ability of journalism in this country to fulfil its civic potential and who would like to use "the crisis in journalism" to turn those concerns into action. We also hope these discussions will themselves open opportunities to recognize and negotiate important differences between the many stakeholders of journalism in Canada. The vast territory and array of cultures from coast to coast to coast can present enormous challenges to anyone considering a project of this kind. Our concluding chapter considers ways that those wishing to take up this project might make it a genuinely diverse undertaking. Recognizing and negotiating differences need not, however, be seen as a burden; these differences have, in fact, been an important impetus for the kinds of creative policy-making being suggested in this book.

PART ONE

New Thinking about Journalism

1 Who Needs Objectivity? Journalism in Crisis, Journalism for Crisis

PINAR GURLEYEN AND ROBERT A. HACKETT

The freedom of the press consists primarily in not being a trade.

Karl Marx

Freedom is the recognition of necessity.

G.W.F. Hegel

We live in a world of multiple and intersecting crises (see, e.g., Cottle 2009a, 1–25). In particular, these include climate change and resource depletion; actual and potential political violence, exemplified by a decade of "terror war" (Kellner 2003); stateless refugees and economic migration; financial instability and periodic meltdowns; globalized inequality and poverty; and arguably, under the surface, a crisis of meaning and of confidence in a decent and shared human future, crudely signalled by contradictory catch phrases like "the clash of civilizations" and "overlapping communities of fate."

We may have already passed certain tipping points that put the continuation of human civilization in question. But if there is hope for avoiding an irreversible nosedive, no solutions that are both effective and just can be imagined without the sustained attention, prioritization, and mobilization of social movements to challenge the inertia of institutions and the self-interest of elites.

As the most important form of storytelling in our culture, journalism is integral to that process. It is not only "the textual system of modernity" (Hartley 2008, 312), but it also constitutes "a dominant force in the public construction of common experience and a popular sense of what is real and important" (Schudson 2003, 13). Hence journalism plays a twofold role with respect to crisis communication. On the one hand, news media contribute to the discursive construction of crisis by selecting and defining certain issues over others to be characterized as crisis (Cottle 2009a, 165). On the other hand, news media occupy a crucial role in preventing or overcoming the destructive impact of crisis by providing the public with adequate information and consequently mobilizing government and civil society initiatives. The 2008 financial crisis in the United States and its inadequate coverage by the news media show clearly how devastating the effects can be when journalism falls short of fulfilling this latter role (Schechter 2009).

In this chapter, we argue that with respect to the critical challenges human society faces, journalism should be reoriented as a self-reflexive crisis discipline, one that accepts an ethical obligation to help inform, engage, and empower publics. Yet certain established norms and practices of conventional journalism may hinder this process significantly. Among these, "the regime of objectivity" (Hackett and Zhao 1998) deserves particular attention. Research shows that some aspects of journalistic objectivity, such as balanced reporting and over-reliance on elite sources, can cause misinformation in crisis coverage.

While pointing out its shortcomings, we do not argue for abandoning journalistic objectivity. Such an approach would leave us with epistemological relativism, the philosophical idea that all knowledge is so context-dependent that there is no neutral way to choose between competing knowledge claims. Instead, we suggest adopting a critical realist position that "upholds one, positive side of the journalistic regime of objectivity – the impulse towards sceptical, investigative, critical examination of contemporary events – but also exposes the other, negative side – the sacrifice of investigative spirit to routine, safe, standardized, and therefore superficial practices, such as 'balance'" (Hackett and Zhao 1998, 134).

It is now commonplace to regard journalism itself as in a state of crisis (e.g., McChesney and Nichols 2010). Dimensions of this crisis include legitimacy and credibility; economic sustainability (rich media corporations, but decreasing investment in journalism); cutbacks to public service broadcasting; a shift from a public service ethos and "serious" civic news, to commercially driven infotainment; and declining and fragmenting audiences who are less interested in political engagement than were previous generations.

But this is a Western/North American–centric view. In terms of economic strength and institutional autonomy, journalism is growing new legs in some of global capitalism's "emerging markets" and "transition societies." Even in the West, new and experimental forms of journalism are emerging, such as citizens' journalism, the blogosphere, public journalism 2.0, and a reinvigorated alternative journalism (Atton and Hamilton 2008). David Skinner and his co-authors elaborate on this point in chapter 3. We argue that what is in crisis may not be journalism as such, but a particular paradigm with its associated institutional forms: the regime of objectivity.

Hackett and Zhao (1998) suggest that in contemporary North American journalism, objectivity constitutes a kind of multifaceted discursive "regime," an interrelated complex of ideas and practices that provide a general model for conceiving, defining, arranging, and evaluating news texts, practices, and institutions. They identify five dimensions in this regime.

First, objectivity comprises goals that journalists should strive for. These can be divided into values concerning journalism's ability to impart information about the world (separation of fact from opinion, accuracy, completeness), and values concerning the stance that reporters should take towards the value-laden meanings of news (detachment, neutrality, impartiality and independence, avoiding partisanship, personal biases, ulterior motives, or outside interests) (McQuail 1992).

Second, such values are assumed to be embodied in a set of newsgathering and presentational practices, such as "documentary reporting practices" that allow reporters to transmit only facts that they can observe or that credible sources have confirmed (Bennett 2009, 193), and the separation of "fact" from "opinion" in newspaper pages.

Third, these values imply a set of assumptions about knowledge and reality. On the one hand, the ideal of "accuracy" entails a positive faith in the possibility of faithful descriptions of the world-as-it-is, through the careful observation and disinterested reporting of events. On the other hand, the practice of providing "balance" between contending viewpoints implies a concession to the epistemological position of conventionalism, which holds that human perception of the world is always mediated by our mental categories and our procedures of knowledge production.

Fourth, objectivity is embedded in an institutional framework. It presumes journalism is conducted by professionals with appropriate skills, employed within specialized institutions (news organizations, usually corporate-owned, but with separated editorial and marketing functions). In their relations with the broader society, journalists and news media are assumed to enjoy legal guarantees of speech and press freedom and independence from the state as well as political parties and other outside interests.

Fifth, objectivity is an active ingredient in public discourse. Objectivity provides the language for everyday assessments of journalistic performance. This language includes synonyms, such as "fairness" and "balance," which some people see as more flexible and achievable substitutes for objectivity. Objectivity is often counterposed to "bias," most frequently political partisanship, as well as propaganda.

The regime of objectivity was subjected to many political and academic critiques in the polarized climate between the 1960s and 1980s. Critics argue that it led journalism to an over-reliance on official sources, to collude with and/or amplify the dominant ideology to the benefit of elites, to distort public issues by reducing them to two-sided, zero sum contests, to adopt practices that undermine democratic public life (such as a stance of cynical negativism divorced from coherent analytical perspectives), to frame politics as a game of insiders motivated only by electoral success, and to prioritize facts and events over processes, conditions, explanations, or context. Implicitly, the critics thus identified many facets of journalism that would impede effective crisis communication.

To some extent, these critiques are now moot, as the regime has been hollowed out and undermined by a number of developments, including the deregulation of broadcasting; cutbacks to public service broadcasters; the decline of the public service ethos in favour of commercialism; the eroding economic basis of the news organizations that constituted the bastion of the objectivity regime; the swallowing of news organizations by conglomerates more interested in short-term profits than investing in "prestige" journalism; the return of partisan journalism; and audience fragmentation and the dispersal of "the public" (as Greg Nielsen addresses in chapter 2); political disengagement; the irruption of the Internet with its capacities to replace the mediators of official perspectives with first-person accounts and unconstrained opinion.

In some ways, the forms of journalism – or post-journalism – unleashed by these developments are as problematic for democratic empowerment as the ossified regime they undermined. The influence of Rupert Murdoch's Fox TV network on news facilitates not only the disintegration of publics into opinion tribes, but arguably removes the very expectation of reasoned argument, evidence-based conclusions, and respectful dialogue. No less than the regime's old conventions of "balance," the rant-ridden blogosphere reinforces epistemological relativism. That is, truth is in the eye of the beholder; all that is needed is "credibility" (or, in satirist Stephen Colbert's memorable neologism, "truthiness"), well-constructed narratives "designed not to represent reality but to bolster a political agenda" (Baym 2010, 139). Infotainment and the emotive/human-interest stance of much reportage (such as the "journalism of attachment" in reporting conflicts like NATO's intervention in Kosovo, or Christie Blatchford's flush-faced accounts of court proceedings in Postmedia newspapers) reinforce a personalized, blame-assigning view of public affairs, divorced from structure and context (Calcutt and Hammond 2011, 114–15). A sneering attitude towards politicians in general, characteristic of "mad dog" or "attack" journalism (Sabato 1991), generates political cynicism and withdrawal as much as reform-oriented engagement.

While market-based alternatives to the regime of objectivity do not respond to the needs of crisis-oriented journalism, the paradigms of peace journalism and environmental communication appear to be more promising.

Peace Journalism[1]

Like objectivity, peace journalism is a multifaceted paradigm. Peace journalism is an analytical method for evaluating reportage of conflicts, a set of practices and ethical norms that journalism could employ in order to improve itself, and a rallying call for change. In sum, peace journalism's public philosophy "is when journalists make choices – of what stories to report and about how to report them – they create opportunities for society at large to consider and value non-violent responses to conflict" (Lynch and McGoldrick 2005, 5).

Peace journalism draws upon the insights of conflict analysis to look beyond the overt violence that is the stuff of conventional journalism, which is often tantamount to "war journalism." Peace journalism calls attention to the context, of attitudes, behaviours, and contradictions, and the need to identify a range of stakeholders broader than the proverbial two sides engaged in violent confrontation. If war journalism presents conflict as a tug-of-war between two parties in which one side's gain is the other's loss, peace journalism invites journalists to reframe conflict as a cat's cradle of relationships among various stakeholders. It also calls on journalists to distinguish between stated demands, and underlying needs and objectives, to move beyond a narrow range of official sources to include grassroots voices, particularly those of victims and peace builders. Peace journalism seeks to identify and attend to voices working for creative and non-violent solutions, to keep eyes open for ways of transforming and transcending the hardened lines of conflict, and to pay heed to aggression and casualties on all sides, avoiding the conflict-escalating trap of emphasizing *our* victims and *their* atrocities. Peace journalism looks beyond the direct physical violence that is the focus of war journalism, to include the structural and cultural violence (e.g., racism, militarism) that may underlie conflict situations (Hackett 2006; Hackett and Schroeder with NewsWatch Canada 2008).

One of peace journalism's prescriptions is to expand the horizons of conflict reportage, from the immediate conflict arena and the most prominent adversaries, to broader venues and time frames that multiply the potential causes, instigators, outcomes, and solutions. As one example of peace journalism's approach, Lynch (2008) analysed British press coverage of the Iran nuclear crisis from this perspective, suggesting that full coverage would – but usually did not – include these topics: the Nuclear Non-Proliferation Treaty; Iran's right to develop civil nuclear power under the NPT's terms; the failure of the UK and US governments to engage in negotiations to disarm their own nuclear arsenal, as required under the NPT; any evidence that Iran is not actually developing nuclear weapons; Iran's possible reasons for seeking a nuclear arsenal, if it were to do so, in terms of deterrence against outside threats.[2]

Peace Journalism and the Regime of Objectivity

Does peace journalism constitute a fundamental challenge to either the practices of journalism, or the broader social structures that help comprise the objectivity regime? In some respects, it does. Peace journalism stands between the fields of established media and oppositional social movements. Consider the contrasts between conventional journalism and the peace movement as paradigms for structuring thought and action. The peace movement values long-term peace-building processes, collective decision making, political commitment, human solidarity, social change, and low-cost grassroots mobilization. Conventional journalism favours timely events, official hierarchies, a stance of detachment, dyadic conflict, a consumerist world view, and costly production values (Hackett 1991, 274–5). While peace journalism should not be equated with the peace movement, it shares some of the above-noted incompatibilities vis-à-vis dominant news discourse.

First, peace journalism constitutes an epistemological challenge to the objectivity regime. In this view, journalism inherently involves choices; it is a matter of representation, not of reflection. Notwithstanding its professed disinterestedness, conventional "objective" journalism enshrines practices that predictably favour some outcomes and values over others, including, too often, war over peaceful conflict transformation. Objective journalism is thus "irresponsible," in that it shuns Max Weber's "ethic of responsibility" in public affairs, the idea that "one should take into account the foreseeable consequences of one's actions … and adjust one's behaviour accordingly" (Lynch and McGoldrick 2005, 218). In conflict situations, far from being passive observers, journalists are often caught in a feedback loop with political players. For instance, based on their previous experience of the media, powerful sources create "facts" that they anticipate will be reported and framed in particular ways. Thus, every time journalists recreate those frames, they influence future actions by sources. By focusing on physical violence divorced from context, and on win-lose scenarios, conventional "objective" news unwittingly incentivizes conflict escalation, impeding a morally and professionally justifiable incentivization of peaceful outcomes (Lynch and McGoldrick 2005, 216–18).

Peace journalism thus challenges the very epistemological basis for a stance of detachment, calling instead for journalists to be self-reflective about the institutionalized biases of their routine practices, the inescapability of framing and sourcing choices, the non-passivity of sources, the interventionist nature of journalism, and the potential of its becoming an unwitting accomplice to war propaganda (Lynch 2008, 10–14). That said, peace journalism is not renouncing the commitment to truthfulness, only questioning why some kinds of facts and sources are privileged, and how they feed into conflict cycles (ibid., 9). Peace journalism rejects both the positivist stance that journalism simply reports self-evident facts, and the relativist position that there is no independent basis to separate truth from propaganda. Instead, peace journalism offers interdisciplinary intellectual anchorage in peace and conflict studies, pursues the rigour of social science, and is reflexive, explicit about its normative commitments, open to justification, and aware of participant/observer interaction (ibid., xv, 21).[3]

Second, beyond epistemological differences that may be implicit, peace journalism explicitly challenges dominant news values, the taken-for-granted criteria that routinely guide journalists in selecting and constructing news narratives. Some peace journalism scholars point to the specific failures of relying on these news values in specific cases, such as the "peace euphoria" framing of the Oslo peace process in Israeli media (Mandelzis 2007). Yet aspects of peace journalism surely clash with dominant news values. In a recent update of a classic study by Galtung and Ruge (1965), Harcup and O'Neill (2001) identify ten dominant characteristics of newsworthy stories in the British press: power elite, celebrity, entertainment, surprise, bad news, good news (events), magnitude or scope, relevance (to the audience), follow-up (continuity), and the newspaper's own agenda. Peace journalism's emphasis on conflict formation and resolution, on win/win positive outcomes, on long-term processes and contexts, and on grassroots sources challenges the news values of violence, negativity, unambiguity, timeliness, elite nations, and elite people.

Indeed, peace journalism's advocates explicitly challenge some of the *practices* of "objectivity," thus comprising a third dimension of challenge (Lynch and McGoldrick 2005). They critique hegemonic journalism's heavy dependence on official sources, such as corporate and government spokespeople; they call for broadening journalists' range of sources to consciously include voices and options for peaceful resolution. They challenge the construction of conflict as a two-sided, zero-sum affair – a construction that is related to the conventions of balance – in favour of a multiple-stakeholder, win/win approach. And they challenge hegemonic journalism's focus on timely events (such as today's battles) rather than contexts, structures, and processes (such as peace building), areas that hegemonic journalism avoids for fear of introducing bias.

Some observers see peace journalism as offering an even more fundamental challenge, not just to the professional conservatism of journalists who cling to "objectivity" and the routinized, market-building formats of profit-oriented news corporations, but also to the entire global war system and its "deadly forms of propaganda," the "lethal synergy of state, corporations, think tanks, and the media" (Falk, cited in Lynch 2008, v, viii).[4]

And yet, peace journalism can be seen as compatible with "objectivity" more broadly defined. While its advocates ask journalists to engage with concepts and ideas from the academic discipline of conflict

analysis, they often prefer to speak in the language of journalistic professionalism. Indeed, when initiating peace journalism as a reform campaign within the journalism field, Lynch preferred to avoid the term
peace journalism, which for some may imply an illegitimate prior commitment to extraneous values. He labelled the new initiative "reporting the world" (Lynch 2002). Indeed, in justifying peace journalism's
prescriptions, Lynch and McGoldrick (2005, 9, 185, 223, 242) are able to
quote from formal editorial guidelines published by one of the world's
bastions of the objectivity regime, the BBC, and to use its language: balance, fairness, responsibility (Lynch 2002, 3). One scholar characterizes
peace journalism as a prerequisite of good journalism, one "which only
forbids the unacceptable," such as the narrowing of the news perspective to that of "war-making elites" or acting as a conduit for propaganda (Kempf 2007, 4).

In this view, peace journalism embodies the best ideals of professional journalism's objectivity regime – comprehensiveness, context,
accuracy, and the representation of the full range of relevant opinions –
and it critiques actually existing journalism from that standpoint, while
providing practical alternatives (Lynch 2008, xviii).

Environmental Communication

A paradigm remarkably parallel to peace journalism is emerging within
environmental communication. In the context of ecological crises, particularly global warming, one school argues for the field to be defined
as a crisis discipline, centred on certain ethical obligations to the public. These obligations include enhancing society's ability "to respond
appropriately to environmental signals," making decision making
processes transparent and accessible to the public, engaging various
groups to understand and interact with the natural world, and identifying harmful or unsustainable policies and practices (Cox 2007, 15–16).

Like peace journalism, environmental communication calls into
question some of the hegemonic media's practices of objectivity: the
reliance on official sources, whose interests are often opposed to effective climate change policy; conventions of balance, which in the US
press created an artificial debate between climate scientists and deniers,
obscuring public recognition of the scientific consensus; and event orientation, which makes it difficult to tell the story of climate change as
a long-term and uneven process, one to which specific events – like a
particularly vicious hurricane – can only be linked probabilistically, not

definitively. The climate change narrative calls into question the personalized and billiard-ball causality of conventional daily journalism.

That narrative also, potentially, challenges some hegemonic cultural values – individualism, freedom of choice, mobility, consumption – as well as hegemonic institutions, especially the matrix of oil, automobile, and other carbon-emitting industries increasingly hard-wired into the global economy, and the logic of growth that is integral to capitalism itself (see Carvalho 2007).

And yet, environmental communication, like peace journalism, enjoins journalism to act as both an early warning system and a facilitator of dialogue and action. Provision of context, receptivity to signals in the environment, getting to the *truth* of global warming and other environmental issues, pointing the way to solutions, are all goals that can be seen as compatible with a reinvented objectivity broadly understood. Compare crisis communication's goal of inspiring individual and community action with the idea of the informed citizen as the political subject of objective journalism; while the former implies mobilization for collective action and the latter denotes individual choice in a political marketplace, they may not be so far apart. Both paradigms endorse civic engagement and reject passive spectatorship, and there was a liberal reformist impulse behind the emergence of objectivity before it ossified into an institutionalized regime. In the view of some historians, the earliest versions of journalism objectivity emerged in the democratic discourse of the nineteenth-century British and American labour press, a stance that combined political independence with advocacy of workers' interests, political democracy, and social progress through science and education, characteristics not too far removed from those of effective democratic environmental communication (Schiller 1981; Hackett and Zhao 1998).

Journalism as Crisis Communication: Implications for Practice and Policy

To adapt Habermas's list, media in a democratic system need to help us identify and respond to challenges in the social, physical, and political environment; meaningfully set agendas and incentivize broad-based engagement in public life; facilitate pluralistic public debate; and act as watchdogs on private and public power-holders (cited in Jakubowicz 1999a, 33). Peace and environmental journalism would facilitate many of these tasks.

Society needs this kind of journalism, but can the market-driven media provide it? Rodney Benson's 2003 study of alternative weeklies in California shows that "under certain circumstances large media marketplaces may generate alternative voices quite effectively" (cited in Couldry and Curran 2003, 10; Benson 2003). And possibly, commercial media can provide a venue for practising crisis-oriented journalism. Indeed, a crisis orientation, combined with narratives and dialogical forms of news gathering that are psychologically and politically empowering, could actually have market value to some news organizations. It could help alleviate the economic crisis of journalism to the extent that "coherent narratives sell" (Entman 2010, 110). Citizenship and commercialism may not *necessarily* be in conflict in all cases. Greg Nielsen takes up the notion of the dialogic in journalism in chapter 2.

On the other hand, both peace journalism and environmental communication entail substantial changes in daily news routines – in sourcing, research, and narrative practices. Focused (re)training in journalism schools and virtual or material newsrooms would be required. As evidenced in the remarkable work of Lynch and McGoldrick (2005), peace journalism already has succeeded in such training, notably in societies such as the Philippines and Indonesia since the 1990s, where media are perceived to have contributed to socially destructive internal conflict, and where the professional norms of journalism may be more open to self-reflexive change than they are in Washington, London, or other imperial citadels of global journalism (Hackett 2010, 186). In terms of environmental communication, organizations such as the Society for Environmental Journalists (SEJ) provide similar tools for journalists in the form of workshops and resources that would increase their capacity to analyse and interpret complex environmental issues. Supporting and extending such initiatives is a crucial component of crisis-oriented journalism.

But beyond the additional resources it would require, the kinds of crisis-oriented journalism we advocate are in many ways incompatible with some of the institutional structures and dynamics of hegemonic journalism in Canada. It is difficult to construct peace as a compelling narrative that is consistent with dominant news values (Fawcett 2002). Climate change is also a topic potentially difficult to market, given the understandable reluctance of consumers to contemplate doomsday scenarios, or their own role in creating them. Crisis journalism challenges aspects of hegemonic culture – militarism, chauvinistic nationalism, consumerism – in ways that may not be compatible with the commercial media's pursuit of profitable audiences. Both paradigms call for significant diversification of sources, thus challenging the legitimacy of a news net anchored on government and corporate bureaucracies and elites, in particular the military and carbon-emitting industry establishments.

Moreover, there are other fundamental reasons to explain why market-driven media are unlikely to embrace crisis-oriented journalism. Like good public broadcasting, with which it overlaps, crisis journalism is a merit good – that is, it is something that individuals or society require, but that people are unable or unwilling to pay for through individual purchases. As Jakubowicz (1999b, 47) puts it, "Just as with education, training or health, consumers if left to themselves tend to take less care to obtain it than is in their own long-term interests." People need to know about crisis situations if we are to deal with them effectively and collectively, but they may not be willing to pay for information about a threat that is not perceived as immediately present and avoidable, and whose consequences are largely unaffected by their individual actions. For instance, people would doubtless pay for news that enables them to escape an imminent volcanic eruption. By contrast, knowledge about a long-term process like global warming does not bring such direct benefits to individuals, even though the distribution of accurate news about global warming benefits society at large.

Aside from being a merit good, crisis journalism is also in large measure a public good – that is, its use cannot easily be confined to those who pay for it and, unlike food or housing, its consumption by any one person does not diminish the ability of other people to use it (see Baker 2002; McChesney and Nichols 2010). A classic example of a public good is street lighting; it is impossible to limit the use of street lamps to consumers paying on the spot to turn on a light. That is why, historically, street lighting has been financed through taxes collected by city governments, rather than through individual purchases. Journalism has some of the above-mentioned characteristics. It is partially non-excludable – even non-subscribers can gather news from free news sources or word-of-mouth. And it is largely non-rivalrous; my access to a television newscast or online news site does not compromise your access. Even if it were possible to limit access to news through subscription fees and online paywalls, that would not be desirable in the case of crisis journalism. To be both democratic and effective, crisis journalism needs to be a widely shared, participatory, and dialogic medium.

As a merit good and a public good then, crisis journalism is a case of market failure; it is not likely to be supplied in sufficient quantity and quality through market mechanisms. Moreover, in Canada's corporate media, journalists have neither sufficient incentives nor autonomy to transform the way news is done, without strong external pressure and support. Therefore, in revitalizing Canadian journalism in the ways we are suggesting, there is an indispensable role for public policy and extra-market civil society organizations and movements. We propose several policy goals based on the realities we have explained above.

The first is the reinvigoration of public service broadcasting in a new media context. The underlying principles of public service broadcasting are compatible with crisis-oriented journalism in many ways. It approaches the public as citizens rather than consumers in the market economy. It is less dominated by entertainment imperatives compared with its market-driven counterparts. And it aims to foster public deliberation (Curran 2005, 205–7). All of these elements are crucial for informing the public about crisis and enabling their engagement with crisis-generating realities. Yet, in the Canadian context, we have seen a continued erosion of public funding for the CBC, the declining distinctiveness of its television programming, and the timidity of CBC management in defending the independence and diversity of its journalism. Neo-liberal federal governments are not disposed to challenge market relations or corporate power.

This brings us to our next and overarching policy goal: democratic reform of communication and media policy to provide a legal, financial, and institutional framework that is conducive to independent, quality journalism. In accordance with this goal, we suggest that both journalists and academics more actively help forge coalitions for democratic media reform, at local and provincial as well as national levels, and support the critical research and advocacy work of such civil society organizations as the Friends of Canadian Broadcasting and OpenMedia. Skinner et al. discuss these initiatives further in chapter 3.

In this regard, advocacy campaigns that aim to build a structurally diverse media environment must be at the forefront. Besides targeting traditional media like newspapers, radio, and television, these campaigns should also include, and arguably prioritize, the domain of the Internet and its policies. Robert Washburn and Vincent Raynauld describe one such online experiment in chapter 10.

The Internet can amplify the voices of peacemakers, witnesses, and victims in conflict situations, subject disinformation by elite sources to more effective public refutation (Allan 2010, 195–217), and enable communities to discuss collectively responses and adaptation to the impacts of climate change. In addition to this, the Internet allows development of new forms of journalism that can be used for crisis communication. As one of these new forms, online citizen journalism has transformed public discourse in important ways: broadening the range of opinion and eyewitness accounts in the public domain; forcing established news media to react more quickly to breaking events or to correct errors; forcing journalists to spend more time being accountable to "the people formerly known as the audience," in Jay Rosen's phrase (Allan 2010, 242); and sometimes setting the media agenda. For these reasons, affordable access to broadband distribution and basic digital literacy should be considered tantamount to a universal civil right, along with network neutrality (the non-discriminatory, non-hierarchical treatment of network traffic, precluding the creation of privileged "fast tracks" for the sites favoured by large Internet service providers) (McChesney 2011, 62–3; in the Canadian context, see Gasher et al. 2016, 211, as well as Skinner et al., chapter 3, this volume). In the context of the Internet's commercial development, dominated by a handful of telecommunications giants like Shaw and Telus, such preconditions of contemporary democratic journalism are far from guaranteed. Public policy is needed to underpin them. Thus the supporters of crisis-oriented journalism have a direct stake in the success of advocacy campaigns to maintain affordable universal access to an open Internet.

Yet an accessible and universal Internet, while essential, is not sufficient for crisis-oriented journalism. Some of the Internet-based forms of journalism we mentioned above, such as volunteer-based, opinion-heavy citizen journalism "do not replace ... the daily drudgery of reporting; this unheralded labour is what makes possible a record of public life" (Compton and Benedetti 2010, 496). If sustained "objective" reporting on public power-holders requires trained paid labour, that is a fortiori the case for certain aspects of crisis journalism, which at its best would require familiarity with the intellectual disciplines of conflict analysis or environmental science, the cultivation of a wide range of sources, the time to investigate the background to complex processes (like wars or climate change), and the skill of translating technical information into compelling public narratives.

This is why reforming existing media structures and supporting public service broadcasting remain essential policy goals. At the same time, the outcome of such policy battles is long term and uncertain. A more immediate and concrete way to support crisis-oriented journalism that promotes civic engagement is through strengthening local and "alternative" media. If adequately resourced, such media may be fruitful venues for experimenting and incubating new forms of journalism. Skinner et al. (chapter 3), Karen Wirsig and Catherine Edwards (chapter 4), and Sneha Kulkarni (chapter 8) discuss some of these new forms.

Alternative Journalism and Crisis Communication

Local and alternative media have the potential to play an important role in fulfilling the requirements of crisis-oriented journalism. First of all, like peace journalism, alternative journalism originates from dissatisfaction with mainstream journalism and its "epistemology of news" (Hackett 2010, 187; Atton and Hamilton 2008, 1), and offers "a critique in action" (Atton 2009, 284). Both are based "on strong notions of social responsibility" (Forde 2011, 10) and share the double goal of citizens' empowerment and political engagement.

Before we explore how alternative and local media can be used for crisis communication, let us briefly define some of the terms we use in this section and outline the relationship between alternative and local media and objectivity. Here, we distinguish alternative media and local media despite the fact that these two forms are not mutually exclusive. While there can be commercial local media, it is also possible that some local media organizations can be characterized as alternative media. Conversely, alternative media can also operate on national, international, or local levels.

The definition of the term *alternative* also deserves explanation. Given the heterogeneity of practices ranging from individual blogs, social movements, and community media to street theatre, fanzines, and the underground press, it is a very challenging task to develop an all-encompassing definition of alternative media/journalism (Bekken 2008). Scholars of alternative media emphasize different aspects as defining characteristics of these media. One of these characteristics is explained by the challenge they pose to the "existing concentration of media power" (Couldry and Curran 2003, 7). In this sense, alternative media refer to "media production that challenges, at least implicitly, actual concentrations of media power, whatever form those concentrations take in different locations" (ibid.). This particular function of alternative media/journalism is defined as the "denaturalization of dominant spaces" and "dominant practices of mainstream journalism (such as what counts as newsworthy, how stories are framed and how subjects of those stories are represented)" (Atton and Hamilton 2008, 124). Thus, alternative journalists demystify the working of mainstream media/journalism. In order to do that, they "monitor the media power" by "watching the watchers" (Forde 2011, 169).

Alternative media are also conceptualized in relation to their connection with social movements and their ability to "affect large scale social and political reform" (Haas 2004, 116; see also Downing 2001; Streitmatter 2001). According to this view, social movements and alternative media almost live in a "symbiotic relationship" (as in the example of the Indymedia Network and anti-globalization movement) (Haas 2004, 115–16). Accordingly, alternative media function primarily as a platform for social movements to "diffuse" their agendas and by doing this they "bring those agendas to the attention of government institutions and mainstream media" (ibid., 116).

Some approaches define alternative media in relation to citizens' empowerment (Rodriguez 2001; Harcup 2011). As a prominent name within this approach, Clemencia Rodriguez (2001) observes how communities use media as tools to convey their identities, stories, and/or problems. Thus, alternative media or, in her terms "citizens' media," contribute to communities and democracy through "opening social spaces for dialogue and participation, breaking individuals' isolation, encouraging creativity and imagination, redefining social languages and symbols, and demystifying the mass media" (Rodriguez 2001, 63). In this chapter, we adopt a broader approach; by the term *alternative media* we refer mainly, but not exclusively, to independent media/journalism that "attempt to fulfil a broader democratic purpose" (Forde 2011, 174).

Just like the variations in practice, the conception of objectivity in alternative media also takes different forms. Some alternative media organizations adopt certain principles of objectivity like balanced reporting (Meyers 2008, 378), while others may reject it entirely on the basis that it masks unequal relations of power (Atton and Hamilton 2008, 84–7; Forde 2011, 114). They may also reject "the notion of detachment and neutrality" while focusing on "objectivity as the quest for truth" (Forde 2011, 118).

How are alternative and local media/journalism relevant for crisis communication? These media arguably carry a stronger potential compared with their mainstream counterparts to create awareness about crisis and engage publics for mitigation. Scholars emphasize the crucial role that framing plays in crisis communication (Entman 2010; Nisbet 2009). Due to their cultural and physical proximity to the communities they serve, local media often use appropriate language, discourses, and frames that resonate with local culture and values. Accordingly, they could potentially contextualize crisis in relation to the lives of communities, leading to a better understanding of its impacts. Climate change scholars point out a real need on this issue. According to Moser and Dilling (2007, 9), news media have long adopted a scientific frame to cover the issues related to climate change. Consequently, climate change communication has largely remained a scientific debate among experts. Yet, several studies (see Fitzgerald 2007; Grossman 2005; Thomashow 2002; Thompson and Schweizer 2008) show that "using a place-based approach to discuss climate change impacts on specific regions, communities, and locations has promise in making messages more effective" (Schweizer et al. 2009, 269). Similarly, Entman (2010) emphasizes the importance of cultural elements in crisis communication, suggesting "news treatments would engage people by highlighting the concrete stakes for *them*, their values and interests and identities, in the outcomes" (114, emphasis added).

Offering a localized context is not only crucial for better understanding crisis and enabling people's engagement with the crisis-generating issues, but also plays a very important role in mitigation. According to Segnit and Ereaut (2007), "addressing people as members of a located community ... positions them as having more power to act" (32). In line with this, local media not only raise awareness on issues like climate change, but also guide citizens towards possible venues of action (Gunster 2011; Leiserowitz 2005; Lorenzoni and Pidgeon 2006; Segnit and Ereaut 2007). Extensive audience research conducted in Australia reaches similar findings: "In practical terms, audiences explain that local news and information empowers them to participate in the political life of their communities. At a number of regional community radio stations, for example, local council members have a weekly spot where they speak about community issues and events .... [I]n metropolitan Melbourne, listeners emphasized that their station was the only place where you could find out about local political rallies and activities" (Meadows et al. 2009, 162).

Do we need alternative media to provide that kind of locally meaningful forum? What about metropolitan daily newspapers? Or what about the community newspapers in the suburbs and smaller towns? These media can sometimes play a useful role in covering climate change issues. One silver lining to the dark cloud of cutbacks to corporate investment in journalism is that it has arguably become easier for environmental advocacy organizations and other citizens' groups to place articles in newspapers that have become hungrier for free content. British research suggests that local weekly papers pride themselves on being a voice for, and booster of, the community. They offer more space for local opinion journalism than does the national press, in some cases printing almost all the letters to the editor they receive (Wahl-Jorgensen 2008, 75).

But they also face considerable limitations as vehicles of crisis communication. They are typically, after all, corporate-owned, advertising-dependent, profit-oriented businesses. They are not likely to report enthusiastically on campaigns that challenge corporate power, an economic system premised on endless growth, or a culture of consumerism – arguably, all crucial impediments to effective climate justice action. The British research has identified more specific shortcomings of local papers. They have long relied heavily on information subsidies from authoritative institutions and public relations firms, and on editorial copy from press agencies that service a number of news outlets. That degree of dependence is increasing due to journalists' growing workload (Franklin 2008, 20–1). That means that "community" papers are becoming both less local in content, and increasingly dominated by institutional sources that may feel threatened by carbon taxes or other effective climate policies. Local urban newspapers are also under pressure to tailor their content to the purposes of target marketing, replacing issue-based journalism with lifestyle features oriented towards particular consumer groups (Niblock 2008, 56). And those predominantly rural local papers that can retain a community (rather than consumerist) orientation in the face of such pressures, traditionally try to generate a "journalism of consensus" that highlights and celebrates local individuals and community achievements, while conversely minimizing topics that are divisive, or could give offence to influential groups in the community (Wahl-Jorgensen 2008, 75–6).

To the extent that effective crisis communication needs to be not only local, but critical or oppositional, then corporate and commercial media are inadequate vehicles. By contrast, alternative journalism evinces not only a local orientation and strong community connection, but also several other commitments that make it relatively effective as a vehicle for crisis communication. Alternative media encourage audiences to participate in broader campaigns and politics, select stories that represent "untold" realities and the perspectives of the voiceless and the downtrodden, and critique the frames and processes of the dominant media (Forde 2011, 174–5). Insofar as alternative media challenge "the existing social status quo through coverage of topics not usually addressed by mainstream media because of their commercial nature and hegemonic biases" (Meyers 2008, 376), they can be called "critical media" (Fuchs 2010). Accordingly, the content of alternative media is described as ideally "progressive, explicitly opposed to particular axes of domination (corporate capitalism, heterosexism, racism, state authoritarianism)" (Hackett and Carroll 2006, 58). They question and criticize existing social and economic inequalities, and this questioning is particularly important for crisis communication since not all groups in society are affected the same way when it comes to a crisis like climate change: "Low income and minority populations are faced with a disproportionate burden from the impacts of climate change on both health and economic well-being" (Agyeman et al. 2007, 127). Thus, with their counter-hegemonic content, alternative media can explore these inequalities, highlight injustice, and expose the power of those forces at the root of crisis. Indeed, one of America's leading environmentalists, Bill McKibben (2012), has argued that the movement needs to identify and attack the fossil fuel industries as "the real enemy" of effective climate policy, a project unlikely to garner much sympathy from news media dependent on advertising, spokespeople, and information subsidies from that sector.

What does such alternative journalism look like in practice? Considering some Canadian examples, the Montreal-based monthly newspaper the *Dominion* stresses this approach with respect to its climate change coverage (*Dominion* n.d.). In the twelve months prior to June 2012, it ran six articles focusing on aspects of climate change, five of which privileged the perspectives of affected First Nations. Recognizing that First Nations views are marginalized in dominant media, the *Dominion* consciously sought to link environmental destruction to the colonization of Aboriginal peoples and other forms of structural violence. In one article, "Witnessing the Tar Sands Dead Zone," for instance, the authors write from the viewpoint of a participant in the elder-led Healing Walk for the Tar Sands (Arenas et al. 2011). They portray the mega-project's devastating impact on First Nations through the use of personal narrative, and they connect the defilement and toxicity of land and water to a history of colonialism, capitalism, the fossil fuel consumption of urban dwellers and modes of resource extraction that are symptomatic of these systems. Another article (Cuffe 2012) covered a Vancouver protest against the Enbridge Northern Gateway Pipeline, framing it as community resistance to an intrusive corporate project that would traverse Indigenous territory that is home to delicate ecosystems. A range of First Nations sources were used, but not to the exclusion of union leaders and environmentalists. The author also connected the protest to other proposed pipelines, and notably used an emotive anecdote (the eviction of a 12-year-old Indigenous activist from Enbridge's office) to connote the company's callousness.

"Only connect," as novelist E.M. Forster famously put it. This type of contextualized analysis allows journalists to move beyond the daily spectacles of conventional journalism, to explore the interconnectedness of crisis-generating realities from an explicitly committed standpoint (Hackett 2010, 189). In relation to their critical analysis function, many alternative media organizations also monitor and assess mainstream media's performance. In some cases, like PublicValues, a news site dedicated to the coverage of privatization, they even provide information on the practices of conventional journalism and mainstream media. The website has an entire section entitled "What Is Framing?" where the concept of journalistic framing is not only explained, but also contextualized in relation to the issue of privatization. Accordingly, it is argued that mainstream media use frames that "glorify business and individual achievement and disparage public enterprise" (Public Values 2012).

In contrast to the dominant framing referred to by PublicValues, alternative and independent publications in Canada aim to cover socio-political issues from the perspective of marginalized groups. The *Dominion* covers topics such as climate change, agriculture, and labour, which are often neglected by the mainstream media. Similarly, the online alternative news site Straight Goods states that it reports "with a special emphasis on under-represented voices and views from the progressive side of the political spectrum" (straightgoods.ca n.d.). This goal is primarily achieved by encouraging and enabling non-professionals' participation in content production (Platon and Deuze 2003). Again, emphasis is placed on the participation of conventionally marginalized groups (Atton and Wickenden 2005; Atton and Hamilton 2008). By using alternative media as a platform, these groups voice their concerns and interests in the public sphere(s). The independent news site Rabble's "Babble" section constitutes an example of this kind of practice.

Due to the variety of voices represented, the public sphere(s) created by alternative media can be conceptualized as "more inclusive and less male, less bourgeois and less dominated by the market" (Harcup 2011, 17). It is in the public sphere(s) that alternatives to the existing crisis-generating structures and practices can be imagined and discussed (Hamilton 2000, 363; Harcup 2011).

The type of participation promoted by alternative media/journalism can have a positive impact on crisis mitigation as well. Drawing from Habermas (1996) and Rochon (1998), Brulle (2010) argues that "political mobilization campaigns are more effective and legitimate if they engage citizens in a sustained dialog rather than treating them as mass opinion to be manipulated" (91). In line with this, we can argue that dialogic models of communication employed in alternative media can work more effectively than advocacy campaigns for citizens' mobilization (ibid.).

Their relation to social movements grants alternative media a special role in crisis communication. Alternative media are often described as a "rhizome" for social movements and facilitate "transhegemonic collaborations and partnerships" among them (Bailey et al. 2008, 31). By using alternative media, social movements can create and convey to the public their own frames regarding various crises. This would arguably help mobilization of the public which is, as Tony Haas points out, one of the distinguishing characteristics of alternative media: "In contrast to mainstream media's liberal democratic ideal of the 'informed' citizenry, alternative media promote the participatory democratic ideal of the 'mobilized' citizenry" (Haas 2004, 116).

In accordance with the mobilization goal, alternative media promote individual and collective agency in relation to crisis. For instance, environmental issues, particularly in the context of British Columbia, occupy a significant place in the *Tyee*'s news agenda. These range from safeguarding Canadian water to environmental policies pertaining to BC fisheries. The *Tyee* serves as watchdog of the federal government by closely reporting on its environmental policies. It also emphasizes community agency in the face of environmental problems. For instance, it is quite common to see news articles like "Great Bear Forest to Be Massive Carbon Offset Project" in the *Tyee* (Pollon 2012). The article covers the carbon-offsetting program implemented by Aboriginal groups living in the Great Bear Rainforest.

Shane Gunster's (2011) research on coverage of the 2009 Copenhagen Summit in the BC media shows how this agency is conveyed in alternative media. Gunster points out that compared with their mainstream counterparts, independent publications the *Georgia Straight* and the *Tyee* featured more empowering frames and "solution-oriented" coverage (486): "Alternative media both offered and demanded a far more active and engaged political sensibility in which outrage with existing institutions was cause for action and not despair, a potent fuel with which to energize multiple forms of popular, democratic mobilization. Diagnostic assessments of the limits of conventional politics and existing institutions inspired calls for *more* rather than less political engagement, a demand that citizens actively confront those with power and influence rather than abandon the political field to their control" (ibid., 492). Similarly, PublicValues encourages its readers to share information on "how to fight" the privatization of public services such as "health care, child care and social services" (Public Values 2012).

Solution orientation is a common characteristic of many alternative news organizations. The biweekly magazine *Watershed Sentinel* clearly states this principle on its website: "The *Watershed Sentinel* deserves its reputation for publishing the true story about how BC fits in an increasingly global world, where our trees become phone books and bears are hunted or, worse, poached. Each issue praises stewardship successes and offers constructive solutions to the problems we still face" (*Watershed Sentinel* n.d). An impressive example of the *Sentinel*'s solution-oriented, analytical journalism was authored by Ernest Callenbach (2011). Whereas much environmental news bemoans current realities, Callenbach focuses on viable alternatives. For readers who may be unfamiliar with the issue, he starts with a critique of the oxymoronic concept of "sustainable development," replaces it with "sustainable shrinkage," and identifies overall consumption and population as two critical areas where global society must shrink. He then identifies several key paths to such shrinkage, including creating effective incentives such as carbon taxes, switching from buy-new to long-term maintenance of appliances, planning for renewable and reduced energy consumption, and privileging urban density and conservation. The article concludes with the silver lining to the cloud of global society's inevitable shrinkage: social benefits such as rediscovered sociability, employment in sustainable energy sectors, and happier lives in smaller families. One need not agree with all of Callenbach's analysis to recognize it as an example of challenging, alternative journalism rarely found in corporate media.

Such emphasis on agency, along with a critical analysis of crisis-generating structures, is crucial for the goals of crisis-oriented journalism. Yet alternative and local media face many obstacles in terms of their own sustainability, resulting from a lack of financial and human resources (Atton and Hamilton 2008, 135). Therefore, developing a supportive institutional and policy framework to sustain these forms of journalism remains an important task. Past and current Canadian communication policy offers numerous mechanisms to support such media. Established in 1967 by the National Film Board (NFB), a federal program called Challenge for Change (CFC) (Skinner 2012, 37) aimed to empower communities by providing them with the necessary communication tools and training to use them. Documentary films and video projects to "promote new ideas and prove social change" were encouraged (Raboy 1990, 202). Over the course of ten years, 250 films were produced to this end (Druick 2010, 337). Challenge for Change created "urban media projects that focused public attention on specific problems and issues, such as housing, health care, welfare policies, employment opportunities and recreation" (Wiesner 2010, 99). However, these efforts were negatively affected when the government stopped subsidizing the program due to fiscal restraints (Marchessault 2010, 356).

Similarly, support mechanisms for Aboriginal media have been in place since the 1970s when the Secretary of State's Native Communication Program "helped to fuel the development of Aboriginal newspapers" (Skinner 2012, 37). Yet, the budget cuts implemented in the 1990s resulted in a decrease in the number of Aboriginal newspapers (Shade 2009). The Province of Quebec also provides support mechanisms for the non-profit media sector. The Quebec government supports the Association des médias écrits communautaires du Québec (AMECQ) by providing funds, training, and educational programs for its members (Shade 2009, 226).

The work of independent organizations is also worth mentioning in terms of the existing efforts to support independent and alternative media in Canada. In this regard, the Community Radio Fund of Canada (CRFC) aims to provide additional funding support for campus and community radio (Skinner 2012, 39).

David Skinner (2012) rightfully points out that despite existing, and arguably limited, government support for alternative and independent media in Canada, an important challenge for these media institutions remains at the level of their "access to policy process" (43). Skinner notes, "Canadian regulatory forums today are largely structured to accommodate the needs and interests of large privately owned commercial corporations. In this context, work needs to be done to provide independent media greater access to the policy process and to increase the flexibility of policy initiatives to allow their application to a wider range of organizational forms" (ibid., 43). In this sense, we emphasize once more the need for support for media policy advocacy, including support for advocacy organizations that target the domain of alternative and community media such as the Canadian Association of Community Television Users and Stations (CACTUS) (Skinner 2012, 39). Karen Wirsig and Catherine Edwards provide an extensive discussion of CACTUS initiatives in chapter 4.

We value state policy to support public service broadcasting as well as alternative and community media, but as the previous examples show, government funding is not always dependable. For this reason, development of creative models for financing crisis-oriented journalism is necessary.

As an example, we would like to explore briefly *VoterMedia.org*, a community-based model founded by Mark Latham in Vancouver. The model was implemented by the University of British Columbia's student union (the Alma Mater Society or AMS) in 2006 (Latham 2012). It resembles the renowned participatory budgeting process pioneered in Porto Alegre, Brazil. Accordingly, it envisages representative collective bodies – such as university student societies or municipal governments – empowering voters to allocate a pool of money among competing individuals or organizations that produce civic media, including blogs. Initial experiments indicate success in stimulating media attention to civic issues, as well as voter engagement with their media and political environments (Latham 2012). During coverage of the AMS executive elections in 2006, an increase in new media outlets on campus was observed. Interviews conducted by the founders of the project four years after its implementation also show the contentment of students and bloggers. Justin McElroy, the coordinating editor of the campus newspaper, the *Ubyssey*, thinks that by providing competition and accountability, *VoterMedia.Org* "ensure[s] established publications on campus like *Ubyssey* do a better job in covering the issues related to students' lives." McElroy thinks *VoterMedia.Org* "absolutely increase[s] campus discussion and student engagement" (Latham 2012, 6).

Voter-funded models like this can be extended to other relatively small-scale communities like municipalities. These models carry the potential to render alternative and independent media more accountable to their public and, equally important, offer one more platform for citizens' support. However, these structures alone cannot provide a viable solution for the sustainability problem that plagues these media organizations. Therefore, it is important to re-emphasize the responsibility of governments and the great potential their support can bring to almost all forms of alternative media; to this end all governments can bring to bear numerous mechanisms such as direct subsidies, tax-exempt status for non-profit media, and tax-deductable donations from individuals and organizations.

Conclusion

In this chapter, we have advanced several arguments, each of which needs further development. Canadian journalism is in a state of malaise, arguably of crisis; one of the avenues to overcome that crisis and regain its own relevance is to redefine itself as a crisis discipline. In the process, journalism should discard some of the ossified practices of objectivity that stifle political understanding and engagement, while maintaining a commitment to public truth. The underlying dilemma is that of reversing the Enlightenment rationale for democracy as an underpinning for ever-expanding individual freedom and "progress." Since humans have overshot the planet's carrying capacity, democracy is, paradoxically, now needed to acquire majority acquiescence in placing limits on those forms of freedom that are exploitative, violence-generating and/or ecologically destructive, and to manage the transition to a post-growth economy and a sustainable civilization.

Acknowledgment

The authors would like to thank the following for their contributions to this chapter: Simon Fraser University Vice President's Office for a Small Institutional Research Grant; Shane Gunster for his valuable comments on an earlier draft of this chapter; the Canadian Centre for Policy Alternatives' Climate Justice Project and SFU Dean of the Faculty of Communication, Art and Technology for funding for bibliographic research; Wendee Lang, Vojtech Sedlak, Josh Tabish, Megan Thomas, and Sara Wylie for invaluable research assistance; and Angelika Hackett for editorial assistance.

NOTES

1 This section is adapted from Hackett 2010.
2 For a visual example, contrasting war journalism and peace journalism coverage of a suicide bombing in Israel, see Lynch and McGoldrick 2005, 21–6, or their film *News from the Holy Land*.
3 A critical realist epistemology is evident in peace journalism's call to distinguish truth from propaganda; to distinguish between stated demands and underlying needs, goals and interests; to look beyond direct physical violence to explore its "invisible" effects of violence (such as cultural militarization or psychological trauma), and its underlying patterns of cultural and structural violence (Lynch and McGoldrick 2005, 28–31; Hackett and Schroeder with NewsWatch Canada 2008, 44n18).
4 Some critics fear that peace journalism challenges a liberal value central to democratic journalism – that of freedom of expression. In the view of Hanitzsch (2004), peace journalism implies that "bad news" and controversial topics whose dissemination could contribute to the escalation of conflict should be avoided. There is no evidence, however, that peace journalists actually make such a claim. But in one sense, peace journalism does challenge the currently hegemonic definition of free speech, as the right of individuals to speak without fear of state punishment. Peace journalism implies not just a right to speak freely, but a right of access by all significant voices to the means of public communication. Free speech needs a chance to be heard in order to be effective – a normative imperative that underpins alternative media and media democratization movements. Peace journalism is thus aligned with a model of democratic communication, founded on a social cycle of dialogue and communication that is more radical than the liberal conception of the free press.

2 Critical Theory and Acts of Journalism: Expanding the Implied Audience

GREG M. NIELSEN

The New York Times on the Topic of Undocumented Immigrants

There is the father from Panama, a cleaning contractor in his 50s, who had lived and worked in the United States for more than 19 years. One morning, he woke to the sound of loud banging on his door. He went to answer it and was greeted by armed immigration agents ... There is the father from Argentina who moves his wife and children from house to house hoping to remain one step ahead of the immigration raids. And the Guatemalan, Mexican and Chinese fathers who have quietly sought sanctuary from deportation at churches across the United States. (*Danticat* 2007)

Entire generations of immigrant Americans are kept in a cycle of poverty. They do not have a means to move up in society, participate fully in society or fulfill their life's dreams. (*Freedman* 2007)

Facing the prospect of major layoffs of farm workers during harvest season, growers and lawmakers from agricultural states spoke in dire terms yesterday about new measures by the administration to crack down on employers of illegal immigrants. (*Preston* 2007)

The Montreal Press on Bill 94[1]

"There is a lot of prejudice against people who are not pure laine ... They need immigrants to come here, and then they expect them to become Québécois. If you deny me who I am by imposing a certain culture on me, I don't accept that," Boodajee said. (*Magder* 2007)

Allowing scarves, turbans, kirpans, kippahs, and saris in classrooms, hospitals, courts and government offices has the effect of promoting integration. Excluding immigrants from many activities and jobs leads to their isolation. If we decide to accommodate, very few in the next generation will seek the same privilege, and a large number will have married outside their community. Accommodation is largely a temporary phenomenon. On the other hand, the niqab blocks integration, because it is difficult to form friendships with people whose face we have not seen. The worst accommodations are private, ethnic or religious schools, hospitals, separate court systems, and all forms of accommodation through separateness. (*Grey* 2010)

"Une jeune fille qui porte le voile à Montréal envoie un message clair à la société d'accueil: mon droit à la différence religieuse l'emporte sur l'impératif de mon intégration à la société québécoise telle qu'elle a été historiquement construite avec le français comme langue principale, la démocratie et la laïcité comme piliers. Je le dis d'une manière assez brutale, l'impératif d'intégration doit l'emporter toujours sur le droit à la différence." (*Akkari* 2010)

The quotations cited above are about undocumented immigrants in the United States and debates in Quebec over the need to reasonably accommodate others who have cultural and, especially, religious differences from their host society. Other newspapers have been talking about these same controversies, which prompts the question: why are so many Western-style liberal democracies appearing to retreat from the principles of religious and cultural pluralism as well as refuge from tyranny at this time (Mailhé et al. 2013)? Are deportations, mass incarcerations (400,000 undocumented immigrants imprisoned each year in the US), and putting up walls the new norm (Brown 2011)? Are laws banning the burqa or niqab in public places in some European countries, or the proposed face coverings in Quebec public institutions, exceptional measures? Or have liberal-democratic societies, with the help of the press, and despite their constitutions and human rights charters, always masked paradoxical limits and uneven definitions for the meanings of citizenship, equality, mobility, and freedom of expression and assembly (Rancière 2006; Agamben 2005; Mouffe 2000; Holston 2008)?

The strategy to theorize the relation between the subjects of social exclusion journalists report on and their implied audiences at the level of acts of journalism stems from a triple dissatisfaction with (1) traditional definitions of journalism as a neutral form of communication and as watchdog over powerful institutions; (2) critiques of the mainstream press that too quickly reduce reporting practices to the consequences of corporate ownership and distribution on capital accumulation and ideology; and (3) overstated claims about new media. I will first introduce briefly the key concept of the implied audience, then outline the approach I adapt from critical theory, comment briefly on each of these points while sketching an overview of mainstream acts of journalism, and finally, propose strategies from the tradition of public journalism that could expand the implied audience for the mainstream without sacrificing the rigour of the craft or creating new subjects of exclusion.

Undocumented migrants and religious and cultural minorities are types of "others" who are often discussed by professional journalists, public intellectuals, and activists in mainstream newspapers – as in the examples above – and yet are almost never directly addressed as the ideal readers of stories. Newspapers obviously have real audiences, but aside from the constraints of standard practice that news organizations place on acts of journalism – levels of verification required, balance, editorial autonomy from profit motives, and professional culture – what goes into the framing of a great deal of news comes from who editors and contributors to newspapers think their audiences are and by how they imagine they can sell more newspapers. In almost all acts of journalism – print, broadcast, or online – and in almost all of its organizational forms – mainstream corporate, alternative, citizens', or civic – the someone we are talking to is first and foremost an implied or ideal audience. Each type of news discourse retains a distinct voice as it addresses itself towards a broader demos or "normal people" that far exceeds the empirical reading public or plurality of publics consuming the news. The implied audiences for Fox News and Democracy Now!, for example, may be completely opposed in their interpretation of news events, and yet it is empirically possible that factions of each audience view each program – if only to disapprove. While empirical audiences can overlap, the implied audiences in the range from the left to the right and from the most serious to the lightest forms of journalism tend to remain distinct. A history of these audiences has yet to be written.

I think the most important task of a critical theory of journalism today is to put into question the way the dialogue between news and the implied audience is consummated without actually addressing the subjects themselves as audiences. While it can be argued that the dialogic principle has always been a journalistic ideal (Hornmoen and Steensen 2014), or at least in tension with the ideal of objectivity (Soffer 2009), only rarely has dialogue been between the subjects of social exclusion and the journalist. The dialogic form of journalism I propose in the last section of this chapter would shift the socially excluded from mere objects of reportage to internal addressees of mainstream news coverage. My point is that if media are not constructing their messages with the intent of speaking to their subjects, but rather towards a third party, then the exclusionary nature of these practices is at odds with the strong notion that media in general, and journalism in particular, have a privileged standing as a core democratic institution with a purported mission of public service and a privileged place within a contemporary pluralist public sphere. Such discursive exclusions produced by discrepant articulations of community and audience need to be systematically assessed as they have serious repercussions that undermine journalism's idealized role as a public service and as a democratically oriented communications system, casting aside the very people, it can be argued, whose needs for representation and understanding are greatest (Gasher and Nielsen 2011).

Wolfgang Iser (1974) argues that not all norms can be framed in a text and that there is a selection of which norms are emphasized and how they are voiced. The implied audience incorporates both the "prestructuring of the potential meaning [of norms]" and "the readers' actualization of this potential through the reading process." In other words, the implied audience takes an active, although virtual, role "in the composition of meaning which revolves around the basic (convergence or) divergence from the familiar," at the level of content (ibid., xii). Iser's concern with how the reader discovers the meaning of a novel through pre-established aesthetic and cognitive forms parallels my own interest in understanding how journalists anticipate the ways the audience discovers information. As Iser states, "The convergence of the text and reader brings the work into existence, and this convergence can never be precisely pinpointed, but must always remain virtual, as it is not to be identified either with the reality of the work or with the individual disposition of the reader" (275).

As "others" reported on, the undocumented and cultural minorities are doubly removed from this convergence between the journalist and the implied reader. First, their voices are not joined in the active, two-way conversation. Second, they are absent even when their voices are present in the form of quotes addressed to readers. This is because the voices of the subjects being talked about are most often limited to a personal reference that lends journalistic authority or emotional attraction to the story. Given the role this paradox – and, at times, contradiction – has played in masking the retreat of liberal democracy, as suggested above, and given the changes that journalism is currently undertaking, it is a good time to sketch out a broad critical theory of how acts of journalism frame subjects of social exclusion for an ideal-typical audience.

Traditional and Critical Theory

If traditional theory, to paraphrase Max Horkheimer's (1972) classic essay, applies a discipline to a positive hypothesis until it can no longer be refuted by methods that are repeatable and, in so doing, makes validity claims between the cause and effect of the phenomenon it studies, critical theory juxtaposes disciplines and fields of study, finds incoherencies between their claims of cause and effect, and creates theory from the remaining compatible, but unfinished, elements and seemingly unrelated forces. Whereas a traditional theory might define acts of journalism, especially serious journalism, as a neutral means of reporting on facts and providing balanced opinions so as to complete the democratic process and act as watchdog over powerful institutions, critical theory has come over time to problematize acts of journalism within a culture industry that on the whole favours the dominant ideology of a given period through its overwhelming standardization of style and repetition of form and content. Under certain circumstances, though, acts of journalism can "speak truth to power" and so remain a potential force for resistance or at least a necessary institution for "a democracy to come" (Derrida 2005).

Critical theory requires an immanent understanding of social relations affecting both the phenomenon being studied and the theory being developed. We can see how this doubling epistemology is especially at work in the Marxist tradition. Marx himself began his career as a journalist in 1840s Germany, although his political activities saw him expelled from several countries. He took refuge in England not long after he broke from the left Hegelian version of journalism he had been practising earlier, and managed to learn enough English to work as a foreign correspondent with the *New York Daily Tribune* from 1851 to 1861, where he published an average of two articles a week (Muhlmann 2010). His journalistic method provides a good example of the above description of critical theory: (1) reconstruct the argument of an official report or the introduction of a norm from the point of view of its author and juxtapose it with competing positions; (2) point out a contradiction or incoherence immanent to each argument; and (3) propose an alternative explanation from the compatible, but unfinished, elements for a moral/political imperative oriented towards the emancipation of the subject of exploitation in the story.

We can see examples in Marx's journalism from more than 150 years ago that are remarkably similar to the opening quotes from the New York and Montreal newspapers seen above. In one article on forced Irish and Scottish emigration, he frames the same kind of moral imperative and emotional orientation towards a sense of "justice to come" we see in the stories about the Latino fathers on the run in the United States today: "there acts in England an invisible, intangible and silent despot, condemning individuals, in extreme cases, to the most cruel of deaths, and driving in its noiseless, everyday working, whole races and whole classes of men from the soil of their forefathers, like the angel with the fiery sword who drove Adam from Paradise. In the latter form the work of the unseen social despot calls itself forced emigration; in the former it is called starvation" (Marx 1853). And yet, like the starving immigrants in London to which he refers, neither the undocumented migrants who are discussed in quotes from New York nor the culturally or religiously different folks from Montreal are addressed as an audience.

In another example of the critical method in his journalism from 1861, Marx examines the British government's position of neutrality regarding the American Civil War. By juxtaposing various historical approaches to the question of slavery in Britain, he unmasks an incoherency between the emotional horror expressed by British officials against the slave-ocracy and the policies of economic cooperation and diplomatic collaboration with the Confederacy. Again, he addresses neither the British officials nor the slaves as his audience (Marx 1861).

Ironically perhaps, Marx's only direct address to the subjects of exploitation he writes about are seen where he shifts out of journalism into political communication. For example, I refer to the direct address to the workers who are the subjects of the *Communist Manifesto* he wrote with Friedrich Engels (Marx and Engels 1998 [1888]). But can we call this journalism? Unlike a journalistic account, Marx and Engels employ analytical concepts like the procession of the economic mode of production and progression of a working-class consciousness of exploitation to explain information to readers about the inevitability of an industrial proletarian revolution. Both political communication and journalism look to uncover an original ultimate truth for an implied reader, and yet the two types of truth differ in their modes of address. In favour of Marx and Engels's political communication, we might say that the subjects of exploitation being discussed are also the immediate, implied audience.

The bourgeois demos is the subject being talked *about*, and not *with*, in this instance. In contrast, the journalistic address to the audience, as we will see, is more often than not a third party.

Marx and Engels's analysis of capitalism has worked its way through several generations of critical theorists who continue to charge the corporate ownership of media (and by implication, mainstream journalism) with sacrificing the possibility of a worthy public life (locally and globally) to commercial imperatives (Fuchs and Mosco 2012; Therborn 2008). The early Frankfurt School was one of the first to theorize media as organizations that expand the logic of capital into the intersectional domains of everyday representations, and not just class politics, to explain how culture enters the logic of capital and impacts social struggles of all forms and at all levels (Horkheimer and Adorno 1972). Along similar lines, well-known media activists, from Edward S. Herman and Noam Chomsky (2002) to Amy and David Goodman (2006), have long charged mainstream journalism with "manufacturing consent," "corporate complicity," and the facile "exchange of truth for access to power."

Jürgen Habermas broke from these kinds of critiques early on and shifted instead to the pragmatic argument that journalism serves democracy whenever the journalist draws attention to public opinion concerning how all can fairly voice concerns about norms before they are introduced. His discourse principle includes all pragmatic attempts to achieve unforced understanding together. But in a sense, Habermas's view on journalism and public opinion simply moves backward past Marx and Hegel to the Kantian idea of publicity and the plurality of points of view, with the assumption that, eventually, reason and the best argument prevail. As Habermas puts it, "Only deliberative conflicts support the supposition that the democratic procedure will lead to more or less reasonable results in the long run" (2009, 135). The implication of his argument returns us to the questionable premise that journalism is an impartial form of reporting truth/information, analysis, and dissemination. Indeed, even mainstream journalists question whether the press will be able to continue to fulfil its obligation to democracy by acting as the fourth estate (see Kovach and Rosenstiel 2007).

The question remains: how can we study concrete acts of journalism and think about strategies to change their traditional form of address to expand the implied audience without having some preconceived, naturalist idea about demos or the inevitability of revolution? Let me be clear on my usage of the concept "acts of journalism." For heuristic reasons, I suspend the distinction between the professional journalist who reports or comments on news for an organization and acts of journalism defined more broadly to include any writer (like Marx) who gets to write about any news event or produce a commentary through a recognized news agency towards an implied audience that may or may not include the subject of the event being discussed (including letters to the editor, op-ed articles, articles by citizen journalists accepted for publication, etc.). Although this broadens the scope of what it means to *do* journalism, my unit of analysis remains narrowly focused on the newspaper text itself, that is, in its organized, digital archival form.

My point is not how, or whether, the journalist or writer is motivated, or even if the journalist is aware of her or his intention, and so I also suspend carrying out interviews with journalists, writers, or empirical audiences in order to theorize how their narratives imply images of the audience being addressed. I want to probe the gap between the addressee and the subjects of reports and flush out any contradictory reception each might have for the story being told. To this end, my focus is on what the French sociologist Luc Boltanski (2011) calls a "hermeneutic contradiction," that is, an interpretive contradiction that can happen whenever the subjects being reported on or represented could rise up and object to the way the story is framed for the implied audience. This definition assumes the subjects of the reports on social or cultural exclusion are not being addressed as part of the implied audience. The assumption leads to a focus on the narrative act rather than on field analysis that would examine the combination of political, organizational, and creative forces that "struggle" with and against each other to define the "purest" form of journalistic practice (Bourdieu 2005). This is discussed at length below.

Within the confines of this chapter, the discussion concentrates on mainstream journalism and so sets aside any in-depth consideration of alternative or citizen journalism at this time. Nor do I review the growing literature around the emancipatory potential of social media and their claims to move acts of journalism in a more inclusive direction. Historical attempts to construct domination-free, alternative, or citizen journalism have often meant either speaking to narrower, like-minded audiences, or placing the argument within the future hopes of new media in ways that underestimate the imperatives of capital and the overwhelming presence of the corporate sector. Meanwhile, mainstream journalists continue their conventional acts of naming conditions for tolerance or public hospitality towards the socially excluded, with little interruption or critical study. Instead, I propose a review of the public or civic journalism movement in the final section, in part because it is a model that potentially combines elements of alternative and citizen journalism that could expand the mainstream implied audience.

My point is not to discuss differences within media ecosystems in terms of ownership bias in editorial policies, nor nuances among the various genres of newspaper writing (editorials, columns, news items, op-ed commentaries, letters to the editor, blogs, tweets, etc.), newer technological possibilities, or close ethnographic descriptions of newsroom practices. I am trying to theorize the encoding side in acts of journalism while acknowledging that a decoding approach would provide a supportive counterpart. While I limit my discussion to acts of journalism in what follows, I enthusiastically admit that all of these research tracks need to be developed for a full-blown research program on the subject.

Exclusion from the Implied Audience

There is, of course, a copious amount of reporting on all kinds of socially or culturally excluded subjects who are rarely addressed as implied audiences: the homeless, the local and the global poor, the undocumented, the refugee, the criminal, the insane. This shortlist is hardly exhaustive and would have included the nineteenth-century working class, as well as women and racial minorities well into the twentieth century. At some point, though, the working class, women, and (some) racial minorities became part of the implied audience even as new subjects of exclusion emerged: for example, Muslims, members of Orthodox religions, and/or sexual minorities. We can pose the issue this way: "If mainstream newspapers regularly discuss issues of cultural diversity and social exclusion in supportive but conditionally hospitable terms and their reportage rarely addresses the subjects being reported on as their readers, does it not follow that public understanding of the experience of exclusion or of difference is diminished, even when the press passionately pleas in the name of democracy for greater hospitality or tolerance for the undocumented or culturally different?" (Jackson et al. 2011, 238). One way of avoiding this issue is to say that the quotations that opened this chapter are not about public dialogue, but about selling mainstream corporate newspapers and the audience commodity, or about coming to terms with the impact of neo-liberalism and the effect "the new spirit of capitalism" is having on the industry (Boltanski and Chiapello 2005). In short, the newspaper industry is in the middle of a major shift in its mode of production and therefore in its relations among capital, labour, and the commodity form of information itself. For example, while the print newspaper industries are enjoying growth in India, China, and Latin America (WAN 2008), Downie and Schudson (2009) found that, in the United States, the number of editorial employees for mainstream daily newspapers dropped by 33 per cent, from more than sixty thousand in 1992 to about forty thousand in 2009. Although layoffs and the actual closure of Canadian newspapers (Statistics Canada 2011) have not been as dramatic as in the United States, there are signs that the reduction in news staff is beginning to take its toll, as in the recent announcement of more cuts to the CBC (Canada's largest news operation), and the downsizing from 253 to 62 news and support staff following the long and divisive lock-out at *Le Journal de Montréal* between January 2009 and February 2011 (Gasher et al. 2012, 295). Advertising revenues and audiences in Canada are also migrating from the traditional news platforms of newspapers and television to digital media (IAB Canada 2011; Ha 2008). Those changes are rendering digital media more significant players in the political economy of news production and dissemination, and have the potential to diversify reportage, in terms both of what is covered and how (Québec 2010).

There is indeed a series of multisided pressures that bear against the civic ideals and economic viability of the industry that directly impact acts of journalism on the ground. These include deregulation and increased corporate concentration, media platform convergence, shifting advertising revenue streams, audience fragmentation, citizen journalism (with and without editorial control), fusion of news and entertainment, the disproportionate role the public relations industry plays in the generation of news stories, and the still very limited range of voices granted the opportunity to speak through mainstream media. But it is also important not to reduce multiple levels of cultural meaning for the implied audiences in acts of journalism to the political-economic imperatives and paradoxes of emerging crises.

On the level of political culture, for example, the quotes at the beginning of the chapter from the Montreal press connect intense debates among feminists to a multinational federal context where the French-speaking québécois demos plays the role of a national minority within Canada that is inseparable from a dominant francophone majority ethos inside Quebec. On the level of cultural policy, the quotes recall how the "Quebec question" provokes debate over how much interculturalism can accommodate an ethnic or religious minority practice without eroding a relatively new secular culture for a national linguistic minority and its particular version of liberal democracy. Recall that a source of tension here stems from Quebec's official policy on interculturalism, which requires newcomers to adapt to the host society's French language, while Canadian policy is open to a positive reinforcement of two official languages as it looks to find its way through a fully multicultural and multinational federation that accommodates minority claims without threatening its version of liberal democracy and a fragile sense of unity (Kymlicka 1998). Despite the difference in policy nuance, both levels of government are considering equally inhospitable legislation regarding face coverings in the public sphere.

Acts of Journalism

On the level of the act of journalism – and this is where I situate my own admittedly one-sided analysis, mainly because it addresses directly the issue at hand – the controversies in the Quebec press over face-covering and in the *New York Times* over illegal immigration concern the ways in which mediated societies absorb a hermeneutic contradiction between the implied ideal-typical audience and the minority subjects that journalists observe and report on. The potential hermeneutic contradiction between reports on subjects of social and cultural exclusion and how they might interpret the story about them, on the one hand, and the interpretation that is framed for the implied audience on the other, can both legitimize acts of journalism and discredit them. To paraphrase Boltanski (2011), because the observer is outside the observed, she needs to consider both the simple description in terms of what information to select to report on, and the complex aspects explaining what the story is for and to whom it is addressed. Whereas the simple exteriority of the observer refers to journalists themselves as embodied subjects, complex exteriority refers to the managerial and organizing discourse of the industry. What might be called the institution of journalism has no body, no voice, and no point of view except those of spokespersons who are often journalists and who are themselves "situated, self-interested, libidinous, and hence condemned to the ineluctability of 'the point of view,'" all pretence to objectivity aside (Boltanski 2011, 84).

The contradiction between diverse horizons of interpretation that minorities might experience and those of the implied audiences that newspapers address is easily seen in how the quotes cited from the Montreal newspapers are groping to answer, or give opinions to, questions like the following: "Which rights are more important, individual or collective?" "Should we accept religious symbols in a secular state?" "Does the veil hinder integration?" or "Does prohibiting the veil hinder integration?" It is important to note that those affected by this legislation have already gained the right of residence, they have already gained this right to hospitality. They are already here. This is not a matter of who we should accept, of who has the right to be here, as that right is already granted. Ask yourself, rather, to whom are these quotes addressed as they frame issues that oppose majority and minority citizens? Do they address the girl or woman who would wear the veil? What do we learn about her expectations? Do the expectations of the immigrant regarding rights to difference need to be more modestly asserted to meet the expectations of a majority? A more inclusive form of address would be a more democratic form of communication. It would entail more than the occasional comment from an immigrant or immigrant-support group. It would require that the subjects be addressed in a dialogic manner that would mix external/official/objective and internal/personal/subjective story sources in ways that would not erase the subjects' voices or stop anticipating their responses, in ways that would not deny them the final word or close them out of the zone of address.

The same contradiction can be seen in the acts of journalism from New York, although here again the articles are not about immigration per se, but about undocumented citizens who are already resident in New York. While controversies concerning Quebec's Bill 94 are divided over the integration versus non-integration of immigrants, secularism versus theocracy, or women's emancipation versus freedom of religion, the US context is just as harshly divided between a raging drive for more incarcerations, on the one hand, and gradually watered-down pleas for amnesty (e.g., the Dream Act), on the other. The *New York Times* quotes are about the lives the undocumented lead, and the extraordinary consequences brought by poverty or threats of imminent deportation. By enumerating cases of fathers from multiple nationalities, the journalist sets a strong emotional tone that slips into a moral question about American citizenship. Their cases serve to make a point about an implied "us." These are the unfortunate or different "others" living among "us" and whose lives somehow impact on "us." Accept, tolerate, or deport "illegal aliens" and their children? Is under-paying them using them or dragging down wage labour for American citizens?

In uni-national federated countries like the United States ("One nation under God," as in the Pledge of Allegiance) or legally defined multinational federations like Canada, an abstract struggle over audi-bility among conflicting voices who oppose and who sympathize on a variety of levels with the issues of illegal immigration or reasonable accommodation are playing out in newspapers. And as a result of the binary opposition between them, both sides participate in the con-struction of a conduct that makes unconditional hospitality towards the illegal immigrant or cultural other impossible. Instead there are conditional arguments for amnesty, reasonable accommodation, or other temporary programs and policies. I am not arguing that this is a new contradiction for the state or for journalism, but rather that journalism has increasingly become a central societal mechanism that adjusts the public capacity to absorb difference so as to support a par-ticular sense of a "normal"/"natural" common people as well as a dominant voice or ethos. The contradiction between what journalists say about the subjects of social exclusion, who the implied "normal people" might be, and the offending lifestyle or legal status of the minorities referred to, does not so much hide a corporate agenda. Rather, it indicates unidentified or unspoken constraints journalists face when framing their address towards the implied audience. These constraints provide the parameters for what is possible for them to frame as subjects for the actual news organization and its manage-ment, the empirical reading public, and the "normal people" implied by their address.

Judith Butler defines norms not as rules that guide how we should perform, but as "implicit standards of normalization" that frame us as subjects and, in the process, define what it means "to have a life worth living," to be human or non-human, citizen or non-citizen, insider or outcast. In her book *Frames of War* (2009), she presents sev-eral examples of how media frame war, including "the frame of the photograph, the framing of the decision to go to war, the framing of immigration issues as a 'war at home,' and the framing of sexual and feminist politics in the service of the war effort." She argues that "the frame tends to function as an editorial embellishment" (8). Being framed has the same colloquial meaning as being set up for something you didn't do: "If one is framed, then a frame is constructed around one's deed such that the guilty status becomes the viewer's inevitable conclusion." Framing the frame or undoing the norm that is established shows that the frame can be changed and that a frame never quite determines "precisely what it is we see, think, recognize and apprehend" (ibid.).

Newspapers organize information in a similar way to the reports on the poetry and photographs of the Guantanamo prisoners that Butler analyses. At the substantive level, framing establishes whether the journalists' rational, emotional, and moral tones and judgments support the status quo, or question the event, issue, and agents that are featured in the story. At the procedural level, framing the norm is done in relation to the authority cited in news reports, through debate that forms around sensational individual cases, or through the construction of social facts and their implications for external variables such as policy, legislation, or community lobbying (Entman 2004).

What exceeds the frame and what is most important at substantive and procedural levels is that the implied audiences remain separate from the subjects of discussion. We read about the undocumented and the culturally or socially marginal in the third person, whether it is from external agencies, or internal groups or organizations that speak for them. The rational or moral tones that reporting frames are derived from the authority of independent data, official statements, and/or opinion from scholarly sources, while more emotional tones come from interviews with the subjects themselves. Although journalists often quote their subjects, especially for emotional effect, they rarely address the quotes back to the subjects' communities in any direct way.

From a purely pragmatic stance, the framing contradiction I have been discussing in the press seems banal and without consequence at first glance. After all, when we speak to someone about our support or rejection of other persons or causes we are not addressing those other persons directly. We frame our talk to someone either in support of, or in opposition to, others. In everyday conversation between actual speakers, the voices of "others" being talked about are seen as excluded from turn-taking, unless they are present and ask for rejoinders. When a speaker stops addressing the voices of the reported subject, discourse lodges itself in the to-and-fro of an abstract exchange with the implied audience. Here the speakers stop anticipating rejoinders from the animated subjects in the exchange, freeze their emotional-volitional tones into positions or pieces of information, stop being halfway on the side of the others' discourse, and become closed off, framing a final word about the other, and in the polemical form, stop listening to the subjects in the conversation. Hence we can conclude that one speaks differently when the "other's" voice is present, and even more so if the person gestures for a turn to speak.

After Public Journalism: Dialogic Acts

What would happen if journalism took up this attitude? Or, more radically, what would happen if acts of journalism took up the seemingly impossible attitude that the "other" was the addressee rather than the larger demos? What if the one being tolerated were part of the conversation about the limits of tolerance? What would happen if the subject of social exclusion being reported on would actually be addressed as central to, or even as a part of, the implied audience? What if the socially excluded were shifted from mere objects of reportage to internal addressees of mainstream news coverage – that is, from the third person (them) to the second person (you)?

The ideal demos is an imaginary unity for journalists. Yet, the imaginary unity of the demos comes from the diversity of its parts and not an oracle (Evans 2008). Serious journalism is not simply an official account espoused as a matter of course. Many journalists work against the power of oracles in society or look to investigate the plurality of voices that can be heard from the implied audience against the perceived truths of another implied audience, and yet, even the most decentred journalistic acts are not especially concerned with addressing as their audience the subjects of exclusion about which they speak. I am not able to answer these questions at the level of policy in the conclusion that follows, but I hope to at least formulate the questions better so we can begin a more fundamental discussion, not just on what journalism is for and how to regulate it, but how to think of new ways to practise it.

Could journalists reposition themselves within the hermeneutic contradiction and directly address the subjects they speak of so that a change between the implied audience and the ideal demos can become a possibility for a democracy to come? The multi-sided pressures bearing on acts of journalism in the present context suggest that this is now technologically possible, but economically and ideologically difficult. What new subjects of exclusion might such dialogic acts produce should acts

of journalism move in this direction? After ten years or so of speculation, study, and more speculation and study, no one seems to know
exactly how the macro shift in the mode of production is going to play
out – for the print media especially. At the level of political economy, it
makes one wonder if capital will ever allow liberal democracy to absorb
such acts of journalism as much as whether or not liberal democracy
will be able to continue without them.

In order to reduce the gap at the level of acts of journalism between
groups being reported on and the implied audience, the first point
would be to shift from the principles of objectivity (the view from
nowhere) and balance (the non-position) to a commitment to the
story (the point of view, standpoint, position). Expanding the
address in this direction could still be consistent with traditional
benchmarks of good journalism, but the journalist also needs to
derive reporting from where citizens or non-citizens are enacted.
This does not mean abandoning accuracy or fairness, but rather
engaging the story itself and in the process making assumptions
about bias and framing more explicit. Shifting to a commitment to
the story, from the point of view of the subjects, and addressing the
story back to the subjects in such a way as they might recognize
themselves, would mean undoing the conventional frame. Balance
and accuracy continue to provide guidelines to prevent the serious
press from falling into a pack mentality for the new implied audience of the subjects being reported on. This doesn't mean the journalists' first obligation is to speak truth to power, but it does mean
a new discourse that connects the relation between knowledge and
power in a different way. The type of journalism that speaks truth
to power (à la Marx) assumes that there is an original truth and
so repeats the same mantra as traditional definitions of the craft.
If the alternative means only being adversarial, though, it cannot
be enough of a guideline to turn acts of journalism into a dialogic
force, as it would simply mean another innovation that reinforces
the misleading assumption of the passive transmission of knowledge towards an equally passive receiver.

I think a good place to move back to in order to think about strategies
in this direction is the public or civic journalism movement of the 1990s,
better known in the United States than in Canada (Nielsen et al. 2009).
It is a good example of a journalism that sought to address audience
members as citizens who can engage in dialogue in order to respond
to this kind of challenge. The idea began in a symposium on a question

posed by the Ethics and Excellence in Journalism Foundation in Oklahoma City in 1994. Journalists and researchers were asked to explore the extent to which "the ethical journalist is an isolated 'individualist,'" and the extent to which "he or she is a member of the wider community" (Black 1997, v). Is the journalist an individual who reports on the personal troubles of non-citizens to a community of citizens, and what, if any, responsibility does the journalist have towards the community being reported on?

A series of debates and innovations with focus groups representing communities that had not been previously addressed were carried out with some urban newspapers in various US cities. The debates drew hard-line polemics around the professional principles of objectivity in ways that sought to draw mainstream journalism more directly into the cultures it reported on (Lambeth et al. 1998; Esterowicz and Roberts 2000). At the height of the movement, more than 60 per cent of American newspapers received funding to experiment with the model (Haas 2007). As the movement declined, prominent corporate media editors claimed victory by arguing that public journalism was redundant, given that the mandate of the urban newspaper already included extensive reporting on communities and that the issue was about the majority empirical audience and not a minority implied audience (Rosen 1999). Critics of the political economy of media perceived the public journalism movement as naive, arguing that the news industry is motivated by profit and loss and that stories emerge primarily because they sell, so that the majority empirical audience is actually a commodity (Compton 2000). Those most invested in expanding the role of journalism towards broader public forms of communication have argued that public journalism needs to shift online to citizen journalism, blogging, and crowd-sourcing; in fact, some argue that public journalism grew as a "step toward the current model of citizen journalism" (Kelly 2009). Still others argue the ethical concern about the role of journalists in public discourse "is not about the wondrous addition of citizen media, but the decline of the full-time, professional monitoring of powerful institutions" (Kovach and Rosenstiel 2007, 185).

It became obvious that the movement for public journalism lacked the kind of rigorous and systematic analysis needed to keep pace with the transformations of the more post-industrial form now in place. Moreover, attempts to shift mainstream journalism failed as the scope of the movement was so broad it missed the obvious problem I raise by focusing uniquely on forms of social exclusion via audience address in beats like immigration and cultural difference. I recognize that socially and culturally marginalized actors do not constitute an attractive market for commercial news organizations, and I am equally aware that research has long demonstrated that journalists are reluctant to change habits and set narrative patterns. But the problematics for public journalism and citizen journalism need to be advanced beyond arguments rooted in economic and technological determinism, and communitarian versus information politics, in order to focus on new robust frames of expression that emphasize the way in which journalism needs to change its mode of address.

In my view, this change requires encouragement towards the following five practical shifts from the traditional craft of journalism: (1) from external to more internal sources; (2) from constative to more performative acts; (3) from rational to more adversarial tones; (4) from accuracy to increased editorial autonomy; and (5) from objectivity and balance to more commitment to the story. I quickly comment on each of these before concluding.

If the assumption is correct that journalists do not innocently report on or comment on an ongoing problem without being selective and actively framing the story, would journalism be any less veridical, accurate, and balanced if the craft were turned towards addressing subjects of social exclusion and cultural difference directly as audiences? The first step is to reconsider the traditional way the journalist connects subjects of the reports, and the framing of emotional, rational, and moral tones that indicate the proximity or distance with the implied audience. Dialogue means making not only constative but also performative propositions to keep conversation alive. The first Montreal quote above is a good example in which the journalist appears to speak with the subject about face covering, but actually confirms an expectation with the implied audience that the ideal demos should be accommodated rather than the other way around. Mainstream acts of journalism tend to speak about, rather than with, the voices of the undocumented and the culturally marginal. Such acts are bound to favour the rational orientation of tolerance and its preference that the strong give up something to the weak. In this kind of framing, the implied reader is not encouraged towards unconditional hospitality for the emotional and volitional orientation of the other in his or her time and place. Speaking directly with internal sources does not mean that rigour of procedure and accuracy should be loosened – otherwise how can information be reliable (a major criticism of citizen journalism)?

Reporting from where the subjects are situated, like the last quote addressed to the Quebec immigrant cited above, or the first quote about Latino fathers on the run in the *New York Times*, still doesn't provoke more conversation. What is needed is to gain a greater exchange of rejoinders to problems or solutions. If the journalist could provoke a performative dialogue, the chance of reducing the gap between the implied audience and the subjects being reported on would increase and, by implication, public culture would become more of an unfinished dialogue between speakers. In other words, journalists would need to accept more responsibility to intervene in order to increase the quality of dialogue and the scope of inclusion.

The performative dimension is often seen in reports that express shock about official policies proposed by governments or their oppositional counter-proposals (Nielsen 2009). Yet these reports also frame the same distance between the implied reader and the subjects who are being discussed. The same is also the case in articles that express hospitality towards the most excluded but are also committed to demonstrating the conditions of authenticity placed on them. Using strongly slanted emotional-volitional tones derived from where the subjects themselves are situated in their life-worlds provides an uncanny hook effect, but it alone is not enough to provoke the kind of dialogue I am referring to here. What is needed is to bring the interlocutors together into a deeper exchange in order to expand the criteria of inclusivity and begin to express a greater diversity of voices in the public conversation. To do this, acts of journalism need to become more adversarial. This should not mean more one-sided, ideological, or monologic writing. Journalists' responsibility would, rather, be to contribute openly and directly to the deliberative, multi-voiced democratic process through exercising their skills of research and communicative action to provide fairness in dialogue rather than neutral and passive detachment.

The idea for developing a more inclusive internal dialogue between the journalists and the subjects of their reports is derived from the argument that dialogue is not limited to a conventional exchange of ideas as in a conversation between two speakers that can be decoded according to linguistic rules. It is understood, rather, as the process that takes place in the imagination of the journalist and their idea, however distant or intimate, of the audience (McQuail 2010; Iser 1974; Butler 2009).

Participation in dialogue means that words and phrases anticipate rejoinders from an animated other rather than from a non-responsive audience commodity. Strategies for shifting this process begin not just from where the actors are located, as in much of community, alternative, or emerging citizens' journalism, but in prioritizing a lively anticipated response from the subjects of reports as themselves the primary addressees.

To conclude, I have tried to sketch a definition of the limits within mainstream acts of journalism and have indicated the need for several additions if we hope to expand on the implied audience for liberal democracies to come. These shifts need to be situated against multisided genealogies of norms of address that journalism is embedded in, and not just the political-economic imperatives that drive its industry. Who are the journalists' primary addressees? What is the interpretive contradiction in the address? Second, we need to undo norms of social regulation that orient journalism's framing for the implied societal cultures it is said to reproduce, preserve, or facilitate. Expanding the implied audience needs to mean more than assuring a place for political communication through direct address, but actually changing the form so as to anticipate rejoinders and allow deep conflicts of opinion to enter into deliberation.

In short, the critique of the political economy of journalism needs to be joined with a critical dialogic analysis so as to better demonstrate the aporia present in acts of journalism. Such a deconstruction doesn't start from the question about what acts of journalism are for, nor simply in whose interests they are performed, but rather how and towards whom they are addressed.

NOTE

1 A Bill that would ban face covering in a variety of public spaces was proposed in the Quebec National Assembly in March 2010, after controversies around reasonable accommodation reintensified with the expelling of students wearing the niqab from government-sponsored French-language classes. Another controversy around the veil took place in 2007, when the federal government ruled that women can vote with their faces covered as long as they provide identification. The Quebec chief electoral officer over-ruled that law and banned voting with a covered face in Quebec. A private member's bill was also introduced in the federal

Parliament in February 2011 that would ban voting with a covered face. It has not yet become law. In 2014, the Parti Québécois government convened public hearings into a "Charter affirming the values of State secularism and religious neutrality and of equality between women and men, and providing a framework for accommodation requests." The Liberal Party has since replaced the former PQ government and introduced a bill on "State religious neutrality," including restrictions on face covering, in June 2015.

PART TWO

New Journalism Policies

3 Media Policy Reform as a Foundation for Better Journalism

DAVID SKINNER, KATHLEEN CROSS, AND
ROBERT A. HACKETT

It is impossible to ... exercise meaningful citizenship without access to news, information, analysis and opinion.

Bacon Report

The role of journalism in the struggle for democratic participation and governance is fundamental (Baker 2007). Yet over the past few years, journalism in Canada has faced several disturbing and interacting trends that have undermined its ability to serve this role, as job losses, ownership concentration, changes in management structures, and the influence of public relations have all taken their toll.

For example, both the private and public sectors have been hit with large layoffs. The Canadian Media Guild has estimated that ten thousand Canadian media jobs were lost between 2008 and 2013 through a combination of layoffs and buyouts (Wong 2013). And, since that time, in April 2014 the CBC cut 657 positions (and expected to reduce its workforce by between 1,000 and 1,500 by 2020) (Kane 2014; Bradshaw 2014a). This follows on what already appear to be large losses through the 1980s and 1990s (see Miller 1998). Many of these layoffs can be seen as the product of increasing concentration of ownership and ensuing demands to maintain or increase the profit levels of these large corporate media organizations.

At the same time, the once sacrosanct boundaries between journalism and marketing have eroded. The 1990s witnessed the emergence of the concept of the "Total Newspaper," in which "editorial, advertising, circulation, research, and promotion functions are all coordinated around marketing concerns" (Underwood 1993, 16). One of the less-often noted consequences of this managerial trend is its class bias. Since affluent readers are of greater interest to advertisers than are the less well-heeled, such a market-driven editorial policy disproportionately reflects the political and cultural sensitivities of the affluent. Greg Nielsen alludes to this in his discussion of the implied audience in chapter 2.

The character of journalism has also been shifting. Political diversity has declined along with a slide to the right, especially on economic issues (such as "free" trade, social programs, and privatization) as distinct from social issues (such as same-sex marriage or abortion rights). That shift is associated with the politics of interventionist media conglomerate owners past and present, such as Pierre Karl Péladeau, the Asper family, and Conrad Black (see Edge 2007). But it is also a by-product of persistent corporate propaganda campaigns that have courted journalists, students, and policy-makers with a steady stream of speakers, conferences, and research consciously aimed at popularizing neo-liberal ideology and policies (Gutstein 2009).

The CBC, one of the mainstays of broadcast journalism in Canada, appears to have tilted in this direction as well. For example, the CBC television program *Face Off*, which regularly accessed progressive views, albeit pitted against conservative opponents, was cancelled, and now none of its programs focuses on unions or workers' rights. Meanwhile, programs glorifying business and markets – such as *The Exchange, Dragons' Den*, and on radio, the screedlike *Invisible Hand* – are on the rise. Similarly, the loudest voices on the public airwaves seem to be those of right-wing populists and neo-liberal ideologues (e.g., Rex Murphy, Andrew Coyne), while their left-of-centre counterparts have been largely silenced.

Some of the changes to CBC content can be understood in the light of the economic challenges it has faced over the past two decades. A Nordicity study found that between 1991 and 2009, federal grants to the Crown corporation increased by only 8 per cent. Over the same period, however, spending on other cultural organizations and activities grew by 71 per cent, and total federal government spending increased by 83 per cent (excluding defence and debt payments) (Nordicity 2011, 14). In spring 2012, the federal government announced a 10 per cent budget cut for the CBC, and in July the CRTC shut down the Local Programming Improvement Fund, effectively cutting another $40 million from the CBC's programming budget (Canadian Media Guild 2012). These cuts, combined with loss of revenue from sports programming and shortfalls in advertising revenue, led to the layoffs discusssed above (CBC 2014).

But while the circumstances undermining journalism's role in the process of democratic self-governance may have intensified in recent years, concerns over the kinds of problems now facing journalism are not new. This chapter begins with a historical review of some of these concerns. It considers why comprehensive reform has been elusive. And, drawing from past recommendations, it enumerates some possible contemporary reforms. Finally, it considers three examples of organizations seeking changes in the media and the insights they might hold for advancing a larger media reform movement.

Looking Back

Driven by values such as the need for an informed citizenship, access to a diversity of media, and cultural sovereignty, concern over the circulation of news and ideas in Canada has a long history. With a small population spread across a vast geography, high costs have mitigated against national distribution of Canadian-made media products. At the same time, given the close proximity of the United States – the world's largest producer and exporter of media products – Canadian media have often had difficulty competing with the cost advantages afforded by their American cousins' economies of scale. Put simply, there is much more money to be made importing news and information products that have already recovered their costs in the huge US market, than there is producing comparable Canadian products. Consequently, government regulation has often been used to offset the effects of geography and the impacts that unbridled markets can have on the news and information available to Canadians. Over the years, in the face of these obstacles, broadcasting, newspapers, magazines, film, and book publishing have all enjoyed varying degrees of public support (see Hindley et al. 1977; Vipond 2011; Gasher et al. 2016).

Aided by various forms of government regulation, by the mid-twentieth century many Canadian newspapers and private broadcasters were prospering (Skinner and Gasher 2005, 51–76). But as these industries developed, the advantages of economies of scale led to pressures for rationalization and the formation of increasingly large newspaper and television chains (Audley 1983, 204, 290). But reaping the economic benefits of concentration took a toll on content. As newspapers and broadcast newsrooms shared stories and other material across their respective chains and networks, the overall number of reporters and editorial voices declined. At the same time, newspaper chains allowed more opportunity for owners and managers to shape editorial material, not only by directly influencing how stories and editorials were written, but indirectly as well through hiring decisions and editorial policies. Cross-media ownership, whereby companies counted both newspapers and different kinds of broadcast outlets among their holdings, exacerbated these possibilities.

At the same time, focused on the bottom line and dependent on advertising as the major source of income, the impact of the escalating commercial character of media companies on newspapers and news in general became more obvious. On the one hand, news and commentary were increasingly seen to be shaped by a "consumerist orientation," representing things such as labour-management conflicts and oil price increases in terms of their impact on the cost to individual consumers rather than examining the larger social, political, and economic forces that animated them (Hackett et al. 1992, 14). In taking this perspective, media companies sought to maximize potential audiences but, in the process, income and other disparities between both readers and other social groups were smoothed over and hidden from view. On the other hand, gaps and blindspots in media coverage started to draw more notice. Advertisers were interested in reaching not just anybody, but those people most likely to buy their products and services. Consequently, news and information that was of interest to people beyond their target demographics tended to be glossed over or omitted (see Hackett et al. 2000, 165–217).

Out of concern for the possible effects of escalating concentration on the range and diversity of media content in the broadcasting field, the Board of Broadcast Governors (BBG) – precursor to the Canadian Radio-television and Telecommunications Commission (CRTC) – in 1966 formulated a network ownership policy. But concentration continued to escalate in both the broadcast and newspaper industries and, under increasing public pressure, the Special Senate Committee on Mass Media (the Davey Committee) was struck in 1969 to investigate "the impact and influence" of "ownership and control" on the mass media.

The Davey Committee examined a wide range of Canadian media, including broadcasting, newspapers, and magazines. Its report did not uncover any direct evidence that chain ownership necessarily undermined editorial diversity or quality, but the committee was clear that, driven by market forces, rising concentration of ownership represented a direct threat to media quality (Canada 1970, 69). While no action immediately followed the enquiry, some of the committee's recommendations would eventually find application in regulation. For instance, in the mid-1970s, Bill C-58 brought tax measures to help strengthen the advertising revenues of Canadian-owned media and to ensure Canadian ownership of Canadian newspapers. Over the years, these measures have made substantial contributions to the incomes of Canadian print and broadcast media (CBC 2011c).

Ten years later, a series of share swaps and newspaper closures by the Southam and Thomson newspaper chains prompted the federal government to strike the Royal Commission on Newspapers (the Kent Commission) to investigate conditions in the industry. Like Davey, the Kent Commission was unable to discover much evidence of direct editorial meddling by owners. But, given both the ways in which concentration of ownership foreclosed on the number of journalistic voices and the possibilities for editorial interference it afforded, the Kent Commission did find that "the structure of the industry that has now been created, that existing law and public policy have permitted, is clearly and directly contrary to the public interest" (Canada 1981, 225). Key among Kent's sweeping recommendations was the creation of a Canada Newspaper Act that would limit concentration, protect editorial independence, and establish a Press Rights Panel to oversee the performance of newspapers under the terms of the Act (Canada 1981, 237–55). However, plans for the introduction of legislation were upset by a national election, and the new government failed to act. In an attempt to head off further government regulation, the industry established press councils in British Columbia and in the Atlantic Provinces (see Miller 1998, 42–3). The federal Cabinet also issued a directive to the CRTC designed to limit the cross-ownership of newspaper and broadcasting outlets in the same market. But no divestitures were ever ordered, and following the election of Brian Mulroney's Progressive Conservative government, this order was rescinded in 1985.

Through the 1980s, both the Mulroney government's pro-market stance and threats of US satellite broadcasting fragmenting Canadian markets pressed upon the CRTC to loosen broadcast regulation. And, while government enquiries continued to recommend action to curb escalating concentration because of its impact on journalism, no formal policies were forthcoming (see Canada 1986, 703). Rather, in the early 1990s, a recession combined with shrinking readerships and shifts in advertising markets put serious pressure on publishers' bottom lines and Southam was taken over by Conrad Black's Hollinger Corporation. By 1999, Hollinger-controlled newspapers accounted for better than 48 per cent of the circulation of English-language dailies in Canada, and amid layoffs and charges of editorial interference, concerns over concentration continued to grow (Miller 1998; Taras 2001, 212–13).

While restructuring was proceeding apace in the newspaper industry, the digitization of media content began to blur the technological and regulatory boundaries between the telecommunications, broadcasting, and cable industries. On the heels of similar changes in the United States, the Canadian federal government issued a Convergence Policy Statement in 1996, removing barriers to cross-media ownership and laying the ground for cable and telecommunications companies to compete head to head in delivering telecommunications and broadcast services (see Armstrong, 2010). And, opening yet another avenue to ownership concentration, in 1999 the CRTC announced that it would not regulate the Internet in Canada. It would take several years for these policies to take root in industry, but when they did it would be with a vengeance.

Three major cross-media ownership deals struck during 2000 radically altered the Canadian mediascape. In Quebec, Quebecor's purchase of Sun Media left two companies – Quebecor and Power Corp. – holding 97 per cent of French-language newspaper circulation in that province. A short time later, Canwest, owner of the Global Television Network, purchased the Southam newspaper group. And Bell Canada Enterprises (BCE, Canada's largest telecommunications company) purchased the Canadian Television Network (CTV, the country's largest private television network), and then struck an alliance with Thomson Newspapers to form Bell Globemedia.

From a corporate perspective, the attraction of these mergers was at least twofold. First, they presented the possibility of reaggregating audiences fragmented by the Internet and the proliferation of a range of delivery platforms through owning media outlets in each of those locations. And, second, they provided the ability to reuse editorial content and programming across those different properties. In an attempt to ensure diversity in television and newspaper news production, as a condition of licence for its broadcast outlets, the CRTC ordered Quebecor to keep completely separate news production facilities among its converged media properties (a requirement that has since been eliminated). But both CTV and Global balked at this idea and they were required to maintain only "independent management and presentation structures" (Zerbisias 2001; Hope 2002). At the same time, the CRTC also noted that if the Canadian Broadcast Standards Council (CBSC) adopted "a self-regulatory code of conduct concerning cross-media ownership," the regulator would consider suspending those conditions (CRTC 2007b, 41).

The mergers left these companies saddled with crippling debt, forcing layoffs and other cost-cutting measures. Under the weight of this debt, two of the three new corporate arrangements didn't survive the decade. But, in the meantime, accusations of editorial interference from Canwest employees precipitated another round of government studies (Shade 2005).

The impacts of these mergers on the quality of journalism raised alarm bells with politicians at both the provincial and federal levels, and through the early 2000s a series of high-profile commissions conducted enquiries into the possible effects of escalating concentration (Québec 2003; Canada 2003, 2006a). Drawing conclusions similar to those of Davey and Kent, these enquiries were concerned with the general propensity of concentration of ownership to narrow the range of viewpoints available to the public and the opportunities it provided for meddling owners to shape editorial perspectives. Highlighting both the dangers of escalating corporate control over news production and the importance of CBC/Radio-Canada to the larger media system, they made a set of wide-ranging and comprehensive recommendations to help ensure a diversity of media perspectives and the independence of journalists. These recommendations included the following: strengthening the Competition Act to address mergers of news and information companies; developing a federal policy on cross-media ownership; creating measures to protect the editorial independence of editors and journalists; and increasing the powers of the CRTC to monitor conditions of licence and levy fines where applicable (see Canada 2006a, 23–62; Canada 2003, 410–11). Meanwhile, a number of Canadian studies from the period underscored concerns of corporate influence on news coverage (Hackett et al. 2000; CJFE 2002).

In its response to these reports, the federal government showed little interest in increasing forms of support for news media, claiming that "Canada has a highly diverse, dynamic, and economically viable news sector" (Canada 2006c, 13; see Canada, 2005, 2006a). Meanwhile, industry shakeups continued (Winseck 2010).

Amid these ongoing concerns over the structure and character of the industry, the CRTC announced it would hold a hearing on the diversity of voices in Canadian media, a key element of which would be consideration of concentration of ownership. Following hearings in Ottawa in 2008, the CRTC issued a number of general policy principles regarding permissible levels of concentration. Among these were three key guidelines specifying that no one company might control (1) more than 45 per cent of the total national audience share; (2) all of the broadcast distribution undertakings in any particular market; or (3) a local radio station, TV station, or newspaper serving the same market (CRTC 2008b). While these regulations sought to curb what were seen as the worst excesses of ownership concentration, critics were quick to point out that despite extremely high levels of concentration in several markets, they would require no divestment on the part of current owners. Further, given that very few private radio stations produce original news reports, there was some question as to whether the cross-media restriction would have any real impact.

The CRTC also announced that with some minor adjustments it was accepting the Journalistic Independence Code of the Canadian Broadcast Standards Council. Under the terms of that code, companies are not required to separate their newsrooms, only to maintain separate news management and presentation structures. The code does not contain an enforcement mechanism, nor does it offer any remedy to the kinds of editorial meddling that prompted concerns during Hollinger's and Canwest's tenure as major newspaper proprietors (see CBSC/CCNR n.d.).

Soon after the new rules were put in place, the television industry faced another crisis. Fragmenting audiences, coupled with worsening economic conditions, were squeezing local television markets. In June 2008, the CRTC approved the sale of the bankrupt Télévision Quatre Saisons network and allowed the new owners to lower significantly local news coverage (Canada 2009a, 3). In October of that year, in an effort to spur local production, the CRTC created the Local Programming Improvement Fund (LPIF), financed by a levy on satellite and cable companies. But, in early 2009, before the fund could come into effect, both CTV and Canwest Global announced they would close or sell stations in a number of smaller markets in Ontario, Alberta, and British Columbia.

The Standing Committee on Canadian Heritage struck a committee to examine the local television issue (Canada 2009a). Following hearings, the committee's recommendations focused on public interest measures to bolster the economic viability of local stations and increase the range of perspectives at the local level. For instance, recommendations included mandatory satellite carriage of local signals; increasing the size of the LPIF; and making the LPIF available to Aboriginal, educational, and community broadcasters, as well as to CBC/Radio-Canada and private broadcasters. There were also a number of recommendations to increase regulatory oversight, such as giving the CRTC the ability to fine companies not in compliance with regulations. Overall, the opinion of the Committee was divided, however, with Conservative members attaching a dissenting opinion that opposed increasing regulatory oversight or subsidies (Canada 2009a, 51–4).

Meanwhile, the debt Canwest Global had assumed to finance its convergence bid almost a decade earlier took its toll and, in October 2009, the company filed for bankruptcy. Within a year, the company's newspapers were bought by a group of investors and renamed Postmedia. The broadcast holdings were purchased by Shaw. This shuffle conformed to the new CRTC cross-media regulations, but the Shaw purchase further fuelled concerns over growing vertical integration (CRTC 2010c).

By 2009, levels of cross-media ownership between newspapers and broadcasters, which had drawn the attention of inquiries since the 1970s, had declined somewhat. Although Quebecor's Sun Media chain claimed 23.7 per cent of national daily newspaper circulation, Postmedia, the largest newspaper company in the country with 30.8 per cent of daily circulation, had no significant broadcast holdings (Gasher et al. 2012, 255).

On another front, however, vertical integration between broadcast producers and distributors continued to escalate. In September 2010, BCE purchased full ownership of CTV. Less than a year later, Bell also announced that it had made a deal to purchase Astral Media, Canada's largest pay and specialty television company. The Bell-Astral merger set off a firestorm of concern from both industry competitors and public interest groups alike (Wallace 2012).

Meanwhile a new chair, Jean-Pierre Blais, took the helm of the CRTC. Despite concerns that it might sound the death-knell for local production, including news programs, one of his first orders of business was to announce the phasing out of the LPIF (CRTC 2012c). Prompted by claims from the large, vertically integrated companies – the same companies responsible for providing the fund – that it was no longer necessary, the fund's termination promised to hit the CBC and independent stations particularly hard. For the CBC alone, it would result in $40 million less for local programming annually (CBC 2012c).

A few months later, citing concerns over threats to media diversity, the CRTC blocked BCE's takeover of Astral (Campion Smith 2012). Given the Commission's track record, this was a notable decision. While in the past the CRTC has ordered companies to divest themselves of some holdings acquired in mergers, it had never outright prohibited a deal of this size. A combination of forces seems to have contributed to the decision. On one side, the deal exceeded limits laid out in the *Diversity of Voices* policy. On another, a broad coalition of forces – including many of the largest industry players, a range of consumer and public interest groups (including OpenMedia, discussed below), and individuals – strongly opposed it (CRTC 2012d). However, in June 2013 the CRTC went on to approve a revised, $3.4 billion deal that required BCE to sell off some of the holdings it had acquired (CBC 2013).

From this brief history, it is clear that the current crisis in journalism in Canada has long and deep roots. Ongoing efforts to wring profits from newspapers and broadcast media have tended to undercut the resources allocated to journalism and undermine public interest goals, content diversity, and editorial independence since at least the late 1960s. Most recently, the proliferation of satellite and pay-TV channels, coupled with the digitization of information and the rise of the Internet, has fragmented audiences and undermined traditional advertiser-supported business models. Mergers and acquisitions have been the central strategy for reaggregating audiences and restoring profitability but, in the process, labour costs have been a key cost-cutting target, and investigative journalism in particular has suffered. From this perspective, it is clear that market forces alone cannot solve the problems identified by decades of studies and enquiries.

Will the Internet Solve the Crisis in Journalism?

The Internet has provided some openings for addressing the crisis in journalism. Trained and experienced journalists have begun to create an online presence through blogging and by offering free content, and more commercial outlets such as the *Huffington Post* are developing audiences. At the same time, social media and forms of citizen journalism have underpinned contemporary social movements such as the Arab Spring, the Occupy Movement, and most recently in Canada, Idle No More (Galloway 2012).

However, a number of trends counteract the often-touted potential of Web-based media to replace traditional print and broadcast media. First, and on the most basic level, not all people have equal access to the Web. In 2013, Statistics Canada reported that 98 per cent of households with income of $94,000 or more had Internet access, compared with only 58 per cent of households with income of $30,000 or less (Statistics Canada 2013a, 2013b; CBC 2011b). Moreover, simple access data understate the depth of the digital divide, which is also informed by age, gender, class, income, education level, market size, and other inequalities (Barney 2005, 153–61). Under conditions of commercial development, the digital divide is likely to reinforce other societal inequalities, including those of political participation and influence.

Second, the production of consistent quality content is expensive and the provision of a comprehensive news and information service is typically well beyond the means of small, independent website operators. While there are a few Canadian Web-based news sites that provide good critical and investigative voices, such as the *Tyee*, they are short on resources and thereby limited in scope (see Skinner 2012). A recent victim of apparent economic woes was OpenFile, a news website touted as particularly innovative, but which suspended operations in September 2012. Others, such as Rabble and Straight Goods, operate largely as aggregators of information rather than original producers. Still others, such as the *Huffington Post Canada*, offer some Canadian news and commentary, but are largely American in content and offer very little in terms of regional and local content. Similarly, while they may add a useful ingredient to the various journalisms now on the Internet's menu, individual bloggers and citizen journalists simply do not have the resources to replace professional journalists (Compton and Benedetti 2010; McChesney and Nichols 2010, 81–2).

Finally, the Internet is at risk of being colonized by the same commercial logic and corporate giants that dominate the traditional information media. Those corporations have the resources to marginalize small content providers, including the ability to afford big losses on speculative ventures, the funds to invest in or buy out start-up media ventures (such as the AOL buy-out of the *Huffington Post* in the US), multimedia promotion of their own websites, brand-name recognition, and funding to get the best position on Web portals (McChesney 1997, 30–4; Nichols and McChesney 2005, 180–4). Convergence between newspaper, broadcast, telecommunication, and cable companies gives large media companies substantial power to shape the Internet's architecture to their own advantage, and to censor troublesome content. And, because traditional, segregated advertising does not work well on the Web, content providers have an incentive to integrate advertising and editorial, which may further intensify the commercial character of media content (McChesney 2004).

In short, the journalistic potential of the Internet can only be developed through supportive public policy that ensures a diversity of voices in terms of producers and universal and affordable access.

What Policies Are Needed to Revitalize Canadian Journalism?

As we have seen, over the years a number of policies have been enacted that both directly and indirectly support journalism and news media in Canada. For instance, after decades of recommendations, the CRTC finally implemented a policy on concentration of ownership in 2008, even if it is weak in character. The CBSC's Journalistic Independence Code was implemented at the same time, although it is superficial in terms of focus and lacks teeth in terms of application. Other measures include the following: press councils in some provinces and the National NewsMedia Council (created in 2015), the Canada Periodical Fund to help support magazine publishing, legislation to protect Canadian advertising markets, and a number of rules keeping foreign ownership at bay. However, all of these measures could use strengthening and updating and, drawing from the recommendations of studies and enquiries over the years, there are a number of further steps that might be undertaken to support journalism and help ensure media diversity. These steps include:

1 Lower ceilings on concentration and cross-media ownership in Canadian media. As noted above, the current limits on concentration need to be strengthened. In calculating acceptable limits, radio should not be treated as a comprehensive news source.
2 Enforcement and/or strengthening of foreign ownership rules. The Bacon Report (Canada 2006a, 44–5) notes that Section 19 of the Income Tax Act, which prohibits Canadian companies from deducting advertising expenditures in foreign-owned media, is not being adequately enforced, which means Canadian media may be missing out on substantial revenues. At the same time, there is a looming threat of increased foreign ownership of broadcasting as the federal government considers relaxing telecommunications

ownership requirements to increase competition in mobile communication markets. Given the level of vertical integration between broadcasting and telecommunications companies, such a development would only serve to further undermine media diversity as foreign owners move to exploit economies of scale with media products from their home markets.

3 Creation of a tax regime that supports journalism and Canadian media. Changing the definition of charitable foundations to include not-for-profit media would be a good step in this direction (cf. Canada 2006a, 44).

4 Increased support for alternative and online media. Restrictions on support mechanisms such as the Canada Periodical Fund should be loosened to include alternative and online media (see Ladurantaye 2012).

5 Increased support for public, community, Aboriginal, and educational broadcasters. While the 1991 Broadcasting Act provides for different types of broadcasters, they are not well supported in the larger regulatory framework, particularly in the case of community broadcasters, as argued by Karen Wirsig and Catherine Edwards in chapter 4. To improve local media coverage, public, community, Aboriginal, and educational broadcasters should have access to all production funds as well as be part of basic cable tiers and have "must carry" privileges on satellite services and other forms of broadcast distribution.

6 Reinstatement of the Local Programming Improvement Fund. As was well argued by a number of recipients, the LPIF was an important support for local programming, including news. The fund should be open to all broadcasters, including community and Aboriginal broadcasters.

7 Stabilized funding for the CBC. As a number of studies point out, the CBC is the main provider of local broadcast news, as well as other local fare (see Canada 2006a, 22). Recent cuts will only exacerbate problems in this regard. At the same time, CBC funding should be de-linked from political decisions, as is the case with the BBC in the United Kingdom.

8 Amendment of the Federal Competition Act. As has been pointed out by a number of studies, current competition law does not appraise media diversity (see Canada 2006a, 24–8). The Act should be amended to include such considerations.

9 Creation of a comprehensive code of professional independence and the establishment of a governing body run by journalists – not media owners – to oversee and enforce it. While the CBSC code is a step in the right direction, it lacks adequate protections from management meddling in the news process, as well as an enforcement mechanism (see O'Carroll 2012; Marier 2012).

10 Establishment of a comprehensive national digital strategy. While the federal government did announce a digital strategy in April 2014, it amounted to little more than a rehash of existing programs and previous announcements (see openmedia.ca 2014). A comprehensive strategy must include measures to support and nurture online media and citizens' journalism, as well as address the digital divide (see Geist 2009).

Why Democratic Media Reform Faces an Uphill Battle

Given the long history of studies and enquiries recommending more diverse and democratic media, why are the kinds of policies that we outline above not already in place? Part of the answer to this question might be seen in the structure of regulation, which affords corporate stakeholders several distinct advantages. Another lies in the difficulties in developing enough public pressure to push reforms through (see Salter and Salter 1997; Barney 2005, 27–30; Raboy and Shtern 2010, 88–9).

On the structural side, while the CRTC has some ability to allocate resources contained within the system it oversees, it has no funds of its own to invest in that system. Nor does it have any direct control over the budgets of organizations operating in the system, such as private broadcasters or the CBC. Consequently, the goals and ambitions of regulation are circumscribed by the willingness of corporations and governments to invest in the system. Moreover, commissioners often have industry backgrounds and thus may be more familiar with, and sympathetic to, corporate perspectives. At the same time, the regulatory process itself also favours large, well-heeled stakeholders: in other words, large media corporations. Hearings are generally conducted in Ottawa and, while in some cases the CRTC reimburses the expenses of interveners, for the most part participants wishing to appear at proceedings must do so at their own expense. At the same time, keeping up with the CRTC's regulatory agenda, and undertaking the research necessary to understand the possible social, political, and economic impacts of the issues it addresses, is impossible without the benefit of paid staff, something very few besides major media corporations can afford. This is not to say that the CRTC is necessarily captured by industry, or bound to simply serve its interests; but as a regulatory venue, the CRTC is tilted in favour of corporate and market interests, as noted by Wirsig and Edwards in chapter 4.

That tilt has hardened in recent years. Despite the many reservations expressed by repeated public enquiries towards unrestricted corporate power in media markets, since the mid-1980s both governments and the CRTC have often expressed preference for regulation by market forces over comprehensive government regulation in developing and allocating communicative resources. In this vein, the CRTC's 2012 decision to discontinue the Local Program Improvement Fund stated that it would benefit "Canadians who pay the subscriber fees from which the LPIF is derived" (CRTC 2012c). Such a consumer focus matched the faith of Stephen Harper's Conservative government in market forces, but overlooked the obvious negative impacts the decision would have on the range and character of local programming (Canada 2009a, 51–4). While the new chair of the CRTC expressed interest in going beyond simple market conceptions of regulation to "consider Canadians as creators and citizens" (CRTC 2012g), overcoming the contrary ideological bent of a government in power is a bigger challenge.

Beyond the biases of regulatory processes and government agendas, broader obstacles to democratic media reform are posed by political and legal structures. Jurisdiction over media regulation in Canada is patchwork, making comprehensive media reform difficult. At a basic level, the federal-provincial division of powers limits the kinds of policies that any one level of government might undertake. And jurisdiction at the federal level is also divided. For instance, magazine publishing and the film industry fall under the purview of the Department of Canadian Heritage, while broadcasting and telecommunications regulation are the responsibility of the CRTC. Given that technological convergence and concentration of ownership is increasingly blurring distinctions between industries, coordinating policy actions is difficult. Similarly, while the CRTC is responsible for regulating broadcasting and telecommunications, it has no direct powers over newspapers. As we have seen, the Commission can indirectly influence newspaper organizations through placing conditions of licence on the broadcast or telecommunications holdings of companies that also have newspaper holdings. But comprehensive regulation of newspapers is beyond the scope of the

CRTC. The CRTC has also refused to regulate the Internet. And while there are instances where the Commission might be seen to have bent this rule, such as in the case of Net neutrality or Internet throttling, it has abstained from content regulation in this realm.

Legal and constitutional factors can also limit the potential for exacting reforms from media corporations. Despite the Kent Commission's assertion that "freedom of the press is not a property right of owners," media corporations are private properties, not some kind of public commons (Canada 1981, 1). The chequered history of regulatory attempts to enforce Canadian-content regulations in broadcasting illustrates the difficulties inherent in trying to force owners to establish production practices that contravene their financial interests. As we have seen, the CRTC declined to enforce the separation of television and newspaper newsrooms, and the question of the Commission's ability to enforce newsroom separation clauses in the face of possible legal challenges remains. As Robert Martin (1997) points out, Canadian law speaks only to limitations on freedom of expression by the state, not corporate threats. Consequently, even if, in theory, issues of representation are seen as taking precedence over private property rights, making that leap in practice runs into possible legal barriers.

Given these obstacles, it is no surprise that long-time observers have identified two of the necessary conditions for accomplishing reform as a "conjunction of circumstances [that] creates a will for change" coupled with "intense and sustained public pressure" to help carry reforms through the policy process (Kent 1992, 38–9). For example, in the face of government reticence to institute the Kent Commission's recommendations, the commission's director of research, Tim Creery, concluded that "the absence of organized public concern was the critical factor in sending the Kent recommendations to the boneyard" (Creery 1984). Developing such strong, united, and organized "public concern" to help push for reform has proven to be a difficult task, even though spectacular citizen mobilizations aiming to transform the mediasphere have occurred in several countries recently, as Arne Hintz points out in chapter 6.

One challenge in generating public interest in media reform is to build enduring and effective alliances. Reform advocates can be divided on strategies and goals. While media unions have sometimes supported campaigns for democratic media reform, labour organizations and other social movements and activists typically more often see media issues as secondary to other priorities, and they are therefore reluctant to put scarce resources into reform (see Hackett and Carroll 2006, 202).

Another challenge is the political quiescence of journalists themselves. In the past, many journalists and journalism educators have opposed comprehensive regulation, citing concerns over possible government censorship (see Cribb 2002). At the same time, growing job insecurity and North American journalism's "regime of objectivity" (Hackett and Zhao 1998) both work to dissuade journalists from ideologically challenging corporate control of the media or working with progressive groups who do (Hackett and Carroll 2006, 137). Moreover, Canadian communication scholars have also been reluctant to engage in the nitty-gritty of media policy debates or to conduct policy-relevant research (Savage 2008).

Yet another challenge for media reform campaigns is sustainability. Developing stable funding has been one of the major impediments to establishing an organization focused broadly but exclusively on media reform in Canada. In the United States, some organizations have been able to access philanthropic funding, but that has been less forthcoming in Canada (see Skinner 2012). Several Canadian organizations have succeeded in sustaining themselves, but they have a specific focus; the long-standing Friends of Canadian Broadcasting, for example, concentrates on broadcasting issues, and OpenMedia (discussed further below) prioritizes Internet issues.

Despite the obstacles to media reform, the very survival and occasional policy impact of such reform groups are grounds for optimism. Moreover, comparative research suggests that there are a number of resources and opportunities that can constitute "springboards" for developing democratic media activism (Hackett and Carroll 2006). For instance, in the United Kingdom, the phone-hacking and corruption scandal involving Rupert Murdoch's newspapers created an opening for considerable public debate and a major government enquiry. While the ensuing report focused on promoting ethical press conduct rather than reducing concentrated media ownership, the scandal created an opportunity to gather support and push for reform. Closer to home, possible springboards include openings in the political system (including public consultation processes, noted above), intermedia rivalry, critical journalism, and media education programs, progressive traditions and movements, extensive and flexible networks made possible by the Internet, forward-looking trade unions that are willing to help fund media policy interventions, and much else. And over the past few years there has been growing resistance to corporate power in the media field and the erosion of local, diverse, and investigative journalism rising from these places. We turn now to three inspiring examples of such resistance: Media Democracy Day, OpenMedia, and Reimagine CBC.

Opening the Policy Process: Some Promising Initiatives

Even in the face of these obstacles, there has been a rising chorus of concern about the effects of the growing concentration of ownership and the undermining of investigative and diverse journalism.

Media Democracy Day

Media Democracy Day (MDD) began in 2001 in Vancouver and Toronto, but its roots lie in the mid-1990s when Conrad Black's Hollinger Inc was expanding its newspaper empire. A coalition of concerned journalists, researchers, scholars, and activists saw this unprecedented concentration of ownership as a threat to the diversity of content and founded the Canadian chapter of the Campaign for Press and Broadcast Freedom (CPBF), modelled after the British group of the same name. Working with the Council of Canadians, the CPBF undertook a number of actions to try to limit the scope of media concentration, including a court appeal of the Competition Bureau's approval of Hollinger's purchase of the Southam newspaper chain (Skinner and Gasher 2005, 67).

A few years later in Vancouver, a small group of CPBF members laid plans for creating a support centre for alternative media, including an office to research media policy and lobby governments. Equipped with a promise of $50,000 in seed money from the San Francisco–based Independent Press Association if matching local funds could be found, the activists held a meeting with local social and labour activists. However, a majority of the representatives of organized labour was not supportive of the project. Meanwhile, in Toronto, local members of the CPBF were organizing the first Media Democracy Day, a movement-facilitating event with the goal of information sharing and community building between citizen groups and researchers largely focused on protecting and enhancing the quality of journalism in Canada. In the face of the difficulties encountered in garnering local support for the larger project, the Vancouver activists decided to hold a Media Democracy Day event there as well.

Over the past twelve years, Media Democracy Day events have been held in communities across Canada and the United States, as well as in Argentina, Brazil, Germany, Indonesia, Spain, and the United Kingdom. It has particularly firm roots in Vancouver, where it has evolved into one of the premiere media reform events in Canada. MDD's approach emphasizes the following two goals: (1) to promote the democratization *of* the media structures in Canada, by seeking internal organizational and policy changes that enhance citizen participation and diversity; and (2) to promote democracy *through* the media by helping to support other messages and groups enhancing social justice and democracy. Its plan of action is reflected in the tag line, "Know the media, Be the media, Change the media." To *know the media* refers to the need for evidence-based research on ownership structures, production and distribution patterns, labour practices, and patterns of media content. This forms the basis for effecting change. To *be the media* signifies the commitment to citizen input and alternative media content. MDD activities have always included a media fair of independent media groups, as well as hands-on training workshops. To *change the media* refers to questions of policy, regulation, and laws, including copyright legislation, Internet throttling, concentration of ownership, and supports for culturally important areas such as independent filmmaking and public broadcasting.

Importantly, Media Democracy Day seeks to introduce the importance of media reform to new audiences and organizations every year, and holds the event free of charge at the easily accessible Vancouver Public Library. Organizers have called Media Democracy Day a "gateway" event to issues of media reform, and one that has also been a catalyst for new forms of media activism and independent journalism. For example, seeds for the award-winning online magazine the *Tyee* were planted out of discussions that occurred at Media Democracy Day (www.thetyee.ca).

As a joint university-community organization, Media Democracy Day also collaborates with scholars to provide a link between research and practice. The organizing committee is housed in the School of Communication at Simon Fraser University, and faculty members sit on the steering committee along with community representatives. The UBC School of Journalism has been a supporter of Media Democracy Day and sees the importance of providing more avenues for its students to conduct good journalism. It is this combination of researcher, practitioner, and activist that appears to have helped sustain this movement-facilitating event.

OpenMedia

In May 2007, the Department of Communication Studies at the University of Windsor convened a conference to celebrate the twentieth anniversary of the book *Manufacturing Consent* by Edward S. Herman and Noam Chomsky. Participants, including scholars, media activists, and representatives from social justice organizations (including MDD activists), decided that a network was needed to engender more public participation in the development of Canadian media policy. Several participants called for creating an organization focused on media reform generally, and on public engagement campaigns and movement-building specifically, similar to FreePress in the United States. Another workshop, Media That Matters (MtM), was taking place on the west coast, and participants were reaching the same conclusions. Shortly thereafter, Steve Anderson, an M.A. student at Simon Fraser University's School of Communication, established Canadians for Democratic Media (CDM) in Vancouver. CDM's first campaign – "Stop the Big Media Takeover" – focused on the CRTC's *Diversity of Voices* hearing. Thus, a national network for media reform, comprising a coalition of labour and social-justice groups and academics, was formed.

A campaign around community broadcasting followed and, in 2008, Canadians for Democratic Media began to organize around the emerging issue of Net neutrality. The SaveOurNet campaign brought together citizens, businesses, and public interest groups to protect equal access to the Internet. In 2009, it organized several campaigns, including Open Internet Town Hall Meetings in Toronto, Vancouver, and Ottawa. In the face of these actions, the CRTC adopted new traffic management guidelines, some resembling those put forward by SaveOurNet and the Canadian Internet Policy and Public Interest Clinic.

In 2010, Canadians for Democratic Media was rebranded to reflect the growing strength of the "open" movement, aimed at advancing the causes of innovation and democracy in governance, both in the public and private sectors. The new name, OpenMedia, reflected the organization's commitment to pursuing and creating an open, accessible media system in Canada. OpenMedia launched the "Stop The Meter" campaign in 2010 to intervene in a CRTC decision to allow wholesale Internet providers the power to impose "usage-based billing" (pay per byte) on independent Internet service providers, and thus, many Canadian Internet users. The campaign garnered over four hundred thousand signatures on its Stop The Meter petition – an unprecedented level of public engagement around telecommunications policy in Canada – and led to the CRTC reversing its decision on the case.

OpenMedia emerged from a loose association of like-minded groups and individuals to become what the organization refers to as a "citizen-driven" movement. While much of the attention of OpenMedia has shifted to Internet-related issues, it still retains a concern for the need for good journalism and public interest media.

Reimagine CBC

Along with partners Leadnow and Gen Why Media, in January 2012 OpenMedia launched a campaign to "support, revitalize and reimagine the CBC" (Reimagine CBC 2015). The campaign came in the face of an impending licence-renewal hearing at the CRTC and increasing attacks on the public broadcaster by Conservative Party MPs. It was designed to engage Canadians in a discussion about the value of the CBC and encourage suggestions for making it more responsive to the interests of Canadians. Focused primarily online, the campaign sought to develop a "crowd sourced plan to enable the CBC to take on a leadership position in the digital era" (Reimagine CBC 2015). It began with a website asking Canadians to submit their ideas about the kind of public broadcaster they wanted the CBC to be. Almost fifteen hundred people took part in this exercise. Amid rumours of deep cuts to the CBC budget, Reimagine CBC also created online and hard-copy petitions that called on the government to "stop the cuts." This petition garnered more than twenty-five thousand signatures and was delivered to thirteen MP constituency offices.

Meanwhile, organizers developed a modular survey of the central ideas their initial survey reflected, and in a second phase of consultation, people were encouraged to rank the values in order of importance. At the same time, the campaign created local gatherings across the country (28 in all) to seek feedback from those who may not have had a chance to comment. Almost eleven thousand people participated in the public survey and contributed to the final report, entitled *Make It Yours*, submitted to the CRTC at CBC's licensing hearing on 23 November 2012. It was clear that the majority of Canadians were deeply supportive of the public broadcaster, and put their highest priority on "courageous" and "in-depth" reporting as a central CBC purpose. The campaign earned praise from the CRTC chair as a model of citizen participation (CRTC 2012g).

These three examples represent important avenues for engaging people in media reform. All three emphasize the importance of coalition building across organizations, combining scholarly, activist, and practitioner interests in garnering public interest and bringing pressure on the policy process. All three emphasize participation in their campaigns, providing people a range of possible ways to become involved, from organizing and creating campaign materials, to directly voicing specific concerns, to attending public events, to simply signing a petition. All three have also illustrated that public meetings can serve as means of developing and galvanizing public interest in reform. OpenMedia.ca and Reimagine CBC have shown that online activism can help break down traditional barriers to the regulatory process and enable large numbers of people to make their voices heard.

Conclusion: Beyond the Democratic Deficits of Market-Driven Journalism

The current crisis of Canadian journalism sharply foregrounds tensions between market-driven media and the requirements of democratic communication. As we have seen, those tensions have been noted in one public policy review after another. Building from the recommendations of those reviews, we have suggested that Canadian journalism needs a supportive institutional framework; amateurs and citizen-volunteers alone cannot address the democratic deficits of corporate media. We have further argued that it is a responsibility of public policy enacted by elected governments to help provide that framework.

But, despite the long history of evidence and concern that the market is unable to deliver diverse and comprehensive media fare, increasingly the dominant justification for the commercial media system is that of "consumer sovereignty," the idea that the media respond effectively to consumer choice and thus "give people what they want." There are several problems with this argument.

Perhaps the first problem is that it conjures an image of determined consumers conveying their considered preferences to compliant media corporations. That is profoundly misleading. Profit-driven private media companies generally look to the largest returns for the least investment. News and current-affairs programming, particularly at the local level, is expensive compared with imported American game shows or reruns of *The Simpsons*. Similarly, as we have seen, the savings arising from reusing programming and other materials in as many outlets or venues as possible is one of the major drivers behind media mergers – another factor mitigating against local and regional production. Underpinned by these kinds of economics, the range of media fare offered to consumers is confined long before audience members ever get to make news or program choices.

A second problem with the consumer sovereignty argument is that news and information are not simply commodities like soap or towels. Rather, they are essential to the democratic process. As expressed by the Bacon Report, echoing the sentiments of its many predecessors, "it is impossible to … exercise meaningful citizenship without access to news, information, analysis and opinion" (Canada 2006a, 65). In this regard, journalism displays the characteristics of what economists call a "merit good," something that society requires, but that people are unable or unwilling to finance adequately through individual purchases, a point Pinar Gurleyen and Robert Hackett made in chapter 1. If during much of the twentieth century Canadian journalism was underwritten financially by advertising, today that business model appears to be collapsing and public policy is needed, not only to offset the undemocratic biases inherent in the commercial media system, but to supplement or replace that system. Privately owned and corporate media arguably do have their place in a pluralistic society; they are adept at providing popular entertainment, representing particular political perspectives, and potentially contributing to critical oversight of political power (Curran 2000, 146). But supportive public policy, as well as alternative, non-profit, and community media, are needed to counterbalance the democratic deficits of corporate media, and to ensure institutional underpinnings for citizen-oriented journalism – particularly in the current moment of crisis in our media system. Good journalism won't often happen without good public policy. But given the uneven playing field we described above, good policy won't often happen without sustained public pressure and grassroots campaigns.

In that respect, Media Democracy Days, OpenMedia, and Reimagine CBC are very hopeful initiatives. The latter two, in particular, are pioneering new modes of organizing that have succeeded both in engaging large numbers of previously apolitical youth and in winning some policy victories. Making full use of social media and the Internet, they use humour, entertainment, and public events to attract younger participants. Perhaps most importantly, they recognize the need for public sector involvement in ensuring journalism is in the public interest and thus have targeted the formal policy process, by organizing online petitions, presenting briefs at CRTC hearings, and lobbying members of Parliament.

Such citizen-led mobilization, combined with journalistic support for policy change, is the kind of energy needed to reinvigorate Canadian journalism. More than any specific set of policy reforms, it has the potential to reinvent democracy itself.

4 Public-Community Partnerships to Improve Local Media in Canada

KAREN WIRSIG AND CATHERINE EDWARDS

Local Media in Canada

Local media have been transformed dramatically over the past decade in much of Canada. New technologies and consumption patterns, private ownership consolidation, cuts to public media, and a muffled community sector have conspired to favour centralized content creation and distribution over independent local voices in the mainstream media. As a result, many communities have diminishing access to original local news reporting and content.

This chapter provides an overview of the policy and market failures undermining healthy local media in Canada and examines ways in which the community and public media sectors could collaborate to improve local media infrastructure in Canadian cities, towns, and rural areas. It concludes by suggesting policy directions to support these efforts.

Definitions

Canada's Broadcasting Act (Canada 1991) gives equal importance to the "public, private, and community elements" in the broadcasting system. For the purposes of definition – not always clear in the Act itself – we adopt a property-based definition of the sectors: that is, public broadcasting is owned, managed, and funded by public bodies; private broadcasting is owned and managed by private, for-profit entities; and community broadcasting is owned and managed by not-for-profit, community-based organizations.

Along with differing ownership structures – and in large part because of these differing ownership structures – the three sectors have different mandates. Private sector media are profit-driven enterprises that depend largely on advertising and/or subscription revenues and must answer to shareholders. Public media, such as CBC/Radio-Canada, the national public broadcaster that operates English- and French-language services, are supported in large part by tax revenues and programmed with a public service mandate.[1] Generally speaking, public media try to serve not only mass audiences, but also underserved audiences to the extent possible within their budget, and to offer services that might not be undertaken by the private sector. The CBC is expected to reflect the whole of the country and must meet high levels of professionalism and journalistic standards.

Community media have an additional mandate not shared by either public or private sector media: to enable audience members to participate directly in production and to shape the finished media content. They are meant to provide a democratic platform for free expression as well as a low-cost alternative to generating local content, since much of the content is produced by volunteers. Community media offer audiences a greater range and diversity of points of view, since every viewer is a potential producer. Community media tend to be local in focus, given that production facilities must be available locally to enable citizen access, but many countries have also launched national "community media" services that distribute content created at community production facilities, content that has regional or national relevance.

Funding

The funding dedicated to national public and community broadcasting is marginal in Canada relative to other countries. In constant dollars, government funding for the CBC/Radio-Canada has dropped markedly since the late 1980s[2] and represented $29 per capita in 2014, or less than half of the average per capita funding for public broadcasting among OECD countries (Nordicity 2011). As noted by David Skinner, Kathleen Cross, and Robert Hackett in chapter 3, the CBC faced in 2012 its first major federal budget cut (10 per cent of its overall budget) since the 1990s. These data are presented in Figure 4.1.

Spending on the community sector is more difficult to assess. While the Canadian Radio-television and Telecommunications Commission

Figure 4.1 Federal government funding to CBC, 1992–2014* in 2010 dollars (millions)

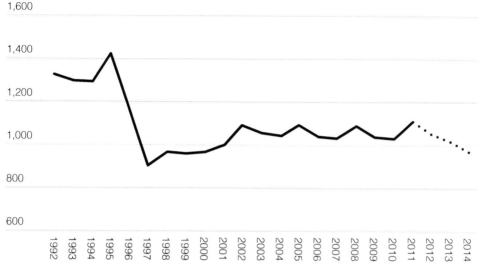

*As projected in federal budget 2012.

(CRTC) requires cable operators to set aside between 1.5 and 5.0 per cent of their revenues to support "community television" (which amounts to more than $130 million annually and is sufficient to the sector's needs), this money is in fact directed mostly towards private, for-profit, cable-administered, professional and regional TV services, not to genuine community broadcasting as it is understood internationally (Edwards 2009). In the twenty-eight other countries where a "community broad-casting" sector is recognized as distinct from public and private broad-casting, its defining characteristics are ownership and management by community-based entities. This principle has been recognized formally in Canada's community radio policy since 2000: "A community radio station is owned and controlled by a not-for-profit organization, the structure of which provides for membership, management, operation and programming primarily by members of the community at large" (CRTC 2010d, para. 13).

Since their inception in the late 1960s and 1970s, however, community television channels in Canada have been placed under the stewardship of the cable companies that distribute them. The cable company holds the licence, owns the production facility, and controls access and the programming aired. This situation is in marked contrast to the United States, for example – whose community TV system evolved at the same time and from the same National Film Board of Canada "Challenge for Change" model – where cable company revenues are directed to non-profit community groups to administer community TV (called "public access" channels).

When cable companies were relatively small operations, headquartered in their communities, it can be argued that they were generally faithful to the CRTC's expectations of offering an open access platform to community members to express their views and air programming of their own creation. When satellite TV came to Canada in the late 1990s, conditions changed, however. Cable companies faced competition for the first time. Since local channels could not be carried by satellite cost-effectively, cable operators saw an opportunity to promote community channels to customers as a competitive advantage. In an effort to improve the technical look of what had formerly been primarily volunteer-produced programming, the cable company took over much of the production. In order to fund the additional staff to pursue this professional production model, many community production studios in smaller markets were closed, and the staff was consolidated in larger centres.

Economic and technical shifts within the cable industry also reduced support for community production studios. Cable companies have been consolidated into a few national networks and are no longer headquartered in most of the communities they serve, so their incentive to serve those communities is less. In addition, it was once necessary for each community to have a cable "head end," a technical reception booth for microwaved programming signals, which were distributed to houses in the community via coaxial cable. A single cable employee might maintain both the head end and the adjoining community production studio in a small community. The recent interconnection of multiple cable-licence areas using fibre optic cable has eliminated the need to send microwave programming signals and to maintain head ends. As a result of this restructuring, it has become cost-prohibitive for cable companies to maintain far-flung production facilities.

The result of all these forces is that the majority of cable companies today offer heavily regionalized and professionalized content to their subscribers on "community television" channels. They can neither be considered "community channels" according to the ownership test, nor by mandate, despite the fact that their community access and hyperlocal programming expectations are still stipulated as licence expectations in CRTC Broadcasting Regulatory Policy 2010-622. Therefore, while there is money available in the system to fund a robust community television sector, five different CRTC audits and two policy reviews have raised questions about how much of this money actually funds production by community members.[3]

Regulatory Support

Regulatory support for public and community broadcasting is also lacking. In the past five years, the vast majority of broadcast policy hearings at the CRTC have dealt primarily or exclusively with the private sector. A few have involved public broadcasters, notably the introduction of the subsequently cancelled Local Programming Improvement Fund (LPIF) for small-market TV stations. However, the LPIF excluded community broadcasters, despite the recommendation in the 2003 Lincoln Report, *Our Cultural Sovereignty*, that an LPIF-like fund be created for "community, local and regional broadcasters" (Canada 2003, 367).[4] A number of other policies announced for the private sector, including group licensing rules, permission for private broadcasters to seek "value-for-signal" payments from broadcast distributors, and the Small Market Local Programming Fund (SMLPF) exclude both public and community broadcasters. In this context, CBC/Radio-Canada's 2015 strategic plan – focused, in part, on improving local and regional programming – appears vulnerable to both government austerity measures and regulatory neglect (CBC 2011a).

Community broadcasting has been dealt with only once in the past decade as an exclusive focus of the CRTC. The CRTC reviewed its community radio and community TV policy in 2010. While some advances were made in community radio policy – notably the establishment of the Community Radio Fund of Canada[5] – there were only token improvements to community TV policy. Despite a strong public call for the funding that is currently tied up in cable community channels to be redirected to community-run organizations, the CRTC left this funding under cable administration. CRTC data posted during the public consultation also indicated that viewership to cable community channels is low, suggesting that audiences don't see them as relevant, even when they have few other local TV options (CRTC 2009c).

While a licence class exists for community groups to operate over-the-air television channels (introduced in response to the call for community-owned and -administered TV channels in 2002), the CRTC's expectation that these licence-holders finance themselves with advertising runs counter to the non-commercial mandate of community television. Like public television, community television is generally understood by practitioners around the world to provide a public service to viewers, rather than a platform to deliver audiences to advertisers. In addition, content on community TV is expected to reflect the individual views of the community members who create it. This mandate can be compromised if management makes programming decisions with a view to revenue generation, in the same way as the national public broadcaster is sometimes criticized for developing commercial programming as a consequence of its hybrid public/commercial funding structure.

Expecting community broadcasters to survive on advertising is also unrealistic when public and private sector local channels have periodically been given specific financial support for local programming: for example, via the Local Programming Improvement Fund as well as the Small Market Local Programming Fund, both of which recognize the failure of the advertising model to support local content in an environment of audience fragmentation. The SMLPF was set up specifically to offset the impact of direct-to-home satellite service on local advertising revenues.

The clearest indication that Canada lacks a viable funding model for community-owned and -administered television channels is that there are only nine in Canada, compared with almost two hundred community radio channels.

The lack of frequency set-asides for community broadcasters has also limited their proliferation. While the public broadcaster has always had two frequencies reserved in every market for both radio and television (one for English service, one for French), there has never been a set-aside for the community sector. Frequencies are allotted on a first-come, first-served basis, with the result that in many big cities close to the US border, would-be community TV and radio organizations cannot get on the air.

In the meantime, Canada's private media sector has remade itself. There are now four major private media/communications companies: Bell, Shaw, Rogers, and Quebecor. Each controls a variety of media holdings (some combination of TV, radio, Internet, publishing) and distribution systems (some combination of cable, satellite, wireless) and are thereby considered horizontally and vertically integrated. These companies thrive by securing rights to well-promoted content – the vast majority from the United States for the English-language market – and repurposing it for various media and distribution services. Figure 4.2 captures this process of consolidation, which continues apace.

Private media ownership in Canada in 2015

THE CABLE+ GUYS

BCE INC. (BELL MEDIA)
BCE

- **TV** Conventional: CTV, A-Channel Specialty+Pay: 39 channels (eg. TSN, MuchMusic, Bravo, CP24, Comedy).
- **TV distribution** Bell ExpressVu, Fibe
- **Newspaper** 15% owner of Globe and Mail
- **Radio** 106 radio stations
- **Internet, phone & wireless service**

ROGERS COMMUNICATIONS
Rogers Family

- **TV** Conventional: citytv; OMNI TV Specialty: 3 channels Shomi over-the-top TV (in partnership with Shaw)
- **Radio** 55 stations
- **Magazines** 50+, inc. Macleans, Chatelaine

SHAW COMMUNICATIONS
Shaw Family

- **TV** Conventional: Global network Specialty: 19 channels (eg. HGTV, Showcase, Slice, History) Shomi over-the-top TV (in partnership with Rogers)
- **Cable** biggest cable system in Western Canada
- **Satellite** Shaw Direct
- **Internet & phone service**

QUEBECOR
Péladeau Family

- **Print** 30 daily newspapers and dozens of community newspapers in Québec; 37 magazines
- **TV** Conventional: TVA Specialty: 9 channels
- **Cable** Videotron
- **Internet & wireless service**

> Note: This chart does not include public and public-service media, including CBC/Radio-Canada, TVO, TFO, Knowledge Netwoørk, Télé-Québec, APTN, or independents.
> Canadian Media Guild, 2015 | www.cmg.ca

THE REST

WOODBRIDGE *Thomson Family*
- **Globe and Mail**
- **Thomson Reuters** (financial wire service and trade publishing)
- **Canadian Press** (in partnership with Gesca and Torstar)

TORSTAR
5 families, descendants of founder J. Atkinson
- **Newspapers** 5 dailies & 95 community papers (Ont.)
- **Canadian Press** (in partnership with Gesca and Globe and Mail)
- **Internet:** Toronto.com

GESCA LTD. *Desmarais Family*
- **Newspaper** La Presse
- **Canadian Press** (in partnership with Globe and Mail and Torstar)

POSTMEDIA
- **Newspapers** 21 dailies (inc. Ottawa Citizen, National Post and Sun chain); 4 free dailies (Metro and 24 Hours)
- **Internet** canada.com, FPinfomart.ca

BLACK PRESS *D. Black Family*
- **Newspapers** 170 daily and weekly newspapers in Western Canada and the US

BRUNSWICK NEWS *Irving Family*
- **Newspapers** All 3 English language dailies in NB and a handful of weeklies

TRANSCONTINENTAL
- **Newspapers** 10 dailies, 200+ weeklies/ community; 15+ magazines

CORUS *also Shaw Family*
- **TV** 3 CBC affiliate stations 28 specialty & pay channels
- **Radio** 39 stations

COGECO *Audet Family*
- **Radio** 16 stations in Quebec
- **Cable**
- **Internet & phone**

NEWCAP RADIO
- **Radio** 95 stations, mostly small markets

MARITIME BROADCASTING
- **Radio** 25 stations in NS, NB and PEI

Figure 4.2 Private media ownership in Canada in 2015

Ahead of the 2008–09 financial crisis, the private media mergers that built these empires resulted in hundreds of layoffs that affected local newsrooms across the country.[6] Since the crisis, the Canadian Media Guild has calculated that more than three thousand jobs have disappeared at newspapers, TV, and radio stations. Local private TV stations in Brandon, Manitoba, and Red Deer, Alberta, were closed, while newspapers across the country lost hundreds of feet on the street.[7] Blaming the migration of advertising dollars on new-media platforms, traditional local news media – printed newspapers, TV, and radio – remain lean operations.

In this policy and market environment, quality local news reporting will likely continue to decline unless the sectors with a specific public service mandate – i.e., the public and community sectors – can find innovative ways to fill the gap. Since they are the sectors given the least financial and regulatory support, creative solutions are needed.

Why Public-Community Partnerships?

While there have long been partnerships between CBC and private broadcasters through affiliation agreements,[8] and what has become an unworkable partnership between community channels and cable companies in the community television sector (described above), there has been almost no collaboration between public and community television broadcasters in Canada, despite the fact that both have public service mandates. Both answer to Canadians as citizens first, consumers second. Given these commonalities, we begin with the assumption that partnerships between public and community media might have the potential to:

• Improve the quality, quantity, and diversity of local media
• Improve the quantity, quality, and diversity of viewpoints
  (i.e., democratizing national public media, by leveraging
  community diversity and creativity)
• Develop the next generation of artists and journalists from a wider
  pool, representing more regions of the country
• Create media jobs in smaller communities and the regions.

The remainder of this chapter proposes models for such partnerships, and case studies where the models have been or could be applied.

International Precedents for Public-Community Media Collaboration

There are precedents for public and community broadcasting partnerships internationally. In the Netherlands, there are only two categories of licence: public and commercial, available nationally, regionally, and locally. Holding a "local public broadcasting" licence is roughly equivalent to holding a community over-the-air TV or radio licence in Canada, and does not imply an affiliation with a national public broadcaster. Although a few local public TV and radio channels are open access platforms (in larger cities such as Amsterdam), most are not. They are run by local, not-for-profit boards designated by the municipality. Volunteers assist employees with production and provide input into content out of financial necessity and to encourage pluralism, but final decisions about production and programming are made by the board (Edwards 2009).

In the United Kingdom, known for its dominant and centralized public broadcaster, the BBC, local TV licences of any kind (private or community) have struggled to survive and have only been available since the mid-1990s. Nonetheless, the BBC operated a Community Programme Unit between 1972 and 2004, which enabled selected ideas from viewers around the nation to be recorded by BBC staff and aired nationally. The BBC has also discussed in several policy papers since the 1990s its intention to establish community TV units on the ground. The most successful was established in 2005 in Havant's Leigh Park, the site of a famous 1969 hunger strike. Although the BBC has since pulled its support from the project, the community has continued to produce videos from the facility. These examples demonstrate that the line between community and public broadcasting is often blurred, and models for collaboration depend on local financial, cultural, and regulatory conditions, as is explored in the case studies that follow.

Forms Collaboration Could Take in Canada

In Canada, public-community broadcasting partnerships could assume a variety of forms.

Model A: Sharing Transmission Infrastructure

The Canadian Media Guild (CMG) and the Canadian Association of Community Television Users and Stations (CACTUS) began working together in the lead-up to the transition from analogue to digital, over-the-air (OTA) television. In the absence of dedicated government funding for the digital upgrade,[9] CBC/Radio-Canada's transition plan was to upgrade only twenty-seven of more than six hundred TV transmitters.[10] These twenty-seven transmitters are located in the twenty cities where the CBC and/or Radio-Canada have a local TV station. In seven of the cities, both French and English signals are available free to air. More than a thousand analogue TV transmitters existed in Canada prior to the digital transition, which represents a significant loss of over-the-air infrastructure as a result of the transition; 658 of these transmitters belonged to the CBC and were decommissioned.

Because of Canada's vast geography, the challenge for Canada's cash-strapped national broadcaster of maintaining an aging, over-the-air public transmission infrastructure, and the difficulty of building out fibre optic networks to replace this infrastructure, there is an increasing and widening digital divide between Canadians in urban areas, who have access to free-to-air television, cellular service, cable television, high-speed Internet, and satellite service, and many rural Canadians, who may soon have access only to satellite TV and high-speed Internet at elevated rates.

The CMG and CACTUS saw an opportunity for partnerships between communities and CBC/Radio-Canada to upgrade and share transmission equipment in smaller markets that were left off the public broadcaster's transition plan. For example, rather than CBC transmitters and towers being decommissioned or pulled down, the proposed partnership would allow communities to maintain analogue transmission for the price of the power to supply the transmitter.[11]

Alternatively, the partners could have shared the expense of the upgrade; the cost of digital transmitters starts at about $10,000. Once upgraded, a single digital transmitter could multiplex CBC/Radio-Canada with one or more other TV or radio channels, including a community channel, or with wireless Internet for communities that lack broadband.

Communities and the CBC could also have shared costs to multiplex the second official language service in markets where only the majority language service has been upgraded. For example, while Calgary's CBC television transmitter was upgraded to digital, its Radio-Canada transmitter was not, and French service free-to-air has ended in that city. Similarly, English service is no longer available in predominantly French-speaking Quebec City. The cost to add a multiplex (an additional piece of hardware to the basic digital transmitter) starts at approximately $10,000. For $10,000, TV viewers in thirteen of Canada's biggest cities could regain access to the minority-language service.

Unfortunately, CBC's analogue TV transmission sites have now been decommissioned and the opportunity to share this publicly funded infrastructure with community media organizations was lost.

Model B: Sharing of Production Facilities

In smaller communities that cannot afford a community TV and/or a CBC local bureau, facilities could be shared. There might be separate licences and broadcast channels, but the stations could share a studio, equipment, even personnel. Or, new affiliation models with community stations could be explored in areas in which there is a single broadcast channel. The licence could be the CBC's, with blocks of time set aside for community-generated content, or the community's, with inserts of CBC network content. The latter model is similar to the early development of the Canadian television system in which privately owned local stations were outlets for distribution of CBC's national service, but provided their own local content. In those early days, the system was developed to overcome the challenges of distributing national content across a vast geographical expanse using over-the-air transmitters. With today's distribution systems (including cable, satellite, and Internet Protocol TV), national distribution is no longer the problem. The current and serious challenge is to create and broadcast *local* content to communities that are losing it, or never had it. CBC's 2015 plan proposed expanding local programming to communities that have never had their own CBC station (CBC 2011a). New local services have opened up in Hamilton and Kitchener-Waterloo, Ontario, and Kamloops, BC. With federal budget cuts, further CBC expansion is on hold. Local content partnerships between community and public media might offer an innovative way out of the impasse.

Model C: Sharing of Content, Personnel, and/or Production Methodologies

Even without affiliate status, partnerships between community channels and regional or national public broadcasters could be fruitful and dynamic. Community-generated content could gain greater exposure if supplied to regional or national public broadcasters, while bringing in

revenue for the community broadcaster. Regional and national broadcasters could access content in communities where they have no journalistic presence. For example, raw footage or short edited stories might
be uploaded by communities to a common server, where the national
broadcaster could access them for a fee.

Aside from cost advantages, the quality of the content could improve
for both parties. For the community, internships with the national
broadcaster and the need to meet its journalistic standards would stim-
ulate professionalism. For the national or regional broadcaster, access
to a grassroots diversity of voices would enhance the depth of discussion on complex issues. This model of collaboration was recently proposed in the Payette Report, suggesting that Télé-Québec (the public
educational broadcaster for the province of Quebec) acquire local and
regional content from independent community producing groups in
Quebec (Québec 2010).[12]

The long-term development of community relationships and partnerships as a means to improve content for the national broadcaster
is already considered a "best practice" by Joan Melanson, executive-
producer for CBC Radio in Toronto:

> We strategically reach out to the many diverse communities that make up
> our city in order to reflect, in an authentic way, their stories and issues.
> Part of that outreach takes the form of two to four public townhalls a year.
> The point is to explore a particular issue, often sensitive, through the lens
> of one community. One recent example was called Turning Point, about
> domestic violence in Toronto's South Asian communities. These commu-
> nities are used to the mainstream media coming to them for negative rea-
> sons. We want to build trust, so we invite them, before we ever turn on a
> microphone or a camera, to have a discussion and we really listen. We get
> an agreement on an approach, and the word gets out that "the CBC is OK.
> You can talk to them." Then people show up and say remarkable things
> that they wouldn't otherwise say. Over the long haul, this approach makes
> my job a lot more productive. (Personal communication with Catherine
> Edwards, 14 Feb. 2012)

While the CBC has a presence in Toronto, it cannot have that presence in
every community across the country. However, the quality of the relationship that Melanson describes between the CBC as a broadcaster and
the Toronto community is routinely built between communities and
their local community stations. The viewing public is already in charge

of "the approach" because it is members of the community themselves who wield the recording equipment and shape the content. The content developed through these partnerships could be made accessible to the national broadcaster.

This is not to imply that community and public media would create or air identical coverage on an issue such as domestic violence in Toronto's South Asian communities. On the contrary, time constraints and expectations for journalistic objectivity might constrain a national broadcaster's approach to such an issue. For example, the completed story might be a few minutes long and would likely feature interviews with members of the affected community as well as experts or community workers for perspective. A community media program on the same issue might be produced by volunteers who identify as belonging to the South Asian community, exploring the issue at greater length from an insider perspective. With a partnership in place, the more in-depth, point-of-view community footage might be made available to the national broadcaster as source material, lending a depth and level of frankness that can be difficult and time-consuming to secure under mainstream media practices, as Melanson describes.

Case Studies for Community-Public Media Collaboration

In late 2011, we began exploring how these ideas might be applied with community media organizations and representatives of CBC/Radio-Canada in several communities. We focused on communities in which concrete challenges for local media have either always existed or have been accentuated in recent years due to the aforementioned technological, regulatory, and market trends.

Model A: Shared Transmission

When the CBC's local private affiliate in Kamloops, BC, disaffiliated in 2006 and stopped airing CBC programming, residents who wanted to watch CBC free-to-air organized a lobby group called "Save Our CBC." When it purchased Canwest Media/Global Television in late 2010, Shaw Media committed to share Global transmission towers and its broadcast frequency with local broadcasters in smaller markets as part of its tangible public benefit package.[13] CACTUS saw an opportunity for Kamloops to regain access to the CBC over the air by multiplexing it as a subchannel of the Global signal. The CBC has indicated that it would provide its signal as long as no local substitutions are made to content.[14]

Kamloops is also home to Thompson Rivers University, which has both a campus-community radio channel, CFBX, and an undergraduate journalism program focused on print. TRU staff members are discussing the potential to extend learning opportunities to their students in television, and reaching the community at large on an additional platform. The community is therefore exploring the possibility of multiplexing both a community TV channel and the CBC as standard definition subchannels of Global's signal. For example, when Global upgrades its Kamloops repeater to digital, Global's signal might be broadcast on channel 6-1, while the CBC and a community channel from Thompson Rivers University might be on 6-2 and 6-3, respectively.

The sharing of public and community sector frequencies predates the introduction of digital technology. In Arichat, Nova Scotia, Telile Community TV has been replaying two local CBC radio programs produced in the town of Sydney. The audio plays behind the television channel's text-based community bulletin board service, enabling residents in parts of Nova Scotia to listen in beyond the range of CBC's Sydney transmitter. Many community radio broadcasters also lease space on CBC transmission towers.

The CRTC also gave the green light to the first instance of digital multiplexing in the summer of 2012. The Commission approved an application by the community TV broadcaster CFTV of Leamington, Ontario, to multiplex four television services from a single digital transmitter.

While any community can consider installing its own towers and transmitters – three CACTUS members in British Columbia have been doing this since the 1980s[15] – the impending loss of CBC service, the efficiency of digital transmission (one "box" can be used to multiplex several services on a single frequency), and the need for transmission infrastructure for wireless broadband make rebroadcasting especially viable and attractive at the present time. Several communities that have lost free, over-the-air CBC TV are particularly well positioned to take advantage of these options, thanks to pre-existing community-run video co-operatives or post-secondary media training programs. Examples include Saskatoon, Saskatchewan (the home of PAVED Arts),[16] Lethbridge, Alberta (Lethbridge Community College's broadcast journalism program), London, Ontario (the journalism program at the University of Western Ontario), and Victoria, British Columbia (the Independent Community TV Co-operative).

In the summer of 2011, the CACTUS partnership with the CMG resulted in publication of a brochure for communities entitled *The Transition to Digital Over-the-Air Television: New Opportunities for Communities* (CACTUS 2011). It was made available both through the CACTUS website and was linked from the Department of Canadian Heritage's official website on digital transition. On the official Canadian digital transition date of 31 August 2011, broadcasters in Canada's largest cities (cities with populations over 300,000, and provincial or territorial capitals) were required to switch off analogue transmitters. Outside these major cities, analogue transmissions were allowed to continue.

On 18 May 2012, the CBC and Radio-Canada submitted applications to the CRTC to shut down all remaining 623 analogue TV broadcasting sites across Canada, leaving rural and small-town Canadians without free access to the public broadcaster. To continue to access its programming, Canadians outside large urban centres where the CBC/Radio-Canada has upgraded transmitters to digital have to subscribe to cable or satellite, or download the CBC's programming over the Internet. Cable and satellite subscriptions range from $500 to $700 per year. High-speed Internet connections that would be required to watch the public broadcaster's content are often not available in rural areas that formerly depended on free-to-air analogue transmission. Where they are available, users are charged for downloading content. Furthermore, only a part of the CBC program schedule is available online.

By 18 June 2012 (the deadline for the CRTC's public consultation regarding the CBC/Radio-Canada's application), CACTUS, the CMG, public interest groups such as Friends of Canadian Broadcasting and the Public Interest Advocacy Centre, along with more than twenty-two hundred individual Canadians, had filed submissions with the CRTC proposing that analogue equipment and broadcasting towers be donated to communities to maintain and repurpose. Instead, CBC/Radio-Canada was simply allowed to shut down the transmitters on 31 July 2012, and has proceeded to offer them for sale through a commercial process. However, it is unlikely the public broadcaster will be able to sell all of its surplus infrastructure, and there could still be opportunities for communities to maintain or repurpose these sites over the next couple of years. For example, the CBC has already given the Hay River Community Service Society in the Northwest Territories the CBC (English), Radio-Canada (French), and APTN analogue transmitters formerly maintained by the CBC.

In parallel to the CBC analogue decommissioning process, APTN and TVO have also decommissioned analogue transmitters and towers since 2011. Unlike the CBC, TVO immediately saw the value of its over-the-air transmission structure to communities, and wrote letters directly to municipalities where they intended to shut down transmitters and towers to offer the towers for free. According to TVO, more than 60 per cent of communities accepted them. CACTUS is in the process of assisting communities that accepted TVO towers to repurpose them.

*Models B and C: Shared Production Facilities
and/or Content and Personnel*

Any community that does not enjoy or cannot support a community and/or a public radio, TV, or new-media production facility (typically smaller communities) is a potential candidate for a shared community-public production facility (Model B), or a community production facility that shares content with a public broadcaster (Model C). Both models offer the potential to reduce costs, cross-fertilize one another's content, and enable more local media diversity.

Sporadic sharing of content occasionally occurs already between community and public broadcasters. For example, the independent community TV licence holder in Neepawa, Manitoba, was contacted by CBC Winnipeg in early December 2012 to collect footage and interviews from a basketball game for inclusion in a story on CBC national radio and TV.

To explore the potential for more lasting partnerships, we have chosen three communities in which residents have identified specific problems with the quality and quantity of local media, where we believe innovative public-community partnerships could help.

HAMILTON

Hamilton, Ontario (with a population of just over 500,000), is the largest city in Canada to have neither a local CBC radio nor television station. Hamiltonians have long been frustrated by the fact that their proximity to Toronto results in less quantity and diversity of local information specific to Hamilton. Since 2004, the non-profit Centre for Community Study in Hamilton has hosted the Hamilton Media Project, which seeks ways "to increase the amount of Hamilton coverage in the mainstream broadcast media."[17] The CBC launched an online/mobile news service for Hamilton in March 2012. According to Sonja MacDonald of the

Centre for Community Study: "Since this isn't a 'traditional' model ... it has left many in the community without any real sense of what this means. Is it a cheap way to shut up those of us here that have been making a lot of noise about their lack of presence without too much effort or a truly new model of convergent media that connects different platforms with a real local flare?" (personal communication with Karen Wirsig and Catherine Edwards, Feb. 2012).

The potential for a robust community-public partnership in Hamilton is great, both because of the obvious demand for more news and community coverage on mainstream radio and TV, as well as the presence of:

- The Factory, a film and video co-operative that already offers the community media training and studio production facilities via a partnership with Gallery 205
- Two campus radio channels, one at Mohawk College and the other at McMaster University, as well as video production equipment and studio facilities at Mohawk College
- Hamilton Public Library, one of many public libraries beginning to experiment by offering the public access to digital media creation facilities, including green screens, and audio and video production equipment and editing suites.

The possibility that the CBC might partner with existing community-based resources had been raised in the early planning stages for the CBC's new digital service. City administration had encouraged Mohawk College to consider moving its studio facilities downtown to create a central street presence, with the idea that the CBC might share the facility and also the college's existing licensed radio frequency (an example of Model B). That partnership did not materialize, however, in part because the parties could not agree on access to prime time within the combined broadcast (both wanted control of suppertime news).[18] Time will tell whether Hamiltonians seek out the CBC's new digital service as a viable alternative, or whether a full radio or TV broadcasting solution in partnership with existing community resources proves more viable.

KINGSTON
The Kingston, Ontario, region has a population of nearly 200,000, a diverse local economy, and higher-learning institutions, but it is not

well served by professional local media. The city has a local private TV station – a Corus affiliate of CBC with a local newscast – a cable TV station owned by Cogeco, three private radio stations, campus community radio and TV stations, and a professional online news site. It also has a daily newspaper, the *Whig-Standard*, now owned by Postmedia. Nonetheless, there has been a decline in the number of professional journalists working in Kingston, resulting in a perceived decline in the quality of local information.

For example, at its peak in the late 1980s, fifty-five people worked in the *Whig-Standard* newsroom; in 2012 there were seventeen (personal communication with Karen Wirsig, Feb. 2012). A campaign was launched by the Communications Workers of America-Canada in 2011 to "Make the Whig Great," which highlights the concern about centralized news-gathering: "These days, the *Whig* is sadly lacking in the sort of useful Kingston-centric information it used to provide. Its pages are crowded with generic wire copy of little relevance to Kingstonians. Most days there are only three or four letters to the editor. Investigative reporting has all but vanished. Overall, the Kingston that the *Whig* portrays bears little resemblance to the vibrant, creative and diverse community that exists in reality."[19] As one local activist put it, "If you want to become an informed local citizen, you have to work harder than you used to."[20] According to the activist, citizen journalism has filled some of the void, but it is largely issue-based and contributes to a sense of fragmentation of information and involvement.

Meanwhile, the Queen's University campus radio channel CFRC has been broadcasting for over ninety years and is one of the oldest broadcasting organizations in the world. Queen's TV is a student-run station that webcasts and distributes a weekly program on Cogeco's cable community channel.[21] CFRC functioned as part of a tri-partite partnership with the CBC and the *Whig-Standard* from 1934 to 1938, so innovative community-public-(and private) partnerships have a long history in this city.[22] Our contacts at both university channels – while aware of the crisis at the *Whig* – did not immediately see how a decrease in quality in the local print press might present opportunities for them as community broadcasters, however.

A small investment in a public-community media partnership in Kingston could result in a local news renaissance. If CBC/Radio-Canada were to establish even a small digital station of the type launched in Hamilton for online and mobile content, professional journalists could provide training and mentorship to local citizen journalists to improve the quality of their contributions and could provide an online clearing house for community-generated media content.

For its part, Queen's TV acknowledged that while at one time students had gained valuable hands-on experience at Cogeco's community channel, the opportunity for public involvement at the cable channel has waned in recent years, as has student viewership of cable TV (citing high costs for a cable subscription). Queen's TV has largely redirected its efforts to online platforms. An online CBC partnership could both leverage the university's studio resources, energy, and creativity to generate content for the national broadcaster, while offering students experience and contact with the CBC.

VANCOUVER

The metropolitan Vancouver region has two daily newspapers (both owned by Postmedia), several local private TV stations, and a Shaw-controlled cable community TV station, as well as public radio and TV stations in both official languages (the CBC/Radio-Canada and the Knowledge Network, British Columbia's provincial educational broadcaster). It also has a vibrant, though financially fragile, community media scene, including Vancouver Co-op Radio, several independent producing groups that contribute content to Shaw's community channel, and (formerly) W2 in the Downtown Eastside. W2 was a multipurpose production facility that did not itself hold a broadcast licence. It was located in the poorest part of the city and broadcast a radio program on the Co-op Radio channel, a TV program on the Shaw community channel, and live-streamed on the Internet on W2 TV.

Although there appears to be a healthy range of media in all three sectors (public, private, and community), practitioners in both the public and community sectors acknowledge that there would be more value for the public if more collaboration took place of the kind described in Model C (sharing of content, personnel, and/or production methodologies). For example, the severity of the social and economic challenges facing residents of the Downtown Eastside is well known, yet the mainstream media fail to provide adequate coverage of them. In a city as socially, economically, and culturally diverse as Vancouver, the public broadcaster cannot be all things to all people.

Community media in Canada, as in many other countries, play a different role in large cities than they do in small towns; in smaller population centres they can assume the mantle of "mainstream" content providers. In the busy media ecosystems of large cities, community media tend to become voices of groups not otherwise served by public and private sector media. Serving residents of Vancouver's Downtown Eastside is therefore the natural preserve of community media.

In Vancouver's Lower Mainland, there used to be more than a dozen cable community TV neighbourhood offices. However, the current cable incumbent – Shaw – has shut all but one studio in suburban Surrey and produces everything else from its corporate tower downtown. The latter facility is difficult to access by citizens, and virtually impossible for a resident of the Downtown Eastside. Anyone entering the building needs to apply for an access card, which is often denied without explanation, there is no parking for quick equipment pickups and drop-offs, and meeting spaces inside the building that community groups require to plan productions are neither readily available nor publicized. The fully independent and community-based W2 was trying to step into the gap, but had to survive from month to month on donations and internal fund-raising activities such as renting meeting space, staging performances, and running a small cafe. In 2013, W2 was evicted from its premises by the City of Vancouver for failure to pay a "community amenity fee," and has so far failed to relaunch.

This environment is ripe for the kind of collaboration that Joan Melanson's "best practice" suggests; the public broadcaster could develop better ties with communities by collaborating with community-based facilities such as W2. An opportunity for collaboration exists in Vancouver, where a redevelopment of the CBC broadcast centre resulted in several new community facilities. Two of these new facilities, Studio 700 and the Outdoor Stage, are used by both the CBC and outside community and cultural organizations to host community outreach events. However, the third and largest facility, a space with an area of 790 square metres, on the main floor, initially dubbed the Vancouver Festival Centre in press releases, and originally intended to house community-based cultural groups such as Vancouver's International Jazz Festival, International Children's Festival, and Folk Music Festival at low cost, remains idle, with the city paying its operating costs. No community tenants have been found due to the high cost of renovating the space. With a concerted effort by CBC, the City of Vancouver, and community media organizations, this space could be developed into a partnership between public and community media to improve local media for the benefit of the people of Vancouver.

Conclusions and Policy Recommendations

From our discussions with citizens, journalists, and thinkers connected with these case studies, it is clear that some infrastructure is needed to make community-public partnerships possible. Community and public media are two underfunded sectors that can barely keep up with what they are doing today.

Furthermore, the people working in these sectors would need to embrace the notion of partnering to improve their respective local programming and presence. Several projects with good intentions and potential benefits to both parties – CBC disposition of its analogue assets to communities and facility- and/or frequency-sharing in Hamilton and Vancouver – have not realized their full potential to date, because of a lack of understanding on the part of one or both of the public or the community broadcaster of what these benefits might be.

As noted by Skinner et al. in chapter 3, Canadians urgently need to ensure that public sources of funding for public and independent community media are stabilized and adequate, and that public policy supports strong and stable media institutions. In addition, we suggest that a fund could be established and made available to both the CBC and to local community media organizations to create new and/or enhanced local service in underserved communities (e.g., Hamilton, Kingston, Kamloops).

One way such a program could work is that ideas for collaboration originate with non-profit community groups that already produce community media, or wish to. They would approach their nearest CBC location to pitch an idea for collaboration and to refine the idea. Together, they would go to the fund for support for the additional personnel and technical infrastructure for both organizations to make the project happen. One criterion for funding could be the project's long-term sustainability. Either the project would demonstrate proof of concept to the CBC – that collaboration results in a greater quantity and diversity of content – and become part of its normal operating procedures in that region, and/or it would demonstrate proof of concept at the community level, and benefit from long-term support from a municipality, subscriptions or collaboration with existing community facilities (such as a library).

Finally, a national body such as CACTUS, working in partnership with public broadcasters, would be needed to promote and develop awareness among practitioners about the benefits of public-community partnerships and the availability of funding to support them.

NOTES

1 Approximately 65 per cent of CBC/Radio-Canada's revenues come from a parliamentary appropriation, while 35 per cent is self-generated from advertising, subscription fees, and leasing.
2 Based on unpublished CBC finance data shared with the Canadian Media Guild.
3 Public complaints about cable community channels were first raised in volume in the run-up to the CRTC's 2001 review of community TV policy. Audits by cable staff were conducted each year from 2002 through 2005 to see whether cable companies were observing the production quotas for local programming and for community-produced programming in the new policy. More than 3,000 Canadians complained about cable community channels in the lead-up to the 2010 community TV policy review, and the most comprehensive audit of cable community TV channels ever conducted by the CRTC was carried out in 2011 in response to a complaint by CACTUS.
4 As Skinner et al. note in chapter 3, the LPIF has been discontinued.
5 The Community Radio Fund of Canada provides funding for special projects and initiatives of community radio channels, not operational funding. Community radio channels are expected to survive primarily on the sale of advertising.
6 There were 300 layoffs at CHUM the day its sale to CTV was announced in 2006 (Summerfield 2006). In 2007, there were 200 layoffs at Canwest-owned Global TV and additional cuts at Canwest-owned newspapers prior to the Canwest purchase of specialty TV company Alliance Atlantis (Canadian Press 2007). More layoffs followed as Canwest began to sink under the massive debt it incurred to buy Alliance Atlantis. In 2010, when the company was on the brink of bankruptcy, the Canwest TV assets were bought by Shaw Communications.
7 See http://www.cmg.ca/en/wp-content/uploads/2013/11/Preliminary -numbers-Broadcast-Job-cuts-between-2008-2013-CMG.pdf. See also the CRTC *Diversity of Voices* proceedings (CRTC 2008a), in which hundreds of Canadians voiced dissatisfaction with local media, and Broadcasting

Public Notice (CRTC 2008b), announcing the creation of the Local Programming Improvement Fund.

8 See an overview of the development of the Canadian television industry here: http://www.broadcasting-history.ca/index3.html?url=http%3A// www.broadcasting-history.ca/specialized/network_histories/histories .php%3Fid%3D3 . A patchwork of public and privately owned stations developed across the country, beginning with the launch of CBC production centres in Toronto and Montreal in 1949 and the first live broadcast from Montreal in 1952. The private stations were considered "outlets" of the national service and broadcast CBC content, a situation that has continued to this day at a reduced number of affiliated stations. See CBC's Affiliated Station policy from 1993: http://www.cbc.radio -canada.ca/en/reporting-to-canadians/acts-and-policies/programming/ program-policies/1-1-24/ <AU: updated url here now>Current CBC affiliates include Corus-owned CKWS in Kingston, Ontario. There are two Radio-Canada affiliates in Quebec, including RNC Media-owned CKRN -TV in Rouyn-Noranda.

9 Unlike the Accelerated Coverage Program, adopted by the federal government in 1974 to provide dedicated funding to extend CBC/Radio -Canada's analogue TV and radio signals to unserved communities.

10 http://www.cbc.radio-canada.ca/en/media-centre/2010/08/6a/.

11 It can cost from a few hundred dollars to a couple of thousand dollars to power an analogue television transmitter annually, depending on its range.

12 The "independent community producing groups in Quebec" referred to in the Payette Report are not-for-profit associations created for the purpose of producing community television. Approximately 45 such associations exist in Quebec. They do not themselves hold licences from the CRTC and do not own distribution infrastructure. They supply content for playback on private, cable-controlled "community channels."

13 When changes in ownership occur within the Canadian broadcasting sector (most recent transactions have created increased concentration in ownership), a percentage of the transaction value (usually 10 per cent) must generate "tangible public benefits." For the particular transaction discussed, see http://www.crtc.gc.ca/eng/archive/2010/2010-782.htm.

14 Personal communication between Catherine Edwards and CBC.

15 Valemount Entertainment Society in British Columbia, CHEK-TV in Dawson Creek and Chetwynd, British Columbia, and AshCreek TV Society, British Columbia.

16 PAVED Arts is a non-profit, community-based organization that provides training and equipment access for community members to express

themselves through photography, audio, video, electronic, and digital media.

17 For more information, see PAVED Arts' web site at http://www.pavedarts .ca. For more information, see http://communitystudy.ca/?page_id=323.

18 Interviews with Hamilton city and college officials, February, 2012. The names of all interviewees are withheld by mutual agreement.

19 For background on the Great Whig campaign, see: http://www.cwa -scacanada.ca/EN/news/2011/110524_greatwhig2.shtml.

20 Interview by Karen Wirsig with anonymous source, Jan. 2012.

21 This is a community channel in name only; it is owned and controlled by a private company.

22 For more information, see the CRTC's web site at http://www.cfrc.ca/ history

5 Understanding Canadian Local News Ecosystems: An International Comparative Approach

CHRISTOPHER ALI

"Localism" in media policy has been, and continues to be, a contested area of regulation, not only in its progenitor, the United States, but in many countries struggling with how to understand the nature of "the local" in a digital, neo-liberal, and global age (Napoli 2000, 2001a, 2001b; Tinic 2005). As Appadurai (1996, 52) asked almost twenty years ago, "What is the nature of locality, as a lived experience in a globalized world?" This question stretches deep within communication policy, as sovereignty over national communication systems is in jeopardy in an era of transnational media and capital (see Barney 2005). Coupled with the deregulatory and liberalizing forces of the hegemonic narrative of neo-liberalism (Freedman 2008; Harvey 2005) – forces that have deeply impacted the practice of journalism in Canada, as David Skinner, Kathleen Cross, and Robert Hackett observed in chapter 3 – many are left wondering whether, and how, to protect media systems at the local level (Stavitsky 1994; Calabrese 2001; Napoli 2001a; Cowling 2005). This is particularly true of regulators and stakeholders in the United States, United Kingdom, and Canada, whose media systems and traditional media outlets have been greatly impacted by the 2008–09 recession and the ever-growing popularity of digital media (Tinic 2010; Waldman 2011; Ofcom 2009a). In response, the overwhelming declaration has been that "localism" in media systems – in particular, local news and information – is vital to a well-functioning democracy and deserving of more attention. For instance, a 2009 report on local news and information in the United States noted, "America needs 'informed communities,' places where the information ecology meets people's personal and civic information needs. This means people have the news and information they need to take advantage of life's opportunities for themselves and their families" (Knight Commission 2009, xi). In the United Kingdom, a similar sentiment was expressed: "The link between geography and citizen participation suggests that local and regional media play an important role by informing the geographic community" (Ofcom 2009a, 15). Canada too has come around to the idea that local news and information play a vital role in the democratic health of the citizenry: "It is from the local media that most Canadians receive the information that is critical to their understanding of local, regional, national and international issues. Local media help to shape Canadians' views and to equip them to be active participants in the democratic life of the country" (CRTC 2008a, para. 57).

Nonetheless, the relevance of traditional local news outlets has been thrown into question in the United States and the United Kingdom, where local newspapers have closed, and the quality of local newscasts challenged (Waldman 2011; Ofcom 2009a). That Canada has not been immune was demonstrated in 2008 when the private television networks CTV and Global closed or sold several small-market stations and decreased local coverage at others (Tinic 2010, 194; Robertson 2009; Akin 2009). Where these three countries differ, however, is in their regulatory approach to these challenges. Over the past three years, both the Federal Communications Commission (FCC) in the United States and the Office of Communication (Ofcom) in the United Kingdom launched omnibus research projects to understand not only the health of broadcasters and newspapers, but to gauge the status of what is dubbed the "local news ecosystem," or "local media ecology" (Waldman 2011; Ofcom 2009a). Titled *The Information Needs of Communities* (Waldman 2011)[1] and *Local and Regional Media in the UK* (Ofcom 2009a), respectively, these reports strove to understand the various types of news and information media serving disparate communities, in recognition of the fact that consumers no longer look exclusively to traditional outlets for local news and information. In contrast, the Canadian response, directed primarily by the CRTC, has focused almost exclusively on broadcasting, and the private sector in particular (see CRTC 2008a, 2008b, 2009b, 2010a, 2011a). While creating such projects as the Local Programming Improvement Fund (LPIF),[2] and lending rhetorical support to the importance of local news and information, Canada seems to lag behind in its understanding of its local media ecosystems when compared with the United States and the United Kingdom (see Burgess 2011).

Using the aforementioned reports as comparisons, this chapter argues that while the CRTC has attempted to bring attention to localism in recent years, such attempts are piecemeal without a comprehensive understanding of Canadian local media ecologies (see also Ali 2012c).[3] More specifically, I argue that an assessment of local news and information ecosystems akin to those undertaken by the FCC and Ofcom is needed, from a distinctly Canadian perspective, incorporating the unique relationship to "the local" and domestic challenges facing local news production (see also Burgess 2011). Interestingly, this is not a new suggestion. In fact, a 2011 article in the online trade magazine *Wire Report* ran the headline, "Canadian Broadcasters Can Take Lessons from FCC Report on Local News, Critics Say" (Burgess 2011).[4]

In this spirit, I ask, therefore, what Canada can learn from these two studies, and which specific characteristics might be adapted to suit the Canadian media landscape? I expand my search, moreover, to encompass not only broadcasting, but also what regulators and policy-makers can learn about Canadian local media ecosystems as a whole. To address this question, I will examine three themes shared by the two aforementioned reports, and explicate how they have been – or not been – addressed in Canada, and where any dearth of knowledge remains. I will examine how these studies identify and define localism and the various related concepts, the holistic approach taken by regulatory researchers towards media platforms, and the players identified as key stakeholders in reviving this supposed paucity of local news and information.

Three justifications point to the necessity of this proposed study and its implications for the future of Canadian local journalism. First, from a regulatory perspective, a consideration of the definitions of the local and regional are needed to underpin regulations concerning such broadcasting elements as local news quotas, licensing commitments, and a diversity of editorial voices. Second, from a liberal-democratic perspective, the CRTC has rightly claimed that a "diversity of voices" is necessary for the democratic well-being of the country, and in 2008 argued that such diversity was being fulfilled in Canadian communities (CRTC 2008a). This assessment, however, omitted online platforms, and served only to count traditional editorial voices. As such, a study is needed both to update this 2008 research and, more importantly, to move beyond nominal assessment so as to understand both the voices and the content informing Canadian communities. The results of such a study could have substantial implications for how funding is allocated in any future subsidy programs, such as the now-defunct Local Programming Improvement Fund. Third, from a normative perspective, if we agree that local news and information is necessary for a well-functioning democracy, for community cohesion, and for civic participation (Friedland 2001; Aldridge 2007; Dewey 1927; Hutchins 2004), then we need a better understanding of the institutions providing this democratically vital service. To reiterate the point made above, we need a deeper understanding than a simple counting of outlets provides.[5]

To reinforce these justifications throughout my analysis, I will pay close attention to the 2003 report of the Standing Committee on Canadian Heritage, *Our Cultural Sovereignty: The Second Century of Canadian Broadcasting*, known as the Lincoln Report (Canada 2003), as it engaged with many of these issues, identified a distinct lack of localism in Canadian media, and despite its lack of impact, set an important precedent for concerns of Canadian local media. It also demonstrates some of the larger challenges of studying Canadian media localism, particularly the exclusive focus on broadcasting, and a lack of impact (see Raboy 2006, 302; Raboy and Taras 2004).

This chapter thus has the following two goals: (1) to review recent Canadian regulation impacting local news and information providers through a comparative lens; and (2) to argue that a review of Canadian local media ecosystems is necessary. To contextualize this argument, this chapter will begin with a consideration of localism in the abstract and then specifically within the Canadian policy milieu. I will then turn my attention to the three aforementioned themes and assess their suitability for application in Canada. The conclusion of the chapter will consider which federal body should be responsible for this proposed undertaking.

Localism Defined

"The local" has been a heavily contested topic in recent years, not only in policy discourse, but also from a conceptual perspective (Ali 2012a). Issues, for instance, have concerned the apparent divide between the local and the global (e.g., Wilson and Dissanayake 1996a; Cvetkovich and Kellner 1997), challenging the notion of an unadulterated or authentic "local culture" and the "romance of communities" (e.g., Dirlik 1996; Haugerud 2003; Kraidy 2005; Joseph 2008) and, above all, interrogations of the relevance of place-based communities in a globalized world (e.g., Dirlik 1996, 1999; Escobar 2000; Wilson and Dissanayake 1996b). Recent scholarship in interrelated fields such as critical theory, critical geography, and the newly emergent critical regionalism, however, reinforces the point that, rather than being associated with the parochial, the provincial, and the backward, the local should instead be understood and analysed as a space for experimentation and innovation, in conversation with, rather than in opposition to, the global (Dirlik 1996, 1999; Wilson and Dissanayake 1996b; Kraidy 2005; Powell 2007). Importantly for current manifestations of localism policy, this move towards an inclusive definition of the local continues to support the idea that place still matters as a seminal component of the human condition (Tinic 2005, 157; Howley 2005; Dirlik 1999; see also Ali 2012a).

Drawing from this connection between people and places, localism in media policy articulates the relationship between a broadcast licensee and a specific geographical community (Napoli 2001a; Ali 2012a). More specifically, "localism is defined in general terms as 'covering local issues, reporting local news, doing local programming, providing an outlet for local voices'" (Tristani, cited in Napoli 2001b, 373; see also Cole and Murck 2007). Coupled with programming responsibilities, localism can also mean television or radio stations be licensed to a specific community, that their physical location be within that community, and/or that they have local ownership (Napoli 2001a; Cole and Murck 2007). This is a distinctly place-contingent policy, underscoring the belief that "local communities and nations continue to define their selves and their aspirations within territorial parameters [and that] [t]he media provide them with the essential ideas and means of expression to do so" (Cowling 2005, 354; see also Napoli 2001a).

The provision of local news and information is the cornerstone of these policies. It is suggested that local news fulfills numerous normative democratic functions such as enhancing civic engagement and deliberative democracy (Calabrese 2001; Friedland 2001; Aldridge 2007; Habermas 1989; Dewey 1927), supporting community cohesion and solidarity (Ewart 2000; Hutchins 2004; Lowrey et al. 2008), and assisting citizens in their everyday lives (Kaniss 1991; Knight Commission 2009). Local news and information, supported by localism policies, is thus the foundation of what Friedland (2001) calls a "communicatively integrated community."

This idealistic visioning, which found its American roots in the myth of the Jeffersonian town hall and Tocquevillian notions of local governance, has been under threat in recent years due to the porous nature of digital communication technologies, which allow users to circumvent their immediate geography (Napoli 2000, 2001a; Cowling 2005; Stavitsky 1994).[6] In light of the ubiquity of these placeless digital platforms, some argue that the "spatial aspect of localism" be abandoned altogether, in recognition that today "communities ... mobilize in terms of commonality of taste rather than commonality of place of residence" (Stavitsky 1994, 8). Others, however, contend that localism will continue to exist, tied as it is to our political and electoral frameworks, but must adapt, taking into account communities of interest and taste, rather than solely communities of geographical convenience (Napoli 2000, 2001a). As Calabrese (2001, 252) argues, "It seems that we can either abandon localism and local participation as a core value in a social policy that is aimed at democratic communication, or we can redefine and defend it in order to enliven its historical relevance." In response, Calabrese argues that localism must continue as a facilitator of political participation and democratic engagement, but must be expanded into a form of "translocalism" so as to recognize "the direct communication that increasingly takes place between and among active participants in organizations, coalitions, and social movements that may or may not have significant memberships in a single locale, but whose collective membership across potentially great distances makes for an increasingly important form of participation" (262).

The idea of connecting disparate places and spaces provides a bridge to the Canadian understanding of not only localism, but of the very notions of nation and region. Canadian media policy has historically been waged at the level of the nation state, at the expense and obfuscation of regional and local identities (Ali 2012a; Raboy 1990; Tinic 2005). Rightly so, some would argue, considering Canada's proximity to the United States, US hegemonic influence on Canadian consumption of popular culture, and the anti-federalist sentiments of Quebec; Canada was in need of a strong and unified national identity, aided by communication (the CBC) and transportation infrastructure (the CPR) (Barney 2005; see also Raboy 1990; Tinic 2005). This prompted the idea that Canada is a country of "technological nationalism," whereby various technological platforms have been used to bind the country together – a country that is inherently regional (Charland 1986; see also Barney 2005).

Demurring slightly, however, many have commented on the distinctly regional nature of Canada. Laba (1988, 82) argues, "The keenest observations of the conditions of Canadian culture have invariably concluded that regionalism – the development (economic, political, cultural) and limits of 'local culture' – has been, and continues to be, the fundamental nature of cultural process in Canada." These critics argue that regionalism has been historically and detrimentally set aside in favour of nationalism (see Tinic 2005, 4; Laba 1988). Indeed, as was previously noted, to unite these "local cultures," a national communications framework was implemented: "National broadcasting policy in Canada developed from the same model as the periphery-centre economic relationship that defined the confederation and the subsequent political structure of the country. In both federal politics and broadcasting, the concentration of decision-making power in central Canada led to the formation of policies that often neglected the incorporation of regional voices in policy formation" (Tinic 2005, 4).

The introduction of commercial television in 1960 and the passage of the 1968 Broadcasting Act, however, began to bring about a renewed regional presence in Canadian communication policy (Tinic 2005, 62–3). The 1968 Act, for instance, directed broadcasters to serve "the special needs of geographic regions" (Canada 1988, 375). Since then, Parliament and the CRTC have attempted – with varying degrees of success – to implement localist or regionalist policies. The 1991 iteration of the Broadcasting Act, for instance, not only includes mention of the regional and the local, but adds "community broadcasting" as one of the three core elements of the Canadian broadcasting system (Canada 1991). As the Lincoln Report explicates, the 1991 Broadcasting Act identifies – but fails to define – community, local, and regional elements, and directs broadcasters to serve these localities (Canada 2003, 346). Three sections of the Act point to localism:

1 Section 3(1)(*i*)(ii): "the programming provided by the Canadian broadcasting system ... should be drawn from local, regional, national and international sources."
2 Section 3(1)(*t*)(i): "broadcasting 'distribution undertakings ... should give priority to the carriage of Canadian programming services and, in particular to the carriage of local Canadian stations.'"
3 Section 3(l)(*t*)(iv): "distribution undertakings ... may, where the Commission considers it appropriate, originate programming, including local programming, on such terms as are conducive to the achievement of the objectives of the broadcasting policy ... in particular provide access for underserved linguistic and cultural minority communities" (Canada 2003, 346; Canada 1991).

Section 5(2)(b) of the Act also directs the CRTC to "take into account regional needs and concerns" (Canada 1991). This legislation underscores the CRTC's requirement that television broadcasters demonstrate commitments to local news and local reflection as part of their licence renewals, or to be eligible for certain regulatory support mechanisms (e.g., LPIF).[7]

More recently, the CRTC has praised the importance of localism and local news and information, calling it the "cornerstone" of the industry (von Finckenstein 2007) and "one of the major building blocks of the community and of the broadcasting system" (Cram 2003). In keeping with this, the CRTC has been concerned with the amount of local news and information provided by commercial broadcasters, particularly after increased corporate consolidation and, more recently, the closure of stations and newscasts in 2008 and 2009 (see CRTC 2008a). In response, the Commission initiated a study called the *Diversity of Voices* in Canadian media in 2008 (CRTC 2008a) and that same year implemented the Local Programming Improvement Fund as a mechanism to fund local news and information programming at small, "non-metropolitan" (i.e., centres with fewer than 1 million people) stations, regardless of public or private affiliation (CRTC 2008b, 2011a).[8] The House of Commons Standing Committee on Canadian Heritage echoed the concerns of the CRTC and conducted its own study of local television, the Schellenberger Report (Canada 2009a), while the Senate's Standing Committee on Transport and Communications conducted a study, *The Canadian News Media* (the Bacon Report) (Canada 2006a, 2006b).

In addition to the CRTC, the House of Commons and Senate, the CBC, and private broadcasters have taken note of local news and information. For the latter, this manifested itself in the campaign "Local TV Matters," which pitted broadcasters against broadcast distribution undertakings (BDUs) for the right of broadcasters to charge a fee for their signal (Marlow 2009; Tinic 2010).[9] For the CBC, this meant the release in 2011 of its policy document, *2015: Everyone, Every Way – CBC/Radio-Canada's Five-Year Strategic Plan*, which recommitted the Corporation to "being the leader in regional presence in all served markets using a multimedia approach" (CBC 2011a, 4).

Notwithstanding such steps, two issues continue to plague a dedicated push towards Canadian localism. First, Canada still lacks a coherent localism strategy and policy (Canada 2003, 362). Instead, it is spread thin between various regulations such as the 1999 Television Policy (CRTC 1999a), the Broadcasting Distribution Regulations (CRTC 2012a), the *Diversity of Voices* proceedings

(CRTC 2008a), the Community Television Policy (CRTC 2010b), the LPIF (CRTC 2009b, 2011a, 2012b), and individual licence mandates. In addition, there is an "absence of a common understanding of key terms and the bewildering array of policies that the CRTC has developed over time" (Canada 2003, 362). As a result, the Lincoln Report recommended "that the Department of Canadian Heritage develop a Community, Local, and Regional Broadcast Policy in consultation with key broadcasting industry stakeholders, including public, private, community, educational, and not-for-profit broadcasters and related interest groups" (ibid.). To be sure, the CRTC has made progress in drawing attention to localism since the release of the Lincoln Report, but has fallen short in implementing this pressing recommendation.

The second issue is the CRTC's approach to digital media, specifically at the local level. Despite acknowledging that Canadians are "increasingly" relying on digital platforms to access local news and information (CRTC 2008b, para. 338), Canada has yet to see a study that assesses both traditional and digital local media platforms equally (see Burgess 2011). This strikes at the heart of the present discussion – that a study is needed to understand the complex dynamics underway within a local media ecosystem – and it will be difficult, if not impossible, to regulate broadcast localism without a more comprehensive understanding of "the local" in Canadian society.

Theme 1: Definitions and Contradictions – What Is the local?

One of the more salient aspects of the US and UK local media studies is the attention paid to defining and delineating "local" from "community," "regional," and "national." As we have seen, this remains a challenge for the Canadian regulator. While both the US and UK reports note the difficulty in defining "local" in a digital age, their focus is some element of geographical or physical proximity. The United States outlines four types of news and information:

1   Hyperlocal News (neighbourhood-based). Here, they recognize that "information is better than ever. Technology has allowed citizens to help create and share news on a very local level – by small town, neighborhood and even block." One may presume as well that community broadcasting and community news falls into this hyperlocal category.

2 Local News (municipal and state). Here, the report notes, "Information is struggling mightily – with a measurable decline in certain types of accountability reporting."
3 National News. Here, the report is more optimistic, observing that it is "vibrant and dynamic: There are certainly many areas of concern. But national newspapers have increased their reach and Web sites operating on a national level … are showing the potential to develop business models that will sustain a variety of national news."
4 International News, which the report describes as "a mixed picture: The contraction of newspapers, newsmagazines, and network news severely undercut traditional ways of getting foreign news. But other media organizations … have expanded their overseas presence." (Waldman 2011, 21)

The UK report is more explicit, drawing a connection between types of media and geography. The report identified five types of local media:

1 Ultra-local: "the individual's immediate geographic community."
2 Local: "the individual's city, town or local district."
3 Regional: "associated with either metropolitan, the county or broader geographic area, e.g. East Anglia/West Midlands."
4 National: "associated with the devolved nations i.e. Scotland, Wales and Northern Ireland, particularly due to their strong sense of cultural identity and devolution at the national level."
5 UK: "the UK as a whole." (Ofcom 2009a, 20)

To be sure, strictly territorial definitions of "the local" are becoming ever more questionable in what Castells (1996) has called our "network society," and the UK report stressed these blurred definitional boundaries among ultra-local, local, and regional (Ofcom 2009a, 19). For instance, it observed that while "consumers find it easy to distinguish between the concepts of 'national' (as in the UK context) and 'regional' […] there are differences in how people classify different levels of localness" (ibid.). Nevertheless, the report held fast to the association between localism and "specific geographic area[s], rather than being of general interest or utility to the wider population, although local content and service may be consumed by individuals outside the geographic area to which the content and services relate" (ibid., 21).

Like the United States and United Kingdom, Canada has tradition-ally relied on a geographical definition for its approach to community, local, and regional media. As was previously noted, however, Canada has struggled historically with defining and integrating these concep-tualizations (Canada 2003). What exists at the moment is an amalgam of disparate terms spread across numerous regulatory initiatives (ibid.). As such, community television is thought to "ensure the creation and exhibition of more locally-produced, locally-reflective community pro-gramming ... [and] a greater diversity of voices and alternative choices by facilitating new entrants at the local level" (ibid., 332; CRTC 2002, para. 5; 2010b, para. 5). This is accomplished through an emphasis on citizen production as an impetus towards greater local reflection (CRTC 2010b, para. 3.) In contrast, a local television station has been defined less by programming and more by signal reach as "an over-the-air broadcast undertaking that reaches a particular audience via a transmit-ting antenna (or antennae) within a particular contour (i.e. footprint) as defined in an undertaking's condition of licence by the CRTC" (Canada 2003, 368). More recently, however, the CRTC employed a far less tech-nical definition: "A local television station is a commercial television station licensed to operate in a market where the licensee is expected to provide local news and information" (CRTC 2008a, para. 66). Similarly, the Commission defined a "local program" as "programming produced by local stations with local personnel or programming produced by locally-based independent producers that reflect the particular needs and interests of the market's residents" (CRTC 2009b, para. 43). The CRTC has also made note of the importance of "local presence," includ-ing the provision of local newscasts, full-time journalists in the mar-ket, and a local news bureau (ibid., para. 46). While the Commission seems to have adopted a more colloquial definition of "local stations," regional television stations continue to be defined in technical terms: "A licensed television station, other than a local television station, that has Grade B official contour that includes any part of the licensed area of the undertaking" (cited in Canada 2003, 355). Regional *programming*, how-ever, has its own definition:"Canadian regionally-produced programs [are] English-language programs at least 30 minutes long ... in which the principal photography occurred in Canada at a distance of more than 150 kilometres from Montreal, Toronto or Vancouver. Programs in which the principal photography occurred on Vancouver Island will also be considered regionally produced programs" (cited in Canada 2003, 377).

As we can see, the Lincoln Report was not incorrect to note that Canadian localism policy is spread among a disparate spattering of regulatory undertakings without a coherent and precise understanding of what the terms "community," "local," or "regional" mean (Canada 2003).[10] The report seems correct, then, in recommending that Canada needs an integrative approach to localism in its media policy to cut through the regulatory clutter.

Perhaps more important than where these scattered definitions are found is the need for an in-depth conversation about the value of these terms. For instance, many of the aforementioned definitions of local television rely on a tautological approach. That is to say, the CRTC has defined "local" in terms of what is "local" (i.e., a local television station is one that provides local news). Such circular reasoning obfuscates the potential of a larger conversation about the nature of localism in Canadian media policy and why it is important. In keeping with this, some have expressed concerns with the lack of definition of local news. In a dissenting opinion in 2008, for instance, CRTC Commissioner Peter Menzies rightly asked, "Is a person on the street interview with local people conducted by a local reporter still considered local news if the topic under discussion is the sub-prime crisis in the United States or an earthquake in China?" (Menzies 2008, ix). Similar expressions were noted at the 2012 CRTC hearings on the Local Programming Improvement Fund. Here, several terms were used to describe related, but ultimately different, broadcasting elements: local programming, local news, local newscasts, and local news segments. As one witness noted, "The only thing is, as we discussed on the threshold issue, before we can answer that question, we need to know whether or not we are talking about local news segments, local news programming, local and regional news segments – it's a different number, depending on which one we are talking about" (CRTC 2012d, para. 1080). Similarly, Commissioner Elizabeth Duncan asked the pointed question to another witness: "Do you think that the definition of local news is specific enough, narrow enough, precise enough to allow us to be able to analyze all across the country and compare the results or do you think we need to fine-tune that?" (CRTC 2012d, para. 1564). These questions are far from trivial, as definitions of local news have consequences for regulations through licence renewals, quotas, and diversity of voices.

In addition to "local news," regulatory ambiguity also rings true for the term "region." This is particularly apparent given Canada's distinct geographical and demographic composition, and the historic tensions over regionalism and regionalization (Friesen 2001; Tinic 2005; Laba 1988). For instance, is the Canadian media system best served by policies directed towards localism, regionalism, or a combination (see Canada 2003, 356)? The CRTC, for instance, has recognized the role of "the regional nature of some conventional stations operating in Canada" (2009b, para. 44).[11] But since Winnipeg is the only city with television stations in Manitoba, should these stations be labelled "regional" rather than "local" in order to better serve the people beyond the borders of its most populous city (see Canada 2003, 356)? A witness from Prince Edward Island during the Lincoln committee's hearings echoed these concerns for his community: "The problem with discussing the Island as an example is that the population is so small. It is a province, it is a unit, it is a unity, but the point that is being made here is that the question of what is local, what is provincial, and what is regional is blurred a little bit here. In P.E.I. clearly you need to have what may appear to be local broadcasting, but it is also provincial broadcasting" (Helwig, cited in Canada 2003, 356). Taking note of the confusion, the Lincoln Report acknowledged, "Part of the problem with the term regional is that one person's regional can be someone else's local, regional or provincial, and depending on one's location, it can be all three" (ibid.). These issues have only served to further weaken and confuse the objectives of localism policy in Canada through regulatory ambiguity.

In concert with these issues, any new study of media localism must take into account not only the definitional boundaries of local and regional as they pertain to Canada, but also the epistemological issue of how to define these terms in a globalized, networked society, where communication technologies and people's day-to-day lives are no longer tethered to physical or political boundaries (Napoli 2001a; Calabrese 2001; Castells 1996; Anderson and Curtin 1999). Given that traditional notions of localism are under siege, however, perhaps it is better, then, that the boundaries remained undefined (Friesen 2001). As Friesen (2001, 544) argues, "The absence of a single, fixed institutional role for 'region' is, in the Canadian case at least, a useful and flexible quality that contributes positively to the conduct of local and national conversations because it introduces more complex appointments of reality."

Most importantly, before any regulatory definitions can even be considered, it is necessary to think critically about how we choose to understand these pressing terms. As the quote from Friesen about "region" suggests, a conversation about the complex nature of these terms is required. Without more critical thought, we risk being left with the tautological definitions as discussed above. Indeed, whatever definitional direction is taken, we may conclude that a conversation within media policy in Canada about localism and regionalism is both severely lacking and desperately needed in the digital age (see Ali 2012c).

Theme 2: Towards a Holistic Approach
to Local Media Ecologies

While underscoring the necessity of definitions, the US and UK reports also underpin the importance of examining local media from a holistic perspective. That is to say, not concentrating on one particular medium (e.g., television) but accounting for the multitude of media platforms that comprise a community's local news and information ecosystem. While it is true that both the US and UK reports were launched by communications regulators, it was argued in both cases that while neither the FCC nor Ofcom have regulatory jurisdiction over newspapers, mobile apps, or websites, failing to understand these media in an era of convergence does future regulation a severe disservice. As the FCC reported, "It is impossible to understand the information needs of communities – a clear statutory focus of the FCC – without taking a holistic look at all media ... The Commission has not only the authority but the affirmative duty to look at these issues" (Waldman 2011, 9). In keeping with this holistic ethos, the FCC's report addressed public and private television and radio, satellite and cable distribution, newspapers, the Internet and mobile devices, foundations, journalism schools, and the non-profit sector. In more than 350 pages, it not only studied these elements individually, but also how they operate in concert within a local media ecosystem. The UK report, while shorter in length, continued this ecological trend:

> Our range of duties, some of which relate directly or indirectly to the local and regional media sector ... mean that we need to understand the issues affecting local and regional journalism. Such journalism is delivered on a wide range of platforms, including local and regional newspapers, local radio, regional television, some local television, and the Internet. In order to understand the local and regional media ecology as a whole, we believe that we need to consider all of these platforms,

even if some, such as newspapers and the Internet are not regulated by Ofcom. (Ofcom 2009a, 12)

There can be little doubt that we are living in an era of digital convergence, and it is almost impossible to enforce regulatory silos around disparate media (Bar and Sandvig 2008; Shade and Lithgow 2010). Bar and Sandvig (2008) argue that communications policy needs to move away from the historical trend that sees "a new medium [treated] with the policy previously applied to whatever it seemed to resemble" (e.g., cable regulation was based on television, which was based on radio) (532). Instead, in this era of digitalization, we require innovative regulatory strategies that understand that media consumption habits are less about specific *media* and more about *formats*.[12] In the Canadian context, for instance, many, including the Lincoln Report and former CRTC chair Konrad von Finckenstein, have suggested the need to merge the existing Broadcasting Act, Telecommunications Act, and the Canadian Radio-television and Telecommunications Act into a single piece of legislation to be better equipped to deal with the challenges posed by a converged mediascape (Canada 2003, 583; von Finckenstein 2011).

This ecological approach is as true for local media as it is for national communication policies, and it is the duty of the regulator to understand these shifts in usage. As the FCC and Ofcom reports underscore, it is impossible to comprehend a specific media sector without understanding the broader ecological context. This is something the CRTC has lacked (see Murdoch, cited in Burgess 2011; Canada 2003). That said, there is precedence within Canadian media policy to support the argument made here for a holistic study of localism. For instance, in 2008 the Commission studied thirty-one Canadian communities as part of its *Diversity of Voices* enquiry (see CRTC 2012b). Addressing public and private television, radio and newspaper outlets, as well as community and ethnic broadcasters, the study concluded, "Within the private element, Canadians currently have access to a reasonable plurality of commercial editorial voices in most local markets. In addition, most markets are served by undertakings representing the public and community elements. In this regard, the Commission notes that while the CBC and educational broadcasters do not always provide a local service, they do provide important regional programming" (ibid., 6). While perhaps true, the study is limited to commenting on the quantity of outlets and not on the quality of the local content produced by these outlets. In addition, in a new media environment, the study has not been updated to include mention of new local journalistic platforms such as hyperlocal, or citizen-run websites, which have grown in recent years (see Washburn 2010; Marotte 2009). Despite these potential drawbacks, in a 2009 submission to the CRTC, communications lawyer Peter Miller (2009) recommended using the "Diversity of Voices framework" to assess the amount of news and information in a community, and from that, set requirements for broadcasters.

Historically, Canadian policy documents have considered the larger communication landscape: for example, the 1951 Royal Commission on the National Development of the Arts, Letters and Sciences (the Massey Commission, Canada 1951), the 1970 Special Senate Committee on Mass Media (the Davey Committee), and the 1982 Federal Cultural Policy Review Committee (the Applebaum-Hébert Report, Canada 1982). As such, it would not be out of place for a new study to incorporate media not regulated by the CRTC.

Theme 3: Key Stakeholders in a Local News and Information Ecosystem

The final theme is identifying key players in the provision of local news and information. While acknowledging the contributions of the private and public sectors, both the US and UK reports overwhelming look to the private sector to correct the dearth of "local accountability reporting" (Waldman 2011; Ali 2012b). The US report, for instance, notes, "The commercial sector has been uniquely situated to generate the revenue and profits to sustain labor-intensive reporting on a massive scale. But nonprofit media has always played an important supplementary role" (Waldman 2011, 147). The UK report witnessed a similar dependence on commercial media, acknowledging that "local and regional content will be delivered by a healthy and vibrant commercial media sector, but also by organizations employing a range of different ownership models, including public sector and not-for-profit, delivering public value to communities throughout the UK" (Ofcom 2009a, 85). From these excerpts, we can conclude that the public and non-profit media sectors continue to play important roles, but consistent with the tide of neoliberalism (Harvey 2005), it is to commercial media that regulators look as the primary providers of local news in the United States and the United Kingdom (Ali 2012b).

It is clear that any Canadian iteration would have to consider which sector – private, public, or community – or which combination of these, would be best suited to advance localism. While the FCC and Ofcom seem determined to anoint the private sector as the bastions of localism, the Canadian context departs from these conclusions. The CBC, for instance, released its five-year, *Everyone, Every Way* strategy, recommitting itself to the goals of local and regional news and information programming (CBC 2011a). To date, the CBC has made good on this promise in developing new radio and digital programs in several cities such as Kamloops, Kelowna, Victoria, Toronto, Calgary, and Saskatoon (CBC 2012a).[13] Not to be shut out, both BCE and Shaw pledged increased financial commitment to local news as a condition of their respective purchases of the CTV and Global television networks (CRTC 2011b, 2010c). As noted by Karen Wirsig and Catherine Edwards in chapter 4, there have also been calls for a greater recognition of community broadcasters in the local news and information ecosystem. The 2006 Senate Report (the Bacon Report) recommended "that the CRTC revise its community television and radio regulations to ensure that ... a diversity of news and information programming is available through these services" (Canada 2006a, 33).

As previously demonstrated, the CRTC also has an important role in forwarding local news and information through such initiatives as the Small Market Local Programming Fund and the Local Programming Improvement Fund, the latter of which was designed to foster local news in non-metropolitan markets (CRTC 2003, 2011a, 2012b). In line with a holistic approach, we might question, as some have done in the United States, whether the jurisdiction of a fund akin to the LPIF could be expanded to include non-broadcast local news platforms.[14] In the United States, policy scholar Ellen Goodman (2009) has argued that federal funding for public broadcasting should be revised to be available to a multitude of media platforms on a competitive basis. This is to better recognize the shift from public *broadcasting* to public *media* (see also Lowe and Bardoel 2009).

Could the same be done in Canada? To answer this question, and to better understand the roles and responsibilities of incumbent and emerging media providers, a comprehensive overview of Canadian local media ecologies is necessary, incorporating both incumbents and new entrants in the provision of local news and information such as

OpenFile, as discussed by Skinner et al. in chapter 3, and the many hyperlocal news portals springing up across the country.

Conclusion: Committee, Commission, or CRTC?

In this review of Canadian localism as articulated within media regulation and policy, I have argued that Canada is in need of a comprehensive and holistic review of localism and local news and information ecologies. Moreover, through a comparison of recent FCC and Ofcom local media ecology studies, I have argued that three salient components would also need to be addressed in a Canadian iteration. First, a consideration of the definitions of "local" and "regional" is necessary in order to understand the embedded dynamics at play within a local media ecosystem. Second, a holistic mindset needs to be adopted, one that considers together all platforms and institutional models. Third, we need to identify the key actors within the local news and information ecosystem, a task unrealizable without an understanding of the system as a whole.

The final aspect will be to consider which organizational body would conduct such a study. Canada has a rich history of royal commissions, standing committees, and CRTC-appointed task forces, all of which have undertaken key studies of the Canadian media landscape. In 2003, for instance, the House Standing Committee on Canadian Heritage released the Lincoln Report, while a smaller report on Canadian local television was released in 2009 (Canada 2003, 2009a). The most recent CRTC-appointed task force occurred in 2007, concerning the Canadian Television Fund and before that, the Task Force on Cultural Diversity (administered by the Canadian Association of Broadcasters) in 2001 (CRTC 2001, 2007a). Royal commissions are rare in communications, having most recently occurred in 1980–81 (Royal Commission on Newspapers) and 1957 (Royal Commission on Broadcasting). Given such scarcity, the question truly comes down to a decision between committee or task force? There are advantages and disadvantages to both. While true a parliamentary committee "can do extraordinary work" and mandates government response within 150 days, it is also subject to partisan politics, and potential neglect by government, as was the case with the Lincoln Report (Raboy and Taras 2004, 67; Canada 2003, xiii). Moreover, a government response may not be what is actually needed. Instead, a CRTC-appointed task force might breathe new life into an institution on the edge of obsolescence. Recent events have indicated that the Commission is willing – for better or worse – to take a more interventionist approach to the Canadian media sector.[15] The study proposed in this chapter could complement this renewed activist impetus. Indeed, despite a lack of jurisdiction over non-broadcasting elements (e.g., newspapers, mobile news apps, and hyperlocal websites), in a digital age the CRTC must nevertheless account for them in order to properly regulate the sectors under its jurisdiction (broadcasting and telecommunications). Some might disagree that the Commission is the appropriate choice to assume responsibility for such an undertaking. What is more certain, however, and more important than which federal body takes on this proposed challenge, is that as Canada moves forward into a digital twenty-first century, localism, and local news and information, cannot be left behind. An understanding of their resonance and relevance is not only warranted, but necessary.

NOTES

1 The author served as an intern with the FCC, working specifically on this report.

2 Before the LPIF was created in 2008–09, the CRTC also established the Small Market Local Programming Fund to assist small-market, independently owned television stations (see CRTC 2003).

3 In 1999, the CRTC exempted broadcasting in "new media" from its regulatory jurisdiction (CRTC 1999b). Nevertheless, while the CRTC today only has jurisdiction in matters related to broadcasting and telecommunications (as does the FCC and Ofcom), the FCC is correct in noting that regulators must "have an understanding of developments within the broader sphere where radio, television, cable and satellite media outlets operate" (Waldman 2011, 367). In addition, the CRTC has investigated Broadcasting in New Media (CRTC 2009a), however, this was not done with a specific local focus.

4 The article, however, focused only on broadcasting, and I argue in this chapter for the need for a holistic study of local media platforms.

5 This point needs to be tempered somewhat, since local media *mapping* is a vital element of recent assessments of "Information Community Case Studies" (Durkin and Glaisyer 2010; Ofcom 2009b).

6 As Anderson and Curtin (1999) remind us, it is not just digital communication technologies that have disrupted a geographical

understanding of localism in policy. In fact, they contend, "It is difficult to talk about localism in broadcasting – in spite of its importance as a regulatory principle – because the media have helped to reorganize the dimensions of time and space in modern society, reconfiguring personal time and creating new forms of space and new social relations that make it virtually impossible to theorize – or to regulate – 'the local' in a way that is consistent or coherent" (295).

7 In 2009, the CRTC harmonized the local programming requirements for television stations at seven hours per week for small market stations, and 14 hours per week for large-market stations (CRTC 2009b, para. 51–60).

8 During the writing of this chapter, the CRTC announced that it would phase out the LPIF by 2014 (CRTC 2012c). According to the Commission, "While the implementation of the LPIF was appropriate to address the issues facing local stations at the time at which the LPIF was introduced, the Commission is of the view that reliance on LPIF funding is not sustainable in the long term in the context of the new broadcasting environment" (2012b, para. 15). It is uncertain as to how the cancellation of the LPIF will impact local stations in the short to medium term (see Morison 2012).

9 We might question, however, whether this campaign was really a plea to save local television, or an opportunity to derive a stable revenue source from BDUs (see Tinic 2010).

10 It should be noted that the *Diversity of Voices* report does indeed define market, local newspaper, local radio station, and local television station in a single document (CRTC 2008a, para. 66).

11 An example of a regional station is CTV's Sudbury affiliate (CICI-TV), which services northeastern Ontario.

12 While Bar and Sandvig do not state it explicitly, an example of a transition from medium to format could be to view the local media ecosystem through video, audio, and text, rather than through television, radio, online, and print (Bar and Sandvig 2008, 533–44; see also Rennie 2007, 29). Such a change would be sure to have an impact on how we assess local news within specific Canadian communities.

13 That said, with the 2012 federal budget cuts to the CBC of $115 million, we do not know the fate of this strategic local and regional plan (see Dixon 2012).

14 Interestingly, before the LPIF was phased out, the Campaign for Democratic Media recommended the expansion of LPIF to include "not only the affiliated networks but ... community broadcasters, independent program producers, and on-line local media groups," during testimony

to the Standing Committee on Canadian Heritage's 2009 review of local television (Canada 2009b, 3).

15 I refer here to the CRTC's October 2012 decision to deny the $3 billion takeover of Astral Media by BCE for fear that "it would have placed significant market power in the hands of one of the country's largest media companies" (Blais cited in CRTC 2012g; see also CRTC 2012e, 2012f; Ladurantaye 2012).

6 Enabling Future Journalisms: Policy Challenges and Advocacy Initiatives in the Digital Age

ARNE HINTZ

The media landscape is changing rapidly, and so are the forms of journalism that we have become accustomed to. "The people formerly known as the audience" (Rosen 2006) are using new digital platforms to produce their own media messages on a scale far beyond the classic instances of alternative and participatory media. The practice of interpreting – and providing knowledge about – the world is thus expanding from the confined sphere of professional journalism to the broader field of popular blogging and tweeting. Amateur and citizen journalists are often the first to report on major stories such as conflicts and natural disasters (Allan and Thorsen 2009). The use of social media during the Arab Spring and other protests and mobilizations has demonstrated the role of these media in democratic action and alternative information exchange (e.g., Gerbaudo 2012). Enthusiastic accounts of such "liberation technology" (Diamond 2010) have placed the latter at the centre of political change. In the words of Egyptian activist (and Google employee) Wael Ghonim, "If you want to free a society, just give them Internet access" (Khamis and Vaughn 2011).

Many of the new citizen journalism channels interact with established news media and professional journalism. Citizen journalists link to mainstream media articles, professional journalists use social media as sources for information and story ideas, and the exchanges between both lead to new forms of "ambient journalism" (Hermida 2010) as a constant flow of news and information, a constantly changing and unfolding truth. Sneha Kulkarni provides a case study of precisely this kind of interplay in chapter 8. Some citizen journalism projects are changing sides to become major news enterprises (e.g., the *Huffington Post*), and some established media organizations are incorporating user-generated content (e.g., CNN's iReporter). WikiLeaks has demonstrated how new media platforms can quickly emerge and occupy key (even though contested) roles in the media landscape by filling gaps in news processes and providing information that established media (and the public) would not otherwise be able to access (Brevini et al. 2013).

The media landscape is thus subject to ongoing shifts, dynamics, and transformations. What may emerge as the outcome of this process is what scholar Yochai Benkler (2011) has called the "networked 4th estate." This model of a contemporary media environment combines different forms of media and journalism towards a layered and inter-connected structure. It includes the following: the traditional news media; new major news blogs and news aggregation sites; civil society organizations that produce and disseminate news; new transparency and whistle-blower platforms like WikiLeaks; partisan and alternative blogs, print products, and community media; and the broader reaches of amateur citizen journalism and individual peer-to-peer information production. Each of these, according to Benkler, has a role to play in the networked media ecology as each has specific characteristics and can provide valuable information both to other parts of the broader news network and to the public.

If the media environment is changing, the legal environment that enables it has to adapt, and safeguards as well as restrictions have to be reviewed. New obstacles may emerge as digital platforms and citizen journalism become more prominent. Government responses to, for example, the uprisings in the Arab world and to WikiLeaks have highlighted the increasing use of online content filtering and electronic surveillance, the vulnerabilities of non-commercial information providers have been exploited through the denial of vital resources (such as Web space and financial services), and infrastructure decisions – from Net neutrality to radio-frequency allocation – have moved further to the centre of policy deliberations.

This chapter will explore the question of which policy environment the "networked 4th estate" would require to thrive, and which restrictions currently inhibit its flourishing. What new (and old) aspects do we need to consider as components for an enabling legal framework? What are the current challenges to freedom of expression online, and what is the nature of restrictions and limitations? Which issues have emerged on the global level, and how are these reflected in Canada? And what can be done to address these challenges?

In the first part of this chapter, I will outline several dimensions that, arguably, deserve attention as we consider the policy environment of new forms of journalism. The second part of the chapter will turn to policy initiatives based in civil society that address these challenges and explore the issue of necessary policy environments from their perspective. Complementing Canadian campaigns and organizations that are presented elsewhere in this book, I will discuss the Icelandic Modern Media Initiative – since 2011 renamed the International Modern Media Institute (IMMI) – as an exemplary case of a civil society campaign that seeks to circumvent restrictions to journalism and free expression by transforming a national policy environment. I will add insights from similar initiatives and experiences elsewhere, and identify strategic lessons, conditions for their success, thematic gaps, and international connections. Together, these dynamics and experiences demonstrate the requirements, as well as current restrictions, for enabling future forms of networked, digital, and citizen-based journalism. Further, they highlight key struggles and contestations on freedom of expression in the current digital media environment.

Policy Challenges

Information Control

The freedom to publish relevant information, and the limits to this freedom, have long been at the centre of journalists' concerns. Digital platforms for disseminating news have allowed for new means to circumvent traditional information restrictions, and they have also been subject to new obstacles and interventions. In particular, the filtering of Web content has become common practice across the globe. According to the OpenNet Initiative, 47 per cent of the world's Internet users experience online censorship, with 31 per cent of all Internet users living in countries that engage in "substantial" or "pervasive" censorship (Open Net Initiative 2012). While the Chinese "Great Firewall" and filtering practices in other authoritarian countries are well documented (e.g., Deibert et al. 2008), filtering is also common in Western democracies, often initiated with the rationale of restricting illegal or otherwise unacceptable content such as child pornography, but increasingly expanding to other fields. Access to WikiLeaks cables was banned from US state institutions, and blacklists from countries such as Australia, Finland, and Sweden have included critical and oppositional civil society–based websites and alternative media. Furthermore, filtering technologies may block access to content that is unrelated to banned topics because of the imperfections or technical configuration of the software (Villeneuve 2006).

Increasingly, intermediaries such as Internet service providers (ISPs) and search engines are enlisted by governments to control and restrict access to Internet content. Intermediaries thus become "proxy censors" (Kreimer 2006, 13). Recent examples include agreements between the government and ISPs in the United Kingdom to filter pornography, and between the content industry and ISPs in the United States to monitor and restrict access to file-sharing services because of alleged copyright infringements. Canadian politicians have applauded the UK approach, and campaigners have argued that the Trans-Pacific Partnership (TPP) trade agreement, which at the time of writing is being negotiated between Canada and eleven other countries, will include further content restrictions (Centre for Law and Democracy 2013; see also http://ourfairdeal.org).

Intellectual property protection has become a key motivation for restricting content. On the one hand, new digital platforms have served as new channels for distributing copyrighted content. Yet, on the other hand, the reach of intellectual property law has been expanded radically, and therefore provides challenges to publishers and disseminators of information. Scholars have observed a trend – also called the "second enclosure" (Boyle 2008) – towards the commodification of knowledge and its removal from the public domain. Enforcement of intellectual property law has been at the centre of recent legal initiatives such as the Stop Online Piracy Act (SOPA) in the United States, the international Anti-Counterfeiting Trade Agreement (ACTA), and most recently the Trans-Pacific Partnership (TPP) free trade agreement.

A further legal construct that has existed in the offline world but has gained new prominence in the online era is libel and anti-defamation law. In countries such as the United Kingdom, strict libel laws have become a tool for businesses (and celebrities) to prevent critical reporting, and thereby constitute a new form of private censorship. The whistle-blower platform WikiLeaks has highlighted this phenomenon as some of its most celebrated scoops have concerned information that had been banned from being published by other media for libel reasons. In 2009, for example, WikiLeaks published documents that proved illegal toxic waste dumping in Côte d'Ivoire by the British company Trafigura, thereby keeping information about the case in the public realm at a time when the *Guardian*, the BBC, and others were legally banned from discussing it. That same year, WikiLeaks published accounting details documenting widespread fraud by the Icelandic Kaupthing Bank. It thereby circumvented an injunction Kaupthing had been granted against the national public broadcaster RUV; the injunction blocked an extensive report by RUV about these fraudulent financial dealings, which had contributed to the collapse of the Icelandic economy (Brevini et al. 2013).

WikiLeaks, of course, also points us to the persistent issue of governmental restrictions on the publication and circulation of content. The state's interest in preventing its citizens from accessing information that is collected about them or in their name has been significant. Secrecy laws (such as the Official Secrets Act in the UK, originally established in 1889) continue to classify large quantities of information held by government bodies and to apply harsh sentences for any public disclosures by officials. Journalists and whistleblowers continue to be punished for revealing information deemed to be sensitive, even if the revelation is arguably in the public interest (Banisar and Fanucci 2013). Freedom of information acts and whistleblower protection laws have been adopted in many countries to improve the right of access to information held by public authorities and to protect the disclosure of vital information against detrimental pressures by employers. However, such laws typically have significant exemptions, are sketchy at best, and political pressures have quickly emerged to reduce their scope and reintroduce restrictions. In Canada, an Access to Information Act has existed since 1983, albeit with major loopholes; it allows the government to withhold most information that it wants to keep secret (Shochat 2010).

Technical Infrastructure

The role of intermediaries in current censorship regimes, as highlighted above, points us to a second level at which restrictions occur: the infrastructure level. In digital environments, the technological infrastructure that enables communication exchange and allows for the storage of relevant data is occupying an increasingly prominent role in enabling, or limiting, information dissemination. New projects such as WikiLeaks attest to the centrality of infrastructure by placing servers in countries with laws that prevent or reduce the risk of censorship, filtering, and surveillance. Points of access to infrastructure are becoming prime points of control where people, media organizations, and information can be stopped and prevented from participating in communication exchanges.

The vulnerability of the supposedly borderless cyberspace was highlighted by the almost complete Internet shutdown in Egypt and elsewhere in the Arab region in 2011 and 2012. It represents the most fundamental challenge to digitally mediated information dissemination. The US debate over an Internet kill switch, and UK proposals on temporary blockages of specific online services such as Facebook and Twitter in times of political turmoil, have further demonstrated the willingness of governments to interfere with online communication. Observers of these trends have started to question whether we can even speak of one Internet in light of these interventions (Goldsmith and Wu 2006). As Bambauer (2009, 481) notes, "Technological censorship by countries worldwide means that how the Net appears depends upon where you access it."

The Net neutrality debate has pointed to the role of network providers as potential gatekeepers who have an interest in favouring the content and applications of some information sources and services over others, and who might block access to disfavoured sites or require a special fee. This provides particular challenges for those members of the "networked 4th estate" that provide non-commercial content, for small businesses, and for oppositional and dissident news sources, but it may affect all media organizations as network providers may favour particular business partners (Balkin 2009). As David Skinner, Kathleen Cross, and Robert Hackett note in chapter 3, Net neutrality has been widely debated in Canada, and the CRTC provided a regulatory ruling in 2009 that upholds Net neutrality in principle but allows slowing down some traffic (so-called traffic "shaping" and "management") in particular circumstances. The framework has been criticized as weak, and Canadian telecommunications operators such as Rogers have been found to slow down certain Internet traffic in violation of the rules (Blevins and Shade 2010; CBC 2012b).

Beyond the most fundamental necessity of an openly accessible information infrastructure, online publications and services require a broader set of resources, such as funding, and an infrastructure that allows people to generate, access, and use those resources. Actors that are able to block access to such infrastructure and thus cut off critical resources constitute important gatekeepers. Their role became particularly apparent in December 2010 when Amazon, Paypal, and others closed the services they had previously provided for WikiLeaks, depriving the leaks platform of its domain name and of access to necessary funds in the middle of a major release that required both. This "denial of service," as Benkler (2011) has put it, propelled the providers of critical services into the spotlight of the debate on WikiLeaks and on freedom of expression. The actions by Amazon, Paypal, and company were poorly justified and likely triggered by pressure from members of the US political elite, both inside and outside government. They demonstrate the vulnerability of these services to political pressure, as well as the crucial position they occupy and the gatekeeping function they possess. So did Apple's removal of the WikiLeaks app at around the same time. Computer application stores have emerged as a further powerful set of gatekeepers with the ability to enable, or restrict, the access of a growing number of Internet users – particularly on mobile platforms – to the Web.

More crudely, governments have been considering physical restrictions to online access for certain users. "Three strikes" rules are now widely discussed, and have been implemented in countries like France. They restrict people's access to the Internet in cases where they have been found to repeatedly violate, for example, intellectual property law by downloading copyrighted content. In the United States, content owners and Internet service providers have agreed to the Copyright Alert System, a "six strike" plan that includes sending educational alerts and potentially hijacking browsers and slowing or temporarily blocking the Internet service of users accused of copyright infringement. The mechanism bypasses governmental and judicial oversight and, therefore, puts both the definition of, and the punishment for, copyright infringement in the hands of content owners and ISPs (Flaim 2012).

While new sets of restrictions appear online, the more traditional questions of who has, and who is denied, access to broadcast infrastructure and the radio-frequency spectrum are not necessarily resolved. Karen Wirsig and Catherine Edwards describe numerous obstacles faced by community broadcasters in Canada in chapter 4. In fact, community broadcasting – i.e., participatory and non-profit radio and TV self-managed by a civil society association or a citizen group – remains outlawed in many countries, while in others it has to compete for frequencies with commercial broadcasters, or is severely limited due to discrimination regarding its reach and funding (Coyer 2006; Coyer and Hintz 2010). Meanwhile, a number of countries in, for example, Latin America, South Asia, and Europe have adopted new laws for the legalization of community media and are thereby starting to recognize and support this new sector (Hintz 2011). As Wirsig and Edwards also recount in their chapter, the transition from analogue to digital broadcasting provides new challenges; while the US digital radio system inband on-channel (IBOC) discriminates in favour of incumbent licence holders, the European system of *digital audio broadcasting* (DAB) focuses on standardized national coverage and introduces a new set of private sector gatekeepers – the multiplex operators – that may be able to make decisions on who is carried on the multiplex and who is excluded (Hallett and Hintz 2010).

Surveillance

At the intersection of content and infrastructure, further aspects deserve attention. In particular, this includes the vastly expanding practice of digitally mediated surveillance, as the Snowden leaks have demonstrated. Not only the US National Security Agency (NSA) and the British Government Communications Headquarters (GCHQ) have been implicated in the spy scandal that was uncovered in 2013, but also the Communications Security Establishment Canada (CSEC), which targeted, for example, the Brazilian government (Freeze and Nolen 2013). Close collaborations between the NSA and CSEC, furthermore, allow for the surveillance of citizens' communication and the bypassing of national privacy laws (Miller 2014).

Prominent surveillance practices pre-Snowden have included social media monitoring by governments in, for example, the Middle East and North Africa, to generate information on protesters and dissidents. Authorities have collected Facebook and YouTube user data, and have used malware to capture Web-cam activity and record key strokes (Villeneuve 2012). Companies like Google and Facebook are regularly requested by governments to hand over user data. Google received 7,969 such requests by the US government in the first six months of 2012 alone (i.e., an average of more than 44 requests per day), a number which has grown dramatically over the years (Google 2015). This shows, again, the role of private sector intermediaries in interventions into digital communications.

Cases like these are embedded in a broader trend. With the ubiquity of electronic communication, the "capacity of the state to gather and process information about its citizens and about the resources and activities within its space is growing by orders of magnitude"

(Braman 2006, 314). We are witnessing a trend to (1) replace the dedicated gathering of specific data with the systematic and ongoing retention of all data and (2) enable law enforcement to access data without judicial oversight and established notions of due process. Legislation such as the European Data Retention Directive, "lawful access" rules in Canada, and the proposed Cyber Intelligence Sharing and Protection Act (CISPA) in the United States demonstrate these dynamics. Not all such policy proposals make it to the stage of legal implementation, but they demonstrate an urge by lawmakers to expand digital surveillance. Even though the monitoring of communication does not directly restrict information exchanges, it affects both individual users of digital media as well as journalists. The chilling effect of surveillance leads users to consider carefully whether to exert their rights to freedom of expression, and places burdens on investigative journalists. Threatening any confidential communication between journalists and their sources, mass surveillance provides a fundamental risk to journalism and the existence of a free press (Bell et al. 2013).

Repression

A much cruder yet persistent threat for parts of the "networked 4th estate" encompasses criminalization, physical violence, imprisonment, and other forms of direct physical repression. The imprisonment of bloggers in the Arab world, China, and elsewhere has long been documented. Globally, Internet activists who provide communications infrastructure for social movements or publish oppositional content have been subject to police operations such as house raids or have been incriminated through the use of anti-terrorism legislation. Servers and other technical infrastructure have been seized, often with dubious justification (Hintz and Milan 2009).

The imprisonment of whistleblowers such as US Army soldier Chelsea Manning, the global hunt for Edward Snowden, and the attempts by the US government to charge Julian Assange, editor-in-chief of WikiLeaks, demonstrate how serious repression also affects more traditional forms of journalism and their sources. The wake of the Snowden scandal has seen serious attacks on press freedom, including a raid on the offices of the UK newspaper the *Guardian* by British security agents and the detainment of *Guardian* collaborator David Miranda at Heathrow Airport on terrorism charges. Linking investigative "watchdog" journalism with terms such as "terrorism" provides a difficult context for the media (see Greenwald 2014).

Advocacy Initiatives

While the trends and cases described in the previous section provide us with a picture of the challenges faced by networked media enterprises, citizen journalists, and new digital projects, civil society campaigns and initiatives have emerged that translate these threats and restrictions into positive agendas for enabling new forms of journalism. In the following, I will discuss, in particular, one of these: the Icelandic Modern Media Initiative (IMMI).

IMMI's Background and Rationale

The Icelandic Modern Media Initiative emerged in the context of the collapse of the Icelandic economy in late 2008. As a national initiative for policy change, it was set up to transform the development model of the country that had, until the collapse, thrived as a safe haven for banks and financial services, and to turn Iceland into a haven of transparency and a favourable environment for media and investigative journalism. Local social and media activists, supported by international civil society organizations, created a bundle of legal and regulatory proposals to "protect and strengthen modern freedom of expression" (IMMI 2010).[1]

IMMI's understanding of "modern freedom of expression" is influenced by the context, the people, and the organizations that fostered its emergence. The story of Iceland's financial collapse uncovered the crucial role that secrecy had played in the country's reputation as a safe haven for banking, as well as the dangers of secretive financial dealings for not just its economy, but its democracy. The blocking of relevant information about corruption in Icelandic banks during the crisis served as an important trigger for growing public dissatisfaction with the problematic role of the finance industry. The injunction against public broadcaster RUV and the role of WikiLeaks in keeping relevant information publicly available, as noted above, served as key moments in this emerging awareness. WikiLeaks also had a more direct influence on IMMI's thematic focus and practices; WikiLeaks activists originally raised the idea of a transparency haven, provided knowledge on relevant laws in other countries, and developed the outline of the IMMI initiative together with local and international experts (Jonsdottir 2013).

Modern Freedom of Expression

Not surprisingly, IMMI's understanding of "modern freedom of expression" thus focuses on the area of information control. At its core is the concern to prevent the suppression of content by both public and private actors. IMMI has initiated the development of a new Freedom of Information Act to enhance access for journalists and the public to government-held information and to end the previous culture of secrecy. It has proposed measures to limit the abuse of libel laws for censoring legitimate information, and has initiated new laws on source protection and whistle-blower protection, which make it illegal for media organizations to expose the identity of sources for articles, books, etc., if the source or the author request anonymity (IMMI 2012). The goal is to provide a legal environment that protects national and international publishers and journalists' organizations from restrictions to the content they wish to publish.

This concern with allowing the free circulation of information is directly linked to an awareness of the key role that digital infrastructure plays. IMMI has developed policy proposals on intermediary protection, thus responding to the privatization of media policy and to concerns regarding repression and critical resources. It has initiated proposals on protecting Net neutrality, and IMMI activists have engaged with debates on the European Data Retention Directive and, more broadly, surveillance. Even more than the specific legal components of the package, the overall approach places the characteristics and opportunities of digital technology at the centre; the new laws will govern all information originating from, or routed through, Iceland. In a new media environment, this will not necessarily require the physical relocation of publishing houses to Iceland, but merely the posting of content on Web servers hosted in the country. Blogs, websites, and all kinds of online publications would thereby fall under Icelandic jurisdiction and would be safe(r) from censorship (Bollier 2010).

IMMI's understanding of "modern freedom of expression" relates closely to the ideas leading to the concept of the "networked 4th estate." Despite an emphasis on traditional journalism and on classic challenges such as restricted access to government information and private censorship through the use of libel and defamation laws, it considers a broader environment that includes non-professional citizen journalists, publishers of blogs, and civil society groups. It does not distinguish between journalists and non-journalists, but instead refers to the wider range of information producers, amateur and professional, that use digital platforms.

Strategies and Practices

IMMI has applied a strategy that we can call "policy hacking" (Hintz 2013). It did not build a legislative proposal from scratch but cherry-picked laws and regulations from other countries, creating a puzzle of tried-and-tested components. For example, the IMMI proposal uses parts of the Belgian source protection law, the Norwegian Freedom of Information Act, Swedish laws on print regulation and electronic commerce, the EU Privacy Directive, the New York Libel Terrorism Act, and the Constitution of Georgia (IMMI 2010). Quite in line with its WikiLeaks influence, IMMI has assembled, revised, and upgraded legal instruments – just as hackers and technical developers would upgrade code – towards a new "legal code." This relation between technical and legal expertise has also been observed in other networks, such as the open source movement, as "tinkering" with technology and the law requires similar skills and forms of reasoning (Coleman 2009).

The IMMI experience underlines the validity of several concepts and advocacy strategies that social movement and policy scholars have highlighted. The post-crisis policy window – a temporary opening in which established social orders become receptive to change and new actors can enter the field and advance their agendas (Kingdon 1984) – has been an important condition for raising the proposals and generating support. As the economic breakdown affected large parts of the population and the secrecy of banks was widely debated and criticized, an overwhelming segment of the public was in favour of a radically new model. Parts of the old political class were delegitimized, new social actors were swept into politics, and thus traditional "policy monopolies" (Meyer 2005) were broken. In a sophisticated effort of framing their proposals to make them resonate with the ideas and perceptions of target audiences, IMMI emphasized the likely international reputation for Iceland as a haven of transparency, the international attractiveness of the legislative package as a model for other countries, and its attractiveness for media companies to locate part of their infrastructure in Iceland or use Icelandic services. Overall, IMMI maintained it would "promote the nation's international standing and economy." Further, the IMMI case confirmed that the presence of sympathetic individuals inside the institutional or political space where relevant decisions are made is a key factor for successful policy intervention; the experienced campaigner and IMMI member, Birgitta Jonsdottir, was elected as parliamentarian and subsequently facilitated IMMI's adoption.

Other Initiatives – Further Agendas

Across the globe, policy initiatives based in civil society, such as IMMI, have responded to challenges that are particularly pertinent in their respective social, political, and economic contexts. Access to technological infrastructure has taken centre stage in many of these campaigns. A prominent example is the struggle over Net neutrality in North America. Groups such as Free Press (US) and OpenMedia (Canada) – as discussed at length by Skinner et al., in chapter 3 – have focused their advocacy on this issue (see also Blevins and Shade 2010). Elsewhere, the debate is still in an earlier stage, but is slowly emerging. The Dutch and Slovenian governments have adopted laws in favour of Net neutrality, and the Council of Europe has drafted a declaration in support of Internet freedoms, including Net neutrality (Council of Europe 2011). European advocacy organizations such as La Quadrature du Net in France and Bits of Freedom in the Netherlands have started to mobilize on the issue, and a European campaign "Save the Internet" (https://savetheinternet.eu/) has been modelled after earlier campaigns in North America.

Campaigns for the legalization of community broadcasting have targeted a key infrastructure challenge faced by community journalists. In Latin America, policy initiatives based in civil society have helped to transform a largely hostile policy environment into global showcases for advanced community media laws. In Argentina, the Coalition for Democratic Broadcasting, formed in 2004, developed guidelines for a new national media law and drafted a proposal. After numerous open hearings and the inclusion of further civil society comments, a demonstration of twenty thousand people brought the final text to the parliament where it was adopted in 2009, making it a true "law of the people" (personal communication with author, 11

Feb. 2011). It not only legalizes community and non-profit media, but reserves one-third of the radio-frequency spectrum for these media. According to the World Association of Community Radio Broadcasters / Association mondiale des radiodiffuseurs communautaires (AMARC), the law has "transformed Argentina into one of the best references of regulatory frameworks to curtail media concentration and promote and guarantee diversity and pluralism" (AMARC 2010, 10). Similar policy developments have taken place in other Latin American countries and around the globe, including the countries with the largest populations in South Asia (India) and Africa (Nigeria) and, most recently, the United States.

Mass protests against the Data Retention Directive in the European Union have addressed the increase in data gathering and surveillance. Mobilized by Internet activists, privacy advocates, and civil liberties groups, numerous campaigns and initiatives have emerged across Europe to change the new policy. They have benefited from strong national campaigns, such as the German AK Vorrat, which have inspired activists in other countries, and from international NGOs, such as European Digital Rights (EDRi), which have raised awareness across the region (EDRi n.d.). Demonstrations and protests have brought to the streets tens of thousands of people since 2007, including over fifty thousand people in Berlin alone in September 2009 and 2010. Constitutional complaints have challenged data-retention laws in several countries. For example, more than thirty thousand people signed a legal challenge before the German Constitutional Court, making it the largest constitutional complaint in German history (EDRi 2010). Following the Snowden revelations, national advocacy organizations, including OpenMedia, started campaigns against mass surveillance, and international mobilizations have included several "Stop Watching Us" rallies (http://rally.stopwatching.us).

In the field of intellectual property, the Anti-Counterfeiting Trade Agreement has drawn criticism from various civil society groups. As ratification and implementation of the agreement became imminent, protests erupted and stalled its adoption; in Poland and Germany, an estimated hundred thousand people took to the streets in February 2012 (Boghani 2012). Earlier, campaigns by European Net activists against the introduction of software patents led to widespread online and offline protests in 2005 (https://www.stoppt-softwarepatente.de/). More recently, Canadian groups have advocated against the tightening of copyright laws as part of international trade negotiations such as the TPP.

Conclusions and Outlooks: Enabling Future Journalisms?

As the media landscape changes and new forms of journalism emerge, we need to reconsider which aspects of the legal environment of journalism provide challenges and obstacles for journalism practices, and which are necessary preconditions for enabling the latter. In this chapter, I have outlined a set of issues that the various members of the "networked 4th estate," including both citizen and professional journalists, are facing in a new media environment. I have drawn, in particular, from the experiences of new media organizations, such as WikiLeaks, and from a wide range of international cases and perspectives.

Concluding this journey across different practices, places, and platforms, we can see that creating enabling policies for new journalisms requires attention to both aspects of content and infrastructure. Regarding the former, classic issues such as libel, source protection, and whistleblower protection enjoy renewed prominence. Some traditional concerns, such as censorship, need to be translated to new environments where content filtering is practised by intervening into the infrastructure through which information is disseminated. New issues that may affect journalism include Net neutrality, access to critical resources such as funding and apps, and digitally mediated surveillance. It becomes apparent that contestations over the availability of, and access to, information are expanding to the level of technical infrastructure and cannot be addressed without considering the opportunities of circumvention, as well as the risks of access restrictions that this infrastructure entails.

Campaigns for policy change, such as the Icelandic Modern Media Initiative, now the International Modern Media Institute, have transformed both these risks and opportunities into policy agendas for enabling future journalisms. With the goal to safeguard "modern freedom of expression," IMMI has proposed to use national legislation to make Iceland a "safe haven" for free expression and investigative journalism. The initiative advances our understanding of necessary journalism freedoms by pointing to current control points in information flows; it transcends the traditional state/government focus of free expression concerns by highlighting the role of private actors; and it includes non-professional citizen journalists and civil society in the remit of journalism. Further, it responds to an increasing understanding that decisions about technological design, and specific legislative and administrative regulations, are at least as relevant for freedom of expression in networked environments as is constitutional law (Balkin 2009). Finally, it shows us that even in times of globalized information streams and the supposedly borderless cyberspace, national legislation can be used to protect core aspects of freedom of expression and to provide models for other countries such as Canada.

IMMI and the other initiatives portrayed in this chapter also allow us to identify important conditions and strategies for their success. They have applied key components from the toolbox for policy advocacy which social movement and policy studies have provided – from framing to alliance building, and from street protest to involvement in institutional fora and the development of legal proposals and legislative frameworks. Unlike classic understandings of civil society advocacy, some have moved beyond advocating for change, and towards the active creation of new policy environments. Practices of "policy hacking," which involve collecting and upgrading policy examples from other jurisdictions, point us also to the international dimension of reform initiatives. Even those initiatives that operate within a specific national context and with the dedicated goal of national policy change borrow from legislative models and regulatory practices developed and implemented elsewhere, and they benefit from existing experiences and, sometimes, concrete reform efforts in other countries. They demonstrate the need to consider policy interventions happening even in a small peripheral country, and they illuminate cornerstones for safeguarding and developing journalism in the "networked 4th estate."

Canada, as we have seen, can provide interesting contributions to the debates on both challenges and solutions. It was one of the earliest countries to provide legal provisions for freedom of information, to open up the spectrum to community broadcasting, and to discuss the issue of Net neutrality. At the same time, some of the regulations on these very issues have been weak and would require significant updates, and Canada has been very much part of the recent criticism over international copyright changes and the storm over mass surveillance. Fortunately, Canadian advocacy organizations and research institutions have been part of the reform agenda that has emerged as a jigsaw puzzle in different parts of the world and on different themes and issues.

NOTE

1 A parliamentary resolution in June 2010 was adopted unanimously and the International Modern Media Institute, successor of the Icelandic Modern Media Initiative, was founded in January 2011 (see https://immi.is/immi -resolution).

PART THREE

New Journalism Practices

7 Rendering the Post-Integration Newsroom Right Side Up

CHANTAL FRANCOEUR

Sens dessus dessous signifies a troubled state – a state of turmoil. Resembling the English term "topsy-turvy," it describes aptly how journalists at Radio-Canada in Montreal were feeling in the aftermath of integration of the newsroom in the summer of 2010. Integration, also known as convergence, referred in this particular instance to the merging of Radio-Canada's radio, television, and Web-based news teams. It was a merger that opened the door to a multimedia and multiplatform world, a world where a journalist would write a news story that would subsequently end up being distributed on television, radio, and the Web.[1]

It heralded a major change in broadcast culture, not to mention in how journalists who were used to producing copy for just one medium saw themselves and their role within that culture. Radio-Canada, for its part, described this new paradigm in terms of a change in organizational structure; henceforth, all journalists would be Radio-Canada reporters, not radio reporters or television reporters. "We're all part of the same tribe," announced a senior member of the management team (Interviews, 24 Feb. and 29 Apr. 2010).[2] It was a paradigm shift that was part of a much broader movement of media convergence at the global level (Winseck 1998; Quinn 2006; Bernier 2008; Puijk 2008; Mitchelstein and Boczkowski 2009; Soderlund et al. 2012) and triggered largely by changes in technology (McKercher 2002; Boczkowski and Ferris 2005; Sparks et al. 2006; Brooks and Pinson 2009).

As for the state of turmoil that Radio-Canada reporters found themselves in as integration was taking place, this was linked to feelings of loss with regard to their identity and their expertise, and to a fear that the quality of their work would be compromised. An ethnographic study conducted in Montreal's Radio-Canada newsroom during this period (Feb. to May 2010) meant that what these reporters experienced was observed first-hand and documented (Francoeur 2011a).

In the first part of this chapter, the parameters of this research project are described briefly, and the conclusions pertaining to the "topsy-turvy" state brought on by integration are summarized. I then go on to discuss the findings of a subsequent and complementary research project based on interviews conducted over a six-month period with Radio-Canada reporters eighteen months after integration had been introduced (Oct. 2011 to Apr. 2012). What these findings suggest is that integration did not alter, at least not significantly, the day-to-day working practices of reporters, nor indeed did it lead to a new multiplatform reality at Radio-Canada.

On the contrary, a year and a half into integration, reporters were still working largely in their original medium and providing copy to a single broadcast platform. Furthermore, their actual working methods had hardly changed. What these findings indicate is that Radio-Canada reporters had not adapted themselves to integration; rather, integration had adapted to them (Francoeur 2012). Their state of turmoil had, in effect, provoked a kind of folding back on itself, precipitating a determined and, some might say, even more resolute return to working methods organized around a single medium.

These latter findings inform the argument advanced here: that an alternative approach to implementing integration might have, and still could, lead reporters to more readily embrace multiplatform working methods while at the same time remaining relatively turmoil-free. And what would this alternative approach look like? How might the "topsy-turvy" state of affairs provoked by integration at Radio-Canada be rendered "right side up"? In the latter part of this chapter, I discuss the findings of an examination of a regional news initiative, entitled *Projet 450*, as well as briefly survey a number of innovative sound- and image-based artistic ventures, all of which suggest that the answers to these questions lie in allowing media reporters to remain experts within their own domain, producing a range of products (special news reports, interviews, investigations, etc.) that, once transformed into image-based, sound-based, or text-based formats, could be distributed on a multitude of platforms. Such an approach to integration is, I argue, distinctly different to the approach that was actually taken: redefining journalists as multimedia reporters and expecting them to distribute the same news story to a wide range of media platforms.

Integration of Radio-Canada's News Teams

The winter of 2010 found managers, administrators, and reporters at Radio-Canada preparing for integration. Moving radio reporters out of their own newsroom and into the CDI – the Centre de l'information, or News Centre – where they would join their television and Web colleagues was the most visible manifestation of the changes underfoot. The physical merging of these three distinct news teams was intended to herald a new way of producing the news at Radio-Canada. Gone was the old single-platform approach, where radio, television, or Web-based reporters supplied stories to their respective media. From now on, every story produced in the newsroom would be shared on a multitude of platforms.

As the first experiments in this new way of producing news were diffused to the public, the atmosphere at Radio-Canada was buoyant, almost effervescent. Newsroom managers described the integration process in terms of "an internal revolution" and "a major cultural change" (Francoeur 2012). A study was launched to document this transformation in how the news was being produced and distributed at Radio-Canada. The three questions underlying this study were as follows:

1 Why had Radio-Canada opted to merge the three news teams?
2 How were Radio-Canada reporters reacting to integration?
3 How was news reporting changing at Radio-Canada as a result of integration?

The methodologies used to conduct the study were discourse analysis (Foucault 1966, 1969, 1993, 2004) and ethnography (Kondo 1990; Van Maanen 1988; Born 2004). Time was spent in the various locations affected by integration between the months of February and May 2010, and special attention was paid to the comments and feedback of the various players involved in the process, as well as to their actual working practices. Twenty meetings were attended and documented. Twenty-six interviews were conducted. Hundreds of pages of internal documentation were read and analysed. Three notebooks, thick with observations, were filled. Many of the findings were explored in detail in a doctoral dissertation (Francoeur 2011a) and a subsequent book (Francoeur 2012). Those findings that pertain to the day-to-day working practices of Radio-Canada reporters inform the argument put forward here.

Loss of Expertise, Loss of Identity

From the beginning, working in a multiplatform environment did not, on the whole, please Radio-Canada reporters. Among the complaints were the following: not enough time; a lack of expertise; having to modify ways of working that had stood the test of time; too much focus on the technologies carrying the content and not enough on the content itself; the homogenization and "dumbing down" of news stories; an over-reliance on news sources. In other words, supplying a range of platforms – each with its own specific characteristics and demands regarding the creation of narrative and the delivery of content – presented an almost impossible challenge. In the words of one radio reporter:

> It's crazy, the amount of energy it takes to produce stories for both television and radio. You've got no more life. Just recently, I did an 8 a.m. live radio piece, followed by a live hit for RDI, then worked on a taped story for the noon broadcast, gathered reactions to it that afternoon, next an interview in the east end of the city, back to Radio-Canada with the material, redo parts of my taped story, redo a "stand up," take part in *Désautels* late that afternoon, leave the studio, finish off the revised version of the 4:30 p.m. news … I was exhausted. I didn't even have time for lunch. I told the editor-in-chief, "If this is integration, I don't want anything to do with it." Not every day, anyway. It just doesn't make sense. (Interview, 23 Mar. 2010)[3]

Radio-Canada reporters were quick to point out how working methods differed from one medium to the next. In radio, for instance, reporters often work alone, expediency is paramount, and the telling of stories relies heavily on sound and the creation of an ambient atmosphere. In television, reporters tend to work in teams, the technical aspect is heavier and much slower, and the emphasis is on imagery. Finally, in online journalism, work patterns are more flexible and the overall organization less regimented, in large part because reporters are less likely to be working against a deadline, or else they are facing constant deadlines. The working cultures that result from these specificities have little in common, according to reporters, and are not easily reconciled. As evidenced in their remarks, as well as in their day-to-day working practices, reporters see their identity *as* reporters as tied to a single medium. In the words of a reporter whose primary medium is radio:

> I feel like I just don't have the necessary tools at my disposal to make good television. It took me years to become a good radio reporter. When I listen to some of my old radio pieces, all I can think is, "Wow, I've come a long way." Take my writing, for example; it's so much more polished these days. There's a lot more finesse in the way I use sound, and my personality comes through better now. This doesn't happen overnight, you know. Rather, it's a case of becoming so comfortable with the tools of your trade that your personality can't help but come through when you're on the radio, you can't be anybody *but* the real you. And that's where it starts to get interesting. And that's why doing television scares me ... I'd have to begin that process all over again. (Interview, 23 Apr. 2010)

The frustration that certain radio reporters felt as a result of this reframing of their job and their working reality was palpable. They complained that their own medium was being neglected, expressing concerns over the loss of what makes radio unique and special: namely, that sense of intimacy, of immediacy, and of proximity that comes from a medium that is oral, rhythmic, and atmospheric. Over and over again, radio reporters newly transformed into multiplatform reporters complained about the amount of time and energy they had to devote to producing stories for television, to the detriment of their own medium. If, in their opinion, this meant that radio was fast becoming television's poor cousin, the explanation lay in the degree to which television is labour-intensive, relying as it does on a combination of audio and visual material, demanding as it does a high level of production not required of stories destined for radio or the Web (Francoeur 2012). In other words, once a radio reporter in the new guise of multiplatform reporter has put together the material required to satisfy the many and varied needs of television, it is simply a matter of redirecting that same material to all the other platforms. Expedient, perhaps. But the downside of all of this is that television is perpetually in the driver's seat. As Radio-Canada radio reporters were quick to point out, the so-called integrated newsroom was just another way of saying the "television-dominated" newsroom. It was just another example, as far as many of them were concerned, of the insidious hegemony of television culture.

These reproaches on the part of Radio-Canada radio reporters echo those of reporters in other news organizations undergoing convergence and/or the integration of their news teams (Cottle and Ashton 1999; Singer 2006; Quandt and Singer 2009). With the odd exception, the multiplatform approach, with its makeover of the single-medium reporter into a "jack of all trades," has not been successful (Brooks and Pinson 2009). Killebrew (2005), for example, brings attention to the uneasy marriage between television and newspaper teams at the *Tampa Tribune* when he cites its president, Gil Thelen: "We have learned that trying to create omnicompetent journalists is impossible. They may be very good in one platform, pretty good in another, but never (or rarely) excellent in both" (51). In other words, the "omnicompetent" journalist does not exist, and Radio-Canada reporters are no exception to this rule.

Minimal Multiplatformism

An additional study undertaken in the Radio-Canada newsroom between October 2011 and April 2012 gave me the opportunity to take part in three assignment meetings as well as conduct twenty-three interviews – some recorded and some not, with notes taken during the latter. The purpose of the research was to see how reporters were adapting to integration eighteen months after the fact. This return to the Centre de l'information affirmed, among other things, that reporters had remained loyal to their original medium and that their working methods had altered very little. Reporters (along with their bosses) admitted that very few of them had adopted a multiplatform approach. In the words of one administrator, "You'll find the odd journalist producing stories for both television and radio, but this certainly isn't the norm" (Interview, 21 Oct. 2011). A radio reporter who had not produced a single story for television during the eighteen months since integration commented, "Us oldies, they leave us alone" (personal communication, 21 Oct. 2011). Another radio reporter declared, "I don't want to have anything to do with television. I just won't do it" (personal communication, 21 Oct. 2011). One manager confessed, "When it comes down to it, not much bi-platform or multiplatform work is happening on a regular basis" (interview, 29 Oct. 2011).

Primary among the reasons given for resistance was a lack of time, but also – and this is key – out of a sense of respect for each of the media platforms concerned. In other words, a multiplatform approach had never taken off at Radio-Canada because of the usual time constraints, yes, but even more significantly, because each medium had been found to have its own personality and, associated with that personality, a distinct set of working practices. On the topic of radio, one television reporter remarked, "It's a whole other culture. And the truth is, I'm no good at it. I don't play around with sound enough. And as a result, I don't tell my story in the 'language' of radio" (interview, 21 Mar. 2012). Another reporter provided a specific example to illustrate the cultural differences between television and radio: "When I'm doing a *vox pop*[4] for television, people either become fixated on the camera or quickly back away. When I do one for radio, and it's just me and my microphone, people look me in the eye – they engage with *me*, not my equipment" (personal communication, 12 Jan. 2012). In other words, approaching a passerby with a microphone elicits a different response, and hence creates a different kind of relationship, to that elicited by approaching him or her with a television camera. In line with this point, one member of the assignment team said that, in her opinion, "Television demands a lot more organization than does radio; you need to spend more time dealing with logistics, with getting things all set up ... You've got a reporter, a cameraman, a TV van – all that takes planning. Whereas with radio, you hand out the assignments and, after that, you'll only see your reporter one more time" (interview, 29 Oct. 2011).

According to this same assignment team member, radio reporters are able to turn a story around faster than their television counterparts; they're also more autonomous. She also had something to say about how these two media differ: "Radio is more intellectual, it's a lot more descriptive. Television is more about the visuals, about making the big impact." As for the Web, "Producing copy for the Web is a whole other story. You write in a completely different way, and the timing is different too. If you're writing for TV, for example, and the deadline is 6 o'clock, you have to be in the editing process by 3, because it had better be ready for the newscast" (interview, 29 Oct. 2011). In other words, deadlines – central when it comes to writing for television or radio – are much less of an issue when it comes to writing for the Web. Furthermore, a Web report can be supplemented – reporters can continue to develop the story – after it has been posted online. Not so with writing for television, where the report has to be finely polished when it hits the airwaves.

In short, eighteen months after integration had taken place at Radio-Canada, multiplatform journalism was the exception and not the rule. In the words of one member of the management team, "Radio privileges sound. You can get in there and get the story – that eyewitness account – and it is relatively discrete. Television has its own strengths, but you can't hide from the fact that having a television camera there impacts the kind of relationship you're going to be able to develop [with an interviewee] ... And it goes without saying that sending just one reporter out [to cover a story] means that one of these media gets the short end of the stick" (interview, 21 Oct. 2011). Another administrator provided an illustrative anecdote: "To cover a recent conflict in the construction industry, I sent out a cameraman with my radio reporter. But as my radio reporter made clear, what he'd collect by way of material was not going to be the same with a cameraman there" (interview, 29 Oct. 2011). As it turned out, the construction workers did behave differently in the presence of the television camera. Appearing relatively reserved while being filmed, they became more open the moment the camera disappeared; at that point, their comments about their bosses and the gestures that accompanied their words became clearly hostile. So much so, in fact, that when it came to broadcasting the story on television that evening, Radio-Canada played the radio reporter's soundtrack – a soundtrack that effectively conveyed the aggression and tensions the workers were feeling – over the images of a benign workforce (Radio-Canada 2011). What all of these comments and anecdotes speak to is the difficulty inherent in creating a harmonious working arrangement between the various media cultures.

At the same time, a small number of determined Radio-Canada employees succeeded in producing multiplatform news reports, especially those who had an exclusive story that they wanted to disseminate to as wide an audience as possible. Investigative journalists, who generally have more time to develop a story than their newsroom counterparts, were among those who adopted a multiplatform approach. To do so, as one investigative journalist explained, "gives your story better exposure, spreads it farther, adds to its overall impact. And all of this adds value to your story" (interview, 21 Mar. 2012).

Another group who adopted a bi-platform or multiplatform approach were reporters assigned to cover foreign visits made by provincial and/ or federal political leaders. One such reporter noted, "It isn't ideal, but given the decline in newspaper coverage of these kinds of international trips being made by the prime minister and other dignitaries, at least the multiplatform option is better than nothing" (interview, 12 Jan. 2012). This same reporter hastened to add, "Audiences are getting the same version of the story on radio and television. Unfortunately, I just don't have the time to rewire my brain so I can rewrite history in accordance with the specificities of each medium." In other words, although this reporter's preference would be to write two separate reports, one for radio and one for television, a lack of time meant this wasn't an option.

Other reporters adopting a multiplatform approach echoed this preference for writing for a specific medium, rather than writing to a one-size-fits-all formula: among these were two reporters who had had temporary jobs at Radio-Canada for a number of years, and had finally been offered permanent positions doing multiplatform work. In the words of one of them, "My full-time position comes under the title of 'radio-television-Web.' So I spend a lot of time thinking about how best to produce stories designed both for radio or television. The process is so different for each of these media, it's a fabulous intellectual exercise – a great mental challenge – working it all out. And I love it" (interview, 12 Jan. 2012). A few journalists working in a multiplatform capacity mentioned that to do so was to give their career and their reputation a significant boost, as well as to heighten their visibility.

It remains, however, that apart from these few exceptions, the majority of reporters who found themselves gathered together in the same newsroom following integration had, in fact, continued to work in their original medium. In other words, if integration at Radio-Canada had opened the door to a multiplatform workplace, very few journalists had stepped through that door.[5]

At the same time, other aspects of integration were more readily embraced: in particular, working in teams and pooling resources. Some radio and television reporters travelled together to cover a story and conducted their interviews side by side. Some even divvied out the interviews required for the same story and then shared the material in order to save time. Moreover, by their own account – and as revealed through my research findings – reporters often appreciated having the opportunity to discuss a particular story or event with a colleague in order to sharpen their understanding of a given subject and take their journalistic research to a new level. In the words of one radio reporter, "To be able to exchange ideas – to brainstorm together – on this topic or that, it's really helpful" (personal communication, 12 Jan. 2012). In the words of a television reporter, "We talk about what angle to take with a story, what details are especially pertinent, and which news story should take precedence that day over the others … [Integration] also means that our circle has widened; we have a bigger cohort than before" (interview, 21 Mar. 2012).

A multiplatform reality has yet to be fully realized at Radio-Canada, remaining a medium- to long-term goal. "We are constantly in a state of change," commented one manager, adding that, in his opinion, integration has yet to be achieved (interview, 19 Apr. 2012).[6] Many managers and administrators see integration as a work in progress, something that will come with a changing of the guard. Their sense is that younger journalists will find it easier to work on a range of platforms and be trained that way. In the words of Alain Saulnier, Radio-Canada's former head of news who oversaw the integration process, "Time will change things. A new generation of journalists will see to that" (interview, 15 Mar. 2012).

As for what happens in the meantime, the way Radio-Canada reporters have responded to integration – crystallizing their journalistic identity around a single medium, refusing to alter their working practices – echoes how integration, or convergence, was received in news organizations that underwent the same process at an earlier date. Kraeplin and Criado (2009), for example, have tracked media convergence in the United States, focusing on two successive phases (2002–03 and 2004–05). What they discovered was that, after an initial period of acceleration towards a multiplatform reality, the process of convergence slowed down. For example, during phase I (2002–03), the portion of print journalists producing copy for a televised news segment or for a television program was 13 per cent; by phase II (2004–05), it had dropped to less than 3 per cent. As for television reporters, 17 per cent wrote copy for the print media during phase I; by phase II, this figure had dropped to just 2 per cent.

Likewise, Singer (2004) has observed that convergence has not necessarily had much impact on newsroom culture, even if everybody is now working in the same space: "In terms of newsroom culture, an 'us' and 'them' attitude remains common" (850). She claims that although the various media realms might now come in contact and occasionally even intersect, the differences between print culture and television culture, for example, remain firmly entrenched: "Medium-driven variations in professional practice – notably issues related to newsroom structures and storytelling norms – may well separate newspapers, television, and on-line products and producers for the foreseeable future" (852).

Findings like these give pause for thought, and prompt some serious questions regarding the integration of journalistic teams at Radio-Canada specifically, and in twenty-first–century newsrooms more generally. Among these are: How could integration be approached and implemented differently? And how do you safeguard the kind of expertise that only distinct journalistic identities and cultures have, until now, seemed capable of generating, and allow it to shine forth in our multiplatform world? In the section that follows I put forward some tentative answers to these questions, proposing an approach to integration that provides an innovative and productive way out of the deadlock that many newsrooms seem to be finding themselves in today as the initial excitement around convergence and the promise of a multiplatform future gives way to a conflicted and uneasy retreat back to the old.

A New Kind of "Expert" in the Multiplatform Age

What would happen if newsrooms like Radio-Canada's adopted a multiplatform approach to journalistic work, while at the same time preserving the proficiencies of their original journalism cultures? What if, rather than having a workforce composed of multiplatform, radio-television-Web reporters, the newsroom became home to "audio journalists," "video journalists," and "text journalists" – all of them distributing their work on a range of platforms? Could such an approach ensure that the expertise of individual journalists trained in a specific medium would continue to be put to the best possible use? By maximizing the degree to which journalistic identities would be maintained through placing the emphasis on the actual skill sets and talents (audio, video, or text) that journalists currently associate with their journalistic culture of origin, would integration stand a better chance of working? Moreover, would this novel way of approaching integration help to curb television's troubling hegemony in our new multiplatform age?

Take, for example, your typical "audio journalist." With sound equipment in hand and a knowledge of what makes radio tick tucked safely under her belt, she produces content for the radio, the Web, and numerous other digital services within this new scenario. She immerses herself fully in audio culture; she lives and breathes sound. Likewise, the "video journalist" – immersed, for his part, in a realm of powerful images – who, continuing to work with a director and a cameraman, maintains his identity as a television reporter while producing stories for a wide range of platforms. As for those journalists whose expertise lies in the written word, they, too, could stay true to their medium of origin, remaining expert textual practitioners who, like their audio and video counterparts, could be relied upon to produce high-quality copy for a plethora of media platforms. To reiterate, the point here is to create an environment in which the strengths of each individual player could be drawn upon, not to turn those same players into multiplatform neophytes. Picking up on the natural course that the majority of journalists working in the new multiplatform reality would seem to be taking – that is, a return to their medium of origin – it is an approach to integration that doesn't fight against the current, but rather, goes with the flow.

Feedback supplied by those heading up a special project at Radio-Canada, *Projet 450*, indicates that this might well be the best route to take. Comprised of ten people – journalists, researchers, someone on the assignment desk, and another in charge of "data visualization"[7] – *Projet 450* is responsible for the multiplatform coverage of regional news to the north and south of Montreal (off-island regions where the telephone area code is 450). Set up as a laboratory, the aim of the project is, as the manager connected to it explains, "To explore new ways of working" (interview, 29 Oct. 2011). Concerned primarily with the possibilities opened up by multiplatform journalism and with developing an ongoing conversation with the audience, *Projet 450*'s main media focus is the Web – bringing together, as it does, text, audio, and video. That same manager offers a glimpse into how it all works:

> It's like a table around which a dialogue unfolds between reporters and the audience. The starting point for a reporter will be a local problem – say, for instance, safety on the cycling paths in the area. The reporter conducts an interview with somebody about this issue. He posts his interview on the *Projet 450* website. The Webmaster then picks it up: supplying some background information, assuring balance by throwing in some other points of view, getting a buzz going around the piece. Once people start to respond, the Webmaster follows up on this, digs deeper into the story. Sometimes this results in more coverage of the issue – another report being posted, for instance – or sometimes, if there isn't much interest, the story is allowed to just fizzle out. (Interview, 29 Oct. 2011)

Reporters who are part of *Projet 450* work with audio, video, and text. Though most of their stories are produced for the Web, an occasional story will be broadcast on radio, or appear on television. What matters here is the vocabulary used to describe the different forms their work can take: audio, video, or text. As a manager connected to the project explains, "It's a case of finding the right language with which to tell your story. As a reporter you have to ask yourself what language [audio, video, or text] makes the story the strongest – best brings out its salient points" (interview, 11 Apr. 2012). The first step, he says, is to "conceptualize the idea of the report. You're thinking: Will visuals make it work? Are words needed here? How about a photo? – does that add something? What about a soundtrack?" Next, he says, "You ask yourself the question: What form does this story take? Is it a radio clip? Or is it a tweet – short, sweet and to the point?" A reporter can choose "to divide up the material, getting the main points of the story straight out there via Twitter, then turning some of it into audio material, and finally, developing the story more fully for television." Through all of this, he adds, "Your primary working tool is your smartphone. After that, the other media kick in, and things like the quality of your material come into play."

In other words, for every story covered, the reporter must determine whether the story would be better served by relating it in audio form, in video form, or in text form. And it doesn't stop there. Decisions must be made about whether certain parts of the story wouldn't lend themselves better to text, while others might find a right fit with audio or video. The critical point is that these decisions are determined by the stories being told, not the platforms being supplied.

One could say that *Projet 450* is a kind of experimental bubble, a space where existing work practices are not firmly entrenched. As a result, and in the words of one manager, "We get to see where the possibilities [inherent in multiplatform journalism] lie, and stretch those possibilities based on what kind of people we have available to us and what kind of competencies they bring to the table" (interview, 11 Apr. 2012). This spirit of freedom to innovate within a special project echoes the experiences recounted in the chapters by King et al. (chapter 9) and Robert Washburn and Vincent Raynauld (chapter 10). Elaborating on the kind of knowledges a space like this can generate, the manager says, "We ask ourselves questions such as, 'what kind of timeframes are we talking about when we engage in multiplatform journalism?' and 'when does working this way start to feel natural?' These are the kind of things that we want to find out more about." As for training, he notes that it is offered "when people aren't as strong in a certain area [video, audio, or text]. We help them out with it."

Referring to another challenge facing *Projet 450* – the question of journalism ethics – he remarks, "Say, for example, I've got two people on opposing sides commenting on an issue – one comment I've caught on video but the other is just a text. I know that the video one is going to attract a lot more attention, give the speaker a lot more visibility. So what do I do? If I run them both, am I going to be accused of unbalanced reporting?" At the same time, he says, certain social media can have powerful interest groups behind them: "During the student strike, for example, certain activists just took over the social media platforms. So we were scrambling to find people on the other side, to get a counter-voice out there, and fast. Or take fracking; citizen groups fighting against it have far more of a presence on the social media networks, are way more fired up about it and hence attract a lot more attention, than the big oil companies" (interview, 11 Apr. 2012.

Clearly, the kinds of questions being asked by the *Projet 450* team, and the issues preoccupying its members, point to what is at stake when it comes to multiplatform journalism. For this reason, *Projet 450* can serve as a prototype for the model multiplatform newsroom: each journalist working within it is capable, in principle, of producing multiplatform news reports, the choice of which platform to use for a given story being decided on a case-by-case basis. Hence, the observation on the part of a manager at *Projet 450* after coming to the end of the project's second trimester, in April 2012: "You can't expect any one individual to do everything. You have to take stock of the talent around you and hand out assignments according to who does what best. For example, when a sound-based assignment comes up, you're going to make sure that your reporter with the 'magic ear' is covering it" (interview, 11 Apr. 2012). In other words, a reporter with a special talent for gathering and editing sound clips should be the one sent out to cover a story where sound plays a crucial role. "That," remarks this same manager "is the sign of an integration approach finally coming of age." He adds that, in essence, the omnicompetent journalist does not exist. "Rather, we say to each of our reporters, 'go with your own strengths ... draw on whichever of your senses work best for you.'" If a journalist has a flair for audio, he will be the first one sent out to cover a sound-based story. If his flair is for video, then he gets first choice of the story that requires good visuals. This way of allotting assignments doesn't so much exclude the possibility of multiplatform news coverage as play to the strengths of each reporter – putting the reporter's own talents first. In fact, this privileging of the story's needs over multiplatforming's demands is so important to those running *Projet 450* that they will sometimes send two reporters to cover the same story: for example, a journalist with little video experience but with a good feel for the story accompanied by a cameraman or a photographer. In some cases, they will send out that same journalist with a camera – fully aware that the quality of the images coming back to the newsroom might not be the best, but equally aware that, as one manager put it, "a video clip has a short life, so even if it is a bit shaky, it's not the end of the world" (interview, 11 Apr. 2012). He went on to say that for him, "The goal is to create hybrid journalists who are also particularly gifted in one area." In other words, it's important that reporters aren't expected to produce a combination of audio-video-text all the time. Rather, they should be encouraged to focus in on what they are particularly good at, so as to develop their expertise in one of these areas. At the same time, journalists have to be prepared to leave their own comfort zone and branch out into areas with which they are less familiar. This might mean that the quality of this or that story might be compromised. But given the short shelf life of most news reports, this might be a concession worth making.

What, then, can we conclude about how *Projet 450* manages the day-to-day functioning of its multiplatform newsroom?[8] Certainly, two questions would seem to surface here, and each pertains to form. The first is: What form – audio, video, text, or photography – best lends itself to effectively covering this news story? And based on the answer to that question, the second question is: Which reporter currently available to us is most accomplished in that form? From there, other issues come into play, all of them linked to the relative importance of form to the story itself. If the story lends itself to a variety of forms, then the question might be: What is the preferred form of this particular journalist: audio, video, or text? On the other hand, if the quality of the visuals makes little difference to the story, then any reporter could be sent to cover it.

This summation of how things work, and moreover work *well*, at *Projet 450* – cobbled together, as it is, from a series of exchanges with those who are running the project – suggests that what I am proposing here in terms of a single-medium, multiplatform approach to journalism could be the way forward. One senior member of the Radio-Canada management team who has also given integration a good deal of thought would seem to echo these sentiments: "I have more faith in vertical integration," she explained – contrasting this latter approach to Radio-Canada's current fusion of radio, television, and the Web. According to her, an approach to integration that would merge all the primary components of radio – news, general programming,

Web-based audio – and bring them together under one "roof" would meet with more success than multiplatform integration in its present form at Radio-Canada. She added, "It would certainly be easier to manage, given that there isn't all that much difference between programs like *L'Après-midi porte conseil*, *Désautels* and the news – not in terms of the kind of work being done by program directors or journalists, that is. Vertical integration or single-media integration ... whatever you call it, it would definitely be more efficient" (interview, 29 Oct. 2011).

In concrete terms, single-medium multiplatform journalists would have to create content that could be adapted to each of the various platforms. For example, an audio journalist could broadcast highlights from an interview on the radio, post the full interview on the Web, and send a short extract of it out to smartphone users. This way of working would give the power back to media creators themselves and it would go some way to repairing those feelings of fragmentation, of identity loss, that journalists are currently experiencing. It would allow them to exert more influence over how technologies get introduced into the workplace, what methods are used by media institutions, and which processes become part of the journalist's daily grind. Furthermore, it would give reporters more room to manoeuvre, enabling them to discover new ways of working, new networks of similarly experienced people with whom to work, allowing them to maintain and further develop their strengths in their given medium.

In effect, this proposition goes further than simply recognizing people's expertise in a single medium. It acknowledges the importance of developing innovative journalistic formats designed to work in tandem with the plethora of newly emerging media platforms. Moreover, audio, video, and text-based multiplatform journalism as it is being proposed here has to be able to effect a change in existing journalistic formats that have become outdated, and to strive towards entirely new and original ways of delivering the news. The emergence of new platforms encourages the emergence of new journalistic practices, new ways of relaying the news, and new formulas for telling the story. In other words, the emergence of a range of new platforms has paved the way for a whole new range of journalistic "codes" (Andersen 2003). And it follows that single-medium multiplatform journalism should be in the driver's seat when it comes to developing these new codes.

Towards a Plethora of New and Innovative Journalistic Formats

A number of researchers and scholars inform the ideas put forth in this chapter – in particular, those authors who have reflected upon journalistic formats, on the different ways that journalists can tell a story, on methods that can be used to arouse the interest of audiences and Internet users alike, and on ways that journalists can surprise those same people – even destabilize them. Vincent Giret is correct in saying, "Thanks to the Internet, we have been given the opportunity to discover new ways of delivering the news, new formulas for telling our stories" (cited in Rebillard 2009, 142, author's translation).[9]

Géraldine Muhlmann (2004) offers some worthy suggestions for getting started. Inspired by Walter Benjamin, she proposes that we embrace an "aesthetic of shock." She writes, "Benjamin's thinking around the aesthetic of shock, which is a central characteristic of modern art, and the ultimate aim of the *flâneur*, could be taken, perhaps, as the ideal trope – and a hugely fertile one at that – for thinking through the practice of journalism today" (139, author's translation).[10] Muhlmann urges us to push our journalistic curiosity to the limit: constantly searching for a fresh and unprecedented point of view; oscillating, in our positioning as journalists, between the detective and the curious onlooker (139).

Benjamin's aesthetic of shock also resonates with Roland Barthes' *texte de jouissance*. Barthes (2000) sets up the latter in relation to the *texte de plaisir* – the text that pleases us, fulfills us, reassures us, providing us as it does with a comfortable reading experience affirming our cultural values, offering nothing to challenge what we already know and recognize. The *texte de plaisir* conforms, in other words, to our standard journalistic formats. In contrast, Barthes's *texte de jouissance* "provokes a state of loss and discomfort, disrupting those things we take as historical, cultural and psychological givens, rupturing how we read, shattering what we take to be our tastes, our values and our memories, creating a crisis around our very relationship to language" (92, author's translation).[11] In the context of my current proposal, you could say that Barthes's *texte de jouissance*, like Benjamin's aesthetic of shock, provides the reader or audience member with a novel brand of news, and a novel way of engaging with it. In chapter 11, Michael Meadows addresses the challenge posed by traditional knowledge-management processes in Indigenous societies – where storytelling, art, and music play an important part – for non-Indigenous journalistic inquiry.

Where does this pursuit of the *texte de jouissance*, the aesthetic of shock, lead us in journalistic terms? There is no easy answer to this question, but I would venture that integration – if approached the right way – could open the door to new journalistic codes, new journalistic formats. Those reporters interviewed while undertaking my research into integration at Radio-Canada certainly seemed to be anxious when it came to trying out something new and innovative. One radio journalist who was also involved in a few Web-based projects spoke excitedly of "doing some multimedia stuff combining photographs and text" (interview, 23 Apr. 2010). The managers with whom I spoke were also encouraging of this kind of exploration and experimentation. Comments such as, "We're lucky, we've never seen so many opportunities, we're in a period of revolution, so many changes and so quickly" or "We've got a right to make mistakes" were common (Francoeur 2011a). As far as the management team was concerned, the door was wide open to new ways of doing journalism at Radio-Canada.

Take, for example, an audio journalist who could find inspiration in the ideas and practices of sound artists when it comes to thinking through new formats and products that could be accommodated on a range of different platforms in her own work. To be so inspired would not be all that surprising: after all, one of the primary goals of sound artists is to undo conventions, to "challenge the half-hour format, the packaged radio voice" (Augaitis and Lander 1994). Radio and sound artist Anna Friz embodies both worlds, and as such is a good example of the audio journalist of the future. She works hard to defy what has gone before her in radio: "I am striving to reimagine radio in order to challenge current conventions-restrictions in terms of form and content" (cited in Waterman 2007, 129). The same applies for radio-creator Marie Wennersten, who insists that the traditional radio voice covers up a number of sins, making the fact that it can be "boring" the least of its problems: "When we started, it felt important to disrupt the manners of the spoken radio voice. We did not want to imitate or encourage a professional tone. The 'good radio voice' is not simply boring, it hides insipid power structures, it speaks with a questionable authority and a false intimacy" (Wennersten 2007, 88). Clearly, innovators like Friz and Wennersten would be a breath of fresh air in the world of audio journalism.

Those working innovatively in other fields – like performance artists Coco Fusco and Guillermo Gomez-Pena, who mix languages in order to throw a wrench into the works of existing linguistic structures and formats – can also be a source of inspiration for adventurous audio journalists: "Our pieces contain Spanglish, Inglenol, various dialectical forms of English and Spanish tongues ... What we are actually doing is healing the language by forcing it to open its structures" (cited in Augaitis and Lander 1994, 231). Remaining attentive to additional information contained in sounds, voices, intonations, rhythms, pauses, and repetitions can also lead to the creation of new journalistic products (Augaitis and Lander 1994; Arkette 2004). Certain authors, for example, have drawn attention to the differences between the voice of reason and a more bodily voice (Dyson, cited in Augaitis and Lander 1994) or between so-called official languages and those of the heart (Drobnick 2004). It is up to journalists to play with these differences, to bring them out into the open. Doing so not only allows them to highlight the role played by those often unacknowledged aspects of language; it also helps audience members to become more aware of the impact of tone, for example, as we listen to an interview with an official who delivers the conventional line in short, snappy sound bites, and then compare it to an interview with an ordinary person who has suddenly been pushed into the limelight because of a cause, and blurts out her message in a tumble of passion, urgency, and rage.

Alvin Lucier is a sound artist who opens up an equally interesting path for journalists. He plays with repetition and juxtaposition in a performance entitled, "I Am Sitting in a Room." We witness him reading a text, recording himself reading it. He plays his recording back at the same time that he is reading the text for a second time, continuing to record himself reading as he does this, continuing to reread and rerecord and replay this increasingly layered recording back to himself as he reads (LaBelle 2007). Could Lucier's performance piece serve as an inspiration for journalists? Could we draw something from it that enhances the way we deliver the news?

More food for thought comes to us courtesy of a piece by Jean-Sébastien Durocher, entitled "Mémoires enfouies, mémoires vives" (Buried Memories, Living Memories). In this piece, Durocher plays with extracts taken from Québécois radio. As we listen, we recognize certain voices, certain eras, certain topics. We hear, quite literally, the soundtrack of québécois culture. There is no narrative accompanying it, just this collage of radio extracts. Created to accompany a book on Quebec's sound heritage (La Rochelle 2009), Durocher's piece, with its potent mix of sounds and voices, radiophonic tones, and alternating rhythms – he occasionally lets an extract run on for a very long time – could serve as a model for a new genre of journalistic reportage.

For my own part, I have attempted to push the boundaries of both journalistic reportage and academic research in a sound piece entitled, "From Radio to Audio while Exploring Journalistic Formats" (Francoeur 2011b). The idea for this piece took root while I was conducting my research into integration. A lot of the research involved interviewing Radio-Canada personnel, and as I listened back to the interviews, many of the same elements kept surfacing: lack of time; suspicion that integration would herald a decline in the quality of news reporting; fear that radio's special identity would be lost; strong identification on the part of journalists with a single medium. Comments like, "I'm a radio journalist," or, "Me, I think TV," kept popping up. The same justifications for integration – its celebration of teamwork, the importance of pooling expertise – inevitably crept into any discussion with a manager or administrator. What the material contained was an endless stream of recurring litanies and themes; a traditional radio report based on my findings would have contained a very small sampling of actual quotes, with my own narrative voice providing a summary of how Radio-Canada employees were reacting to integration.

In an effort to create a different kind of audio experience for listeners, "From Radio to Audio while Exploring Journalistic Formats" brought those recurring litanies and themes to the fore, my interviewees' words ringing out in all their repetitive glory; their comments juxtaposed and intermeshed to the point that the litanies became insistent, almost amplified. In place of a narrative voice-over stating, "Journalists are worried about losing their identity and expertise," what listeners experienced through the juxtaposition of voices was the tangible evidence of this worry – my interviewees' words, quite literally, speaking for themselves. The piece also included the soundscape of the newsroom in the hope of giving listeners the sense of being right in the middle of the action. In its totality, the piece is a condensation of many of my actual observations and research findings. The listener quickly grasps the stakes involved in integration: the arguments being used to justify it and the impact it is having on journalists' lives. The piece only lasts about three minutes, but in that time, information about integration is offered to the listener in a whole new way. As an audio piece, it cracks open current journalistic formats in this area; in the context of multi-platform journalism, it complements more traditional and conventional ways of telling a story on radio.

This blend of information delivery and sound creation is not new. Radio-Canada's cultural channel, for example, has aired programs that present an eloquent exploration of sound. Director Mario Gauthier, in his program *L'espace du son* (Sound Space) has, in his own words, "attempted many radio-phonic experiments" (personal communication with author, author's translation). Likewise, director Hélène Prévost (2012) has come up with numerous examples of sound creation. For her part, sound artist Chantal Dumas (n.d.) has created an array of unconventional audio pieces. All three of these trend-setters are doing exciting things in this realm, and are there to inspire us as we strive to establish a greater link between journalistic information delivery and the realm of sound creation, as we strive to push journalistic information delivery centre stage in the move towards more exploratory audio formats.

We might well ask if there is also a space opening up in the press for this kind of pushing of traditional genre and format boundaries. If the talent and creativity of newspaper reporters is anything to go by, then the answer would be a definitive yes. At the heart of every newspaper there are innovative people who, given the time to do it, would welcome the opportunity to spearhead new initiatives. At Radio-Canada, an informal group of avant-garde journalists is currently testing the waters in terms of what possibilities might lie in multiplatform journalism, and they regularly come forward with new ideas, ideas that would not require many infrastructural changes. One member of the group described the initiative as Radio-Canada's "multimedia sphere of influence" (personal communication, 29 Oct. 2011), composed of artisans eager to experiment with different ways of working, and prepared to inundate new-media outlets with Radio-Canada products. All that would be required now is to hand these technology "aficionados" (Bélanger 2005) a mandate and they'd be on their way to a promising future. The addition of young journalists, who have grown up in a multiplatform environment and are at ease with it, would give the movement an important boost. In its capacity as a public broadcaster, Radio-Canada could play a pioneering role in transforming the way we do journalism in our multiplatform age.

Waddell (2009) maintains that the survival of the newspaper industry is linked in part to the kind of initiatives I have discussed in this chapter – among these, "innovation in storytelling" (21). For her part, Singer (2004) also supports such initiatives, suggesting that one of the outcomes of convergence could be to propel journalists towards finding more creative ways of doing their work: "As creative professionals continue to expand their definition of who they are and what they do, they will find an expanding number of ways to provide new outlets for their work and fulfill the professional goal of quality public service" (852). Singer twins the word "convergence" with "divergence," eager to point out the kind of combinations – some compatible, some less so – that can be brought into being in this new media age. In her opinion, television and the Web make for a good marriage, whereas print journalism and the Web are less compatible. As she explains it, "Online and television journalism share three complementary strengths: immediacy, brevity and visual impact" (375). On the other hand, "Journalism based primarily on the power of words works best, and will continue to work best, on paper. The print medium offers greater legibility and flexibility as well as fewer distractions, inviting relatively slow reading as opposed to relatively quick viewing" (376). What is critical, she argues, is that those implementing convergence, or integration, take into account these compatibilities and incompatibilities.

Ultimately, these experimental initiatives and exploratory inroads can lead to the emergence of new journalistic identities. Other studies on convergence – notably in the newspaper industry – have shown this to be the case. For example, reporters who combine journalistic backgrounds with information technology skills are appearing on the scene. Ursell (2001) calls them "server managers." Referring to this "new species of editorial worker," she describes them as "an occupational hybrid of journalist and computer expert" (186). Quinn (2005) has written about the emergence of "news resourcers," reporters who are called in to do supplementary research on a news story, so that additional content can be added as the story migrates from platform to platform. These journalists combine the roles of writer, researcher, and copyeditor. Ideally, they have library skills and background in information management (94). Whizzes at putting their finger on whatever information is required, and quickly, they are as adept as librarians when it comes to searching "through archives and databases of the news organization, and the Web, and public and government records" (95). Moreover, they can be relied upon to put a news story in context and supply it with depth. They are also able to find, amid the plethora of online responses to a trending story, those points that should be followed up on in order to generate more interest around the topic and keep the story in the news. In short, these new and emerging roles like "news resourcer" and "hybrid journalist" could be tweaked and adjusted to lend themselves to journalistic identities such as "sound journalists" or "imagery journalists."

What is clear is that those journalists who become integrated change their identity. They find themselves swimming around in a culture that has yet to be fully defined, a culture that, as a result of this fluidity, they have the opportunity to shape, determine, and even create. "We're forming a new culture," declares Jennifer McGuire (2010), and with good reason. As the person who presided over integration at the CBC in 2010, she is well aware that journalists must now engage with a wide range of media platforms. The act of doing this is forcing them to see both their material and their journalistic practice in a very different light. So here you have it: if we remove the blinkers, change up those formats, just imagine what might surface in the way of new journalistic knowledges and practices and products – in the way journalists *do* news. Certainly, it is the kind of imagining that every media organization should be doing if they are serious about tackling the *sens dessus dessous* currently plaguing the post-integration newsroom, and rendering things *right side up*.

NOTES

1 For the purposes of this chapter, the term *multimedia* refers to the combination of radio, television, and Web-based media, and the term *multiplatform* refers to both multimedia and the full range of distribution possibilities and digital platforms engendered by it: radio, television, the Internet, smartphones, tablets, etc.

2 The English-language public broadcast counterpart of Radio-Canada, the Canadian Broadcasting Corporation (CBC), had gone through the same process of integration one year earlier, and provided the same line of reasoning.

3 Because they support the argument being advanced here, certain quotes from my book, *La transformation du service de l'information de Radio-Canada*, (Francoeur 2012) reappear in this chapter. Quotations from the interviews and conversations with Radio-Canada journalists were translated from the original French by the author. The names of all interviewees are withheld by mutual agreement.

4 Also known as "*micro trottoir*," this is a practice whereby reporters take to the streets to gather reactions from passersby about a given issue. The classic opener is: "What do you think about …?"

5 On the other hand, integration did lead to significant changes at the level of the newsroom: for example, the allocation of assignments (who covers what) – previously done on a medium by medium basis (a radio assignment, a television assignment, a Web-based assignment) – are now all multimedia assignments. These, in turn, are handled by a regional, national, or international assignment desk, with radio, television, and Web-based journalists falling under one or the other's supervision. Thus, in assignment meetings, you'll hear these kinds of statements: "For the Ministry of Health announcement, let's send Rochon in television and St Louis in radio" (Assignment Meeting, 8 Oct. 2011); "I've got two features in editing this weekend, one in radio, one in television"; "I'm sending Eve for radio, Louis-Philippe for television"; "Liette will send a camera with her radio person" (Assignment Meeting, 12 Jan. 2012). Before integration, each medium organized its own news coverage. A television team would not consult a radio team or a Web-based team when it came to covering a story; it was each team for itself. Integrating the allocation of assignments has, as one manager explained, resulted in "news coverage that is more cohesive, more coherent. Reporters find themselves working the same territory, and this means they exchange information" (interview, 21 Oct. 2011). Sharing news coverage in this way has also reduced operating costs.

6 This same manager added that, "In the outlying areas, they've been doing multiplatform journalism for the past 15 years" (interview, 19 Apr. 2012). In fact, multiplatform journalism is the norm in newsrooms outside of Montreal. Many hypotheses have been advanced to explain this disparity between the regional stations and Montreal. Among them: smaller teams at the regional level resulting in journalists taking on a heavier and more diversified workload, not to mention more responsibility; younger journalists – better versed in multiplatform technologies – tending to be those finding jobs in the regional stations; trade unions differing from area to area and, with them, the nature of journalists' work contracts; the larger workforce in Montreal, meaning that these journalists can present a more united and powerful front when it comes to resisting change. With respect to this latter point, one manager at Radio-Canada was overheard referring to his workforce as "specialists in resisting the global trend" (Comment overheard, 23 Mar. 2010). Finally, a Montreal journalist alluded to the possibility that the criteria used to define quality reporting at the regional level and for Montreal might not be the same: "In Calgary, I watched a regional guy cover a demo. First he's filming, then he's dumping his stock in the machine, then he's doing a voice-over, and next he's putting together his piece for the radio. I couldn't believe how much he was doing. Of

course, I didn't get to see the end result" (Informal Conversation, 12 Jan. 2012). In short, the hypotheses regarding the relative success of integration at the regional level (as compared with Montreal) are many and varied, and no doubt warrant further research.

7 Creating visual representations of facts.

8 *Projet 450* concluded in the spring of 2014. Some of those involved are now part of a team of Radio-Canada "Web format specialists" helping journalists adapt their stories for the Web. Others have been integrated into Radio-Canada's regular news production operations. In the words of one senior manager at Radio-Canada: "The spirit of *Projet 450* lives on" (interview, 23 Feb. 2015).

9 "Nous avons, à travers l'Internet, à trouver de nouveaux modes de narration de l'information, de nouveaux modes de récit."

10 "La réflexion benjaminienne sur l'esthétique du choc, caractéristique centrale de l'art moderne, visée ultime du flâneur, constitue donc, peut-être, un idéal-critique très fécond pour penser aujourd'hui la pratique journalistique."

11 "Met en état de perte, déconforte, fait vaciller les assises historiques, culturelles, psychologiques, du lecteur, la consistance de ses goûts, de ses valeurs et de ses souvenirs, met en crise son rapport au langage."

8 The Tweets That Bind Us: A G20 Case Study

SNEHA KULKARNI

Pictures and updates from ordinary citizens are instantaneously shared among millions of people every day, but the extent to which this information is reliable and valuable to news organizations needs to be examined. The Internet's environment of immediacy challenges news organizations to deliver information to their traditional audiences as well as the large audiences seeking information online. The new media landscape has marked a significant change for journalism; in order to stay relevant and connect with new audiences, journalists have needed to better understand how to make sense of, and utilize, information shared by citizens online.

In 2009, when a US Airways plane made an emergency landing on New York's Hudson River, Janis Krums, an ordinary citizen with an iPhone, was the first to spread the news to the world and to media outlets. He posted a dramatic photograph on Twitter using an online application called Twitpic and with the simple caption: "There's a plane in the Hudson. I'm on the ferry going to pick up the people. Crazy" (Deards 2009). The photograph was subsequently retweeted, and the sheer number of people wanting to view the image crashed the website. According to the founder of Twitpic, it was the greatest volume of activity his site had ever seen, with close to five hundred requests to view the photograph every 15 to 20 seconds, and seven thousand people having viewed the picture before the site went down (Terdiman 2010). Since 2009, the use of Twitter has increased exponentially, and breaking news events such as political unrest and disasters continue to showcase the public's desire to share and access information; during these times, an explosion of information, images, and commentary from citizens proliferates on the Internet.

New media advocate Clay Shirky (2008) argues that the Internet is shifting the definition of news from an institutional sphere to a communications ecosystem co-habited by a mix of organizations and individuals. He suggests the gatekeeping role long enjoyed by news organizations is becoming obsolete. Current research portrays the field of journalism in a conflicted state, in which professional ideologies are clashing with the growing consumer acceptance of a do-it-yourself culture enabled by the Internet (cf. McChesney and Pickard 2011). While online communication alters news cycles and gives audiences the power to participate in the news-gathering and -delivery business, there is little guidance on how useful social media platforms can be for journalists, and how journalistic values can be upheld in the new media landscape.

Some critical theorists argue media simply serve as tools for disseminating dominant ideology, but what is happening in the digital world challenges assumptions about the relationship between public and media agendas. New research suggests that social media users and news media organizations have established an interdependent, rather than hierarchical, relationship (see Reese et al. 2007).

Through a thematic content analysis of Twitter messages posted during the 2010 G20 protests in Toronto, this chapter sets out to gain greater insight into how social media impact the way journalists and citizens experience breaking news events, and how journalists can adapt their reporting skills to incorporate the network of information available through social media. This study uses foundations from gatekeeping theory (Shoemaker 1996) and the "ambient journalism" framework (Hermida 2010) to analyse how social media impact the way major news events are understood collectively, and the implications this has on the way news organizations approach social media as tools for research and publishing.

Changing Boundaries

A large body of research surrounding social media and citizen journalism perceives Internet use as a democratizing force (cf. Poster 2001; Nip 2006; Deuze 2008). Collaboration between participatory and mainstream journalism is encouraged, yet a struggle exists between journalists' ability to uphold their professional ideology and practices, and audience members' desire to play an active role in the reporting and sharing of news. Researchers have identified two distinct camps within journalism: those who feel the news industry is threatened by the cult of the amateur, and those who see collaboration with online communities as the route to self-preservation.

Essential to the debate is the notion that mainstream news organizations have long enjoyed a dominant position in the production and delivery of information. For decades, a lack of competition afforded media outlets the luxury of developing and maintaining a distinct and institutionalized presence as the trusted and authoritative voices on public issues (Williams and Delli-Carpini 2000). Gatekeeping theory is central to explaining the power granted to journalists on behalf of the public to filter information, and select which messages should be seen in newspapers and on the nightly news (Shoemaker 1996). However, some see technological innovation and the rise of computer literacy as pivotal forces shifting the hierarchy, granting the public gatekeeping powers. Poster (2001) views the Internet as a democratizing force, opening up a previously restricted and largely one-way conversation into an open ring of opinion with multiple avenues for participation. Similarly, Jenkins (2006b) describes the audience as shifting from passive, predictable, and isolated individuals into active, socially connected citizens with declining loyalty to conventional news networks.

Consequently, there is considerable pressure on mainstream news organizations to look at Web communities as valued outlets for news in order to stay relevant to an audience that values technological connectivity. A new intermediary layer has risen in the media landscape in which citizens have free rein to write, publish, and distribute information as they see fit (Bowman and Willis 2003). As Bennett (2009) points out, the greatest changes in news content over time have come from developments in communication technology; photography, television, personal computers, and now the Internet have all resulted in changes to the way we share information and consume news.

Professional Ideology

To understand how social media impact journalists' storytelling and news-gathering practices, it is important to look at the professional ideology of journalists. Altheide and Snow (1979) use the term "media logic" to refer to the ways in which social affairs are viewed and interpreted in the news. Media logic theory implies that specific processes guide and structure the features of a medium, and adhering to a professionally ingrained format creates a socially constructed interpretation of news and reality. Journalistic ideology is similar around the world, and values such as objectivity, immediacy, public service, and the quest for the truth help legitimize the practice (Deuze 2005). Critical analyses into journalistic practices have revealed that mainstream media often rely on professional routines as crutches; one result of this is an overdependence on professional and political sources of information at the expense of new voices and alternative sources (Williams and Delli-Carpini 2000). Even in this era of technological innovation, Livingston and Bennett's (2003) study into event-driven news stories discovered that during unpredictable breaking-news events, the reliance on official spokespeople as news sources was a consistent factor, and this dependence served as further proof of the organizational routines that define journalism as a practice.

Conversely, improved access to technology and rising computer literacy are increasing the possibilities for audiences to participate in the flow of news. The rise of participatory journalism is viewed as a direct response to what some see as shortcomings within the mainstream media (Deuze et al. 2007). Industry leaders argue that television cannot continue to operate in its conventional ways, because today's viewers want and expect greater influence over the media they consume (Jenkins 2006b). News organizations must look at how the "do-it-yourself" culture fits into the delivery of news and information programming. While journalists have the task of informing the public, they must also search out new ways to gather information and offer it through various media platforms. In chapter 7, Chantal Francoeur looks at one news organization that has embraced multiplatform reporting and the tensions this has produced in the newsroom.

Bowman and Willis (2003) recognize that the journalism profession is facing an identity crisis; journalists are no longer the sole gatekeepers and technology is allowing audiences to become new kinds of participants in the processes of news production and dissemination. It should be noted that audience members are increasingly plugged in and no longer willing to wait for the morning newspaper or the evening newscast; engaging them now requires going beyond typical news deadlines and formats and allowing them to help play a part in the news delivery process.

Participatory Culture

A key theme emerging within journalism research is the notion of participatory culture, which Jenkins (2006b) defines as a culture with low barriers to entry and increased civic engagement. Web logs (blogs) are considered a popular means of participation, since they require little to no start-up costs, beyond a computer and an Internet connection, to allow an ordinary citizen to play a role in public discourse. While the impact of this role depends on the quality of the blogger's interventions, researchers consider blogs significant sites within the journalism field because of their ability to promote independent, alternative news reporting (Haas 2005). For example, Internet bloggers gained notoriety for breaking explosive stories, such as the Clinton-Lewinsky affair, US Senator Trent Lott's racist comments (Williams and Delli-Carpini 2000), and, in 2011, social media were cited for their contribution to the rejection of Egypt's long-standing Mubarek regime. Williams and Delli-Carpini (2000) describe the new media environment as one that can increase the volume of information available, audience and message interactivity, and the collection, transmission, and reception of information by operating in a 24-hour cycle, unfettered by deadlines. The rise in popularity of blogging, citizen journalism, and online communities demonstrates that citizens relish the opportunity to be a part of the information-sharing process (Skoler 2009). Examples of this are cited in the chapters by Gretchen King and her co-authors (chapter 9) and by Robert Washburn and Vincent Raynauld (chapter 10).

During the the 2008 Mumbai terror attacks and the 2009 Iranian election protests, websites such as the *New York Times* (nytimes.com) and the *Guardian* (theguardian.com) published a mix of unverified video and eyewitness accounts from social media as sources of breaking news information, alongside reports from professional journalists (Hermida 2010). Journalists are not always on the scene of breaking news and at other times – e.g., civil war in Syria, nuclear testing in North Korea – they are denied access. Opinions are ever-changing and news stories can take many directions, especially in developing situations, before they are published or broadcast. The ability to blend real-time, online reactions with traditional reporting showcases a more organic form of journalism and shatters the conventional idea that a news report must be a polished and formal type of communication. Hermida (2010) argues that news models are in transition, and that social media technologies like Twitter facilitate information dissemination, enabling millions of people to share and discuss events instantly as an expression of collective intelligence.

Jenkins (2006b), Poster (2001), Beers (2006), and Howe (2008) are among those who identify the driving dynamic behind this change to be a shift from a vertical, top-down model through which the audience is a relatively passive recipient of information, to a horizontal structure whereby citizen journalists share information with many others and rely on crowdsourcing or collective wisdom to shape their views. These findings suggest that mainstream journalists must be an active part of this new media process, in which interaction and sharing take precedence over process and hierarchy. The term "ambient journalism" is proposed as a new framework for understanding social media platforms as news delivery platforms. Hermida (2010) describes ambient journalism as a "broad, asynchronous, lightweight, and always-on communication system," in which the value does not lie in the individual news and information fragments, but instead in the mental picture created by a number of messages over a period of time (301). This mental portrait is a personalized understanding of the world, constructed and influenced by various communication platforms, such as personal interactions, news media, and online or social media conversations.

Deuze (2008) and Nip (2006) regard participatory journalism as a means to reinvigorate public engagement and democracy. However, Nip (2006) points out that while blogs have broken a small number of big news stories, these stories make little impact until the mainstream media follow them up. This raises the question of whether bloggers and citizen journalists require mainstream media to legitimize what they do, to assume the role of "sense-makers." Nip (2006) suggests that journalists should not perceive participatory journalism as a threat. Instead, she highlights collaborative citizen journalism as an opportunity for news media to change and strengthen their relationship with everyday citizens, since news audiences are increasingly using social or citizen media platforms to supplement traditional news media. In the same vein, Reese et al. (2007) show that social media networks promote discussion by linking individuals and anchoring their discussions to a stream of analysis and information distributed by mainstream media outlets. Social media users, it appears, don't restrict themselves either to mainstream or to citizen media, but tend to use both, especially those users who are most interested in news.

An increasing number of journalists and news organizations have created online profiles on social media sites, but further analysis is needed to understand whether journalists are playing a role in social media communities and creating the collaborative sphere touted by so many researchers, or whether they merely use social media to scan and sift online data to serve their own interests. The idea of a so-called media democracy facilitated by online access is not without its sceptics, and to understand the basis of criticism we must examine the role of journalism from a historical context.

Ideals and Criticism

During the colonial period in the United States, publicans picked up information overheard in public houses and taverns, and provided it to publishers to record and circulate (Carey 1993). This was an early element of what critical theorist Jürgen Habermas referred to as the "public sphere." He noted the importance of free discourse in coffee houses and homes as a place *between* society and the state, where citizens could gather in inclusive environments to discuss public matters, and organize as the "bearers of public opinion" (Habermas 2006b, 75). The public sphere as described by Habermas is a virtual space created solely by participation, assembly, and critical dialogue. Some researchers wonder whether the participatory nature of social media and their ability to allow audiences to participate in news production and delivery bring us closer to Habermas's utopian view of a public sphere. Reese et al. (2007) argue social media networks and blogs blend citizen journalist voices with established mainstream journalists to shift the boundaries and extend the public sphere beyond traditional borders. Others maintain that new media and blogs have created a "hyper-aggressive news environment," in which being the first to break the story takes precedence, often resulting in the widespread reporting of inadequately sourced information (Farhi 2010, 3). Thus, there are concerns over how journalists can uphold professional values such as thoroughness, accuracy, and verification in the new media world, where the gratification of instant information can trump the value of well-researched and accurate reporting, which a modern-day public sphere would seem to require. Chantal Francoeur addresses these concerns directly in chapter 7, in the context of a news organization engaged in multimedia reporting in an accelerated news cycle.

Dahlgren (1996) points to two opposing reactions that can arise from the Internet's potential. The first is "cyber euphoria," in which technology enhances democracy by giving the public a platform for open deliberation. Alternatively, there is "digital dystopia," in which power elites use technology to maintain their positions with more effective control (Dahlgren 1996, 60). McChesney and Nichols (2002) take the latter, more critical view, and note that journalistic integrity is at the mercy of commercial interests, and that conglomeration and centralized ownership in the news industry continue to make a mockery of the traditional free press.

While existing research advocates a collaborative approach between citizen and professional journalists, there are still gaps in how this collaboration is materializing in contemporary news organizations, and what, specifically, journalists can achieve by becoming active members of new media platforms, such as social media.

A Social Snapshot of History

To gain a greater understanding of how social media impact the way citizens and journalists experience breaking news events, a qualitative case study using thematic analysis was conducted to examine the interactions between citizens and journalists on Twitter during the G20 protests in Toronto in June 2010. Thematic analysis is a useful process for encoding qualitative information, since it serves as a bridge between researchers of different fields (Boyatzis 1998). Dey (1993) argues that qualitative analysis places a strong emphasis on describing the world as different observers perceive it, hence the main concern is not the construction of texts, but rather how "actors define situations and explain the motives which govern their actions" (37). The analysis of emerging themes within Twitter messages helped reveal how social media impacted the ways in which individuals made sense of the G20 protests and violence. The ambient journalism framework (Hermida 2010) and gatekeeping theory (Shoemaker 1996) were used to analyse journalists' roles in the new media world, specifically how news-gathering techniques can be adapted without compromising professional ethics.

The data set for this study is comprised of Twitter updates, or tweets, aggregated through the #G20 hashtag, and sent on the afternoon of 26 June 2010. Hashtags are community-driven labels used to organize and group Twitter messages under a specific topic or keyword (Messina 2010).[1] The 26 June time frame is significant because it represents an evolving news story, during which time a peaceful protest turned chaotic. Police cars were set ablaze, storefronts were damaged, and mass confusion and vandalism ensued in downtown Toronto. When searching the chosen four-hour time span, Google's Twitter archive provided 460 tweets under the #G20 hashtag. The messages included in this data set do not constitute a clear and flowing conversation, nor do they represent all of the tweets sent within the four-hour time span. Rather they serve as a cross-section of the online messages and activity posted during the chosen timeline.

Analysing Social Media

Case studies offer an avenue for multiperspectival analyses, since they allow researchers to consider the voice and perspective of the actors as well as the relevance of the groups of actors and the interactions between them (Tellis 1997). In their study of the user intentions of micro bloggers, Java et al. (2007) discovered that Twitter users used social media sites for four main functions: daily chatter, conversation, information sharing, and news reporting. These descriptors served as preliminary labels for organizing the individual #G20 tweets for this study.

This study aimed to uncover the basic social processes that underlie online behaviour by "allowing commonalities and contradictions to naturally emerge" within the data (McLeod 2001). Gatekeeping theory and Hermida's (2010) framework of ambient journalism served as foundational lenses through which the experiential impact of social media communication on citizens and journalists was examined. To provide greater context to the individual tweets within the #G20 hashtag, each sender was identified through his or her publicly available Twitter profiles to determine whether the sender self-identified as a citizen, as a journalist for an independent publication, or as a journalist for a mainstream news organization. From there, the data were categorized under Java et al.'s (2007) categories for micro-blogging uses: daily chatter, conversation, news reporting, and information sharing. The following two codes were then used to further analyse the data: Mental Models and Authority.

The Mental Models code is based upon Hermida's (2010) framework of ambient journalism, in which the multitude of messages and short bursts of information help users form a mental portrait of an event or their surroundings.

The Authority code is based upon gatekeeping theory (Shoemaker 1996), which describes journalists and news organizations as being in a position of power, based on their decisions about what information is newsworthy for their audiences.

The Tweets That Bind Us

Analysis of the Twitter commentary in this study revealed the primary intent of posting tweets during this breaking news event was to report and share information. This shows that in a technologically connected society, Twitter can be a front-line information site, especially in a developing situation. However, this study's findings also show that, while citizens play a significant role in sourcing information, providing eye-witness accounts, and publishing photographs of the event on Twitter, it appears journalists maintain their authoritative voice and preserve their journalistic ethics and commitment to accuracy.

A significant theme that arose within the Twitter commentary, under the conversation label, was the shifting dynamic among online users, from a sense of pride to helplessness with respect to the vandalism and a perceived hijacking of the city by some protestors. It appeared Twitter users, which included a mixture of citizens involved in, or witnessing, the protest, and those at home, found the means to gain a collective media voice by using the micro-blogging site as a venue to speak out about a perceived loss of ownership of their city.

In the first part of the data set, during which the peaceful protest had just begun, posts focused on the reasons for the initial protest, and messages conveyed pride in those exercising their democratic rights to gather and be heard. A citizen, AntoninPribetic, wrote, "I am proud to be a Torontonion today. Peaceful protests against political tyranny and economic injustice." Another citizen, tonydurke, wrote, "What is the difference between soldiers and protestors? One is a state sponsored fight, while the other is not. Both are heroic." While these two users were not directly messaging each other, their posts were retweeted and shared by others, and their participation under the #G20 hashtag immediately linked them to a greater community of individuals, all of whom were expressing views in an open environment. Hermida (2010) describes the sharing of Twitter posts as both a form of data sharing and as a system for creating a mediated conversation. And although this public space only exists online, it appears to help frame what human-computer interaction researchers Harrison and Dourish (1996) refer to as an "understood reality" through conversational and collaborative user experience.

The legitimacy of the information and opinions shared on Twitter appears to increase as more and more people join the conversation, and retweet previous posts. This notion follows Metcalfe's law of networking, which states that the value of a network – in this case, a social network – exists in the square of the number of users (Harrison and Dourish 1996). Furthermore, if online legitimacy is based on the "share-ability" of a comment, then professional journalists cannot assume their affiliation with a news organization guarantees a sense of authority, especially in the new media world. Being an active member of a social media community requires one to share and discuss ideas. For professional journalists, this means expanding their social network beyond that of officials and spokespeople. Expanded networks also open up the potential for new voices to be heard in mainstream news stories, providing an opportunity for more robust storytelling.

As more images and textual information flooded the #G20 hashtag, a changing dynamic emerged in the expressions of users posting general comments. Posts went from expressing pride over peaceful protests to fear and disgust over the vandalism and violence that unfolded. At the height of the protest violence, messages ranged from, "Tossing journalistic impartiality aside ... I'm ashamed to be a Canadian today. Riots out of hand in #Toronto #g20," and, "Toronto lost its innocence today ... I'm disgusted," to "Pray tell, what do those committing acts of violence at the #g20 demonstrations hope to achieve? Violence is not the answer," and "Media, mayor [sic] have no idea what is going on in downtown Toronto. Only social media makes sense now." These comments indicate a collective response of frustration and helplessness from both citizens and self-identified journalists. This also demonstrated a marked change from posts that inferred pride in the protest just a few hours earlier. This presents an interesting example of Putnam's (1995) notion of social capital created through online communication, in which dense networks of interaction broaden a participant's sense of self, converting an individual "I" into a collective "we." This further reveals that online discourse helps shape a user's mental model of an event, which is important for journalists to consider, since capturing the public reaction to and impact of an event is a key part of telling a story.

Mental models help us understand the world around us, and are part of a process in which discourse leads the human mind to construct reality, conceive alternatives, and seek the consequences of assumptions (Johnson-Laird 1996). News reports are considered to be a major influence on mental models; through the story selection and editing process, journalists help shape the way the world is seen (Shoemaker 1996). However, it is clear that conflicting and alternative mental models can be created online, and journalists must be cognizant of these varying views in order to provide more complete and accurate reports of how major events influence the public.

For journalists, online commentary found on social media can serve as a temperature gauge or immediate glimpse into the *vox populi*. Skoler (2009) and Overholser (2009) suggest social media are not just tools, but windows into how today's citizens make sense of events in real time. Typically, journalists have resorted to doing "streeters" – interviews with ordinary people in the street – to inject into a news report a sense of what the average person is thinking and feeling about an issue. However, hashtags like #G20 can serve as a rudimentary and immediate glimpse into public attitudes and trends surrounding a specific topic. In addition, the immediate and short bursts of commentary on Twitter signify a captive audience that not only wants to comment, but is also seeking a means to speak out, as indicated by the barrage of posts surrounding the G20 protest. Online conversations also showcase shifts in public opinion during an event, such as the sudden transformation from pride to helplessness and disgust among Twitter users during the G20 protests. By viewing the online community as a partner, rather than a competitor, journalists can immediately tap into a wealth of new sources to help bolster their final reports. In addition, creating personal connections through online conversation can potentially draw more people into the journalistic process, and give them a vested interest in becoming loyal viewers or readers.

Who Is Minding the Gate?

The Authority label used to code the G20 data stems from gatekeeping theory, which is often used to explain the power and authority granted to news organizations to select what information deserves to be called news and is worthy of public consumption (Shoemaker and Vos 2009). While the bottom-up movement touted by new media researchers, in which the audience helps produce and disseminate news, is highly evident in the G20 tweets, it appears that even online journalists maintain a sense of authority over citizens as purveyors of information.

Java et al. (2007) identified news reporting as one of the primary functions of Twitter in a study of the micro-blogging site. Similarly, in the G20 data set, reporting and sharing information accounted for the majority of Twitter posts. As outlined in Figure 8.1, 60 per cent of the tweets focused on either spreading information, links, and photographs, or reporting news through eyewitness or other collaborative means. This corresponds to Farhi's (2009) finding that Twitter users are extremely engaged in news; in fact, his research finds these online users to be two to three times more likely to visit a news site than the average person.

Figure 8.1 Twitter user intentions.

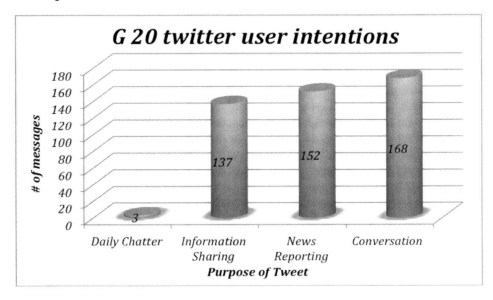

Figure 8.1 provides further evidence that, in a breaking news event, citizens turn to Twitter to seek and provide information. This is why news organizations and journalists must look at social media sites, such as Twitter, as essential platforms for disseminating updates, reports, and information. While traditional publishing and broadcasting processes play an important role, it is clear that social media are emerging as a new front line for information. Journalists must consider social media as an additional platform for disseminating breaking news information and promoting value-added context on their own websites and newscasts. Otherwise, they risk ignoring a wide audience of potential readers and viewers, people who are eager to play a role in the journalistic process by sharing information of their own.

McCombs and Shaw (1972) established that, in the gatekeeping process, mainstream media decide what information should be broadcast or published, and determine which images and issues the public should think about and consider to be important. In contrast, the information and posts published on the #G20 hashtag served as a community newswire through which different players had a say, searched for answers, and posted commentary and information. Without a single organizer or leader, the gates of information were left relatively open. This collaborative and largely unrestricted environment allowed users to help one another by sourcing and spreading updates and links pertaining to road closures, building lockdowns, protest routes, photographs, and even the history of the Black Bloc group, which was believed to be largely responsible for the damage and violence during the protest. Ordinary citizens researched the Black Bloc, and posted information from online encyclopedias and other sources to help answer questions presented by members of the online community. Howe (2008) uses the term "crowdsourcing" to describe this kind of collaborative action, in which a job traditionally performed by a designated agent – for example, a journalist – is outsourced to a large group of people on a voluntary basis.

However, upon closer examination of the information being shared and the type of posts being retweeted, it appears professional journalists maintained an authoritative voice, even in the highly collaborative and open-sourced environment of Twitter. The task of a journalist on the scene of a breaking news event is to give eyewitness accounts to the audience, to portray the basic facts of what has happened, and to provide context and meaning. At first glance, there were few differences between the eyewitness posts made by journalists and those made by citizens who were watching the protests unfold, or were in the thick of it as participants. Both groups provided succinct updates, with far more individual users than journalists uploading photographs to accompany their updates. However, the news reporting on Twitter was not limited to eyewitness accounts. Messages posted by citizens included relating what mainstream news outlets were reporting. Users appeared to be scanning mainstream media websites, and watching the 24-hour news channels for information, which they then updated in the form of posts on the #G20 hashtag. Updates included direct quotes from news reports or retweeted posts made by established news organizations or mainstream journalists. For example, anndouglas tweeted, "CBC TV reporting less than 100 violent protestors out of total crowd of 10000 protestors." Her tweet was picked up and retweeted numerous times. Posts made by the *Toronto Star* and *National Post* newspapers' official Twitter accounts were also frequently retweeted within this hashtag. The *Toronto Star* focused on providing frequent updates regarding specific locations and intersections such as, "Eaton Centre locked down. Protestors now outside police headquarters" and "Reports that tear gas has been deployed near Sheraton Centre hotel, on Queen." As the violence and vandalism spread, the *Toronto Star* dutifully sent out links to a photo gallery on its website. Meanwhile, citizen witnesses uploaded similar tweets and pictures, and provided links to online photo galleries created by ordinary citizens. Yet it appeared that when given the choice, Twitter users still granted more authority to mainstream news organizations by frequently retweeting journalists' posts over other citizens' eyewitness accounts.

Another interesting observation arising from the posts was the balance of professional and informal tones used by journalists on Twitter. Professional journalists were careful to attribute their information, by using qualifiers like "reports" and "Toronto Police say." This further demonstrates how professional journalistic conventions and ethics can be carried over to the social media world, and accuracy and proper sourcing can be practised. However, within the Twitter feed, journalists included updates with less formal tones. This added to the online conversation with colourful commentary and portrayed the impact of the event on a personal level. *Toronto Star* reporter @balkissoon mused, "OH a dad explaining dif between corporations and 'small companies' to little daughter as glass is cleaned up from Yonge St" and "women with bullhorn saying don't be violent 'it makes them right.'" Another *Toronto Star* reporter, @RaveenaAlukah, tweeted, "Why did no one think of mobile toilets for this march. Bladder is bursting," while newspaper columnist @AntoniaZ remarked, "Who was the bonehead who lit the flare," when unruly protestors lit flares in the streets to create police distractions.

This casual language humanized the journalists and helped break the perceived authoritative hierarchy between journalists and citizens. Twitter users frequently spread the word about which journalists were most active in providing updates, pictures, and interesting commentary; recommendations to follow certain journalists began to appear consistently in the latter part of the data set.

This kind of community-based media monitoring shows that even in the new media world, mainstream news organizations and journalists are still perceived as authoritative voices when it comes to reliable information, but the journalists that garnered the greatest following among Twitter users offered more than the typical news updates; they took more active and social roles in online conversations and commentary.

This further showcases the value for journalists to consider Twitter as a promotional tool and a bridge to online communities.

Moving Forward

Social media have become a cultural force and while they are changing the way journalism is practised, they are not rendering professional journalists obsolete. With more and more information available to the public, journalists' roles are broadened beyond, and greater emphasis is placed on, making sense of all the information available (Hermida 2010). The fact that links to news organizations' websites and mainstream news reports are overwhelmingly shared and distributed on Twitter reveals that many social media users continue to turn to established news organizations for reliable information. The issue at play is not who is minding the gates of information, but rather who can best make sense of all the information available.

It does not appear that social media users seek to replace mainstream news organizations, but instead aim to assist established organizations and, in turn, expect immediate information through online platforms. The Internet affords news consumers choice, and the collaborative approach employed by Twitter users to source and share news reports can only foster greater public engagement within the news community. By viewing social media users as partners, rather than competitors, journalists can tap into a wealth of new sources to enrich their final reports. In addition, journalists must go beyond tweeting headlines to create personal connections through online conversation. The findings show that establishing connections draws more people into the journalistic process, and gives news audiences a vested interest in becoming loyal viewers or readers.

The new media world isn't simply an intermediary virtual layer; it has become an integral part of society, where lasting connections are made between individuals. Dourish and Brewer (2008) describe technologically mediated spaces, such as micro-blogging sites, as places within which new cultural practices are conditioned. Furthermore, mobile technology gives new meaning to connectivity and participation. The photos instantly uploaded by citizens who witnessed the G20 protests and vandalism illustrate the immense opportunity social media provide for journalists to facilitate citizen engagement. News organizations must perceive the accessibility and affordability of mobile technology as an enormous benefit. It is recommended that newsrooms create and promote ways in which viewers/readers can participate in news stories vis-à-vis a newsroom Twitter feed, publicizing individual reporters' Twitter handles, soliciting photographs or comments via official newsroom Facebook accounts, or conducting live chats during breaking new stories. It is not enough to solicit viewer email, but instead news organizations must make a concerted effort in real time to show people that the newsroom is engaged with online communities.

At a time when newsrooms are struggling with cutbacks and diminished resources, the opportunity to strengthen online relationships with active bloggers and Twitter users opens up great potential for collaboration and content enrichment, especially in breaking news situations. The newsroom's Web team can no longer be relegated to repurposing stories for the Web platform and posting Web polls. Instead these journalists can serve as a front-line team tasked with engaging social media users and sourcing photos, contacts, and information from social media for further verification and potential use in broadcast and published reports.[2]

It is evident that established organizations like government offices and police organizations are using social media to reach out to citizens for public awareness purposes and requesting social media users' assistance in investigations. Public relations professionals are also tapping into social media. A Canada Newswire and Léger Marketing poll found a 300 per cent increase in social media use among PR professionals between 2009 and 2011 (Canada Newswire 2011). While the journalist's role remains to inform the public, no longer is a simple email request or waiting for a return phone call enough to find information. Our sources and potential sources are increasingly engaged in social media, and journalists must use these new avenues to keep a pulse on who and what people are saying. For a journalist, maintaining a social media presence also enhances personal visibility within the community and provides increased opportunities for self-promotion, feedback on stories, and potential tips and pitches for future stories.

Moreover, this study shows that social media users are engaged in the search for news and information. Reaching out to these active online users, and having a social media program in place for breaking news events, is important for the future of news organizations. This study's findings make it evident that Twitter users are interested in news and they are active in gathering and sharing information when news breaks. Ignoring this demographic is a poor business decision.

Conclusion

This analysis into how journalists and citizens interact through social media during a breaking news event helps us to understand the role social media play in how we experience news. Primarily, online contact strengthens interactions between citizens and journalists. In turn, these online conversations help feed the demand for information between the time a breaking news event occurs and when comprehensive reports are published or broadcast or posted to a website. Further research is required to understand whether the connections gained from social media sites are being incorporated into mainstream news stories.

This research was based on posts made during a four-hour span within the #G20 hashtag, and as a thematic analysis, it is limited in that it does not consider the individuals' personal reasons for uploading or seeking information online. Nor does it account for individual journalists' reasons for using or not using Twitter during the protests. Further ethnographic research into how individual journalists and citizens use Twitter during a breaking news event would help shed more light on how technology is impacting the ways in which journalists and citizens report, disseminate, and consume information, specifically in breaking news situations.

Workflow practices must also be examined, with consideration of how newsrooms prioritize when and how information is fed through and collected via social media versus the reliance on traditional deadlines. In order to capitalize on the collaborative efforts already found in social media, it is critical that news organizations and their stakeholders view these online communities as assets to be leveraged for the purpose of improving the message itself and its reach. It is also evident that greater integration is needed between newsroom Web teams and field reporters and producers. The Web team must be seen as having an integrated role in the newsroom with responsibilities that go beyond repurposing reports for the website. This team can play a crucial role by sourcing and providing material for stories, while helping to drive social media traffic to the news organization's own website.

One of the greatest challenges presented in the new media world is not the increased power given to citizens to produce media content, but rather the greater demand and expectation for immediate information access. Putnam's (1995) famous essay on the decline of social capital posed the notion that "electronic technology enables individual tastes to be satisfied more fully" (74). Simply put, the conversations and social interactions that were once conducted through face-to-face interaction now also occur online and at a much faster pace.

NOTES

1 Hashtag labels are chosen organically by online users, and become effective when an increasing number of people utilize them to identify their tweets. Tweets under a hashtag are automatically grouped by the Twitter service, but the labels are created by online users.
2 It is also worth noting that in the Ontario Auditor General's report into civil liberty breaches by police at the G20 Summit, the province for the first time used social media as investigative tools to reach out to witnesses and to track the event as it unfolded. In his final report, Ontario Auditor-General Andre Marin made special note of the role of social media in his investigation (Marin 2010).

9 *GroundWire:* Growing Community News Journalism in Canada

GRETCHEN KING, CHRIS ALBINATI,
ANABEL KHOO, CANDACE MOOERS,
AND JACKY TUINSTRA HARRISON

Launched in 2008 by the National Campus and Community Radio Association (NCRA), *GroundWire: Community Radio News* is a biweekly community news radio magazine. Each twenty-nine–minute edition offers a community radio report or spotlight on local music, as well as headlines and feature stories, presenting engaging critical analysis on under- or mis-represented issues and communities. Produced by a national network of community radio journalists, story submissions come from contributors from all over Canada. This community news project garners participation from nearly every region in Canada through its rotating production and shared governance practices. *GroundWire* programming is carried on more than thirty campus and community radio stations in Canada and each edition is released online at the *GroundWire* website (groundwire.ncra.ca). This chapter focuses on our collective efforts to build a national community news network among community radio stations and volunteers in Canada, prioritizing public engagement, training, and localism.

Although the past decade has seen a rise in academic reflection on alternative media and community radio (Rodriguez 2001; Atton 2002, 2003; Carpentier et al. 2003; Couldry and Curran 2003; Rennie 2006; Meadows et al. 2007; Milan 2008; Howley 2005, 2010a, 2010b; Coyer 2006, 2011; Coyer et al. 2007; Downing 2001, 2002, 2008, 2010, 2011), there is a lack of focus on the challenges that national community-based journalism poses to traditional journalism practices, whether public or commercial, national or local. In addition to reviewing the way the category "community media" has been conceptualized in the academic literature, this chapter summarizes *GroundWire's* approach to community journalism, which is seeking to transform the mediascape in

Canada. We focus on four policies developed by a network of volunteers involved with local campus and community radio stations across Canada. These policies put into practice our vision of community-centric journalism and include (1) priority bureaus that clearly identify our community and social justice news values; (2) an editorial policy that defines principles of diversity, participatory engagement, balance, integrity, and accuracy; (3) a governance structure that is transparent and collaborative as well as largely drawn from volunteer participation; and (4) a collective production process that rotates among stations and regions in Canada.

Planting the Seed

Long before the conceptualization of *GroundWire* in 2004 at the National Campus-Community Radio Conference (NCRC) in Edmonton, alternative media had garnered the attention of academics. The first scholars to conceptualize alternative media include Paul Lazarsfeld and Robert Merton of the 1940s Columbia School, and Theodor Adorno and Jürgen Habermas of the Frankfurt School. Each provides insight into the social and political structures that contextualize mass media in the West in the twentieth century, and each also points out practices for alternative spaces in the media system. Some of these potential openings for alternatives include blurring the lines between audiences and producers; engaging with some or all of the conditions conducive to powerful media effects; avoiding "culture industry" trappings and scientific management organizational structures; and lastly, contributing to the Habermasian public sphere (Adorno 2008; Lazarsfeld and Merton 2008; Habermas 2008). This Habermasian theory of the public sphere as a function of mass media has been applied to studies of alternative media and community radio by many scholars, including Atton and Wickenden (2005), van Vuuren (2006), Elson (2007), Atton and Hamilton (2008), and Jurriens (2009). *GroundWire*, in its community-centric approach to journalism, is committed to many of the theories of early alternative media theorists.

GroundWire's community news policies and practices exemplify these observations made by media theorists nearly a century ago. A departure from traditional media presentation is clear from the start of any *GroundWire* edition. Each episode is produced at a different campus and/or community station and hosted by different volunteers. The producing station collects and executes presentation and unique sound design of the edition within suggested guidelines. *GroundWire* anchors have included francophone voices, east-coast accents, youths paired with elders, and people who sound like friends and neighbours. Such a format flies in the face of traditional media wisdom that dictates the audience wants a connection with a charismatic and dependable host or sound presentation. Chantal Francoeur addresses the question of innovative sound design at Radio-Canada in chapter 7. Even progressive news programs abide by this formula, thus the independent US broadcast program *Democracy Now!* owes much of its brand identity to host Amy Goodman (www.democracynow.org/). In addition, *Ground-Wire* encourages producers to contribute sources in languages other than English. Its editorial policy points to the importance of representing a diversity of linguistic communities and outlines the commitment to "featuring Aboriginal languages as often as possible" (*GroundWire* 2014). For example, several producing stations have scripted Aboriginal place names into their editions of *GroundWire*, such as CKUT Radio from Tiohtià:ke (also known as Montreal).

This difference in sound is further elaborated within *GroundWire's* editorial policy, which outlines programming priorities and responsibilities. Of particular interest is the focus on challenging the divisions between audiences and producers, by encouraging self-representation and media training as key to meaningful participation. For example, *GroundWire* contributors are encouraged to produce first-person pieces with no external reporters. Indeed, many of the primary sources at GroundWire are drawn from movements – "the person or people closest to the issue; the ones directly affected by it" – whereas "secondary sources" are identified as "authors, professors, governmental or community workers" (*GroundWire* 2014). This has resulted in many first-person features being aired on *GroundWire*. Having no reporter to speak to the listener is a rogue convention of journalism practised sparingly by most news organizations. For example, *GroundWire* presented a special, double-length feature in 2011 on midwifery, produced with only the voices of mothers, midwives, and health care stakeholders. A year earlier, *GroundWire* aired a report featuring only Native voices commemorating the twentieth anniversary of the defence of Kanehsatake during the so-called Oka Crisis.

Indeed, the editorial guidelines prioritize engagement with sources and listeners by mandating that "*GroundWire* will seek to train and provide skills to communities to make their own media contributions, recognize the power of the media as a tool for education, and inspire listeners to reflect upon injustice and oppression" (*GroundWire* 2014). The edition produced by FlemoCity Media, based in Toronto, provides an example of *GroundWire*'s approach to blending training and production. A participatory peak for *GroundWire*, this training project for at-risk youth simultaneously provided training and produced content for air. In one feature of the program, the topic was the FlemoCity project itself, and the youth were the sources, the producers, and the trainees all at once. This practice exemplifies the approach to accuracy identified by the editorial policy: "*GroundWire* is responsible to our listeners and to our interview subjects to be as accurate as possible in our reporting. We encourage journalists to orient themselves to the facts as defined by the communities they are reporting on, and due diligence will be practiced" (*GroundWire* 2014). Orienting facts presented in *GroundWire*'s news within the communities we report on and the hands-on experience of producing *GroundWire* (and in so doing, telling one's own stories) offer the opportunity to direct public discourse towards the root causes and everyday realities that are often left out of policy or decision making.

This two-way relationship between the listener and reporter fits with Susan Forde's findings on what is at the core of localism: empowerment through process, moving beyond the mere content of the medium (2011, 79). In addition, the practice of training "local community people" as producers was specifically recognized by the Council of Europe's Declaration of the Committee of Ministers on the Role of Community Media in Promoting Social Cohesion and Intercultural Dialogue (Council of Europe 2009). Furthermore, in focusing on training and skill sharing with the goal of self-determination, *GroundWire* takes the work of redefining public priorities beyond the neo-liberal framework of the "citizen." While Clemencia Rodriguez (2001) coined the term "citizens' media" to convey a spirit of open access and the facilitation of social change, *GroundWire* seeks to actively confront the past and ongoing legacies of colonialism in Canada and globally, which often entails featuring voices from people without official citizenship or who do not recognize the legitimacy of the Canadian state as a determinant of their identity. For this reason, *GroundWire* prefers the terms *grassroots* or *community-based* media.

These priorities result in a major difference not only in the voices heard on *GroundWire*, but also in how our content is oriented to the issues. In a news data analysis conducted by CKUT's Community News Department in June 2010, the coverage characteristics of *GroundWire* and CBC radio reporting were compared for four key stories: the G8/G20 Summits; the 20th Anniversary of the Oka Crisis; the Attack on the Freedom Flotilla; and Haiti – After the Earthquake. *GroundWire's* coverage was historically contextualized, offered rights-oriented perspectives, and featured voices from those directly affected or involved, as opposed to sources who comment on the story from an outsider's or status quo perspective. The CBC's coverage of Haiti after the 2010 Earthquake, by contrast, did not offer critique of the aid industry, or any discussion of the history of Canada's complicity in Haiti's financial debt or damaging militarization. Further, the analysis found that the CBC did not frame its reporting concerning the G8/G20 summits around human or constitutional rights. The full news data analysis is available online at *GroundWire's* Wiki space (*GroundWire* 2010).

GroundWire's community news practices are rooted in a long tradition of journalism advocating social justice. Emphasizing the voices of primary sources has roots in feminist journalism, going back to the 1970s, and inspired the Women's International News Gathering Service (www.wings.org). Operating for twenty-six years, WINGS is produced by various women around the world and emphasizes that the people covered speak for themselves. In addition, two popular community radio programs in the United States, Sprouts (www.independentreports.net/sprouts) and Free Speech Radio News (fsrn.org), are also inspired by social justice and have also been built by sharing production responsibilities within a network of stations. Each of these programs influenced *GroundWire's* early structural formation. These programs work in ways that exemplify John Downing's radical alternative media theory (2001). Downing, one of the foremost theorists on contemporary alternative media, attempts to narrow Nick Couldry and James Curran's definition of alternative media. In 2003, Couldry and Curran defined alternative media in their book *Contesting Media Power* as "media production that challenges, at least implicitly, actual concentrations of media power, whatever form those may take in different locations" (7). Downing maintains that this type of media practice is a form of contestation, but suggests the term "radical alternative media" (2001, ix). In 1984, and again in 2001, Downing defined radical media as "generally small-scale and in many different forms, that express an alternative vision to hegemonic policies, priorities, and perspectives" (ibid., v). Ultimately, Downing locates radical media within – or in the service of – radical social movements "to express opposition from subordinate quarters directly at the power structure and against its behaviour and to build support, solidarity and networking against policies or even against the very survival of the power structures" (xi).

In a move to narrow considerably the focus of what may or may not constitute alternative or radical media, Mitzi Waltz (2005) evokes two major alternative media theorists: Michael Albert's (1997) definition whereby the "alternativeness" is located in how the institution is organized and works; and Rodriguez's (2001) preference for "citizens' media," a term aiming to encompass "a means of production characterized by open access and volunteerism, goals inviting social change, and a not-for-profit orientation" (Waltz 2005, 3). Waltz further identifies a kind of "activist media," whereby audiences are implicitly encouraged to get involved in social change (ibid.). *GroundWire*, in its organizational structure, touches on these points. Andrea Langlois and Frédéric Dubois (2005) further raise organizational structure as a key element in defining autonomous media. In their definition, they seek to elicit a move beyond issues of content to offer a focus on organizational infrastructure, participation, and "empowerment" (ibid., 9–10). Within this definition, we can locate *GroundWire* as an autonomous medium, operating independently of dominant institutions (such as the state, corporations, the church, the military, and corporatist unions). Such media, Langlois and Dubois argue, seek to "encourage the participation of audiences within their projects" (10). Autonomous media also challenge the subordination of audiences to the role of passive receivers, and upset the binary between producer and consumer. The authors further maintain that true alternative discourses can only be fostered through open, transparent, and non-hierarchical media organizations.

As outlined in the anti-oppression section of its editorial policy, *GroundWire*'s approach to community news is inclusive, "internally amongst members, and externally in all aspects of *GroundWire* production" (*GroundWire* 2014). This structure is rooted within an anti-oppressive framework that ensures its production practices are participatory, collaborative, decentralized, and volunteer-driven. Indeed, *GroundWire* manages to evade macro-level control by financial and political sponsors, while also challenging the working practices of traditional journalism. For example, the steering committee, responsible for *GroundWire*'s oversight and development, is made up of mostly volunteer producers, although it includes one or two NCRA board members (who also typically produce with *GroundWire*). The steering committee reports to the membership of the NCRA annually and hosts an in-person, open meeting at the National Campus-Community Radio Conference every year. Finally, during the production of each episode, collaborative work is the norm; each production typically involves conference calls, Google Docs, and Skype-ing. *GroundWire* encourages these practices even within individual productions. Thus, headlines are often written in one city, recorded in another and edited in yet a third.

While terms like *community news* or *radical alternative media* and *activist* or *autonomous media* may allude to a new or eccentric form of journalism, reporting on issues by those directly affected or invested in social and environmental causes precedes the development of the standard of political neutrality that has become the hallmark for journalistic integrity in dominant public and commercial media. Forde, in *Challenging the News* (2011), notes that alternative news practices are rooted in a long-standing tradition and that it is actually the notion of objectivity that is more recent, having emerged with the dominance of neo-liberalism as a market model in the West. Fuelling economic capitalism by appealing to a broad audience and prioritizing "non-controversial" news is directly linked to the development of objectivity as a journalistic value (Forde 2011, 114). Forde goes further in noting that the basis of objectivity's development indicated a shift in news organizations' priorities away from upholding the collective rights of the public to information, and towards a faith in the individual's freedom of expression or discretion in content (ibid., 115). Along these lines, *GroundWire* aims to challenge the notion that objectivity is a prerequisite for legitimacy in news reporting. While its editorial policy offers definitions of balance, integrity, and accuracy, the term *objectivity* is purposefully omitted (*GroundWire* 2014). By maintaining priority bureaus on under-reported news from a diversity of social movements, and by facilitating the self-representation of marginalized communities, its approach to community journalism moves beyond definitions of objectivity that insist upon political neutrality. Ben Bagdikian (1983) suggests standards upheld by most media organizations for politically neutral content are made at the expense of "intelligent examinations of the causes of events" (132).

Through identifying priority bureaus on under-reported issues, *GroundWire*'s editorial policy locates a central place for social movements throughout Canada's rural and urban regions. The priority bureaus include:

- Labour and Workers' Rights
- Indigenous Perspectives
- Migration, Refugee, and Newcomer Issues
- Student Affairs
- Environment, Agriculture, Alternative Economy, and Sustainability News
- Women and Equality
- Queer and Trans Voices
- Prison Justice Reporting
- Race and Equity Focus
- Poverty and Homelessness Focus
- Disability/Accessibility Issues
- Pro-Peace Reporting

Beyond drawing attention to strengthening social justice movements and promoting a critical analysis of the news, the editorial policy identifies *GroundWire* content as "original, alternative and determin[ing] its news values independently from other media" (*GroundWire* 2014). This point reflects the commitment to marginalized or under-represented voices telling their own stories and bringing attention to social justice movements. Indeed, we aim to cultivate meaningful engagement through our orientation to social movements in Canada. These are movements that engage local, regional, national, and global governance structures, as outlined in the priority bureaus (*GroundWire* 2014). Any program pitch to *GroundWire* concerning any of these movements will likely be accepted. In this way, *GroundWire* defines its news values according to the experiences of social justice movements operating at multiple levels, but always relevant to our largely Canadian-based audience. Cultivating engagement among its listeners is mandated by the editorial policy. Each program will "promote an analysis of the news that will lead to ongoing dialogues and understanding among individuals of different communities across Canada, including providing social justice and historical considerations" (*GroundWire* 2014). In this way, community news at *GroundWire* provides a platform for movements to share their experiences, connect to other movements, and inspire individual listeners.

In addition, through a collaborative and regional production process that rotates between rural and urban campus and community radio stations, *GroundWire* guarantees that each program reflects a

diversity of regions and movements in Canada. Producers emphasize local content, but the broadcast of the program is intended to
share very local stories with other communities, and vice versa, and
to profile communities that are often invisible in media on a national
scale. This growing of local content for the purpose of national exposure is what makes *GroundWire* unique. In the face of all the obstacles,
it is striving to break ground; its very mandate is to create national
connections between local communities and social movements, no
matter how small. In this way, it is challenging the very definition of
national news programming. As the private and public sector news
providers struggle with local coverage, gutting their newsrooms and
centralizing their content, GroundWire is aiming to perfect a 100 per
cent, volunteer-based, collaborative production process that showcases stories from even the most remote communities, and working
to recruit new producing stations. It could be perceived that our collaborative, collective, and regional production ethics have an impact
on the efficiency of producing each edition of *GroundWire*, but in the
digital age, *GroundWire* is more significantly constrained by the need
for human resources, such as paid coordinators, and the need for technical resources to equip community radio stations with newsrooms.
Currently, there are only a handful of paid news staff in Canada's
campus-community radio sector. *GroundWire*, through its practices
and with its limited resources, is attempting to develop and increase
community news production in the campus community radio sector.
While we search for sustainable funding to aid the national coordination of *GroundWire*, we continue to look for funding opportunities to
build local community news departments.

Community news journalism at *GroundWire* is also rooted in the history of campus-community radio in Canada. Charles Fairchild (2001)
examines community radio broadcasting (including what is referred
to as "community-based campus radio" by CRTC policy) in both Canada and the United States. Fairchild argues that community radio can
only be effective as a political public sphere when a series of practical
principles or "constituent elements" are present, namely, democracy,
participation, localism, and accessibility (ibid., 7). He further describes
some of the constraints, tensions, and challenges of community radio
stations as marginal institutions. Fairchild argues that community radio
is marginal because it is "governed by structures that are mostly democratic, because participants engage in media practices whose outcomes
are beyond the control of specific financial and political sponsors, and

because people are inherently treated as potential and actual contribu-tors by these stations" (4). For Fairchild, community radio's alterna-tiveness is located in its participants' "work to expand arenas of public discourse by freeing them, to the greatest extent possible, from the arbi-trary limits set by financial and political power" (5). Fairchild identi-fies community radio's mode of volunteer-driven production, and the socio-economic context that simultaneously enables and constrains the radio sector, as the central locations for community radio's alternative-ness. A decade later, Fairchild's observations still hold true for projects like *GroundWire*.

GroundWire's steering committee grapples with all of these issues in its considerations of content driven by social movements, as clearly stated in its editorial policy, as well as in its deliberations on how to fund the project. *GroundWire* has received limited amounts of financial support from labour unions as well as the Community Radio Fund of Canada (communityradiofund.org), which is supported by the pri-vate sector. Whether its receipt of funding from Astral Media via the CRFC in 2009 negates its role in the service of social movements is debatable. Private funding often comes with guidelines written by the funder; however, in the case of the CRFC, the fund is largely run by the campus-community radio sector. Since 2008, the CRFC has run two programs previously developed by Astral Media. These include the Radio Talent Development Program and the Youth Internship Pro-gram, both of which have been criticized for offering funding options that fall short of the sector's needs. The two inherited programs offer limited-term funding: a maximum of sixteen weeks for the former and up to eight months for the latter. In addition, both programs offer a maximum amount of $10,000.

The funds available through these programs fall short when com-pared with any community radio station's basic expenses. For example, paying one full-time staff person can easily cost a station $30,000 per year and, on top of that, maintaining a transmitter and paying for rent for the studio location can quickly push total expenses over $100,000 annually. More recently, the CRFC developed the Radiometres pro-gram, which accepts applications for longer-term projects (up to nine months) and a higher cap on funding requests (up to $20,000). How-ever, no funding through this program (or any offered by the CRFC) can be spent on capital purchases (such as computers, soundboards, or transmitters). In addition, the maximum amount allowed for tech-nical expenses through any of the CRFC programs is $500, which barely covers the cost of one digital recorder (a professional Marantz digital recorder, e.g., can start at $650). Today, *GroundWire* continues to function without any core funding, and relies entirely on volunteer resources. Its ability to adapt, whether or not it is in receipt of core funding, is a testament to its community-powered strength as a grassroots, autonomous medium. This question of long-term viability for under-funded community media is also addressed by Robert Washburn and Vincent Raynauld in chapter 10.

Making Community News Sustainable

In 2004, when *GroundWire* was simply an idea, no one knew the eventual scope and sustainability of the proposed project. The structure and mandate for a national community news network have been developed annually at NCRCs hosted in different regions of Canada. Currently, the NCRCs provide the only space for *GroundWire* members to meet face-to-face and to produce programming side-by-side. Over the years, *GroundWire* has been developed largely through volunteer power, though the project did secure a grant and several sponsorships enabling the hiring of a national coordinator from 2009 to 2010. To date, our model has been successfully operating through a national network of dedicated community and campus radio volunteers. However, community news models need to be examined not only with respect to practices and policies, but also by exploring the implications of various funding structures. In this last section, we will focus on the challenges *GroundWire* faces in growing a national community news infrastructure in Canada and investigate the possibility for its long-term, financial sustainability.

From developing technology to assist real-time collaboration between dispersed producers editing with Internet-capable cell phone software, to being able to compensate a small, paid staff and offer honoraria for producing stations and contributors, *GroundWire*'s efforts to redefine journalism in Canada require access to financial and technical resources. For example, during the period that it had funding for a national coordinator, the number of episodes, as well as the number of volunteer contributors and producers, rose significantly. Indeed, the number of producing stations increased from just five stations hosting the then-monthly production of *GroundWire* to twelve stations hosting it biweekly. However, when that funding ceased, the production team stagnated, in part due to a lack of resources to provide consistent levels of outreach and training. The need for remuneration for coordination and hosting production is evident in the lack of momentum for growing the project. In 2014, the stations that produced *GroundWire* numbered fourteen (an all-time record): CKDU, Halifax, NS; CFMH, Saint John, NB; CKUT, Montreal, QC; CFRU, Guelph, ON; CHRW, London, ON; CFRC, Kingston, ON; CIVL, Abbotsford, BC; CJLY, Nanaimo, BC; CILU, Thunder Bay, ON; CKUW, Winnipeg, MB; CFCR Saskatoon, SK; CFBX, Kamloops, BC; CiTR, Vancouver, BC; and CJSF, Burnaby, BC. So far, the community sector has been held up as the champion of diversity in the Canadian media landscape, but without core funding this mandate becomes a burden rather than an opportunity.

As the enabling statute for the Canadian Radio-television and Telecommunications Commission, the Broadcasting Act (Canada 1991) establishes the CRTC's mandate and the powers the CRTC may exercise in meeting its mandate. That mandate largely involves regulating the Canadian broadcasting system. The broadcasting system is defined as "comprising public, private and community elements." All three of those elements "constitute a single system and ... the objectives of the broadcasting policy ... can best be achieved" through regulation "by a single independent public authority." That authority is the CRTC. The objectives of the system encompass an obligation to "safeguard, enrich and strengthen" the multicultural and multilingual diversity of Canadian society, including "the special place of aboriginal peoples within that society" in all of its programming and operations. The Act also requires each of the broadcasting system's elements to "be readily adaptable to scientific and technological change" (ibid.).

The language of the Act is clear in its intention to promote the type of programming that originates in the community sector. For example, the Act states, "the programming provided by the Canadian broadcasting system should ... provide a reasonable opportunity for the public to be exposed to the expression of differing views on matters of public concern, and include a significant contribution from the Canadian independent production sector" (1991). The meaning of "differing views" is open to interpretation, but it is arguable that Parliament's intention was much broader than the continuous shuffle of in-house commentators, and government and corporate spokespersons that dominate programming on public and private stations. This results in the community sector largely left to carry this mandate. In this way, *GroundWire*'s programming stands out from the voices heard on the mainstream channels – e.g., CBC Radio and TV, Radio-Canada, and CTV – by featuring news from contributors embedded in social movements across Canada and also offering an inclusive, as opposed to exclusive, range of sources. *GroundWire* presents perspectives that are rarely available through the programming of the public and private broadcasters.

The Act also singles out and prioritizes programming for Aboriginal peoples and disabled persons, stating that it "should be provided within the Canadian broadcasting system as resources become available for the purpose" (Canada 1991). In the community sector, there are examples of programming being produced by these specific groups on the issues and views unique to them, yet very few of the resources available seem to go towards supporting these programs. *GroundWire* has dedicated priority bureaus that address First Nations and the disability communities, but has never been considered for any available resources. The ongoing reality is that the community element continues to be impoverished relative to the other elements in the broadcasting system. Recent attempts to change this funding gap are evident in some of the priorities of the CRFC. As mentioned above, *GroundWire* was the beneficiary of the Radio Talent Development Program from the CRFC for sixteen weeks in the summer of 2009. However, due to changes in the eligibility requirements for the CRFC, *GroundWire* no longer qualifies, as our initiative is a project of the NCRA and is not hosted by a single-community radio station. The experience of trying to develop *GroundWire* in a regulatory environment that neglects core funding for the non-profit community radio sector is one that is frustratingly slow.

Recently, in the revised campus and community radio policy known as the Broadcasting Regulatory Policy, the role of the community sector was further emphasized and articulated: "The programming provided by campus and community radio should meet the needs and interests of the communities served by these stations in ways that are not met by commercial radio stations and the Canadian Broadcasting Corporation" (CRTC 2010d). The policy states that it does not require that community radio embrace or keep pace with new media, but that it should strive to do so. The CRTC has stated through its policy that it recognizes that funding is the greatest barrier to achieving this goal, but believes the solution is to be found in the independent CRFC, stating that "the cost of producing local content, implementing new media approaches and distributing programming by digital means could be offset by funding obtained from the CRFC" (CRTC 2010d). This assertion is both incorrect and demonstrates the CRTC's limited understanding of the needs of the community sector. The statement is incorrect in two ways: First, the CRFC does not apply to upgrading technology; and second, funding requests are limited to less than $20,000 for one program and less than $10,000 for the other two programs (stations are allowed one application, per program, annually). In addition, the statement does nothing to address the barriers faced by *GroundWire*, which is currently excluded from the CRFC because of its project- and station-specific requirements.

To its credit, what this policy does represent is an acknowledgment of the systemic problem that the community sector faces, stating, "Canada, with the exception of the province of Quebec, employs a patchwork funding system for campus and community radio that is generally project-based rather than directed to operational requirements such as staff salaries, technical upgrades and other capital expenditures" (CRTC 2010d). At great expense, the CRTC in 2010 overhauled the policy governing campus and community radio. Although visiting stations offered CRTC commissioners a realistic snapshot of station life, it did not afford them the time to truly engage in dialogue with all the stakeholders. These stakeholders include not just those staff members who were able to make it to the hearings, but also community radio station volunteer producers and listeners. These people should be afforded an opportunity to influence CRTC policy decisions, since they are being impacted the most by them.

In the end, the policy does not present a good understanding of the needs of the community sector that is arguably carrying out a significant share of the broadcasting system's mandate without any representation at the decision-making level. The lack of understanding and representation at the CRTC are two problems that go hand-in-hand.

Recommendations

As Fairchild (2001) noted above, volunteer-driven production has both benefits and drawbacks; it provides for authenticity, but also places the projects in perpetual flux. If a project like *GroundWire* is unable to thrive because of lapses in the funding and application of our framework, then the Broadcasting Act is not upheld. We call on the CRTC to empower, not burden, the community radio sector by consulting regularly and treating those who work within the sector as experts. In light of our experiences in building a community radio news network in Canada for nearly a decade, we offer the following recommendations:

- Appoint a CRTC commissioner from the community sector: The community sector is not being represented on the Commission in the intimate and detailed manner in which the other broadcast sectors are. Implicit in this problem is the fact that currently – and, seemingly, historically as well – CRTC commissioners are chosen exclusively from the private and public sectors, not just in broadcasting, but in telecommunications as well. This disregards both the legal position and the valuable contribution of the community sector in the Canadian broadcasting system. Thus today, the community sector is defined by the Act as one-third of the broadcasting system, but it is not represented proportionately through funding or CRTC membership. Today, commissioners represent proportionally the regions of Canada, yet there is no requirement that mandates cross-sector representation. This must change.
- Recognize *GroundWire* as "locally produced" content for stations that both produce and air the program. While the intention of requiring 15 per cent locally produced spoken-word content is a good one, it fails to consider how this provision actually translates into air time. If the provision is interpreted within the context of the Broadcasting Act and the CRTC's 2010-499 policy, its purpose is to encourage the local members of every station to get involved with making radio. This is exactly what *GroundWire* accomplishes, especially for producing stations. By creating a national forum that connects local communities, *GroundWire* not only informs those listening, but also offers them a platform from which to contribute their own voices. Currently, community news aired on *GroundWire* does not qualify as "locally produced" content, even for stations hosting production. The local production requirement is restricted to content produced solely by the station. A station that produces *GroundWire*, hosts the program, and even contributes a headline and/or a feature story cannot count the 29-minute program as locally produced. This is especially punitive for stations that turn to *GroundWire* because they do not have local news departments. Such stations are already pressed by the 15-per-cent requirement and do not deserve to have their contributions of locally produced content to *GroundWire* go unrecognized. In addition, not

recognizing *GroundWire* as locally produced content (especially for producing stations) could hinder the reach of *GroundWire* as stations prioritize rigidly defined locally produced content. We are asking for this change to ensure stations can commit to collaborating with GroundWire within a supportive regulatory environment.

- Improved framework for funding and strategy. The community radio sector is required to operate with a non-profit mandate. As a result, community radio stations exist in financial limbo. Stations have a limited ability to raise revenue through advertising and are regularly denied the opportunity to apply for charitable tax status. Campus radio stations have, on occasion, faced threats to their existence from university administrations and conservative student groups working to undermine the student fee levies that contribute to station funding. Ultimately, many stations struggle from year to year to find adequate funds needed to ensure operations. The CRFC is limited, inadequate, and imbalanced when compared with the funding available to the private and public sectors. We advise funders to consider longer-term or operational funding options, instead of small-scale, project-based funds.
- Further research and best practices. When it comes to sharing successes and best practices in planning and programming, the sector is limited by the lack of data to build a common strategy. Further research is needed into community news journalism in Canada. This research agenda should include (1) an analysis of the social and economic values of community news; (2) comparisons of case studies on the efficacy of various multiple funding models across a large sample of stations and projects; (3) a long-term tracking of the representation of underserved groups in radio news; and (4) an examination of news and spoken-word content produced under the new (15%) conditions of licence for campus and community stations.

If a project like *GroundWire* is unable to thrive because of lapses in funding and application of its framework, then this regulatory environment, and the resulting resource scarcity, will have failed the community sector. The onus is on all supporters of community radio and community news journalism to demand their government respect the Broadcasting Act and reshape its priorities.

Acknowledgments

This chapter is a collaborative project involving the participation of *GroundWire* members from different regions in Canada. We would like to thank the following contributors for their efforts in producing this chapter: Candace Mooers, Anabel Khoo, Chris Albinati, Gretchen King, and Jacky Tuinstra synthesized the words and ideas presented here; Catherine Fisher, Omme-Salma Rahemtullah, and Trevor Chow-Fraser read with critical eyes, providing insightful feedback.

10 Journalism on the Ground in Rural Ontario

ROBERT WASHBURN AND
VINCENT RAYNAULD

As new and emerging technologies continue to globalize news production and consumption processes (see Reese 2010, 350; Cottle 2009b, 341), the importance of grassroots news cannot be lost in communities across Canada (see also King et al., chapter 9 in this volume). While the news industry is seeking efficiencies and cost-effective solutions in the face of declining audiences and revenues, it should not ignore the value of news within the local context. Certainly, it can be argued that it is important for audience members to gather knowledge and understand the significance of events like the Arab Spring. But it is equally important for them to be aware of community-based news such as losing a crossing guard at the corner of their street, or changes to the local transit schedule. Moreover, there is a need to place international, national, provincial, and regional news in a local context so people can see how world events affect them and how they can, in turn, be effective in the world.

Community journalism has traditionally played this role. As R.D. Chatterton wrote in the inaugural edition of the *Cobourg Star and Newcastle General Advertiser* on 11 January 1831, this local newspaper "is to be esteemed as a friend and welcome guest at every fireside." While the proverbial hearth has been replaced with Internet-enabled mobile devices, Chatterton's original sentiment remains relevant. The purpose of community journalism continues to be to provide local news to audiences, recognizing an intimate relationship among the individual, the news media, and the community.

A bias, however, exists within Canadian journalism. Covering potholes is not perceived as exciting compared with reporting news from provincial or federal capitals. But if journalism is to hold steadfast to its mandate of public service, it cannot flinch when it comes to local news coverage. Audience members are confronted with a tidal wave of information via numerous media platforms. They face a seemingly endless stream of news and information, produced by individuals and organizations with varying levels of credibility. Their challenge is to find information that is timely and accurate, but also important and relevant to them. Conversely, journalists face the Herculean task of competing against a myriad of voices presenting a diverse range of information of varying quality, all calling out to the audience for attention.

There is also a new financial reality. Fragmenting audience markets and intense competition for advertising dollars are among the factors prompting the overhaul of the news industry's economic model. Where once audience and advertising markets were clearly defined and exploited by print and broadcast operations, the marketplace has splintered. Advertisers are inundated with choices for reaching targeted audiences. The intense competition takes its toll as news corporations seek to maintain profit margins to satisfy investors. To increase efficiency and cost effectiveness, companies have bought out competitors and streamlined operations, ever vigilant towards their return on investment.

The consolidation of the news industry in Canada over the past four decades has placed extreme pressures on local media (see Blidook 2009; George 2010). While the ownership of local newspapers is changing, the number of newspaper titles is growing. The number of community newspaper owners in Ontario, both independent and corporate, shrank 26 per cent between 1998 and 2011 according to an Ontario Community Newspaper Association study (see Appendix A). During the same time period, the overall number of titles rose by 22 per cent (OCNA 2011, 20). The growth in publications results from corporate owners expanding to accommodate advertisers, who look to community newspaper chains for convenient distribution networks. This dynamic was confirmed by the final report on the Canadian news media by the Standing Committee on Transportation and Communications in 2006, during testimony by Victor Mlodecki, general manager of Brunswick News (part of the Irving Media Group): "The newspapers are nice, but it is the distribution systems that are important to me" (Canada 2006b, 38).

While this expansion of titles may demonstrate the growth of community newspapers, it also marks a shift away from autonomous ownership. The number of owners classified by the Ontario Community Newspapers Association as "independent" – publishing one to twelve titles – dropped 26 per cent between 1998 and 2011. The number of "independent" publications also decreased by 21 per cent in the same period. Meanwhile, the number of corporate owners who publish more than twelve titles has remained constant at four, but they publish 195 titles, a 44 per cent increase in the decade 2001–11 (OCNA 2011).

This expansion shows a growing confidence in the economic value of community newspaper publishing. This is supported by a ComBase Inc report that looked at 217 markets served by community newspapers between January 2008 and April 2009. It showed that 74 per cent of Canadian adults read their local community newspaper; 82 per cent of those readers identified local news as the main reason they read their community newspaper (ComBase 2009).

On the surface, these can be viewed as positive signs. But the drop in independent ownership and the concurrent rise of corporate publishers have impacts beyond the economic picture. Corporate publishers tend to seek efficiencies through decreases in locally produced content and increases in the use of shared content, content that is often created outside the community and has little direct reference to the audiences being served. This is particularly true of Sun Media, which distributes content for publication throughout its community newspaper chain. Centralized news coverage and the need for greater diversity in editorials and opinion pieces were particular concerns of the Senate committee examining news media (Canada 2006a, 8; Canada 2006b, 67–8).

In seeking economic efficiencies, community newspaper groups tend to treat their publications as regional rather than hyperlocal. A good example would be Sun Media's consolidation of the *Cobourg Daily Star*, *Port Hope Evening Guide*, and *Colborne Chronicle*, three long-standing newspapers in southern Ontario, into a single publication called *Northumberland Today*.

Community journalism not only serves informational needs for its residents, but it is also critical to sustaining a community's identity and enhancing the development of social capital. For example, Meadows et al. determined that community-based news outlets have the unrivalled capacity "to create 'communities of interest,' based on criteria determined, for example, by social, cultural, linguistic or geographical boundaries" (2009, 165). Michael Meadows addresses the topic of community media serving Aboriginal populations in Australia in chapter 11. Ewart et al. (2005) also point out that community-based media platforms can be important sources of social capital because they can make "a significant contribution to culture, communication and life in small towns and regions by helping individuals and communities to make sense of themselves, [their peers,] their world and their place in it" (cited in Richards 2013, 632).

A 2012 Pew Research Center report on the state of US local news reinforces this point. It shows sharp differences between the way people living in suburban neighbourhoods or small urban areas consume news compared with those living in rural areas. Urban residents are more likely to access local news and information via a range of digital activities and platforms (e.g., blogs, news organizations' websites) and tend to be more engaged participants, often sharing local stories online, posting material on social networking sites, and commenting on websites. Residents of small towns and those living in rural areas rely more heavily on traditional news activities and platforms, such as television and newspapers. The study found that civic information is particularly important to small-town and rural audiences, as well as information about local weather and community events (Miller et al. 2012).

An opportunity exists to use new and emerging technologies to provide affordable, cost-efficient content production and diffusion platforms for community news media. If there could be a path for journalists, as entrepreneurs, to find a sustainable model to produce quality coverage for geographically narrow locations across Canada, it could be the start of a movement to reclaim the importance and values of community journalism beyond the corporate model. An example within the public broadcasting system is discussed by Chantal Francoeur in chapter 7. Such community news production could be an opportunity to strengthen the education of citizenry in more highly localized issues of particular relevance to these rural communities. Through a diverse range of technologies, citizens could become more engaged with each other in the discussion of issues happening just beyond their doorstep. All this would be done in the hopes of empowering people to take action on grassroots issues that affect them directly. At the same time, it could restore independent, locally owned news media.

It is within this context that community journalism seeks to find its direction in the twenty-first century. How can rural communities be served at a local level by the news media in the future? One such initiative is hyperlocal news, which refers to "highly locally focused news reporting, now usually delivered online, about issues and events targeted within a well-defined geographic community" (Pavlik 2013, 8–9). This chapter presents research undertaken over a one-year period to explore hyperlocal news as an alternative vehicle for underserved communities, particularly those in rural Canada. The potential to revitalize journalism within a community via online technologies by both professional and citizen journalists is proposed as a positive alternative to the current configuration of large newspaper chains and broadcast conglomerates. It could also challenge community newspapers' reliance on uneven regional coverage too often comprised of boosterism, promotional stories, fundraisers, and advertorials.

Most of Canada's eleven hundred community newspapers have a website. However, most of these sites reflect the regional approach driven by the economics of community newspaper publishing, which demands large geographical areas to create a critical mass for advertising and a level of profitability suitable for a conglomerate. This can come at the cost of diminishing the role news media play in reflecting the cultural and social identities of the communities being served. Many proud, historic newspapers once served small-scale communities by playing an integral role in developing and maintaining local identity and enhancing social capital, as some hyperlocal sites are already doing in many countries, such as the United States and the United Kingdom (Metzgar et al. 2011; Openly Local 2015).

Hyperlocal news sites present an opportunity to provide underserved communities with news and information. In some cases, these sites are the sole source of journalism for their communities. In others, they complement and even compete with existing news organizations. By leveraging the comparatively lower costs of online publishing, along with interactive features to enhance the diversity of voices and discourse, hyperlocal news represents a model worth exploring.

Hyperlocal News

Studies of hyperlocal news fall under the umbrella of community journalism in the research literature, a category featuring two principal themes. The first examines community journalism in its relationship to members of civil society (i.e., citizens, interest groups, etc.), while the second is dedicated to the interaction of community news organizations with the institutions and structural imperatives of local communities. There are a number of subthemes, including forms of community media and definitions of community journalism that go beyond mere geography and start to explore communities of interest. Rural newspapers are typically associated with community journalism, whereas news media serving suburbs, urban neighbourhoods, and cultural communities defined by race, ethnicity, gender, and/or sexual orientation are emerging as part of the research agenda (Rosenberry 2011, 25).

Research conducted in the 1950s looked at community ties between rural newspapers and their audiences. From the work done by sociologist Morris Janowitz (1952), local newspapers were perceived as mechanisms to seek and maintain local consensus through an emphasis on common values, as opposed to sites where conflicting values might be resolved. As forms of mass communication, community newspapers were interrelated with personal communications and social connections, linking the newspaper's personnel, community leaders, and the audience. It was up to local news to help individuals navigate the complicated world of organizations, institutions, and activities at a neighbourhood level. It was up to the news media to emphasize community routines, promote the status quo, avoid controversy, and support social rituals.

Janowitz's arguments were echoed by Keith R. Stamm in 1985. In *Newspaper Use and Community Ties*, he underlines the importance of local news as a mechanism for integrating individuals and social groups, like families, into a community's social network (Stamm 1985). Much like Benedict Anderson (1984), Stamm contends community is an imagined construct and it is up to local news media to represent not merely a range of news items, but also the particular values and aspirations of the community they serve. Stamm argues that community-based news media have a fundamental role in local democracy, ensuring citizen involvement through the presentation of a plurality of ideas, not just those of institutions and elites. His approach has been developed further in recent years as other scholars explore the shared symbolism of meaning facilitated by local news and its ability to ensure a diversity of voices (see Lowrey 2011; Miller et al. 2012).

The public journalism movement in the United States sought to reconnect news media with citizens through direct engagement. Proponents, like New York University professor Jay Rosen and newspaper publisher Buzz Merritt, aimed to re-establish journalism's ties to democratic governance, allowing the interests and concerns of citizens to drive news coverage (Merritt et al. 1997). As a lens for viewing the relationship between news organizations and audiences, public journalism serves as a model for community journalism scholars, even if the practice found little traction among community newspapers.

Other researchers have adopted a political-economic perspective, arguing local news media merely serve their own powerful elite within the community. They argue community journalism is reduced to boosterism for the maintenance of traditional power structures (see Lowrey et al. 2008, 277; Barney 1996). The propaganda and influence models, whereby news media impose the values of the social, economic, and political elite, are placed within the framework of community journalism. The outcome is a type of journalism that avoids controversy, promotes the status quo, and supports existing economic, political, and social structures. Community journalism has the potential to be an ongoing process of engagement where social change and control can be mediated by community journalists who bring disparate views to audiences.

The emergence of hyperlocal news as a form of online community journalism opens the research to discussions of new technologies and their impact. The literature reflects this trend. Hyperlocal news is not just about coverage of a small geographical area, but also the expression of an attitude. It is about providing a voice for the community, a theme already applied to literature related to traditional community-based news media. When websites devoted to hyperlocal news emerged, they were devoted to creating content about important local issues such as education and transportation. More scholarly efforts define hyperlocal news as something beyond the traditional confines of community newspapers merely being published online (see Kurpius et al. 2010; Metzgar et al. 2011). Instead, this research suggests hyperlocal news represents a wide range of community-based activities aimed at supplementing, challenging, and/or changing the operating principles, structures, financing, and cultural forms of journalism and the news industry. It moves away from the boosterism and promotional styles of journalism and works to recapture the watchdog function. In one of the few scholarly attempts to wrestle with a definition of hyperlocal news, Metzgar et al. (2011) state, "Hyperlocal media operations are geographically based, community-oriented, original news-reporting organizations indigenous to the Web and intended to fill perceived gaps in coverage of an issue or region and to promote civic engagement" (774).

New media technologies have opened up numerous opportunities for better interaction between audiences and news producers. Interaction is enhanced by features that create expectations of a news ecosystem where information is delivered via a range of platforms with interactive features, including hyperlinks, live streaming, aggregation, social media applications, live chats, and discussion forums, allowing individuals to explore news as superficially or as thoroughly as they require. This challenges the traditional skill set of journalists and emphasizes new technical skills. It also alters journalistic practices. Rather than seeking to inform, explain, and interpret news, journalists seek to educate, engage, and empower audiences using the technological tools available (see Francoeur, chapter 7, and King et al., chapter 9, in this volume). In this way, journalists interact with audiences as partners seeking sources and expertise. Together, the parties educate each other on issues through engagement, empowering citizens to act both by raising awareness of community concerns and by participating in their resolution (Mensing 2010). Hyperlocal news is well suited to meet these requirements to educate, engage, and empower.

Methodological Approach

This study adopts an action research approach to addressing the practical concerns of people in the community. A hyperlocal news site (http://consider-this.ca) was created by researcher/journalist Robert Washburn for the town of Cobourg, located on the shores of Lake Ontario roughly 100 kilometres east of Toronto, in November 2010. Originally established by Washburn in 1997, the site had previously been used as an experimental online space for professional/personal skill development, a place to publish academic work, archive columns written for a local newspaper, and other journalism projects.

The site was transformed into an independent hyperlocal news site to provide an alternative to the town's two community newspapers, its local radio station, and several news blogs serving the community. The task of providing news coverage for the town of 18,500 people was undertaken by Washburn with the help of citizen journalists. The purpose of the project was to gain first-hand knowledge of the opportunities and pitfalls of the hyperlocal news model.

A series of events and interactions with the community inspired the development and subsequent study, *Consider This*. During the October 2010 municipal election campaign, several regular returning audience members voiced their excitement about the local coverage provided by *Consider This*. An election night panel was created on 25 October 2010 for the purpose of discussing the election results reported by the mainstream media.

A live blogging event on the *Consider This* website was held, using free CoverItLive software, for the purpose of creating a synchronous live chat forum for community members. While the majority of participants were audience members who were present on the site and interested in being part of the election night discussion, two participants were recruited to animate the discussion: a local communications consultant and a former political staff member for the federal and provincial Liberal parties, who was a retired community activist and worked at the local Legal Aid centre. They were selected because of their knowledge of local politics, their high profiles, and the fact they were rarely given voice in the mainstream media. The chat was promoted via social media as a hyperlocal journalism event.

Cobourg used online voting software for the first time in the 2010 municipal election. A major glitch occurred around 6 p.m. and voters had difficulty casting ballots in the last two hours before the polls were to close. There was no real-time mainstream media coverage of the voting problems. One of the *Consider This* chat participants shared the information, discussion ensued, and confirmation was sought. Frustration was growing among some of the chat participants and the communications consultant decided he would go to the town hall to find out what was going on. Armed with his laptop and a wireless mobile "turbo stick," he provided from the returning office live updates on the status of the online voting problem. A lively discussion ensued and several chat participants asked questions. Once the technical issues were resolved, the communications consultant decided to stay and switched to reporting results, acting as a citizen journalist.

Another participant in the CoverItLive event decided to go to the town hall and join the action. The two paired up and expanded the coverage. Together they provided interviews with candidates and commentary, and the live blog audience participated in energetic discussion and analysis of the information posted. For instance, audience members shared their frustrations with the online voting crisis. One woman wrote an email of appreciation, claiming the live blog coverage enabled her to learn of a decision by municipal returning officers to extend the voting deadline. This allowed her to go online and cast a ballot.

For nearly two hours, forty-nine people were involved in the live blog. Beyond the actual returns, the discussion covered a wide range of topics, including voting problems, tourism, and the revitalization of a closed movie theatre. Participants also explored various other community issues and the impact of the results in addressing citizen concerns towards ongoing and future civic matters.

The enthusiasm created by this initial foray was the genesis of a larger initiative to transform *Consider This* into a hyperlocal news site and to

undertake a formal academic research project. With the new municipal council taking office on 11 January 2011, two volunteers, acting as
citizen journalists, joined *Consider This*. One volunteer, the consultant,
offered to attend town council meetings regularly on Monday nights to
record the proceedings in a live blog. The retired community activist
decided to freelance articles on a diverse range of local topics, providing
an alternative voice to mainstream coverage. This included a series on
a train derailment, stories on mental health services in the community,
and social justice issues such as welfare reform. Within a few weeks, a
local business owner joined the project, offering commentary on local
economic issues. He left after two months, citing conflicts between his
contributions and his personal commitments. Another retired community activist with more conservative views joined, but filed only a single
commentary on downtown parking and promptly left, saying he had
nothing else to write about.

During the initial phase, a number of technical changes were made to
the website, which used the WordPress software hosted by an independent Internet service provider (ISP). A new template more suited to the
delivery of news was used, moving away from the previous two-col-
umn blog format. It provided a multiple-block, magazine format associated with major urban news websites. Additional open source tools
were added to provide enhanced functionality, giving prominence to
the live blogs and simplifying technical issues related to sharing content. An events calendar, stronger site security, and tracking tools were
also added. When complete, the site mirrored the look and functionality
of a community news website.

The early role of the researcher/journalist was to provide technical
support, act as editor, and provide training to the citizen journalists
on a part-time basis. Assignments were discussed and agreed upon in
advance with topics originating with the citizen journalists. Beyond the
technical support for the live blogs, the researcher/journalist's role was
to act each Monday night as a facilitator, stimulating discussions and
adding contextual information, links to primary documents, minutes
from previous meetings, historical background on issues, and related
news articles, while the citizen journalist typed the proceedings. This
produced a rich information environment, allowing the audience to follow the council's debates, understand the topics, and participate in a
live discussion.

During some of the earlier meetings, Twitter was used instead of the
CoverItLive chat. This experiment was meant to explore how audiences

used Twitter technology and to determine whether more people might participate. The Twitter feed was imported into Storify aggregation software and presented as alternative event coverage, since it mirrored the format of a traditional newspaper story of a council meeting. Text could be added to form bridges between the various elements. If done in a logical fashion, the materials could form a narrative similar to a news story. It was used quite effectively for background stories or sidebars. *Consider This* published a series of profiles on candidates for the 2011 provincial election.

From the beginning, *Consider This* sought to provide quality journalism using a multimedia approach, with text, images, audio, and video, as well as a more diverse range of stories and formats compared with the existing news media. It presented meeting coverage using Twitter and live blogs, along with alternative storytelling tools (e.g., Storify) for efficiency and to redirect energies towards under-reported or ignored topics to provide depth. The site provided unprecedented interactive opportunities for participation through social media, including Facebook, Twitter, live blogs, comments, features, and email. It also provided content subjected to a more thorough verification process than that provided by local bloggers.

In May 2011, the researcher/journalist joined the project full-time and began reporting as a multimedia journalist, providing mainly political/institutional coverage based on an assessment of staff resources, conversations with citizen journalists, and consultations with audience members via social media. The focus of the hyperlocal news would remain political/institutional coverage, along with some commentary and analysis. The site provided no traditional community features (profiles, stories about non-profits, service clubs, charities, or fundraisers), sports, or entertainment news.

Stories were told via the media form – text, images, audio, video – judged most appropriate to their content. Most stories combined text and images, but several video stories were produced due to the highly visual nature of the content. Meetings were covered using live blogs. One to two stories per day were generated on average.

Consider This sought to provide quality coverage of stories not picked up by the local mainstream press. There are two newspapers in Cobourg. One is owned by Metroland and the other by Sun Media. One newspaper is delivered five days per week, while the other is biweekly. The newspapers have three to five reporters along with numerous contributions from community volunteers and organizations. One publication, called *SNAP*, is a franchised newspaper chain, using only photographs with descriptive cutlines from events in the community. *SNAP* uses volunteer labour and the owners, a husband and wife, do the majority of the work. There are two regional radio stations owned by the same independent company. The radio stations offer minimal news coverage, providing mostly music. Finally, there are three bloggers focusing on Cobourg politics.

Consider This faced a formidable challenge in a relatively media-rich environment. Nonetheless, there were numerous gaps in Cobourg's local news coverage. A good example was the East Pier story involving the local Rotary Club's Canada Day celebrations. It was noted by a member of the town staff at a Monday night council meeting a month before Canada Day that the east pier in the harbour had deteriorated to the point that public safety was a concern. The town hired experts to conduct tests and the pier was deemed safe. However, tensions rose between the Rotary Club and council during the intervening weeks as public concern grew. *Consider This* was the only news outlet to track the story at each stage of its development, providing pictures and following up as discussions took place, until the matter was resolved.

Another under-reported area consisted of the committees of council through which individual politicians consult citizen advisory groups and make recommendations to council. Often, committee deliberations are where policy proposals are developed and first debated. When these deliberations are covered, citizens have greater opportunity to become familiar with community issues, to consider policy proposals, and provide input before the proposals come to full council meetings ready for adoption.

The committee coverage involved creating live blogs for each meeting attended and then following up the coverage with value-added features and analysis. The live blog was used in the place of simple, event-based stories. This freed resources for deeper coverage of specific topics coming out of the committee meetings, as well as providing unprecedented opportunities for live interactive discussions. Several times, when a committee meeting was promoted in advance using social media, audience members commented on topics during the meetings.

For major stories receiving mainstream coverage, it was important to provide greater depth and follow-up. An example of this was the Ontario Heritage Conference, an annual event during which preservationists, planners, and experts share information about saving local buildings of architectural significance. The mainstream media provided advance stories announcing the event and some minor coverage when the conference was over. *Consider This* provided extensive daily coverage over three days with live blogs of keynote speakers and panels. Participants used social media throughout the conference. There were a number of people using Twitter as panelists spoke. Others were posting to Facebook and other websites. At the end of the conference, a number of the participants summarized the key ideas and discussions. These were aggregated into a Storify format and presented as an alternative to a traditional wrap-up story.

Consider This coverage continued for four months. In September 2011, a reassessment was done in consultation with the same individuals involved in the launch, keeping with the action research approach. The role of the researcher/journalist was reduced to part-time once more. Fewer stories were posted, but live blogs of council meetings and freelance articles carried on at the same pace. By November 2011, council meeting coverage stopped due to a lack of time and interest by both the audience and the citizen journalist involved. The citizen journalist's contribution decreased due to time constraints, work, and personal matters. It seemed logical to identify this point as the end of the first phase of the project, as it marked nearly one year of activity.

The site continues to be active on this basis. However, the templates were reverted to blog format and features associated with a news website were reduced. As described earlier, the site functions as an experimental online space for personal and professional skill development and as a platform to publish columns written for a local chain of newspapers. It seemed reasonable to allow it to return to this function once the project ended its first phase.

Monetizing

The news industry continues to seek a sustainable financial model for online journalism. Hyperlocal journalism faces the same challenge of monetizing online news in the face of growing audience interest in digital content of all kinds. In testimony before the Joint Economic Committee hearings on the future of newspapers in the United States, Tom Rosenstiel said the combined audiences of online and print newspaper readers were growing in 2009, thus having positive effects on levels of online advertising revenue (Joint Economic Committee 2009). The challenge is not to attract audiences, but to rethink the traditional advertising-based business model, combined with the high costs of providing online news often associated with large urban news organizations.

As news industry analyst Ken Doctor (2012) suggests, it is easy to get cynical about hyperlocal news in the face of current business conditions within the news industry. The *MinnPost*, a hyperlocal publication in Minnesota, is offered as an example of a successful online news site using an alternative funding model. It raised US$1.5 million in revenue in 2011, giving the company its first surplus of US$21,000 in its four-year history (Phelps 2012). Patch, the franchise of hyperlocal news sites in the United States operated by AOL, is struggling. Early forecasts for 2012 predicted that it would surpass its entire revenue for 2011, just in the first quarter of the new year (Gillette 2012). The company reportedly lost US$100 million in 2011, but it continues to publish in an attempt to reach audiences by offering more participation in gathering news and creating business directories for communities (Carlson 2011).

Success stories are few and far between. Critics argue that hyperlocal news is not financially viable and current projects are unsustainable (Washburn 2011). The recent closures of hyperlocal news projects operated by the *Washington Post*, the *New York Times*, and the Gannett Corporation have sent trembles through the industry.

Consider This did not attempt to monetize the project. Resources and time were limited, and it was perceived to be a huge commitment to identify and implement a fiscal model, while at the same time bringing sufficient resources to managing, producing, editing, and posting news content. However, this is an issue that could be addressed in future studies.

Consider This received no direct funding, but was supported by Loyalist College in Belleville, Ontario, eagle.ca, a local Internet service provider, and the donation of citizen journalists' time and resources. All software used was either free and open source or pre-installed on the computer hardware. Mileage was tracked, along with other small, related costs. The total was less than $250. The matter of how much time an individual would need to pursue any type of business model was identified as a significant problem. It was enough each day to generate content, let alone find time to pursue sponsors or advertisers. However, the research shows there are many alternatives to traditional economic models worthy of investigation.

Hyperlocal news sites' monetizing efforts have been met with mixed results as the implementation of traditional advertising models is not likely to ensure the profitability of online news. Hyperlocal sites are looking beyond advertising to sponsorships, individual and corporate memberships, foundation grants, fundraising, and non-news sources such as staging public events, to become sustainable. Other successful hyperlocal news sites include *Baristanet*, *The Bay Citizen*, *Community Impact*, and the *Voice of San Diego*. Hyperlocal sites can also use themed issues, events, online coupons, and advertising directories as income sources.

Another approach is crowd-funding, whereby entrepreneurs post a proposal to a website and people donate money to realize the project. Two American hyperlocal news sites, *Charlottesville Tomorrow* and *Homicide Watch DC*, used Kickstarter in 2012 to raise money. There are a number of crowd-funding sites, including IndieGogo, Razoo, GoJournalism, and Spot.us, where funding can be raised for a single story or an entire website.

A small survey of local politicians, community opinion leaders, and municipal staff was completed as part of the action research methodology to seek input from stakeholders (see Appendix B). Of the twenty-seven respondents, all sourced their local news via the traditional community newspaper. One-third supplemented this source by reading blogs. In addition, 15 per cent said they accessed social media like Twitter and Facebook for local news. Almost none of the respondents turned to local news sources for provincial, national, and international news, instead using mainstream media for this type of information. Nearly half of the respondents visited *Consider This* during the project, with fewer than 20 per cent visiting several times per week, but not daily. The vast majority, 81 per cent, came on an occasional basis. More than 80 per cent of respondents said traditional local news sources affected their decision making, 51 per cent said blogs or other online news sources, including social media, influenced them. Without question, local news coverage was considered important to the community. Notably, 97 per cent of respondents said online news was an importance source for the community. Finally, 65 per cent said hyperlocal news sites like *Consider This* will be important to the community in the future.

Discussion

The *Consider This* project experienced challenges, but met with enough success to be optimistic about its role. The contribution of citizen journalists was essential to the success of the first phase. The top five hits during this time were three stories by citizen journalists, the live blog coverage of council meetings, and a parking story. The stories most shared via social media (mainly Twitter and Facebook) were three stories done by a citizen journalist on welfare reform. The Canadian federal election in May 2011 received the highest combination of page views (120) and average time spent on a single page (just over 10 minutes), making it a highlight for the project. The live blog of the federal election results, similar to the municipal panel six months earlier, was the day with the single highest number of visits (443). A total of 18,063 page views took place over the length of the first phase, with one-third of those identified as regular, returning visitors; the remainder were one-time visitors. The average time spent on the site was one minute, 56 seconds.

This can be considered a fair performance for a site serving a community of 18,500 people. A Pew Center survey in 2012 showed that about 2 per cent of rural audiences in the United States get news from blogs and similar sites, as compared with 20 per cent who use the local newspaper site (Miller et al. 2012). By this measure, the *Consider This* site drew a reasonably sized audience. The number of returning visitors means there is a core of regular readers. The length of stay indicates people were reading articles and not simply scanning pages.

With the number of free websites, open source software, and abundant training tools online, an individual can create a hyperlocal news operation with little upfront investment and minimal technical skill. Certainly, franchise-style opportunities exist, like Patch in the United States, but there are no similar opportunities in Canada. There is a sufficient number of sites like Blogger and WordPress, where a fully functional, basic site can be created in three clicks of a mouse. An aggressive search of Internet service providers also reveals low-cost opportunities to host sites using open source software like WordPress, Joomla, and Drupal, for the more technically literate. There is a diverse range of free templates for news or magazine-style online publications. Instructions can be found in a multitude of training websites, which are also freely accessible. Tools for creating multimedia content are also freely available, along with a long list of applications for tablets and smart phones for use as a mobile journalist, which seemed to be the preferred method of reporting during the project.

There was a serious effort to use alternative storytelling approaches during the project. Stories were presented with multidimensional digital material, but not all media were used. Given more time and different subject matter, it could be expanded. Highly interactive multimedia or data journalism, even investigative stories, were beyond the time and resources of the project. Aggregators like Storify were excellent tools for creating content in an efficient and cost-effective manner as replacements for event coverage. This allowed for resources to be used to follow up on items arising out of the meeting or event in an effort to increase the quality of journalism. Social media were used to break news and offer interactive opportunities for audience members to share information.

The contribution of citizen journalists was important for the project. The ability to cover the weekly council meetings via a live blog was a worthwhile initiative and could have grown given more time. The audience was not always interested in viewing the event in the moment, but there were a number who read the archived version. Interactivity is an attractive attribute of a hyperlocal site, but it appeared there was a small, dedicated group who attended regularly with a small number coming and going as issues arose on the council agenda. Most were voyeurs, only watching the discussions, as only one or two regulars made comments.

There is no question citizen journalists expanded the audience and reach of *Consider This*. As the community activist wrote pieces, the numbers indicated the items were popular and shared. This seems to support hyperlocal news advocates and theorists who promote the significance of community involvement. Working with volunteers is not always easy, as demonstrated by the two citizen journalists who wrote briefly for the project and quit. However, a good community outreach plan with regular soliciting of potential individuals makes sense, especially when particular issues arise in the community and ignite controversy.

Crisis is a catalyst for hyperlocal news. As the election coverage demonstrates, significant events generate readership. The demand for information increases and hyperlocal news rises in importance. There is nothing particularly surprising here since that is true for all news organizations. While the project did not encounter a hot-button issue, subsequent research has shown how a community will turn to local online resources to mobilize support and debate issues, especially during major events and breaking news moments (see Hu et al. 2013; Paulussen and D'heer 2013).

The decision to focus on political and institutional news due to limited time and resources was a significant one as it brought into stark contrast the notion that traditional community news media often provide diverse content, including social activities, service club events, philanthropic groups, sports, arts, entertainment, and so forth. The notion of creating a paper of record, where one source could be considered comprehensive, seemed daunting. However, while the site lacked the variety typical of community journalism, there was a recognition that the opportunity for many different news sources in a single community could exist. Local bloggers could also play an important role by being involved in the journalistic coverage. The inclination of the reporters is also a factor in limiting coverage if the expertise or interest is not available.

Sustainability is an important element of such a project. Financial, technical, and human resources are huge factors. As the literature shows, the size and sophistication of hyperlocal news operations are scalable. Large corporations find it difficult to cover kittens stuck in trees, yet this is the demand of hyperlocal news. Audiences also want quality, but few sites can afford to provide it. And volunteers are problematic because their interests, skills, and commitment must all be properly managed. The rules of business can be harsh masters, as hyperlocal sites struggle to find workable models. The most tantalizing opportunity was the realization that businesses are interested in supporting hyperlocal news for philanthropic and altruistic reasons, similar to the way they sponsor local sports and service groups. This is worthy of more examination in the future.

Recommendations

If hyperlocal news is going to be successful, regional and national journalism associations must acknowledge it as a category for professional development and awards. These and other journalism organizations already support local and community journalism and should see this kind of backing as reinforcing and acknowledging the expanding types of journalism being practised in this context.

Funding should also be made available to set up an online incubator to help Canadian journalists begin producing hyperlocal news sites under new business initiatives, similar to the Knight Foundation and J-Lab. A homegrown cooperative effort among Canadian academic institutions, the news industry, and government could serve as a launch point. This might provide services such as editorial support, technical training, and business development counselling, as well as identifying communities in need to match them with journalists.

Regional economic development programs, which mainly support manufacturing, retail, and other traditional businesses, need to be expanded to include media enterprises. The Federal Business Innovation grant under the Canada Periodical Fund, which focuses on magazines and digital versions of magazines, could have its parameters expanded to encompass hyperlocal news sites.

Finally, the formation of advertising co-operatives, similar to the Ontario Community Newspaper program AdReach, might open opportunities whereby hyperlocal news providers could pool resources to pursue shared revenues generated through a centralized agency whose sole purpose is to find advertisers looking to target communities.

Conclusion

Hyperlocal news deserves a place within the discourse regarding the evolution of news and its future. It represents a potential alternative for underserved communities in Canada. There is reason for optimism in the face of serious challenges. The *Consider This* project is a first step in identifying the challenges and wrestling with solutions in the context of rural Ontario. The use of new and emerging technologies provides practical tools and potential platforms for the effective and cost-efficient creation and distribution of local news. With sufficient support by industry and governments, hyperlocal news could flourish more quickly than if it is left alone to find its own way within the confusing, often contradictory, efforts of large, mainstream news conglomerates. Innovative approaches like hyperlocal journalism might be drowned out by bigger, better-financed, and higher-profile initiatives of news corporations that do not address the social and cultural needs of communities. Canadians living in rural areas, along with those living in identifiable neighbourhoods of large urban centres, could see hyperlocal news as a means to be informed about issues impacting them where they live, providing opportunities to speak out and be engaged, while also enabling them to find solutions.

The *Consider This* project grew spontaneously out of an identified grassroots response to ongoing activity within a community. The original intent was grand when it was formulated: to explore hyperlocal news as a viable option for news coverage in rural communities. By the end of the study, the goal of viability was deemed to be overly ambitious. The action research methodology was particularly useful in this manner, since the experience of conducting the project exposed the limits of time and resources. It took hyperlocal journalism away from a strictly theoretical exercise into a far more practical one, creating an enlightening praxis. The involvement of citizen journalists was critical and a vital, popular component of the project. But it was difficult to sustain interest and commitment in the face of the participants' everyday lives. The question of long-term viability remains unresolved.

As the news industry continues to be transformed, hyperlocal news should be part of the ongoing discussion about keeping community journalism alive in Canada. Despite its faults and identified shortcomings, having a vibrant, reliable, accurate, informative, and interactive news source remains a vital component of community identity.

Sustainability is critical, but so is innovation. Journalist entrepreneurs and inventive news organizations must come to the table and be willing to take risks and think outside the traditional models to be successful. What will work for one community may not work for others. Further study is critical to further explore sustainability, but also practical applications of the hyperlocal news model.

Appendix A

Ontario Community Newspaper Association Ownership and Titles Statistics, 1998–2011

	1998	1999	2000	2001	2002	2003
Independent owners: 1 paper	96	86	82	79	83	79
Independent owners: 2–5 papers	23	26	24	23	22	22
Independent owners: up to 12 papers	6	3	1	2	2	3
Total independent titles	125	115	107	104	107	104
Number of independent titles		163	135	122	155	147
Corporate groups	4	4	4	4	5	4
Number of corporate titles		101	122	185	117	106
Total owners		119	111	106	112	108
Total titles	266	264	257	257	272	263

2004	2005	2006	2007	2008	2009	2010	2011	Vary
75	68	70	72	78	77	77	76	−21
25	20	19	17	16	15	15	14	−39
2	1	2	3	2	2	3	2	−67
102	92	91	92	96	94	96	92	−26
157	128	140	151	150	145	147	129	−21
4	4	4	4	4	4	4	4	0
118	161	162	173	175	166	168	195	93
106	93	95	96	100	98	100	96	−19
274	289	302	324	325	311	315	324	22

Appendix B

Online Community Survey – January 2012

How often do you consume local news?

Daily
Several times per week
Weekly
Not at all

Where do you source your local news?

Newspapers
Radio
Television
Magazines
Blogs
Social Media
Other

When you are seeking news other than local (provincial, national, international), where do you find it?

Local news sources (*Northumberland Today*, Northumberland News, radio, television)
Major mainstream news sources (*Toronto Star*, *Globe and Mail*, *National Post*, CBC, CTV)
Alternative media sources (favourite bloggers, Truthdig, Reddit, StumbleUpon)

Did you consume news from the *Consider This* hyperlocal news site during any time in 2011?

Yes
No

If you did use *Consider This*, how often did you visit?

Daily
Several times per week
Occasionally

How important are the news media in your decision making as a community leader?

Not important
Neutral
Somewhat important
Important
Very important

How important are blogs or other online media, including social media, in your decision making as a community leader?

Not important
Neutral
Somewhat important
Important
Very important

How important is local coverage for the community?

Not important
Neutral
Somewhat important
Important
Very important

How important are online local news media coverage for the community?

Not important
Neutral
Somewhat important
Important
Very important

How important are hyperlocal news websites like *Consider This* to the community in the future?

Not important
Neutral
Somewhat important
Important
Very important

11 Aboriginal Media in Australia and Canada and the Implications for Journalism Practice

MICHAEL MEADOWS

In this chapter, I will focus on a particular subsector of the Australian community broadcasting industry that serves diverse audiences in Aboriginal and Torres Strait Islander communities across the country. In particular, I want to identify how an Indigenous public sphere operates to authorize and encourage Aboriginal and Torres Strait Islander communities to incorporate media technologies like radio and television into their community social structures and, thus, their lives. A greater understanding of the existence and operation of this "parallel universe" is highly likely to facilitate more informed and reliable journalism practices in relation to this fraught sector of Australian and Canadian society.

There are strong parallels between the Australian and Canadian Aboriginal broadcasting sectors. In Canada, the Aboriginal Peoples Television Network (APTN), along with an estimated three hundred community radio stations, serve Native communities mostly across the North. This complex network has allowed disparate First Nations communities to find their voices despite the plethora of mainstream cable and satellite television channels and radio stations accessible by Canadian audiences. The parallels between Aboriginal innovation and development in Australia and Canada are striking. For example, satellite-delivered radio in remote northern parts of British Columbia helps to link more than eighty Gitskan Wet'suwet'en communities to each other, to the rest of Canada, and beyond, in the same way that a satellite-delivered radio network links Aboriginal and Torres Strait Islander communities across northern Australia. Of course, the communication networks that link Aboriginal communities in both countries extend well beyond these examples (Molnar and Meadows

2001; Roth 2005; Forde et al. 2009; see also King et al., chapter 9 in this volume).

But what does this have to do with journalism? I suggest that an appreciation of Indigenous public spheres and the "parallel voices" (Valaskakis 1993) that constitute them not only offers the opportunity for greater understanding of Aboriginal affairs, but also challenges existing journalism practices to adapt to help audiences to make sense of First Nations peoples' ideas and assumptions about the world. In terms of the latter project, mainstream journalism in both countries has a poor historical record (Avison and Meadows 2000; Meadows 2000; Molnar and Meadows 2001; Forde et al. 2009).

The Australian community-broadcasting sector has experienced extraordinary growth in the past three decades, in terms of both the number of licensed stations and the size of their audiences. In 2012, more than five hundred free-to-air radio and television services reached a national audience of 9.5 million people in an average month. More than 4.5 million listeners tuned into a local community radio station each week, with just over 700,000 Australians identified as exclusive listeners to a community radio station in their area, attracting audience numbers that far exceed those in comparable developed countries globally. The community television audience is much smaller, with the sector struggling since its inception, reaching around four million viewers. The sector has been described as the country's largest media literacy workshop, training more than 7,500 people each year in aspects of media production, administration, and management. There are more than 23,000 volunteers who make a significant contribution to creating, maintaining, and advancing local cultures in various ways. The sector produces more local content, more Australian music, and reflects a greater diversity of Australian cultures than its commercial and government-funded national broadcasting counterparts (Forde et al. 2003, 2009; Community Broadcasting Foundation 2009).

Audiences tune into community radio across Australia for four main reasons: local news and information; specialist and diverse music formats; its ability to connect communities; and to represent Australia's cultural diversity (Forde et al. 2002, 2009; Meadows et al. 2007). The evidence suggests that the community-broadcasting sector in Australia – and radio in particular – is performing a significant cultural role at a number of levels. Drawn from more than a decade of sector research, the evidence suggests that it is the nature of the relationships between audiences and producers that not only defines community radio in

Australia (and elsewhere), but also enables particular community connection processes to function (Forde et al. 2009; Meadows and Foxwell 2011). By association, it suggests that mainstream media – and journalism – has much to learn from the ways in which the community sector has managed to imagine local audiences and to enlist their participation in the broader processes of democracy. At a time when trust of mainstream media in Canada, Australia, the United Kingdom, the United States, Ireland, and Northern Ireland are at an all-time low (Hanitzsch 2013), it is worthwhile exploring the modus operandi of a sector that is perhaps too often overlooked because of its perceived peripheral nature.

As with its Canadian counterpart, the community-broadcasting sector in Australia can be likened to the country's largest language laboratory, broadcasting programs in more than a hundred Indigenous and ethnic community languages. Many of these marginalized communities rely on local, non-profit radio and/or television as their primary sources of information about events that affect their daily lives. This is especially the case for Indigenous people where, in remote communities, English might be a second, third, or fourth language. Like Canada, most First Nations people in Australia live in urban centres with the local, Indigenous-produced radio and television emanating from these sites as important as those emerging from the "bush" communities (Community Broadcasting Foundation 2009; Meadows 2010).

Coming on the heels of almost two decades of research into Aboriginal and Torres Strait Islander media production and processes, the first audience study of the sector, completed in 2007, confirmed that Indigenous media offer an essential service to communities and play a central organizing role in community life (Meadows 1988, 1994, 1998, 2001, 2005; Meadows et al. 2007; Forde et al. 2009; Meadows and Foxwell 2011).

As I suggested earlier, the parallels with – and implications for – Canada are profound. Although the study that is the focus of this chapter was confined to the Australian continent, it reveals much about First Nations audiences' perceptions of media as well as offering a critique of mainstream journalism and media practices that tend to marginalize or ignore Aboriginal perspectives. A growing body of evidence stemming from studies of minority media globally suggests that the voices of the marginalized – whether First Nations or multicultural minorities – should now be acknowledged as integral elements of everyday life (Downing and Husband 2005; Browne and Uribe-Jongbloed 2013, 25–6). In one recent Canadian case, this quest has been advanced; use of social media enabled a higher proportion of Indigenous and alternative voices to be heard by enlisting social media platforms like Twitter (Callison and Hermida forthcoming).

Indigenous (First Nations) Public Spheres

The power and influence of mainstream media – and journalism – continue to transform the wider public sphere, compelling First Nations people to seek access to their own media for various reasons: providing an essential service to communities; maintaining social networks; providing education, particularly for young people; offering alternative sources of news and information that eschew stereotypes; building cross-cultural bridges with the non-Indigenous community; and offering a crucial platform for Indigenous music and dance (Roth 2005; Meadows et al. 2007; Forde et al. 2009). Bickford (1996, 4) reminds us that "both speaking and listening are central activities of citizenship," and it is clear that Aboriginal media enable these activities in ways that differentiate them from mainstream approaches.

How effective are existing mainstream journalism practices in this regard? Studies of mainstream representation of First Nations peoples in Australia and North America suggest significant flaws (Alia et al. 1996; Weston 1996; Meadows 2001; Alia 2010). Primarily in response, a global trend of increased use of community media by marginalized groups has been influenced by recognition of the potential for using media as tools for cultural and political empowerment – effectively allowing the dispossessed the capacity to "speak as well as hear" their own stories (Dowmunt 1993; Rodriguez et al. 2009). This process has been driven by several impulses: combatting stereotypes, addressing information gaps in non-Indigenous society, and reinforcing local community languages and cultures.

While in one sense this activity is at the periphery of mainstream conceptions of the public sphere, I will argue here that the implications are highly significant for the operation of the democratic public sphere. Rather than adopting the idea of a single, all-encompassing public sphere, we should think in terms of a series of parallel and overlapping public spheres, spaces where participants with similar cultural backgrounds engage in activities of importance to them. Each of us simultaneously has membership in several different public spheres, moving between and within them according to desire and obligation. In this way, these multiple spheres of activity articulate their own discursive styles and formulate their own positions on issues that are then brought to a wider public sphere where they are able to interact "across lines of cultural diversity" (Fraser 1990, 69; see also Avison and Meadows 2000).

Aboriginal social organization in Australia is bound up in the notion of "the Dreaming," which might be interpreted as referring to the law and a relationship to time and space in which ancestral beings' journeys across the landscape shape natural features and describe "Dreaming tracks." These pathways can also be considered to be information conduits or media, along which information and people travel, carrying goods for exchange and moving between ceremonial sites (Michaels 1986, 508).

Behind much of the impetus for the development of First Nations media production globally is the fear of *further* cultural and language loss because of the influence of mainstream media. Western-style media for most Indigenous people represent a double-edged sword – both a threat and a promise. Media technologies themselves represent a double-edged sword for minorities and have often been identified as purveyors of cultural imperialism; pioneering Inuit politician Rosemarie Kuptana once described mainstream satellite broadcasting into the Canadian North as "neutron bomb television" with her Australian counterpart, Aboriginal linguist Eve Fesl, likening satellite television broadcasts into remote Aboriginal communities to a "cultural nerve gas" (Molnar and Meadows 2001). But such technologies do not necessarily come with instructions on how they *must* be used, with all having the potential to become powerful community cultural resources enabling public sphere activity (Katz 1977). Such alternative media practices extend contemporary ideas of the public sphere and democracy. And there is considerable evidence to suggest Indigenous media producers have appropriated various media technologies to suit their own social and cultural needs. The foundation of this is functionality, that there must be a clear benefit flowing from the adoption of technologies of any kind (personal communication with author, Sept. 2000). This is especially the case in remote Indigenous communities that are commonly required to confront issues of survival on a daily basis. I am suggesting here that Indigenous media production – or "invention" as Michaels (1986) has described it – has contributed to a reconceptualizing of the notion of the public sphere.

A key influence on the quest by First Nations people for media empowerment is a continuing failure by the broader public sphere to account for their ideas and assumptions about the world. This has played a central role in the development of alternative media systems and alternative public spheres, including Indigenous public spheres (Fleras 2009). Audience reception has powerful political and cultural implications, so it should not be surprising to find that Indigenous audiences have responded in this way. At the same time as Indigenous voices remain suppressed in mainstream news coverage of events in which they are deeply implicated, Indigenous agency has been a crucial element of a global push for media access (Meadows 2001; Roth 2005). Valaskakis (1993) echoes the experiences of many Indigenous peoples when she concludes, "Today, we are all caught in a Web of conflicting interests and actions, confrontations constructed in dominant cultural and political process and the Native experience of exclusion, or stereotypical inclusion and appropriation. For people of the First Nations, this involves the subaltern experience rooted in the lived reality and the representation of the 'insider,' the 'outsider,' and the 'other.'" Valaskakis coined the term "parallel voices" to illustrate the idea of separate universes inhabited by Indigenous and non-Indigenous peoples sharing virtually the same physical spaces. The extraordinary differences between Indigenous and non-Indigenous media form and content are further evidence of their existence. Mainstream journalists covering Aboriginal affairs still seem to be grappling with the very existence of an Indigenous public sphere.

A critical element of the notion of the public sphere is in the relationships stemming from a shift in the role of the mass media, from centres of rational-critical discursive activity to commercialized vehicles for advertising and public relations, all of this within the context of the decline of the liberal public sphere in the nineteenth century. Habermas (1974, 29) describes the public sphere as "a realm of our social life in which something approaching public opinion can be formed." This early model was developed with acknowledgment of a strict separation between the public and private realms of society. But for Habermas, unrestricted access to the public sphere is a defining characteristic, with the role of the mass media a central element of the process.

The decline of the liberal public sphere, according to Habermas (1989), was hastened with a shift from the media being a forum for rational-critical debate for private citizens assembled to form "a public," to a privately owned and controlled institution that is easily manipulated by owners. Despite its flaws and critics, this public sphere model does offer ways of reconceptualizing the limits of democracy.

But for Fraser (1990), an important theoretical task is to "render visible the ways in which societal inequality infects formally exclusive existing public spheres and taints discursive interactions with them" (65). So her reconceived public sphere model theorizes it as a space where participants with similar cultural backgrounds can engage in discussions about issues and interests important to them, using their own discursive styles – and genres – and formulating their positions on various issues (Mercer 1989). It is then that these are able to be brought to a wider public sphere in which "members of different more limited publics talk across lines of cultural diversity" (Fraser 1990, 69).

This assumes the existence and operation of multiple public spheres where members of society who are subordinated or ignored – "subaltern counterpublics" (Fraser 1990, 67) – are able to deliberate among themselves. My concern here is with how Indigenous people continue to "make themselves" within their own public spheres and the implications that flow from this. To me, that is how Indigenous public spheres must be defined.

It is clear from the commentary from a wide cross-section of audiences for First Nations media that Indigenous public spheres should not be understood in terms of a non-dominant variant of the broader public sphere. Although they develop in close proximity to, and with a great deal of influence from, mainstream society, they should be seen as discrete formations that exist in a unique context as the product of contestation with the mainstream public sphere: parallel universes, perhaps. This has some resonance with Rodriguez's more recent notion of citizen media (Rodriguez 2002). While they operate within a dominant context, it is their "Indigenousness" that is the defining characteristic (Avison 1996). Indigenous public spheres can thus be seen as providing opportunities for people who are regularly subordinated and ignored by mainstream public sphere processes. They enable Indigenous people to deliberate together, to develop their own counter-discourses, and to interpret their own identities and experiences. This highlights the importance of seeing the notion of Aboriginality, or identity formation, as a dynamic process facilitated through dialogue (Langton 1993; Meadows 2005).

Indigenous public spheres might be defined in various ways: as sites of discursive activity like meetings and media production; as the process of public opinion formation; and as conceptual ideas, focusing on analysis of the phenomenon of the public sphere (Avison 1996; Avison and Meadows 2000; Meadows 2005). Indigenous public spheres are frames to be understood as existing on a variety of levels: clan, community/reserve, provincial/territorial, regional, urban, national, and international. They are also constituted, in some ways, by mainstream media. They are sites where Indigenous people find the information and resources they need to deliberate on issues of concern to them (Forde et al. 2009). In keeping with Habermas's principle of publicity, Indigenous public spheres are accessible to all citizens and, ideally, are spaces where the views of participants are judged and authorized, according to existing protocols, rather than relying on the status apportioned to a source by non-Indigenous journalism practices. In fact, the very nature of non-Indigenous journalistic inquiry – including the notion of editorial independence – is in direct conflict with traditional knowledge management processes in most First Nations societies. Storytelling, art, and music – even silence – are important ways in which people make their positions known, as are the particular ways in which they are presented. An ideal Indigenous public sphere accommodates such varied and culturally specific communicative styles. Indigenous public spheres are spaces that can accommodate a wide range of non-mainstream discursive styles and non-traditional perspectives. They are sites where collective self-determination can take place. They ideally engage in public dialogue where cultural values, political aspirations, and social concerns of participants are introduced into larger public spheres where they might influence discussions there, hence playing an important role in the broader processes of democracy (Avison 1996, 58; Avison and Meadows 2000; Meadows 2001, 2005; Fleras 2009).

Along with the physical size of communities, the values and institutions of oral societies – through practices such as gift exchange and sharing – play a key role in framing public sphere activity. As with the dynamic notion of identity, the nature of "traditional" Indigenous public spheres has waxed and waned according to the nature and extent of the dialogue with non-Indigenous society. It seems evident that many traditional Indigenous public spheres went into decline following European contact as a result of communities being marginalized and disenfranchised through their lack of access to information, land, and the control and management of their lives under colonial government. The enforced gathering of Indigenous people into settlements and missions played an important part in this and has been reflected in overwhelmingly mainstream media representations of Indigenous people since the European invasion of the Great South Land – the Australian continent – in 1788 (Meadows 2001).

However, the evidence from studies of Indigenous media production over the past twenty years or more suggests that community broadcasting in particular is challenging the established power base of mainstream media by empowering participants in various ways (Meadows 1993; Forde et al. 2009; Meadows and Foxwell 2011). It strengthens Rodriguez's (2002, 79) assertion that we should avoid defining alternative media – or in this case, Indigenous community broadcasting – in terms of its opposition to mainstream media and, rather, focus on the "transformative processes they bring about within their participants and their communities."

This directs our attention to considering the impact of community media within the context of people's everyday lives. Indigenous media form a central element in the representation of culture. The dissemination of different ideas and assumptions about the world, and the creation of a space in which to talk about such things, affirms a place for millions of Australians, both Indigenous and non-Indigenous, by validating their "whole way of life" (Williams 1977). This is an outcome that mainstream journalism still struggles to achieve.

Indigenous Media in Australia

The community broadcasting sector has proved to be a major communications outlet for Indigenous voices in Australia with around 130 licensed radio stations in remote, regional, and urban Australia, broadcasting about fourteen hundred hours of Indigenous content weekly. There is one Indigenous commercial radio station, 6LN, in Carnarvon in Western Australia, and one commercial television station, Imparja, based in Alice Springs in central Australia. Aboriginal and Torres Strait Islander people have won access to the airwaves following persistent campaigns. Most major urban and regional areas have an Indigenous broadcaster complementing existing media. In addition to the community stations, there are two Indigenous radio networks. The satellite-networked National Indigenous Radio Service (NIRS) was launched in 1996, enabling Indigenous community radio stations across Australia to either link into national programming or choose to broadcast locally. In 2001, the National Indigenous News Service (NINS) began operating out of Brisbane, providing a general, independent, national news service that features Indigenous stories and Indigenous perspectives on general news (Molnar and Meadows 2001; Community Broadcasting Foundation 2009).

An additional eighty Remote Indigenous Broadcasting Services (RIBS) served their communities in 2013 with a combination of radio and/or television in the most isolated parts of the continent. Most of the small, remote stations are engaged in retransmitting available satellite programming, both mainstream and community-produced. These RIBS units also rebroadcast the National Indigenous Television (NITV) service. Launched in 2007, NITV is similar to the Aboriginal Peoples Television Network in Canada, although its programming does not originate in a range of Native communities as with APTN. In terms of having a central production ethos, NITV is perhaps more akin to the Maori Television model in New Zealand, albeit operating on much less funding.

In 1988, Imparja Television became the first Indigenous-owned and managed commercial television service in Australia and, arguably, the world. Largely for financial reasons, Imparja is able to produce only a few hours of Indigenous content each week, but an Aboriginal-owned and -run Indigenous Community Television service (ICTV) began broadcasting from one of Imparja's spare satellite channels in 2001. This innovative service featured close to 100 per cent Indigenous content, produced mostly by small bush communities and often in local or regional languages. However, a federal government policy decision favoured NITV over ICTV, and the creative "bush" service was displaced from the airwaves, forcing it, initially, onto the Internet. The loss of their voices caused great concern among remote Indigenous communities at the time and led to the launch of Indigitube, a database of Indigenous-produced videos available for viewing online. Late in 2012, NITV moved to a digital channel on Australia's national multicultural broadcaster, the Special Broadcasting Service (SBS). Around the same time, ICTV relaunched on a new digital television channel; however, it is available only to audiences with satellite television access. As a result, most of Australia cannot view this pioneering, innovative Aboriginal television service (Meadows et al. 2007; Forde et al. 2009; Meadows 2010).

The vast majority of Indigenous media operations exist almost entirely on funds from federal government grants. About AU$16 million each year is distributed by the Community Broadcasting Foundation (CBF) for Indigenous community radio and television program production across the country. NITV was allocated AU$15 million as a one-year support grant in 2011, and this level of funding has remained static (Jackson 2010). As I suggested earlier, the numerous roles played by Indigenous radio and television in their communities makes this investment by government seem very modest, particularly when compared with funding for comparable First Nations media organizations. In Canada during the same period, APTN had an annual budget of Can$37.9 million with an additional Can$8 million distributed for National Aboriginal Broadcasting program production by the Department of Canadian Heritage. Maori Television in New Zealand received NZ$36.4 million (APTN 2013; Maori Television 2013; Canada 2012).

Despite concerted lobbying over decades, Indigenous broadcasting in Australia remains on the periphery of political policy-making (Meadows 2012). But while the mainstream continues to have difficulty placing Indigenous media into the broader Australian public sphere, Indigenous communities have long applied their own frameworks in producing media that reflect themselves and their lives. This is clearly evident, too, throughout the Native broadcasting sector in Canada (Molnar and Meadows 2001; Roth 2005).

Creating an Audience-Producer Dialogue

One of the dominant defining characteristics of Indigenous media that has emerged from the Australian audience study of community broadcasting is the absence of a barrier between audiences and producers. One media worker at Yuendumu in the Tanami Desert in central Australia described it like this: "The audience are the producers and we get constant feedback from them as to what they want and also that they're prepared to just get up there and do it themselves and the separation of production processes from audience – it's a unique situation; it's something that the government should treasure" (Meadows et al. 2007, 53). Indigenous audiences express this relationship in varying ways: a sense of ownership, communication, identification with the grassroots, access, and the innate ability for stations to relate to their listeners socially, culturally, and linguistically. Communication between producers and audiences happens in many ways and, perhaps most importantly, in the process of talking about place. One listener to CAAMA Radio in Alice Springs concluded, "It's Aboriginal radio for Aboriginal people; people who take greater pride in being Aboriginal people, especially grassroots people – it gives them something to listen to and play a part of it" (Meadows et al. 2007, 53). The nature of this relationship was also attributed to the open nature of Indigenous radio and television enterprises and, in this case, throughout the islands of the Torres Strait:

"They're very open in their [approach]. If you've got something you want to put on the radio, they call in, you know, talk about your idea. If it's community news or, you know, you go into the studio and do all of that" (ibid.).

The critical role radio plays in maintaining communication links between prisoners and their families, largely through music requests and associated messages, was commonly raised by audiences across the country. Perhaps this is not surprising with Indigenous people making up about 22 per cent of the national prison population in Australia – compared with 2.5 per cent of the total population (Krieg 2006; Australian Bureau of Statistics 2013). The continuing high rates of Indigenous incarceration and deaths-in-custody in Australia alone make radio an essential service.

For many, Indigenous media are defined in terms of simply feeling comfortable listening to and/or watching programs with which Indigenous people can identify and trust. One Palm Island interviewee reflected the views of many when he observed, "Cherbourg Murri radio is very informative. It presents a point of view that we want to talk about – what you people call the blueprints of your world. We know our blueprints … it concerns the whole world and it gives us a sense of identity and direction" (Meadows et al. 2007, 53). One Melbourne listener to the local Indigenous community radio station, 3KND – Kool 'N' Deadly – described how she tuned in: "I heard about 3KND from indigenous friends who I met through work and she, I said to her, 'I want to learn more about indigenous culture,' and she said, 'Listen to the radio station'" (54). Another young Indigenous woman acknowledged that "pretty much all the elders in Inala [a suburb with a high Indigenous population in Brisbane's west] listen to 98.9" (a popular Indigenous-owned community radio station in Brisbane), confirming its "authorisation," like other Indigenous radio stations, by key community figures (ibid.).

Audiences define Indigenous media in many ways – "the electronic message stick of the new millennium" was one eloquent response by a caller to a national Indigenous community radio program, *Talkblack*. But there are many other variants: "our voice" was a simple description from the Torres Strait, the "Murri grapevine," or the "bush telegraph," by others. One passionate Palm Islander explained why he listened to Indigenous radio: "Because it's blackfella listening to blackfella. You know you want to communicate with them. You know!" (Meadows et al. 2007, 54).

Indigenous radio and television represent a first level of service in terms of the provision of news and information for Indigenous communities. But it is also clear that media organizations do far more than this for communities that feel isolated by persistently negative and irrelevant mainstream media representation (Meadows and Foxwell 2011). Indigenous audiences undoubtedly consider their local media an essential service. Some argue that it should be considered alongside other more traditional community services like health and education. The idea that Indigenous media provide an essential service is widespread among listeners and viewers. One response from central Australia underlines this theme: "The radio station [at Yuendumu] itself is, I think, the hub of life. In some places it's the school, but here it's the radio station and they make it very, very relevant … And everybody's playing the radio here in every house you go into and the shops, everything! It's on all the time" (Meadows et al. 2007, 55).

An important role audiences attributed to Indigenous media is linking individuals and groups within communities. This is especially the case where communities are spread over vast areas as throughout remote Australia, including the islands of the Torres Strait. The capacity for people to come together for meetings on a regular basis is limited, but innovative uses of media have managed to overcome this in several regions. One is a unique system of broadcast radio, television, and UHF radio devised by PY Media to maintain traditional processes of decision making by consensus in the Anangu-Pitjantjatjara-Yunkantjatjara (APY) lands in the central desert, straddling the South Australian and Northern Territory border. As this interviewee – an Anangu elder – explains, whenever the APY Council holds a meeting, people out in the community need to know what's happening: "We need to have meetings, not a secret. They've got to be open, on the table and through radio broadcasting, a lot of people are out there listening. Sometimes, when something really important comes up, they ring the meeting and they talk in the meeting. They're way over there in the community but they can be in the meeting here, talking" (Meadows et al. 2007, 56).

It is clear that audiences for Indigenous radio and television see them as essential services. In locations where Indigenous media are active, they play a central organizing role in community life and are critical, organizational hubs. A commonly expressed description of locally produced media was that it is "ours." It is clear from this perception of intimacy that Indigenous community radio, in particular, helps audiences maintain social networks by enabling kinship ties to be strengthened through a range of activities including dance, interviews, stories, prisoners' shows, and by playing music and video requests.

In the eyes of their audiences, Indigenous media are playing a strong educative role in communities, particularly for young people. Indigenous media offer their audiences an alternative source of news and information that avoids stereotyping, promoting self-esteem, epitomized in this comment from Central Australia: "Radio is one of the coolest things that they can do and we usually have a queue of our young people wanting to work with Warlpiri Media all out there but particularly on those multimedia projects ... we have all the same issues as any other community but we also have extremely strong people, not only elders, now the young people they're taking action and they're not accepting those unacceptable ways of life" (Meadows et al. 2007, 61). But Indigenous-produced media are helping to break down stereotypes about Indigenous people for the non-Indigenous community, too, thus playing an important role in enabling cross-cultural dialogue. This is evident in earlier research (Meadows 2001; Forde et al. 2002) and suggests a continuing role for tertiary-level journalism programs around Australia that are linked to local Indigenous radio and television producers. This focus-group member in Brisbane sums it up: "I would say that another reason I like tuning in, too, particularly to 'Let's Talk' show [by Tiga Bayles] because it's a credible alternative to mainstream news that it's more balanced and you're given the truth. And as I say, it's out there – discrimination and the racism – and there's a lot of things that go on that you just don't get a balanced view in mainstream media" (Meadows et al. 2007, 64).

Audiences identify Indigenous radio and television as a crucial medium for specialist music and dance; without this outlet, it is doubtful whether any Indigenous-produced music and video would ever be seen or heard on the Australian broadcast media. Almost every Indigenous community in the country has at least one local teenage band – many have half a dozen or more. Virtually alone, Indigenous community radio and television support the huge Indigenous music industry that remains largely unknown to most of non-Indigenous Australia. The role of music – particularly requests – in cementing kinship ties is evident in much of the discussion with Indigenous media audiences across the country.

Conclusion

The multiple roles that are performed by First Nations broadcasting, in particular, reveal as much about the gulf that exists between the mainstream and Aboriginal worlds as they do about the central, organizing resource they represent in Australian and Canadian communities where they are active. It is important to understand that the processes of such minority media extend well beyond the public spheres themselves that are created. These necessarily encompass the broader public sphere where deliberations – primarily through an increasing variety of media platforms – at the very least have the potential to impact on society as a whole. Viewed in this way, minority media are far from being peripheral in influence (Fleras 2009; Browne and Uribe-Jongbloed 2013). It is this understanding of the role of Aboriginal media, in particular, that mainstream journalists have yet to grasp effectively, and yet the process operates under their very noses. Perhaps a first step towards rectifying this clear imbalance would be for journalists to pay more attention to First Nations media processes and product. Valaskakis (1993), too, is in no doubt of this: "It is through the prism of parallel voices, of competing narratives, expressed in public text – in literature, art, music, ceremony, and media – that we can access the subaltern experience, expand our concepts of inquiry, and approach our points of connectedness." At the centre of democratic life are the public spheres in which private citizens learn about and comment on issues that concern them. These discursive activities take place in varied settings: classrooms, associations, unions, community meetings, and in provincial and national arenas. While most citizens take access to these spaces for granted, a great many other citizens are systematically excluded. The advent of mass democracy and mass media has seen the concept of the "imagined community" (see Anderson 1984) – the nation – become societies of multiple-connected public spheres.

The continuing circulation of ideas and assumptions about the Aboriginal worlds in Australia and Canada – through speaking and listening processes that define local media – contributes to the development of a national Indigenous public sphere. Importantly, Indigenous media also act – most often quite deliberately – as a cultural bridge, linking the "parallel voices" of Indigenous and non-Indigenous society. They provide sites for public opinion formation; sites where citizens can engage in collective efforts to bring their issues to the dominant public sphere; and sites where Indigenous people can attempt to influence the policies of various governments through the pressure of public opinion. First Nations media in Australia and Canada represent important cultural resources that provide their respective communities with an essential service. And it is these media, globally, that continue to play a central role in offering a critique of mainstream media – and journalism practices – and the multifarious roles all of us play in the formation of the democratic public sphere.

Acknowledgments

The audience study to which this chapter refers, Community Media Matters, was conducted by the author with Griffith University colleagues Susan Forde, Jacqui Ewart, Kerrie Foxwell, and senior Aboriginal researcher Derek Flucker. It was funded jointly by the Australian Research Council, the Community Broadcasting Foundation, and the federal Department of Communication, Information Technology and the Arts. The executive summary and first chapter are available as a free PDF download at the Community Broadcasting Foundation's website: http://www.cbf.com.au/projects-and-resources/audience-research-project/.

Conclusion: Strategies Forward – A Future for Journalism in Canada

ERROL SALAMON, GRETCHEN KING,
CHRISTINE CROWTHER, AND
SIMON THIBAULT

This book demonstrates some of the ways in which academics and journalists seek to contribute to research, scholarship, and praxis in Canada. It serves as part of a process to initiate participatory and deliberative policy-making to generate the knowledge necessary to enhance a variety of interacting public spheres that, in turn, can redress a democratic deficit in Canadian journalism. The chapters in this collection pointedly attribute this democratic malaise to several issues, including the following: a dearth of organized concern around key media policy issues to mobilize people to participate in policy processes; a lack of media diversity; an over-reliance on the notion of journalistic objectivity; a preference for market imperatives and private sector media; and asymmetrical access to digital media. In the book, some authors reduce the problems that currently face journalism in Canada to a "relationship between commerce and public service," in the words of Marc Raboy. Raboy warns that we have reached a "global warming" of mainstream media within our broader media ecology. To safeguard our media ecosystem, the book's authors stress the role of public policy to ensure that we have a variety of public institutions, an independent regulatory authority, and public support.

One immediate outcome of a majority of the chapters was key policy recommendations that could support democratic journalism in Canada. Our goal in this concluding chapter is to show that a future for journalism in Canada can and should be reimagined through deliberative policy processes. We first discuss ways in which a participatory policy-making process could redress the democratic deficit in journalism. Second, we introduce an innovative methodological orientation to investigate the deliberative nature of policy-making. Finally, we offer policy recommendations that could lead to a more democratic media environment in Canada.

A Process for Participatory Policy-Making

One key way to initiate a process for participatory policy-making is to forge explicit links among journalism research, praxis, and policy development (Salamon 2012). According to Aslama and Napoli (2011), a weak relationship exists between communication researchers and policy-makers. Important exceptions include connections between research and praxis in the relations between communication researchers and the public interest and advocacy community. Research is vital as a *tool* because "when put into action, it can enhance democracy and build a more democratic society" (333). Habermas (2006a) reminds us of the important links between theory, practice, and the public sphere, embracing the Aristotelian notion of bridging theory and empirical research to enhance democratic imperatives. Another way to initiate a participatory policy-making process is by building on the growing body of engaged scholarship. Engaged research consists of rigorous research by scholars in collaboration with movement actors.

Similar to engaged research, Kidd and Lee (2011) refer to their work on digital inclusion as "embedded research" because of the close relationship between the researchers and the Media Alliance, the advocacy organization out of which their research emerged. Engaged and embedded research is also representative of what McChesney (2007) refers to as "self-reflective research" on media advocacy and activism. These projects have extended traditional notions of academic work, activism, and advocacy. They blur the distinctions among the scholar, the activist, and the advocate. Along these lines, we advocate a deliberative approach that combines the rigorous academic research of students and professors, all of whom have experience in, and links to journalism practice, with a variety of movement actors, including journalists, activists, and policy-makers. This process would include not only formal academic interventions based on participants' research and practical experiences, but also deliberative group consultations so that participants could develop policy recommendations collectively.

A Methodological Tool to Study
Deliberative Policy-Making

In what follows, we offer preliminary evidence that participatory policy-making can create a space that most participants recognize as a significant process to address a future for journalism in Canada. To evaluate the practices and outcomes of deliberative policy-making, we deploy a new methodological orientation that is comprised of consensus qualitative research (CQR) tools and discourse studies.

We analysed the deliberative process of Journalism Strategies, a policy-making event that we organized at McGill University and Concordia University in Montreal from 19 to 21 April 2012. We used a plethora of data from the event archive, including transcripts of four break-out sessions, each of which consisted of between five and ten participants and a facilitator, and was based on a different theme (working definitions of journalism, organizational models, regulatory policies, and financial policies); a live blog on Twitter; and three-minute surveys following the break-out sessions at the end of the event to assess policy recommendations with participants (Journalism Strategies Project 2012). One of our goals was to analyse this attempt at deliberative journalism policy-making in Canada. We reviewed the traditional mechanisms used to evaluate participatory, deliberative, and consensus conferences, such as quantitative and qualitative surveys, interviews, group discussions, and participant observation (see Joss 1995). However, we posit that these evaluative approaches should be complemented with consensual qualitative research methods (Hill et al. 2005, 1997) and discourse analysis (e.g., Fairclough 2005; Fischer 2003).

The CQR approach has been developed and adopted within investigations of phenomena in counselling psychology. We draw on this framework because it reflects the consensual nature of the participatory policy-making of our approach to organizing, facilitating, and evaluating Journalism Strategies. CQR mirrors the policy process that was built into Journalism Strategies in that the CQR coding method is also deliberative. It consists of a process that unfolds over several sessions of coding with a team of coders that engages with a designated auditor. The auditor is not part of the coding process and independently assesses and problematizes the coding. CQR has roots in grounded theory, but differs in that it (1) strives for consensus among a team of coders and an auditor; (2) codes explicit meanings using topics and themes to summarize, rather than interpret, the data; and (3) in measuring frequency, represents data horizontally across domains, rather than in a hierarchy of a single category with subcategories as in grounded theory (Hill et al. 1997, 2005).

Our use of CQR is complemented by attention to power dynamics, as reflected in discourse studies, revealing how control and domination are "negotiated and resisted" (Fairclough 2005, 21) in deliberation. Deliberative democratic practices are inclusive, equitable, pluralistic, reflexive, and accountable (Dryzek 2000, 3; Young 2000, 23–5). These practices include "debate and discussion aimed at producing reasonable, well-informed opinions in which participants are *willing to revise preferences* in light of discussion, new information, and claims made by fellow participants" (Chambers 2003, 309, emphasis added). We also draw on CQR to inform an intertextual analysis of the event archive, using Fairclough's (1992) conceptualization of "manifest intertextuality," to illuminate "where specific other texts are overtly drawn upon within a text" (117). Indeed, manifest intertextuality can illuminate these deliberative *shifts* through participant references to previous discussions or presentations and to other policy processes and documents.

We conducted a preliminary assessment of these practices at Journalism Strategies by using CQR to code the transcript from the final three-hour session in which participants presented and discussed the policy recommendations from the four break-out sessions. During our first phase of coding, topics appeared that are useful to our investigation of the deliberative nature of the event. For example, some of the domains (i.e., topic areas that represent the data) generated include "interruptions," "inclusion/exclusion," and "reflections on the process." Our methodological orientation can therefore help to answer necessary questions regarding power and inclusion that emerged during the coding phase. For example:

1 Were discussions and procedural matters between organizers and participants addressed equitably?
2 Did deliberations reflect the diversity of the policy community?
3 Did participants refer to ideas and experiences offered by other participants?

Our preliminary analysis of this final session provides evidence of the participatory and equitable nature of the discussion and procedural matters. In fact, our CQR coding demonstrates procedural matters, such as "Do we vote now?" expended 34.5 per cent of the discussion time during this session. This figure may demonstrate the willingness of event organizers to facilitate and engage participants in procedures. However, it is also possibly the result of a combined lack of procedural guidelines or a framework for possible outcomes planned for the final session. The coding of this session further reveals the failed attempt to organize a deliberative session that affords participation in French *and* English. Our coding shows that interventions in French took fewer than five lines of a fifty-page transcript. Thus, the final session failed to reflect some diversity of opinion, as it may have limited the capacity of francophone attendees to fully participate in the deliberation process, an issue that we address further in this chapter.

CQR coding also offers rich data for documenting how and when participants took up the ideas of others and referenced earlier Journalism Strategies interventions. In one case, participants collectively revised a policy recommendation presented in the final session concerning audience research:

> FEMALE VOICE: Your wording seems sort of useful – research for audiences, whereas we think of it as research of audiences – the "for" versus the "of."
> FEMALE VOICE: That's an excellent point, yeah.
> MALE VOICE: And if you go back to the wording, you now have two things in there. One is – if you can go back up to the –
> FEMALE VOICE: It's a lot to take all at once, so going back up. Okay.
> MALE VOICE: See, in the top line you have "evaluating," "measuring" audiences. It turns out that's – like that's not what Michael [a presenter the previous evening] was talking about. Michael was talking about what do audiences look for? What do audiences want? What do they want from journalism, you know, which is a different question.
> FEMALE VOICE: Yeah, we can totally change it. I just wrote it really fast.
> (Journalism Strategies Project 2012)

The recommendation was modified from a policy advocating "studying more audiences" to one calling for research "for audiences." Our preliminary analysis of the data, then, illuminates that CQR, combined with tools from discourse studies, complements the consensual nature of deliberative policy-making, extending these practices to the evaluative process and building a framework that can reveal power dynamics. This methodological approach could inform the projects of other people who do engaged or embedded research.

Recommendations

One of the most important aims of the embedded process is to generate policy recommendations that could lead to a sustainable future for journalism in Canada. Below, we provide a variety of recommendations at the intersection of the chapters in this collection that could democratize media in Canada. As we adopt a discursive approach, we contend that it is also important to address issues that were not overtly covered in this book – gaps in policy or "policy silences" (Freedman 2010).

Increased Links, Access to, and Participation in, Formal Policy Processes and Organizations

Although it is important to bring together a diverse group of people of different backgrounds, from different sectors, etc., they must still be linked to, or intervene in, formal policy-making processes. Our policy-making model is built on critiques of, and responses to, these processes, but we recognize that alternative structures of organizing must also interact with, and directly challenge, the processes and power structures they are critiquing in order to impact policy. We recommend, then, that policy-makers and regulators, such as the CRTC, be invited to participate in future projects and be involved in the deliberative decision-making processes.

These links to formal policy processes are necessary, but it is particularly important to address "access to policy process[es]" (Skinner 2012, 43). Related to access is the challenge to mobilize people to participate in these processes. For example, Tim Creery (1984), the Kent Commission's director of research, concluded that the federal government was reluctant to implement the Commission's recommendations in 1981 because of "the absence of organized public concern" (see Skinner et al., chapter 3). Activism and advocacy could redress these issues, engaging people in media reform through coalition building across organizations, linking scholarly, activist, and practitioner interests to generate public interest, and applying pressure within policy processes. Effective media reform campaigns enable people to participate in the campaigns as well as use public meetings and online spaces to develop public concern.

Academics and journalists could also partner with established institutions, like Lead Now (À l'action), the Friends of Canadian Broadcasting (Amis de Radio-Canada), Media Democracy Day, or OpenMedia, which have successfully advocated and lobbied for policy changes and public-led participatory processes (Gurleyen and Hackett, chapter 1; Skinner et al., chapter 3).

Other models for organizing and for broader social change could stem from social movements, some of which are media-centric: for example, the public or civic journalism movement in the United States in the 1990s, which sought to connect journalism with citizens via direct engagement (Nielsen, chapter 2; see also Merritt 1998; Rosen 1999). Although policy advocacy for media change is important, the Icelandic Modern Media Initiative (renamed in 2011, the International Modern Media Institute, IMMI), moves beyond this approach, instead offering a new policy environment (Hintz, chapter 6). This approach demonstrates that journalism needs to expand the criteria of inclusivity, which could increase media diversity.

Commitments to Increased Diversity: Bilingualism and Non-Western Epistemologies

From the outset, stakeholders in Canada must create a model of policy-making that is bilingual (English and French) and culturally diverse (especially with regard to region, sector, and gender). According to Colette Brin (2012), one of the challenges is that, although some people may have at least a passive knowledge of the other language, parts of the process may get lost in translation. A bilingual project forces bilingual people to do more work. Bilingualism also might strain and limit the extent to which people could participate and express themselves in translating journalism and policy-making issues that are difficult to translate, or that have little or even no overlap in another linguistic context. In order to hear and understand the majority of participants, then, one language may become the preferred dominant language.

Language is embedded in broader systems of power, and in Quebec especially, these language politics comprise a reality that is important to acknowledge and challenge. Journalism policy-making should not only be focused on media-centric issues, but also incorporate broader political issues, such as language, into policy reform initiatives. Canadian broadcasting pioneer Graham Spry (1965) reminds us that, as early as the 1920s, the Canadian Radio League, a lobby group that was instrumental in proposing and advocating national public service broadcasting, viewed broadcasting as an instrument of communication that could "strengthen bi-culturalism and bi-lingualism" (138). Likewise, similar initiatives must have a mandate to be more inclusive to people of colour and Aboriginal people (Gurleyen and Hackett, chapter 1; Skinner et al., chapter 3; Meadows, chapter 11).

Future deliberative policy-making projects must also challenge the dominant notion of "policy" and "policy-making" and consider non-Western approaches and anti-oppression frameworks (Dominelli 2002) to consensus building and decision making. Institutions of Canadian public policy have begun, but must continue, to include traditional Indigenous knowledge into the realm of policy development and decision making (Abele 2007). One challenge is that Western journalistic inquiry is in direct conflict with traditional knowledge management processes in Indigenous societies (Meadows, chapter 11). Indigenous people make their positions visible through several important practices, including storytelling, art, music, even silence. For Indigenous communities spread over vast areas (e.g., Canada, Australia), media can facilitate and maintain traditional processes of consensus decision making. These practices could also inform non-Indigenous epistemologies, journalistic practices, and policy processes. As first steps, at the federal governmental level, the Competition Act could be amended to consider these issues of media diversity, and the ceilings on concentration and cross-media ownership could be lowered to expand the types of voices that can participate in production (Skinner et al., chapter 3).

Commitment to Critical-Realist Journalism

Moving forward also entails a shift away from some aspects of journalistic objectivity, such as balance or a narrowly defined "implied audience" (Nielsen, chapter 2), to a critical-realist approach to journalism. Embedded in this latter approach are commitments to the story and to journalism that is reflexive, crisis-centric, environmental, and peace-oriented (Gurleyen and Hackett, chapter 1). This approach is also predicated on a commitment to an ethical necessity to help inform, engage, and empower people who may not hold positions of authority and power. Despite this shift, a critical-realist position would importantly retain some facets of objectivity: for example, the tendency towards investigative and critical journalism. This shift is vital because a strict realm of objectivity could dissuade journalists from building the support and organizing that is necessary to challenge a corporate media system. This modified journalistic framework, then, would be participatory, inclusive, and dialogic: a "performative dialogue" (Nielsen, chapter 2). In addition, it is adversarial in the sense that journalists would actually intervene directly in, rather than merely report on, stories. It is important to note, however, that this issue is complex and part of an ongoing and highly contested debate within the journalism community and academic literature as well as among the editors of this book.

Increased Support for Alternative, Community, (Hyper)Local, and Public Media

Alternative media are well suited to challenge some of the hegemonic practices of objectivity and are an immediate and concrete way to support crisis-centred journalism (Gurleyen and Hackett, chapter 1). Alternative media could not only oppose the objectivity of mainstream media, but also provide "innovative ideas" and "political practices" that could become incorporated into mainstream media (Raboy, Foreword). Local media, which often fall under the umbrella of community (and sometimes alternative) media, could also provide outlets for critical-realist journalism (Gurleyen and Hackett, chapter 1; Skinner et al., chapter 3; Ali, chapter 5; King et al., chapter 9; Washburn and Raynauld, chapter 10; Meadows, chapter 11).

GroundWire, Consider This, and Indigenous media are examples of local media that could challenge journalistic objectivity. *GroundWire* is a social justice–based local news program that receives national exposure and builds national links between local communities and social movements (King et al., chapter 9). Its decentralized reporting "challenges the notion that objectivity is a prerequisite for legitimacy," especially reporting that relies on a vision of "political neutrality." The word "objectivity" is purposely omitted from its editorial policy. *GroundWire* prioritizes not only localism, but also public engagement and training to facilitate community participation. Its news is historically contextualized, offering a rights-based approach and featuring voices from people who are directly affected or involved in stories. *Consider This* featured hyperlocal news through online technology and is important because it opposes a "regional" approach to community news (Washburn and Raynauld, chapter 10). Like *GroundWire*, its dialogic, participatory approach aimed to educate, engage, and empower a well-defined geographical community. Similarly, Indigenous media break down barriers between audiences and producers. Some Indigenous audience members consider locally produced media "ours," an essential service alongside health and education (Meadows, chapter 11). These examples rely on citizen and volunteer journalists who are essential for these projects, but these local and community media, along with alternative media, struggle in large part due to funding shortfalls.

Several funding models could mitigate this issue. Support mechanisms such as the Federal Business Innovation Grant under the Canada Periodical Fund could be opened to alternative media and hyperlocal news sites (Skinner et al., chapter 3; Washburn and Raynauld, chapter 10). Another broad funding strategy was recommended in the Bacon Report (Canada 2006a): the creation of a tax regime that supports journalism and Canadian media (Skinner et al., chapter 3). To sustain local media, in particular, one obvious solution would be to reinstate the Local Programming Improvement Fund, which the CRTC phased out in 2014 (Skinner et al., chapter 3). At the core of potential funding strategies is a need to recommend long-term, stable, and adequate operational funding to help sustain *independent* local, community, and public media as well as online and hyperlocal news (Gurleyen and Hackett, chapter 1; Skinner et al., chapter 3; Wirsig and Edwards, chapter 4; King et al., chapter 9; Washburn and Raynauld, chapter 10). This funding should be dispersed to community media that are made *by* and *for* local communities. Another potentially viable and innovative funding model is participatory budgeting. With this voter-funded model, representative collective bodies (e.g., university student societies, municipal governments) would allocate a pool of funding to public media projects, empowering people to vote on competing projects for available resources. This model carries the potential to make media directly accountable to their publics (Gurleyen and Hackett, chapter 1).

Partnerships could also alleviate funding shortfalls. Hyperlocal partnerships between academic institutions, news institutions, and government (Washburn and Raynauld, chapter 10) as well as public-community partnerships (Wirsig and Edwards, chapter 4) could serve as launching points for these concerns. Communities and the CBC could upgrade and then share transmission equipment in smaller regions. They could also share facilities and content, the latter of which is a type of partnership that is not new to Canadian media. During the early development of the Canadian television system, privately owned local stations were conduits to distribute the CBC's public broadcasting content. The Payette Report (Québec 2010) importantly points to this model of collaboration, suggesting that Télé-Québec gather local and regional content from independent community producers.

To complement the financial support, it is vital to affirm the over-all importance of community, local, and alternative media beyond the private and public sectors. The Standing Committee on Canadian Heritage has already set an essential precedent for concerns regarding local media in its report, *Our Cultural Sovereignty: The Second Century of Canadian Broadcasting* (Canada 2003). The 2009 Local TV Matters cam-paign also highlighted the importance of the local, pitting broadcasters against broadcast distribution undertakings (BDUs) for broadcasters' right to charge a fee for their signals. Despite this recognition, the gov-ernment must strengthen its support. The CRTC should be mandated to appoint a commissioner from the community sector, as commission-ers are selected exclusively from the other two broadcasting sectors. In addition, more research on local and community media may lead to a comprehensive understanding of key terms and the significance of local and community to the Canadian media ecology. A CRTC-appointed task force could be mandated to conduct this holistic research (Ali, chapter 5; King et al., chapter 9).

Commitment to Universal Access, a National Digital Strategy, and Converged Labour

The future of journalism will depend on the Internet and digital media, and digital platforms must remain open and universally accessible. The federal government must therefore develop a national digital strategy to support these principles (Skinner et al., chapter 3). The Icelandic Modern Media Initiative (IMMI; now the International Modern Media Institute) is one such model for digital democracy, addressing issues of both content and infrastructure. It consists of a new Freedom of Infor-mation Act that improves access for journalists, laws to protect sources and whistle-blowers, and Net neutrality. It is based on "policy hack-ing," an international approach to policy-making, in which laws and regulations are informed by the policy experiences of other countries (Hintz, chapter 6).

News organizations and journalists would benefit from open, universally accessible digital media. New and emerging media technologies, such as Twitter, expand networks and open affordable spaces for diverse voices to participate and be heard in news media (Kulkarni, chapter 8; Washburn and Raynauld, chapter 10). These media offer journalists the potential to partner with local communities online and "crowd source." Despite their importance, citizen, amateur, or volunteer journalists alone cannot immediately address the democratic deficits of our media system, especially due to their limited resources, as mentioned above (Skinner et al., chapter 3). In this era of information overload and unpaid journalism, professional journalists are still vital to help people filter essential information about current affairs, because they can be perceived as authoritative and reliable voices (Sauvageau, Foreword; Kulkarni, chapter 8). To tackle these important challenges, a national digital strategy could recommend that newsrooms create and promote ways for viewers and readers to participate directly in news stories of established news organizations and support start-up, online organizations through social media (Kulkarni, chapter 8; Washburn and Raynauld, chapter 10).

With the growth of the Internet and the emergence of digital technologies, traditional news organizations have embraced a converged approach to journalistic labour. Professional journalists' tasks have blurred and expanded, their reports are disseminated on a variety of platforms (radio, television, the Web, mobile phones, digital tablets), and their production rate has accelerated. In this era of immediacy, journalists generally have less time to analyse, verify, and investigate stories. This convergence process may be accompanied by a sense of loss and confusion on the part of journalists, as Francoeur (chapter 7) shows in her analysis of the challenging integration of radio, television, and Web newsrooms at Radio-Canada. Thus, instead of privileging a homogeneous model of multimedia journalists who disseminate the same news stories across different platforms, Francoeur pleads for an approach based on flexibility, innovation, and depth. Journalists should be allowed to focus on their strengths (i.e., their preferred media form) and, at the same time, be encouraged to explore new ways of producing news by, for example, developing new formats, innovative news narratives, and new storytelling modes. By so doing, journalists would be able to assume more tasks and refine their products, which could then be adapted and distributed across different platforms, an approach that Francoeur calls "single-medium multiplatform journalism." The national public broadcaster could serve as an important resource to expand and support this approach.

Conclusions

These policy recommendations could help to ensure that a future for journalism in Canada exists in a media system that is committed to generating awareness and mobilizing people to participate in policy-making processes; expanding non-Western, non-English–language content and approaches to policy-making and media practice; embracing some ideals of critical-realist journalism; increasing support for independent public, community, local, and alternative media; and formulating strategies to strengthen digital media openness and converged labour. They could also ensure that the policy principles of localism, diversity, and universal access guide Canadian media. Ultimately, these recommendations are vital for Canadian media policy because they could help to guarantee that people's fundamental right to freedom of expression, as outlined in Section 2 of the Canadian Charter of Rights and Freedoms, is protected. Linked to this right, the Kent Report (Canada 1981, 1) reminds us again that "freedom of the press [and other media of communication] is not a property right of owners. It is a right of the people." Our recommendations could help to safeguard this right.

References

Aamidor, Abe, Jim A. Kuypers, and Susan Wiesinger. 2013. *Media Smackdown: Deconstructing the News and the Future of Journalism*. New York: Peter Lang.

Abele, Frances. 2007. "Between Respect and Control: Traditional Indigenous Knowledge in Canadian Public Policy." In *Critical Policy Studies*, ed. Michael Orsini and Miriam Smith, 233–56. Vancouver: UBC Press.

Aboriginal Peoples Television Network (APTN). 2013. "Financial Statements 2011." http://aptn.ca/pdf/en/Final-Statements-APTN-2011.pdf.

Adorno, Theodor. 2008. "Culture Industry Reconsidered." In *Media Studies: A Reader*, ed. Paul Marris and Sue Thornham, 31–7. New York: New York University Press.

Agamben, Giorgio. 2005. *State of Exception*. London: Verso. http://dx.doi.org/10.1215/9780822386735-013.

Agyeman, Julian, Bob Doppelt, Kathy Lynn, and Halida Hatic. 2007. "The Climate-Justice Link: Communicating Risk with Low Income and Minority Audiences." In *Creating a Climate for Change: Communicating Climate Change and Facilitating Social Change*, ed. Susanne Moser and Lisa Dilling, 119–38. Cambridge: Cambridge University Press. http://dx.doi.org/10.1017/CBO9780511535871.010.

Akin, David. 2009. "CTVglobemedia Says Its Business Model 'Broken.'" *National Post*, 11 Mar, FP2.

Akkari, Abdeljalil. 2010. "Une lettre à mes amis du Québec." *Le Devoir*, 2 Feb., A7.

Albert, Michael. 1997. "What Makes Alternative Media Alternative?" Subsol. Subsol.c3.hu/subsol_2/contributors3/alberttext.html.

Aldridge, Meryl. 2007. *Understanding the Local Media*. Berkshire: Open University Press.

Ali, Christopher. 2012a. "A Broadcast System in Whose Interest? Tracing the Origins of Broadcast Localism in Canadian and Australian Television Policy, 1950–1963." *International Communication Gazette* 74 (3): 277–97. http://dx.doi.org/10.1177/1748048511432608.

Ali, Christopher. 2012b. "The Local Media Citizen: Citizens, Journalisms, Citizen Journalisms, and Democracies in the Local Media Ecosystem." Paper presented at the 1st International Journalism Studies Conference, Santiago, Chile, 27–9 June.

Ali, Christopher. 2012c. "Of Logos, Owners, and Cultural Intermediaries: Defining an Elite Discourse in Re-branding Practices at Three Private Canadian Television Stations." *Canadian Journal of Communication* 37 (2): 259–79.

Alia, Valerie. 2010. *New Media Nation: Indigenous Peoples and Global Communication.* London: Bergahn.

Alia, Valerie, Brian Brennan, and Barry Hoffmaster. 1996. *Deadlines and Diversity: Journalism Ethics in a Changing World.* Winnipeg: Fernwood.

Allan, Stuart. 2010. *News Culture.* 3rd ed. Buckingham: Open University Press.

Allan, Stuart, and Einar Thorsen, eds. 2009. *Citizen Journalism: Global Perspectives.* New York: Peter Lang.

Altheide, David L., and Robert P. Snow. 1979. *Media Logic.* Beverly Hills: Sage.

AMARC. 2010. "AMARC Deplores Suspension of New Communications Law in Argentina." *AMARC Link* 13, no. 1. https://www.facebook.com/notes/amarc-international-secretariat/amarc-deplores-suspension-of-new-communications-law-in-argentina/113524432011315.

Andersen, Niels Akerstrom. 2003. *Discursive Analytical Strategies.* Bristol: Policy Press.

Anderson, Benedict. 1984. *Imagined Communities: Reflections on the Origin and Spread of Nationalism.* London: Verso.

Anderson, Christopher, and Michael Curtin. 1999. "Mapping the Ethereal City: Chicago Television, the FCC, and the Politics of Place." *Quarterly Review of Film and Video* 16 (3–4): 289–305.

Anderson, Chris W., Emily Bell, and Clay Shirkey. 2014. "Post-Industrial Journalism: Adapting to the Present." New York: Tow Center for Digital Journalism, 2012. Last modified 3 Dec. http://towcenter.org/research/post-industrial-journalism/.

Appadurai, Arjun. 1996. *Modernity at Large: Cultural Dimensions of Globalization.* Minneapolis: University of Minnesota Press.

Arenas, Aidee V., Choo-Kien Kua, Christine Leclerc, and Rita Wong. 2011. "Witnessing the Tar Sands Dead Zone: Asserting the Need to Heal." *Dominion*, 8 July. http://www.dominionpaper.ca/articles/4058.

Arendt, Hannah. 2005. *The Promise of Politics*. Toronto: Random House.

Arkette, Sophie. 2004. "Sounds Like City." *Theory, Culture & Society* 21 (1): 159–68. http://dx.doi.org/10.1177/0263276404040486.

Armstrong, Robert. 2010. *Broadcasting Policy in Canada*. Toronto: University of Toronto Press.

Aslama, Minna, and Philip M. Napoli. 2011. "Conclusion: Bridging Gaps, Crossing Boundaries." In *Communications Research in Action: Scholar-Activist Collaborations for a Democratic Public Sphere*, ed. Minna Aslama and Philip M. Napoli, 333–6. New York: Fordham University Press.

Atton, Chris. 2002. *Alternative Media*. London: Sage.

Atton, Chris. 2003. "Reshaping Social Movement Media for a New Millennium." *Social Movement Studies* 2 (1): 3–15. http://dx.doi.org/10.1080/14742830320000062530.

Atton, Chris. 2009. "Why Alternative Journalism Matters." *Journalism* 10 (3): 283–5. http://dx.doi.org/10.1177/1464884909102582.

Atton, Chris, and James F. Hamilton. 2008. *Alternative Journalism*. Los Angeles: Sage.

Atton, Chris, and Emma Wickenden. 2005. "Sourcing Routines and Representation in Alternative Journalism: A Case Study Approach." *Journalism Studies* 6 (3): 347–59. http://dx.doi.org/10.1080/14616700500132008.

Audley, Paul. 1983. *Canada's Cultural Industries*. Toronto: James Lorimer.

Augaitis, Daina, and Dan Lander, eds. 1994. *Radio Rethink*. Banff: Walter Phillips Gallery.

Australian Bureau of Statistics. 2013. "Aboriginal and Torres Strait Islander Population." http://www.abs.gov.au/ausstats/abs@.nsf/Lookup/by%20 Subject/1301.0~2012~Main%20Features~Aboriginal%20and%20Torres%20 Strait%20Islander%20population~50.

Avison, Shannon. 1996. "Aboriginal Newspapers: Their Contribution to the Emergence of an Alternative Public Sphere in Canada." Master's thesis, Concordia University.

Avison, Shannon, and Michael Meadows. 2000. "Speaking and Hearing: Aboriginal Newspapers and the Public Sphere in Canada and Australia." *Canadian Journal of Communication* 25 (3): 347–66.

Bagdikian, Ben H. 1983. *The Media Monopoly*. Boston: Beacon Press.

Bailey, Olga G., Bart Cammaerts, and Nico Carpentier, eds. 2008. *Understanding Alternative Media*. Maidenhead: McGraw-Hill / Open University Press.

Baker, C. Edwin. 2002. *Media, Markets, and Democracy*. Cambridge: Cambridge University Press.

Baker, C. Edwin. 2007. *Media Concentration and Democracy: Why Ownership Matters*. New York: Cambridge University Press.

Balkin, Jack M. 2009. "The Future of Free Expression in a Digital Age." *Pepperdine Law Review* 36 (2): 427–44.

Bambauer, Derek E. 2009. "Cybersieves." *Duke Law Journal* 59 (3): 377–446.

Banisar, David, and Francesca Fanucci. 2013. "WikiLeaks, Secrecy and Freedom of Information: The Case of the United Kingdom." In *Beyond WikiLeaks: Implications for the Future of Communications, Journalism and Society*, ed. Benedetta Brevini, Arne Hintz, and Patrick McCurdy, 178–90. Basingstoke: Palgrave. http://dx.doi.org/10.1057/9781137275745.0017.

Bar, François, and Christian Sandvig. 2008. "US Communication Policy After Convergence." *Media Culture & Society* 30 (4): 531–50. http://dx.doi.org/10.1177/0163443708091181.

Barney, Darin. 2005. *Communication Technology*. Vancouver: UBC Press.

Barney, Ralph D. 1996. "Community Journalism: Good Intentions, Questionable Practice." *Journal of Mass Media Ethics* 11 (3): 140–51. http://dx.doi.org/10.1207/s15327728jmme1103_2.

Barthes, Roland. 2000. *Le plaisir du texte*. Paris: Seuil.

Battle for the Internet. 2012. *The Guardian*. www.theguardian.com/technology/series/battle-for-the-internet.

Baym, Geoffrey. 2010. *From Cronkite to Colbert: The Evolution of Broadcast News*. Boulder, CO: Paradigm.

Beers, David. 2006. "The Public Sphere and Online, Independent Journalism." *Canadian Journal of Education* 29 (1): 109–30. http://dx.doi.org/10.2307/20054149.

Bekken, Jon. 2008. "Alternative Journalism." In *The International Encyclopedia of Communication*, ed. Wolfgang Donsbach. Malden, MA: Blackwell.

Bélanger, Pierre C. 2005. "Online News at Canada's National Public Broadcaster: An Emerging Convergence." *Canadian Journal of Communication* 30 (3): 411–27.

Bell, Emily, Ethan Zuckerman, Jonathan Stray, Shelia Coronel, and Michael Schudson. 2013. "Comment to Review Group on Intelligence and Communications Technologies Regarding the Effects of Mass Surveillance on the Practice of Journalism." *Tow Center for Digital Journalism*, 4 Oct. http://towcenter.org/wp-content/uploads/2013/10/Letter-Effect-of-mass-surveillance-on-journalism.pdf.

Benkler, Yochai. 2006. *The Wealth of Networks*. New Haven, CA: Yale University Press.

Benkler, Yochai. 2011. "A Free Irresponsible Press: WikiLeaks and the Battle over the Soul of the Networked Fourth Estate." *Harvard Civil Rights - Civil Liberties Law Review*. http://benkler.org/Benkler_Wikileaks_current.pdf.

Bennett, W. Lance. 2009. *News: The Politics of Illusion*. 8th ed. New York: Pearson Longman.

Benson, Rodney. 2003. "Commercialism and Critique: California's Alternative Weeklies." In *Contesting Media Power: Alternative Media in a Networked World*, ed. Nick Couldry and James Curran, 111–29. Lanham, MD: Rowman and Littlefield.

Bernier, Marc-François. 2008. *Journalistes au pays de la convergence: Sérénité, malaise et détresse dans la profession*. Quebec: Les Presses de l'Université Laval.

Besley, John C., and Chris M. Roberts. 2010. "Cuts in Newspaper Staffs Change Meeting Coverage." *Newspaper Research Journal* 31 (3): 22–35.

Bickford, Susan. 1996. *The Dissonance of Democracy: Listening, Conflict and Citizenship*. New York: Cornell University Press.

Black, Jay. 1997. *Mixed News: The Public / Civic / Communitarian Journalism Debate*. Hillsdale, NJ: Lawrence Erlbaum.

Blevins, Jeffrey Lane, and Leslie Regan Shade. 2010. "International Perspectives on Network Neutrality: Exploring the Politics of Internet Traffic Management and Policy Implications for Canada and the U.S." *Global Media Journal – Canadian Edition* 3 (1): 1–8.

Blidook, Kelly. 2009. "Choice and Content: Media Ownership and Democratic Ideals in Canada." *Canadian Political Science Review* 3 (2): 52–69.

Blumler, Jay G., and Stephen Cushion. 2014. "Normative Perspective on Journalism Studies: Stock-Taking and Future Directions." *Journalism* 15 (3): 259–72. http://dx.doi.org/10.1177/1464884913498689.

Blumler, Jay G., and Michael Gurevitch. 1995. *The Crisis of Public Communication*. London: Routledge. http://dx.doi.org/10.4324/9780203181775.

Boczkowski, Pablo J., and José A. Ferris. 2005. "Multiple Media, Convergent Processes, and Divergent Products: Organizational Innovation in Digital Media Production at a European Firm." *Annals of the American Academy of Political and Social Science* 597 (1): 32–47. http://dx.doi.org/10.1177/0002716204270067.

Boghani, Priyanka. 2012. "ACTA Hits Delays in Germany." *Global Post*, 10 Feb. http://www.globalpost.com/dispatch/news/regions/europe/germany/120210/acta-hits-delays-germany.

Bohman, James. 1996. *Public Deliberation: Pluralism, Complexity, and Democracy*. Cambridge, MA: MIT Press.

Bohman, James. 1999. "Deliberative Democracy and Effective Social Freedom: Capabilities, Resources, and Opportunities." In *Deliberative Democracy: Essays on Reason and Politics*, ed. James Bohman and William Rehg, 321–48. London: MIT Press.

Bollier, David. 2010. "A New Global Landmark for Free Speech." 16 June. http://www.bollier.org/new-global-landmark-free-speech.

Boltanski, Luc. 2011. *On Critique: A Sociology of Emancipation*. Trans. Gregory Elliott. London: Polity.

Boltanski, Luc, and Eve Chiapello. 2005. *The New Spirit of Capitalism*. Trans. Gregory Elliott. London: Verso.

Born, Georgina. 2004. *Uncertain Vision*. London: Secker and Warburg.

Bourdieu, Pierre. 2005. "The Political Field, the Social Science Field, and the Journalistic Field." In *Bourdieu and the Journalistic Field*, ed. Rodney Benson and Eric Neveu, 29–47. Cambridge: Polity.

Bowman, Shane, and Chris Willis. 2003. *We Media: How Audiences Are Shaping the Future of News and Information*. Reston, VA: Media Center at the American Press Institute; http://www.flickertracks.com/blog/images/we_media.pdf.

Boyatzis, Richard E. 1998. *Transforming Qualitative Information: Thematic Analysis and Code Development*. Thousand Oaks, CA: Sage.

Boyle, James. 2008. *The Public Domain: Enclosing the Commons of the Mind*. New Haven, CT: Yale University Press.

Bradshaw, James. 2014a. "CBC Plans Massive Staff Cuts as It Shifts to Mobile-First Strategy." *Globe and Mail*, 26 June. http://www.theglobeandmail.com/report-on-business/postmedia-cuts-national-writer-jobs-offers-newsroom-buyouts/article22819241/.

Bradshaw, James. 2014b. "Postmedia-Quebecor Deal Raises Questions on Future of Newspapers." *Globe and Mail*, 6 Oct. http://www.theglobeandmail.com/report-on-business/quebecor-sells-english-papers-to-postmedia-for-316-million/article20941032/.

Bradshaw, James. 2015. "Postmedia Cuts National Writer Jobs, Offers Newsroom Buyouts." *Globe and Mail*, 5 Feb. http://www.theglobeandmail.com/report-on-business/postmedia-cuts-national-writer-jobs-offers-newsroom-buyouts/article22819241/.

Braman, Sandra. 2006. *Change of State: Information, Policy, and Power*. Cambridge, MA: MIT Press.

Brevini, Benedetta, Arne Hintz, and Patrick McCurdy, eds. 2013. *Beyond WikiLeaks: Implications for the Future of Communications, Journalism and Society*. Basingstoke: Palgrave. http://dx.doi.org/10.1057/9781137275745.

Brin, Colette. 2012. "*Roundtable on Journalism Strategies Conference: Discussion of Similar Conferences and Language Issues*." Roundtable conducted at the meeting of the Canadian Communication Association, Waterloo, ON, May–June.

Brock, George. 2013. *Out of Print: Newspapers, Journalism, and the Business of News in the Digital Age*. London: Kogan Page.

Brooks, Bryan S., and James L. Pinson. 2009. *The Art of Editing in the Age of Convergence*. Boston: Pearson Education.

Brown, Wendy. 2011. *Walled States, Waning Sovereignty*. New York: Zone.

Browne, Donald R., and Enrique Uribe-Jongbloed. 2013. "Introduction: Ethnic/Linguistic Minority Media – What Their History Reveals, How Scholars Have Studied Them and What We Might Ask Next." In *Social Media and Minority Languages: Convergence and Creative Industries*, ed. Haf Gruffydd Jones Elin and Enrique Uribe-Jongbloed, 1–12. Bristol: Multilingual Matters. http://dx.doi.org/10.1017/CBO9781139855938.001.

Brulle, Robert J. 2010. "From Environmental Campaigns to Advancing the Public Dialog: Environmental Communication for Civic Engagement." *Environmental Communication* 4 (1): 82–98. http://dx.doi .org/10.1080/17524030903522397.

Burgess, Mark. 2011. "Canadian Broadcasters Can Take Lessons from FCC Report on Local News, Critics Say." *Wire Report*, 14 June. http://www .thewirereport.ca/reports/content/12571-canadian_broadcasters_can_take _lessons_from_fcc_report_on_local_news_critics_say.

Butler, Judith. 2009. *Frames of War*. London: Verso.

Calabrese, Andrew. 2001. "Why Localism? Communication Technology and the Shifting Scale of Political Community." In *Communication and Community*, ed. Gregory J. Shepherd and Eric W. Rothenbuhler, 235–50. Mahwah, NJ: Lawrence Erlbaum.

Calcutt, Andrew, and Philip Hammond. 2011. *Journalism Studies: A Critical Introduction*. New York: Routledge.

Calhoun, Craig, ed. 1992. *Habermas and the Public Sphere*. Cambridge, MA: MIT Press.

Calhoun, Craig, ed. 1995. *Critical Social Theory*. Oxford: Blackwell.

Callenbach, Ernest. 2011. "Sustainable Shrinkage; Envisioning a Smaller, Stronger Economy." *The Watershed Sentinel* 21 (5). http://www .watershedsentinel.ca/content/sustainable-shrinkage-envisioning-smaller -stronger-economy.

Callison, Candis, and Alfred Hermida. (Forthcoming). "Dissent and Resonance: #idlenomore as an Emergent Middle Ground." *Canadian Journal of Communication*.

Campion-Smith, Bruce. 2012. "Bell's Bid for Astral Media Blocked by CRTC." *Toronto Star*, 8 Oct. http://www.thestar.com/news/canada/2012/10/18/ bells_bid_for_astral_media_blocked_by_crtc.html.

Canada. 1951. *Report of the Royal Commission on the National Development of the Arts, Letters and Sciences*. (The Massey Commission). Ottawa: Edmond Cloutier.

Canada. 1970. *The Uncertain Mirror: Report of the Special Senate Committee on Mass Media*. (The Davey Committee). Ottawa: Queen's Printer.

Canada. 1971. *Instant World: A Report on Telecommunications in Canada*. Ottawa: Information Canada.

Canada. 1982. *Report of the Federal Cultural Policy Review Committee*. (The Applebaum-Hébert Report). Ottawa: Minister of Supply and Services Canada.

Canada. 1981. *Report of the Royal Commission on Newspapers*. (Kent Commission). Ottawa: Minister of Supply and Services Canada.

Canada. 1986. *Report of the Task Force on Broadcasting Policy*. (The Caplan-Sauvageau Report). Ottawa: Minister of Supply and Services Canada.

Canada. 1988. *Broadcasting Act 1968*. 16–17 Eliz. 2, c.25. In *Documents of Canadian Broadcasting*, ed. Roger Bird, 374–405. Ottawa: Carleton University Press.

Canada. 1991. *The Canadian Broadcasting Act (1991)*. Statutes of Canada. c.11. Ottawa: Public Works and Government Services Canada.

Canada. 2003. *Our Cultural Sovereignty: The Second Century of Canadian Broadcasting. Report of the House of Commons Standing Committee on Canadian Heritage*. (The Lincoln Report). Ottawa: Communication Canada.

Canada. 2005. Department of Canadian Heritage. *Reinforcing Our Cultral Sovereignty. Second Response to the Report of the Standing Committee on Canadian Heritage*. http://www.parl.gc.ca/Content/HOC/Committee/381/CHPC/GovResponse/RP1726418/CHPC_Rpt02_GvtRsp/GvtRsp_Part2-e.pdf.

Canada. 2006a. Senate Standing Committee on Transport and Communications. *Final Report on the Canadian News Media*, vol. 1. (The Bacon Report).http://www.parl.gc.ca/Content/SEN/Committee/391/TRAN/rep/repfinjun06vol1-e.htm.

Canada. 2006b. Senate Standing Committee on Transport and Communications. *Final Report on the Canadian News Media*, vol. 2. (The Bacon Report). http://www.parl.gc.ca/Content/SEN/Committee/391/tran/rep/repfinjun06vol2-e.htm.

Canada. 2006c. Department of Canadian Heritage. *Response to the Report of the Standing Committee on Transportation and Communication: Final Report on the Canadian News Media*. http://publications.gc.ca/collections/collection_2007/ch-pc/CH44-80-2006E.pdf.

Canada. 2009a. Standing Committee on Canadian Heritage. *Issues and Challenges Related to Local Television*. (The Schellenberger Report). http://www.parl.gc.ca/HousePublications/Publication.aspx?DocId=4005108&Language=&Mode=1&Parl=40&Ses=2.

Canada. 2009b. Campaign for Democratic Media. Testimony given to the Standing Committee on Canadian Heritage, Meeting No. 20, 40th Parliament, 2nd Session. 11 May.

Canada. 2012. Department of Canadian Heritage. *Analysis of National Aboriginal Broadcasting Financial Information and Aboriginal Content, Fiscal Year 2010–2011*. Ottawa: Department of Canadian Heritage.

Canada Newswire (CNW). 2011. "Social Media Reality Check 2.0." http://www.slideshare.net/cnwgroup/social-media-reality-check-20-8459861.

Canadian Association of Community Television Users and Stations (CACTUS). 2011. *The Transition to Digital Over-the-Air Television: New Opportunities for Communities*. June. http://cactus.independentmedia.ca/files/cactus/The%20Digital%20Transition%20-%20New%20Opportunities.pdf.

Canadian Broadcast Standards Council (CBSC) / Conseil canadien des normes de la radiotélévision (CCNR). n.d. "Journalistic Independence Code." Accessed 18 May 2015. http://www.cbsc.ca/codes/journalistic-independence-code/.

Canadian Broadcasting Corporation (CBC). 2011a. *2015: Everyone, Every Way –CBC/Radio-Canada's Five-Year Strategic Plan*. http://www.cbc.radio-canada.ca/en/explore/strategies/strategy-2015/.

Canadian Broadcasting Corporation (CBC). 2011b. "No Internet in 1/5 Canadian Homes." *CBC News*, 25 May. http://www.cbc.ca/news/technology/no-internet-in-1-5-canadian-homes-1.989812.

Canadian Broadcasting Corporation (CBC). 2011c. *Understanding Public Support for Private Broadcasters*. http://cbc.radio-canada.ca/_files/cbcrc/documents/latest-studies/public-value-en.pdf.

Canadian Broadcasting Corporation (CBC). 2012a. *Our Progress Report: Everyone, Every Way*. http://www.cbc.radio-canada.ca/en/explore/strategies/strategy-2015/progress/.

Canadian Broadcasting Corporation (CBC). 2012b. "Rogers Violating Federal Net Neutrality Rules, CRTC Says." *CBC News*, 23 Jan. http://www.cbc.ca/news/technology/rogers-violating-federal-net-neutrality-rules-crtc-says-1.1258560.

Canadian Broadcasting Corporation (CBC). 2012c. "CBC/Radio-Canada Astonished by the CRTC's Decision to Eliminate the Local Programming Improvement Fund." *CBC/Radio-Canada*, 18 July. http://www.cbc.radio-canada.ca/en/media-centre/2012/07/18/.

Canadian Broadcasting Corporation (CBC). 2013. "CRTC Approves Bell-Astral Merger." *CBC News*, 27 June. http://www.cbc.ca/news/business/crtc-approves-bell-astral-merger-1.1367433.

Canadian Broadcasting Corporation (CBC). 2014. "CBC to Cut 657 Jobs, Will No Longer Compete for Professional Sports Rights." *CBC News*, 10 Apr. http://www.cbc.ca/news/canada/cbc-to-cut-657-jobs-will-no-longer-compete-for-professional-sports-rights-1.2605504.

Canadian Journalists for Free Expression. 2002. "Not in the Newsroom!
Canwest Global, Chain Editorials and Freedom of Expression in Canada."
24 Mar. Toronto: Canadian Journalists for Free Expression.

Canadian Media Guild. 2012. "Government, Private Media Take Their Shots at
CBC." 16 Apr. http://www.cmg.ca/en/2012/04/16/government-private
-media-take-their-shots-at-cbc/.

Canadian Media Guild. 2013. "How It Breaks Down." http://www.cmg
.ca/en/wp-content/uploads/2013/11/cmg-infographic-Jobcuts
2008-2013.jpg.

Canadian Press. 2007. "Fears Grow at Newspapers amid Recent Canwest
Layoffs." *CBC News*, 11 Nov. http://www.cbc.ca/news/business/fears
-grow-at-newspapers-amid-recent-canwest-layoffs-1.683026.

Canadian Radio-television and Telecommunications Commission (CRTC).
1999a. *Public Notice 1999-97: Building on Success – A Policy Framework for
Canadian Television.* www.crtc.gc.ca.

Canadian Radio-television and Telecommunications Commission (CRTC).
1999b. *Public Notice CRTC 1999-97: Exemption Order for New Media
Broadcasting Undertakings.* www.crtc.gc.ca.

Canadian Radio-television and Telecommunications Commission (CRTC).
2000. *Public Notice CRTC 2000-13: Community Radio Policy.* http://www.crtc
.gc.ca/eng/archive/2000/pb2000-13.htm.

Canadian Radio-television and Telecommunications Commission (CRTC).
2001. *Public Notice CRTC 2001-88: Represenation of Cultural Diversity on
Television: Creation of an Industry / Community Task Force.* www.crtc.gc.ca.

Canadian Radio-television and Telecommunications Commission (CRTC).
2002. *Broadcasting Public Notice CRTC 2002-61: Policy Framework for
Community-Based Media.* www.crtc.gc.ca.

Canadian Radio-television and Telecommunications Commission (CRTC).
2003. *Broadcasting Public Notice CRTC 2003-37: Direct-to-Home (DTH)
Broadcasting Distribution Undertakings – Simultaneous and Non-Simultaneous
Program Deletion and the Carriage of Local Television Signals in Smaller Markets.*
http://www.crtc.gc.ca.

Canadian Radio-television and Telecommunications Commission (CRTC). 2007a.
Report of the CRTC Task Force on the Canadian Television Fund. www.crtc.gc.ca.

Canadian Radio-television and Telecommunications Commission (CRTC).
2007b. *Broadcasting Public Notice 2007-41-1. Call for Comments on the Canadian
Broadcast Standards Council's Proposed Journalistic Independence Code.* 17 Apr.
http://www.crtc.gc.ca/eng/archive/2007/pb2007-41-1.htm.

Canadian Radio-television and Telecommunications Commission (CRTC).
2008a. *Broadcasting Public Notice CRTC 2008-4: Diversity of Voices.* www.crtc
.gc.ca.

Canadian Radio-television and Telecommunications Commission (CRTC). 2008b. *Broadcasting Public Notice CRTC 2008-100: Regulatory Frameworks for Broadcasting Distribution Undertakings and Discretionary Programming Services.* www.crtc.gc.ca.

Canadian Radio-television and Telecommunications Commission (CRTC). 2009a. *Broadcasting Regulatory Policy 2009-329: Review of Broadcasting in New Media.* www.crtc.gc.ca.

Canadian Radio-television and Telecommunications Commission (CRTC). 2009b. *Broadcasting Regulatory Policy CRTC 2009-406: Policy Determinations Resulting from the 27 April 2009 Public Hearing.* www.crtc.gc.ca.

Canadian Radio-television and Telecommunications Commission (CRTC). 2009c. *Broadcasting Notice of Consultation CRTC 2009-661-5: Review of Community Television Policy Framework.* www.crtc.gc.ca.

Canadian Radio-television and Telecommunications Commission (CRTC). 2010a. *Broadcasting Regulatory Policy CRTC 2010-167: A Group-Based Approach to the Licensing of Private Television Services.* www.crtc.gc.ca.

Canadian Radio-television and Telecommunications Commission (CRTC). 2010b. *Broadcasting Regulatory Policy CRTC 2010-622: Community Television Policy.* www.crtc.gc.ca.

Canadian Radio-television and Telecommunications Commission (CRTC). 2010c. *Broadcasting Decision CRTC 2010-782: Change in Effective Control of CanWest Global Communications Corp.'s Licensed Broadcasting Subsidiaries.* www.crtc.gc.ca.

Canadian Radio-television and Telecommunications Commission (CRTC). 2010d. *Broadcasting Regulatory Policy, CRTC 2010-499, Campus and Community Radio Policy.* http://www.crtc.gc.ca/eng/archive/2010/2010-499.htm.

Canadian Radio-television and Telecommunications Commission (CRTC). 2011a. *Broadcasting Notice of Consultation CRTC 2011-788: Review of the Local Programming Improvement Fund.* www.crtc.gc.ca.

Canadian Radio-television and Telecommunications Commission (CRTC). 2011b. *Broadcasting Decision CRTC 2011-163: Change in Effective Control of CTVglobemedia's Inc.'s Licensed Broadcasting Subsidiaries.* www.crtc.gc.ca.

Canadian Radio-television and Telecommunications Commission (CRTC). 2012a. *Broadcasting Distribution Regulations.* http://laws-lois.justice.gc.ca/eng/regulations/SOR-97-555/page-1.html.

Canadian Radio-television and Telecommunications Commission (CRTC). 2012b. *Local Broadcast Markets: Diversity of Voices.* http://www.crtc.gc.ca/ownership/eng/dov_ind.htm.

Canadian Radio-television and Telecommunications Commission (CRTC). 2012c. *Broadcasting Regulatory Policy CRTC 2012-385: Review of the Local Programming Improvement Fund.* www.crtc.gc.ca.

Canadian Radio-television and Telecommunications Commission (CRTC). 2012d. *Transcription of Proceedings Before the Canadian Radio-television and Telecommunications Commission: Subject: Review of the Local Programming Improvement Fund – Broadcasting Notice of Consultation CRTC 2011-799, 2011 -788-1 and 2011-788-2.* http://www.crtc.gc.ca/eng/transcripts/2012/tb0416 .html.

Canadian Radio-television and Telecommunications Commission (CRTC). 2012e. *Astral Broadcasting Undertakings – Change of Effective Control.* http:// www.crtc.gc.ca/eng/archive/2012/2012-574.htm.

Canadian Radio-television and Telecommunications Commission (CRTC). 2012f. *CRTC Denies BCE's Bid to Acquire Astral.* http://crtc.gc.ca/eng/ com100/2012/r121018.htm.

Canadian Radio-television and Telecommunications Commission (CRTC). 2012g. *Notes for an Address by Jean-Pierre Blais.* http://www.crtc.gc.ca/eng/ com200/2012/s121029a.htm.

Carey, James W. 1993. "The Mass Media and Democracy Between the Modern and Postmodern." *Journal of International Affairs* 47 (1): 1–21.

Carey, James W. 1995. "The Press, Public Opinion and Public Discourse." In *Public Opinion and the Communication of Consent,* ed. Theodore Glasser and Charles Salmon, 373–402. New York: Guilford.

Carlson, Nicholas. 2011. "Exclusive: Now We Know AOL's Patch Revenue – And It's Tiny." *Business Insider,* 16 Dec. http://www.businessinsider.com/ weve-gotten-a-good-look-at-aols-local-ad-revenues-and-they-are-tiny -2011-12?utm_source=twbutton&utm_medium=social&utm_campaign =media.

Carpentier, Nico, Rico Lie, and Jan Servaes. 2003. "Community Media: Muting the Democratic Media Discourse?" *Continuum* 17 (1): 51–68. http://dx.doi .org/10.1080/1030431022000049010.

Carvalho, Anabela. 2007. "Communicating Global Responsibility? Discourses on Climate Change and Citizenship." *International Journal of Media and Cultural Politics* 3 (2): 180–3.

Castells, Manuel. 1996. *The Rise of the Network Society.* Oxford: Blackwell.

Centre for Law and Democracy. 2013. *Analysis of the Draft Intellectual Property Chapter of the Trans-Pacific Partnership.* Dec. http://www.law-democracy .org/live/wp-content/uploads/2013/12/TPP.IP-final.Dec13.pdf.

Chambers, Simone. 2003. "Deliberative Democratic Theory." *Annual Review of Political Science* 6 (1): 307–26. http://dx.doi.org/10.1146/annurev .polisci.6.121901.085538.

Charland, Maurice. 1986. "Technological Nationalism." *Canadian Journal of Political and Social Theory* 10 (1): 196–220.

Charles, Alec, ed. 2014. *The End of Journalism Version 2.0: Industry, Technology, and Politics.* Oxford: Peter Lang. http://dx.doi.org/10.3726/978-3-0353-0563-0.

Christians, Clifford G., Theodore Glasser, Denis McQuail, Kaarle Nordenstreng, and Robert A. White. 2009. *Normative Theories of the Media: Journalism in Democratic Societies.* Chicago: University of Chicago Press.

Cole, Harry, and Patrick Murck. 2007. "The Myth of the Localism Mandate: A Historical Survey of How the FCC's Actions Belie the Existence of a Governmental Obligation to Provide Local Programming." *CommLaw Conspectus* 15 (2): 339–71.

Coleman, Gabriella. 2009. "Code is Speech: Legal Tinkering, Expertise, and Protest Among Free and Open Source Software Developers." *Cultural Anthropology* 24 (3): 420–54. http://dx.doi.org/10.1111/j.1548-1360.2009.01036.x.

ComBase. 2009. "Community Newspaper Readership Remains Strong Across the Country." http://www.combase.ca/wp-content/uploads/2007/12/ComBase-2008-2009_ALL-MARKETS-PROVINCES.pdf.

Community Broadcasting Foundation. 2009. "2010/11 Budget Funding Submission Summary." In *Community Broadcasting and Media: Year 2015.* Funding Strategy Group. http://www.cbf.com.au/files/3013/5546/5327/Community_Broadcasting_and_Media_2015.pdf.

Compton, James. 2000. "Communicative Politics and Public Journalism." *Journalism Studies* 1 (3): 449–67. http://dx.doi.org/10.1080/14616700050081777.

Compton, James, and Paul Benedetti. 2010. "Labour, New Media and the Institutional Restructuring of Journalism." *Journalism Studies* 11 (4): 487–99. http://dx.doi.org/10.1080/14616701003638350.

Cottle, Simon. 2009a. *Global Crisis Reporting: Journalism in the Global Age.* Maidenhead, UK: Open University Press.

Cottle, Simon. 2009b. "Journalism and Globalization." In *The Handbook of Journalism Studies,* ed. Karin Wahl-Jorgensen and Thomas Hanitzsch, 341–56. New York: Routledge.

Cottle, Simon, and Mark Ashton. 1999. "From BBC Newsroom to BBC Newscentre: On Changing Technology and Journalist Practices." *Convergence* 5 (3): 22–43.

Couldry, Nick, and James Curran. 2003. *Contesting Media Power: Alternative Media in a Networked World.* Lanham, MD: Rowman and Littlefield.

Council of Europe. 2009. *Declaration of the Committee of Ministers on the Role of Community Media in Promoting Social Cohesion and Intercultural Dialogue.* 11 Feb. https://wcd.coe.int/ViewDoc.jsp?id=1409919.

Council of Europe. 2011. *Internet Governance Principles, Draft V. 2.0.* https://wcd.coe.int/ViewDoc.jsp?id=1835773.

Cowling, Paul. 2005. "An Earthy Enigma: The Role of Localism in Political, Cultural and Economic Dimensions of Media Ownership Regulation." *Hastings Communication and Entertainment Law Journal* 27: 257–358.

Cox, Robert J. 2007. "Nature's Crisis Disciplines: Does Environmental Communication Have an Ethical Duty?" *Environmental Communication: A Journal of Nature and Culture* 1 (1): 5–20. http://dx.doi.org/10.1080/17524030701333948.

Coyer, Kate. 2006. "Community Radio Licensing and Policy: An Overview." *Global Media and Communication* 2 (1): 129–34. http://dx.doi.org/10.1177/1742766506061847.

Coyer, Kate. 2011. "Community Media in a Globalized World: The Relevance and Resilience of Local Radio." In *The Handbook of Global Media and Communication Policy*, ed. Robin Mansell and Marc Raboy, 166–79. Malden, MA: Wiley-Blackwell. http://dx.doi.org/10.1002/9781444395433.ch10.

Coyer, Kate, Tony Dowmunt, and Alan Fountain, eds. 2007. *The Alternative Media Handbook*. London: Routledge.

Coyer, Kate, and Arne Hintz. 2010. "Developing the 'Third Sector': Community Media Policies in Europe." In *Media Freedom and Pluralism: Media Policy Challenges in the Enlarged Europe*, ed. Beata Klimkiewicz, 275–98. Budapest: CEU Press.

Cram, Barbara. 2003. "Dissenting Opinion of Commissioner Barbara Cram." *Broadcasting Public Notice CRTC 2003–37, Appendix B*. Canadian Radio-television and Telecommunications Commission. http://www.crtc.gc.ca.

Creery, Tim. 1984. "Out of Commission: Why the Kent Recommendations Have Been Trashed: An Insider's Report." *Ryerson Review of Journalism* (Spring). http://rrj.ca/out-of-commission/.

Cribb, Robert. 2002. "Journalists' Association Wants Diversity of Opinions Protected in Wake of Canwest's Editorial Decisions." *Vancouver Sun*, 7 Feb., A19.

Crowther, Christine. 2010. "CBC News: A 'Public' Shift?" Unpublished paper.

Cuffe, Sandra. 2012. "'Stand with Us to Fight': Hundreds Protest Enbridge Pipeline and Oil Tankers at Heiltsuk-Led Rally." *Dominion*, 28 Mar. http://www.dominionpaper.ca/articles/4402.

Curran, James. 2000. "Rethinking Media and Democracy." In *Mass Media and Society*, 3rd ed., ed. James Curran and Michael Gurevitch, 120–54. London: Arnold.

Curran, James. 2005. *Media and Power*. London: Routledge.

Curran, James, and Jean Seaton. 2003. *Power Without Responsibility: Press, Broadcasting, and the Internet in Britain*. London: Routledge.

Cvetkovich, Ann, and Douglas Kellner, eds. 1997. *Articulating the Global and the Local: Globalization and Cultural Studies*. Boulder, CO: Westview.

Dahlgren, Peter. 1996. "Media Logic in Cyberspace: Repositioning Journalism and Its Publics." *Janvost / The Public* 3 (3). http://www.javnost-thepublic.org/media/datoteke/Dahlgren_3-1996.pdf.

Danticat, Edwidge. 2007. "Impounded Fathers." *New York Times*, 17 June, A12.

Deards, H. 2009. "Twitter First Off the Mark with Hudson Plane Crash Coverage." *Editors Web Log*, 19 Jan. http://www.editorsweblog.org/2009/01/19/twitter-first-off-the-mark-with-hudson-plane-crash-coverage.

Deibert, Ronald J., John G. Palfrey, Rafal Rohozinski, and Jonathan Zittrain. 2008. *Access Denied: The Practice and Policy of Global Internet Filtering*. Cambridge, MA: MIT Press.

Derrida, Jacques. 2005. *Rogues: Two Essays on Reason*. Stanford, CA: Stanford University Press.

Deuze, Mark, ed. 2005. "Popular Journalism and Professional Ideology: Tabloid Reporters and Editors Speak Out." *Media Culture & Society* 27 (6): 861–82. http://dx.doi.org/10.1177/0163443705057674.

Deuze, Mark. 2008. "Understanding Journalism as Newswork: How It Changes, and How It Remains the Same." *Westminster Papers in Communication and Culture* 5 (2): 4–23.

Deuze, Mark, Axel Bruns, and Christoph Neuberger. 2007. "Preparing for an Age of Participatory News." *Journalism Practice* 1 (3): 322–38. http://dx.doi.org/10.1080/17512780701504864.

Dewey, John. 1927. *The Public and Its Problems*. New York: Henry Holt.

Dey, Ian. 1993. *Qualitative Data Analysis: A User-Friendly Guide for Social Scientists*. New York: Routledge. http://dx.doi.org/10.4324/9780203412497.

Diamond, Larry. 2010. "Liberation Technology." *Journal of Democracy* 21 (3): 69–83. http://dx.doi.org/10.1353/jod.0.0190.

Dirlik, Arif. 1996. "The Global in the Local." In *Global/Local: Cultural Production and the Transnational Imaginary*, ed. Rob Wilson and Wimal Dissanayake, 21–45. Durham, NC: Duke University Press. http://dx.doi.org/10.1215/9780822381990-002.

Dirlik, Arif. 1999. "Place-Based Imagination: Globalism and the Politics of Place." *Review - Fernand Braudel Center* 22 (2): 151–87.

Dixon, Guy. 2012. "CBC Cuts Current-Affairs Shows, 88 New Jobs." *Global and Mail*, 11 Apr., R2.

Doctor, Ken. 2012. "The Newsonomics of Hyperlocal's Next Round: Patch, Digital First, and More." *Nieman Journalism Lab*, 23 Feb. http://www

.niemanlab.org/2012/02/the-newsonomics-of-hyperlocals-next-round-patch-digital-first-and-more/.

Dominelli, Lena. 2002. *Anti-Oppressive Social Work: Theory and Practice*. New York: Palgrave.

Dominion. n.d. http://www.dominionpaper.ca/.

Dourish, Paul, and Johanna Brewer. 2008. "Storied Spaces: Cultural Accounts of Mobility, Technology, and Environmental Knowing." *International Journal of Human-Computer Studies* 1–4. http://dx.doi.org/.

Dowmunt, Tony, ed. 1993. *Channels of Resistance: Global Television and Local Empowerment*. London: BFI Publishing and Channel Four Television.

Downie Jr, Leonard, and Michael Schudson. 2009. "The Reconstruction of American Journalism." *Columbia Journalism Review* (Nov./Dec.). http://www.cjr.org/reconstruction/the_reconstruction_of_american.php?page=all.

Downing, John D.H. 2001. *Radical Media: Rebellious Communication and Social Movements*. Thousand Oaks, CA: Sage.

Downing, John D.H. 2002. "The INDYMEDIA Phenomenon: Space-Place-Democracy and the New Independent Media Centers." Paper presented to the BUGS Conference, Montreal, Quebec, 24–7 Apr.

Downing, John D.H. 2008. "Social Movement Theories and Alternative Media: An Evaluation and Critique." *Communication, Culture & Critique* 1 (1): 40–50. http://dx.doi.org/10.1111/j.1753-9137.2007.00005.x.

Downing, John D.H. 2010. "Nanomedia: 'Community' Media, 'Network' Media, 'Social Movement' Media: Why Do They Matter? And What's in a Name?" Paper presented to the Mitjans comunitaris, moviments socials i xarxes Conference, Barcelona, 15 Mar.

Downing, John D.H. 2011. *Encyclopedia of Social Movement Media*. Thousand Oaks, CA: Sage. http://dx.doi.org/10.4135/9781412979313.

Downing, John D.H., and Charles Husband. 2005. *Representing Race: Racisms, Ethnicity and the Media*. London: Sage.

Drobnick, Jim, ed. 2004. *Aural Cultures*. Banff, AB: Walter Philipps Gallery.

Druick, Zoë. 2010. "Meeting at the Poverty Line: Government Policy, Social Work, and Media Activism in the Challenge for Change Program." In *Challenge for Change: Activist Documentary at the National Film Board of Canada*, ed. Thomas Waugh, Michael Brendan Baker, and Ezra Winton, 337–54. Montreal: McGill-Queen's University Press.

Dryzek, John S. 2000. *Deliberative Democracy and Beyond: Liberals, Critics, Contestations*. Oxford: Oxford University Press.

Dumas, Chantal. n.d. "Radio: À travers le temps." *Chantal Dumas, artiste sonore*. http://chantaldumas.org/projets-2/radio-_-productions-a-travers-le-temps/.

Durkin, Jessica, and Tom Glaisyer. 2010. *An Information Community Case Study: Scranton: An Industrial City with a Media Ecosystem Yet to Take Advantage of Digital Opportunities*. New America Foundation, May. http://apps.fcc.gov/ecfs/document/view;jsessionid=TvhyTcTMdpqSZgZc84yjn4GpJ3vRlsJrYb W2H8tzpNTtPqPQxBSk!1281169505!1675925370?id=7020450503.

Edge, Marc. 2007. *Asper Nation: Canada's Most Dangerous Media Company*. Vancouver: New Star Books.

Edge, Marc. 2014. *Greatly Exaggerated: The Myth of the Death of Newspapers*. Vancouver: New Star Books.

Edwards, Catherine. 2009. *Community Television Policies and Practices Worldwide*. http://cactus.independentmedia.ca/node/519.

Elson, Shane. 2007. "A Habermasian Perspective on the Alternative Radio Program." *Social Alternatives* 26 (1): 32–8.

Entman, Robert. 2004. *Projections of Power: Framing News, Public Opinion, and U.S. Foreign Policy*. Chicago: University of Chicago Press.

Entman, Robert. 2010. "Improving Newspapers' Economic Prospects by Augmenting Their Contributions to Democracy." *International Journal of Press/Politics* 15 (1): 104–25. http://dx.doi.org/10.1177/1940161209352371.

Escobar, Arturo. 2000. "Place, Power, and Networks in Globalization and Postdevelopment." In *Redeveloping Communication for Social Change*, ed. Karin G. Wilkins, 163–73. Lanham, MD: Rowman and Littlefield.

Esterowicz, Anthony, and Robert N. Roberts. 2000. *Public Journalism and Political Knowledge*. New York: Rowman and Littlefield.

European Digital Rights (EDRi). 2010. "German Federal Constitutional Court Rejects Data Retention Law." 10 Mar. https://edri.org/edrigramnumber8 -5german-decision-data-retention-unconstitutional/.

European Digital Rights (EDRi). n.d. "About EDRi." Accessed 8 May 2015. https://edri.org/about/.

Evans, Fred. 2008. *The Multivoiced Body: Society and Communication in an Age of Diversity*. New York: Columbia University Press.

Evans, Pete. 2014. "Quebecor Sells 175 Sun Media Newspapers and Websites to Postmedia." *CBC News*, 6 Oct. http://www.cbc.ca/news/business/quebecor -sells-175-sun-media-newspapers-and-websites-to-postmedia-1.2788693.

Ewart, Jacqueline A. 2000. "Capturing the Heart of the Region – How Regional Media Define a Community." *Transformations* 1: 1–13.

Ewart, Jacqueline A., Michael Meadows, Susan R. Forde, and Kerrie Foxwell. 2005. "Media Matters: Ways to Link Community Radio and Community Newspapers." *Australian Journalism Review* 27 (2): 87–104.

Fairchild, Charles. 2001. *Community Radio and Public Culture: Being an Examination of Media Access and Equity in the Nations of North America*. Cresskill, NJ: Hampton.

Fairclough, Norman. 1992. *Discourse and Social Change*. Malden, MA: Polity.

Fairclough, Norman. 2005. *Media Discourse*. London: Bloomsbury Academic.

Farhi, Paul. 2009. "The Twitter Explosion." *American Journalism Review* (Apr./ May). http://www.ajr.org/article.asp?id=4756.

Farhi, Paul. 2010. "Lost in the Woods." *American Journalism Review* 32 (1): 14–9.

Fawcett, Liz. 2002. "Why Peace Journalism Isn't News." *Journalism Studies* 3 (2): 213–23. http://dx.doi.org/10.1080/14616700220129982.

Fenton, Nathalie. 2010. *New Media, Old News: Journalism and Democracy in the Digital Age*. London: Sage. http://dx.doi.org/10.4135/9781446280010.

Fischer, Frank. 2003. *Reframing Public Policy: Discursive Politics and Deliberative Practices*. New York: Oxford University Press. http://dx.doi.org/10.1093/01 9924264X.001.0001.

Fitzgerald, Kate. 2007. "Aspen Offers Stark Look at Snowless Slopes." *Advertising Age* 78 (24): 6–11.

Flaim, Sean M. 2012. "Imminent 'Six Strikes' Copyright Alert System Needs Antitrust Scrutiny." *Ars Technica*, 18 Mar. http://arstechnica.com/tech-policy/ news/2012/03/op-ed-imminent-six-strikes-copyright-alert-system-needs -antitrust-scrutiny.

Fleras, Augie. 2009. "Ethnic and Aboriginal Media in Canada: Crossing Borders, Constructing Buffers, Creating Bonds, Building Bridges." In *Media-Migration-Integration*, ed. Rainer Geissler and Horst Pöttker, 143–79. London: Transaction. http://dx.doi.org/10.14361/9783839410325-006.

Forde, Susan. 2011. *Challenging the News: The Journalism of Alternative and Community Media*. Hampshire: Palgrave Macmillan.

Forde, Susan, Kerrie Foxwell, and Michael Meadows. 2002. *Culture, Commitment, Community: The Australian Community Radio Sector*. Brisbane: Griffith University.

Forde, Susan, Kerrie Foxwell, and Michael Meadows. 2003. "The Australian Community Radio Sector." *European Journal of Communication Research* 28 (3): 231–52.

Forde, Susan, Kerrie Foxwell, and Michael Meadows. 2009. *Developing Dialogues: Indigenous and Ethnic Community Broadcasting in Australia*. Chicago: University of Chicago Press.

Foucault, Michel. 1966. *Les mots et les choses*. Paris: Gallimard.

Foucault, Michel. 1969. *L'archéologie du savoir*. Paris: Gallimard.

Foucault, Michel. 1993. *Surveiller et punir: Naissance de la prison*. Paris: Gallimard.

Foucault, Michel. 2004. *Philosophie:Anthologie*. Paris: Gallimard.

Francoeur, Chantal. 2011a. *Choc des cultures, contre-discours et adaptation: L'intégration, le régime de vérité radio-canadien*. Doctoral dissertation, Concordia University.

Francoeur, Chantal. 2011b. "From Radio to Audio While Exploring Journalistic Formats." *Ethnographic Terminalia*. http://ethnographicterminalia.org/2011-montreal/chantal-francoeur.

Francoeur, Chantal. 2012. *La transformation du service de l'information de Radio-Canada*. Quebec: Presses de l'Université du Québec.

Franklin, Bob. 2008. "Introduction: Newspapers: Trends and Developments." In *Pulling Newspapers Apart: Analysing Print Journalism*, ed. Bob Franklin, 1–36. New York: Routledge.

Fraser, Nancy. 1990. "Rethinking the Public Sphere: A Contribution to the Critique of Actually Existing Democracy." *Social Text* (25/26): 56–80. http://dx.doi.org/10.2307/466240.

Fraser, Nancy. 1992. "Rethinking the Public Sphere: A Contribution to the Critique of Actually Existing Democracy." In *Habermas and the Public Sphere*, ed. Craig Calhoun, 109–42. Cambridge, MA: MIT Press.

Freedman, Des. 2008. *The Politics of Media Policy*. Cambridge: Polity.

Freedman, Des. 2010. "Media Policy Silences: The Hidden Face of Communications Decision Making." *International Journal of Press/Politics* 15 (3): 344–61. http://dx.doi.org/10.1177/1940161210368292.

Freedman, Des. 2014. *The Contradictions of Media Power*. London: Bloomsbury.

Freedman, Des, Jonathan Obar, Cheryl Martens, and Robert W. McChesney, eds. Forthcoming. *Strategies for Media Reform: International Perspectives*. New York: Fordham University Press.

Freedman, Samuel G. 2007. "School Records on Special English Classes Are Called Works of Fiction by Critics." *New York Times*, 11 Apr., B7.

Freeze, Colin, and Stephanie Nolen. 2013. "Charges that Canada Spied on Brazil Unveil CSEC's Inner Workings." *Globe and Mail*, 7 Oct. http://www.theglobeandmail.com/news/world/brazil-spying-report-spotlights-canadas-electronic-eavesdroppers/article14720003/.

Friedland, Lewis A. 2001. "Communication, Community, and Democracy: Toward a Theory of the Communicatively Integrated Community." *Communication Research* 28 (4): 358–91. http://dx.doi.org/10.1177/009365001028004002.

Friesen, Gerald. 2001. "The Evolving Meanings of Region in Canada." *Canadian Historical Review* 82: 520–45.

Fuchs, Christian. 2010. "Alternative Media as Critical Media." *European Journal of Social Theory* 13 (2): 173–92. http://dx.doi.org/10.1177/1368431010362294.

Fuchs, Christian, and Vincent Mosco. 2012. ""Marx Is Back: The Importance of Marxist Theory and Research for Critical Communication Studies Today." *Triple C*." *Open Access Journal for a Global Sustainable Society* 10 (2): 127–40.

Galloway, Gloria. 2012. "First Nations #IdleNoMore Protests Push for 'Reckoning.'" *Globe and Mail*, 20 Dec. http://www.theglobeandmail.com/news/politics/first-nations-protests-push-for-reckoning/article6589418/.

Galtung, John, and Mari H. Ruge. 1965. "The Structure of Foreign News: The Presentation of the Congo, Cuba and Cyprus Crises in Four Norwegian Newspapers." *Journal of International Peace Research* 2 (1): 4–91.

Gasher, Mike, and Greg Nielsen. 2011. *Mediating Exclusion through Journalism*. Non-published Standard SSHRC Application.

Gasher, Mike, David Skinner, and Rowland Lorimer. 2012. *Mass Communication in Canada*. 7th ed. Don Mills, ON: Oxford University Press.

Gasher, Mike, David Skinner, and Rowland Lorimer. 2016. *Mass Communication in Canada*. 8th ed. Toronto: Oxford University Press.

Geist, Michael. 2009. "Connecting Canada to the Digital World." *Toronto Star*, 13 June. http://www.thestar.com/business/2009/06/13/connecting_canada_to_the_digital_world.html.

George, Éric. 2010. "Re-reading the Notion of 'Convergence' in Light of Recent Changes to the Culture and Communication Industries in Canada." *Canadian Journal of Communication* 35 (4): 555–64.

Gerbaudo, Paolo. 2012. *Tweets and the Streets: Social Media and Contemporary Activism*. London: Pluto.

Giles, Robert H. 2010. "New Economic Models for U.S. Journalism." *Daedalus* 139 (2): 26–38. http://dx.doi.org/10.1162/daed.2010.139.2.26.

Gillette, Felix. 2012. "AOL's Patch: Big Losses on Hyperlocal News." *Business Week*, 31 May. http://www.bloomberg.com/bw/articles/2012-05-31/aols-patch-big-losses-on-hyperlocal-news.

Gitelman, Lisa. 2006. *Always Already New: Media, History, and the Data of Culture*. Cambridge, MA: MIT Press.

Goldsmith, Jack, and Tim Wu. 2006. *Who Controls the Internet? Illusions of a Borderless World*. Oxford: Oxford University Press.

Goodman, Amy, and David Goodman. 2006. *Static: Government Liars, Media Cheerleaders, and the People Who Fight Back*. New York: Hyperion.

Goodman, Ellen P. 2009. "Public Service Media 2.0." In *And Communications for All: A Policy Agenda for a New Administration*, ed. Amit M. Schejter, 263–80. Lanham. MD: Rowman and Littlefield.

Google. 2015. "Transparency Report 2012." http://www.google.com/transparencyreport.

Greenwald, Glenn. 2014. *No Place to Hide: Edward Snowden, the N.S.A., and the U.S. Surveillance State*. New York: Metropolitan.

Grey, Julius. 2010. "The Accommodation Debate: It's an Argument that Just Won't Die – And There's Plenty of Hypocrisy and Self-Satisfaction on Both Sides." *Montreal Gazette*, 8 Apr., A22.

Grossberg, Lawrence. 2010. *Cultural Studies in the Future Tense*. Durham, NC: Duke University Press. http://dx.doi.org/10.1215/9780822393313.

Grossman, Daniel. 2005. "Observing Those Who Observe." *Nieman Reports* 59 (4): 80–5.

GroundWire. 2010. "News Data Analysis." http://groundwire.ncra.ca/index.cfm/2010/6/15/News-Data-Analysis-2010.

GroundWire. 2014. "GW Editorial Policy." 27 Aug. http://groundwire.ncra.ca/index.cfm/2014/8/27/GW-Editorial-Policy.

Gunster, Shane. 2011. "Covering Copenhagen: Climate Change in BC Media." *Canadian Journal of Communication* 36 (3): 477–502.

Gutstein, Donald. 2009. *Not a Conspiracy Theory: How Business Propaganda Hijacks Democracy*. Toronto: Key Porter.

Ha, Louisa. 2008. "Online Advertising Research in Advertising Journals: A Review." *Journal of Current Issues and Research in Advertising* 30 (1): 31–48. http://dx.doi.org/10.1080/10641734.2008.10505236.

Haas, Tanni. 2004. "Alternative Media, Public Journalism and the Pursuit of Democratization." *Journalism Studies* 5 (1): 115–21. http://dx.doi.org/10.1080/1461670032000174783.

Haas, Tanni. 2005. "From 'Public Journalism' to the 'Public's Journalism'? Rhetoric and Reality in the Discourse of Weblogs." *Journalism Studies* 6 (3): 387–96. http://dx.doi.org/10.1080/14616700500132073.

Haas, Tanni. 2007. *The Pursuit of Public Journalism: Theory, Practice, and Criticism*. New York: Routledge.

Habermas, Jürgen. 1974. "The Public Sphere: An Encyclopedia Article." *New German Critique* 3: 29–35.

Habermas, Jürgen. 1989. *The Structural Transformation of the Public Sphere: An Inquiry into a Category of Bourgeois Society*. Trans. Thomas Burger. Cambridge, MA: MIT Press.

Habermas, Jürgen. 1996. *Between Facts and Norms: Contributions to a Discourse Theory of Law and Democracy*. Cambridge, MA: MIT Press.

Habermas, Jürgen. 2006a. "Political Communication in Media Society: Does Democracy Still Enjoy an Epistemic Dimension? The Impact of Normative Theory on Empirical Research." *Communication Theory* 16 (4): 411–26. http://dx.doi.org/10.1111/j.1468-2885.2006.00280.x.

Habermas, Jürgen. 2006b. "The Public Sphere: An Encyclopedia Article." In *Media and Cultural Studies: Key Works*, ed. Mennakshi G. Durham and Douglas M. Kellner, 73–9. Malden, MA: Blackwell.

Habermas, Jürgen. 2008. "The Public Sphere." In *Media Studies: A Reader*, ed. Paul Marris and Sue Thornham, 92–7. New York: New York University Press.

Habermas, Jürgen. 2009. *Europe: The Faltering Project*. Trans. Ciarin Cronin. London: Polity.

Hackett, Robert A. 1991. *News and Dissent: The Press and the Politics of Peace in Canada.* Norwood, NJ: Ablex.

Hackett, Robert A. 2006. "Is Peace Journalism Possible?"*Conflict and Communication Online* 5, no. 2. http://www.cco.regener-online.de/2006_2/pdf/hackett.pdf.

Hackett, Robert A. 2010. "Journalism for Peace and Justice: Towards a Comparative Analysis of Media Paradigms." *Studies in Social Justice* 4 (2): 179–98.

Hackett, Robert A., and William K. Carroll. 2006. *Remaking Media: The Struggle to Democratize Public Communication.* New York: Routledge.

Hackett, Robert A., and Richard Gruneau, with Donald Gutstein, Timothy A. Gibson, and NewsWatch Canada. 2000. *The Missing News: Filters and Blind Spots in Canada's Press.* Toronto: Canadian Centre for Policy Alternatives / Garamond.

Hackett, Robert A., Richard Pinet, and Myles Ruggles. 1992. "From Audience Commodity to Audience Community: Mass Media in B.C." In *Seeing Ourselves: Media Power and Policy in Canada*, ed. Helen Holmes and David Taras, 10–20. Toronto: Harcourt Brace Jovanovich.

Hackett, Robert A., and Birgitta Schroeder, with NewsWatch Canada. 2008. "Does Anybody Practice Peace Journalism? A Cross-National Comparison of Press Coverage of the Afghanistan and Israeli-Hezbollah Wars." *Peace and Policy* 13: 26-46.

Hackett, Robert A., and Yuezhi Zhao. 1998. *Sustaining Democracy? Journalism and the Politics of Objectivity.* Toronto: Garamond.

Hackett, Robert A., and Yuezhi Zhao. 2005. *Democratizing Global Media: One World, Many Struggles.* Oxford: Rowman and Littlefield.

Hallett, Lawrie, and Arne Hintz. 2010. "Digital Broadcasting – Challenges and Opportunities for European Community Radio Broadcasters." *Telematics and Informatics* 27 (2): 151–61. http://dx.doi.org/10.1016/j.tele.2009.06.005.

Hamilton, James. 2000. "Alternative Media: Conceptual Difficulties, Critical Possibilities." *Journal of Communication Inquiry* 24 (4): 357–78. http://dx.doi.org/10.1177/0196859900024004002.

Hanitzsch, Thomas. 2004. "The Peace Journalism Problem: Failure of News People – Or Failure of Analysis?" In *Agents of Peace: Public Communication and Conflict Resolution in an Asian Setting*, ed. Thomas Hanitzsch, Martin Loffelholz, and Ronny Mustamu, 185–209. Jakarta: Friedrich Ebert Stiftung.

Hanitzsch, Thomas. 2007. "Deconstructing Journalism Culture: Toward a Universal Theory." *Communication Theory* 17 (4): 367–85. http://dx.doi.org/10.1111/j.1468-2885.2007.00303.x.

Hanitzsch, Thomas. 2013. "The Transformation of Journalism in a Global Context." Keynote address at the annual Journalism Education Association of Australia Conference, Mooloolaba, Queensland, 2 Dec.

Harcup, Tony. 2011. "Alternative Journalism as Active Citizenship." *Journalism* 12 (1): 15–31. http://dx.doi.org/10.1177/1464884910385191.

Harcup, Tony, and Deirdre O'Neill. 2001. "What Is News? Galtung and Ruge Revisited." *Journalism Studies* 2 (2): 261–80. http://dx.doi.org/10.1080/14616700118449.

Harrison, Steve, and Paul Dourish. 1996. "Re-place-ing Space: The Roles of Place and Space in Collaborative Systems." *ACM Conference on Computer-Supported Cooperative Work*: 67–76.

Hartley, John. 2008. "Journalism and Popular Culture." In *The Handbook of Journalism Studies*, ed. Karin Wahl-Jorgensen and Thomas Hanitzsch, 310–25. New York: Routledge.

Harvey, David. 2005. *A Brief History of Neoliberalism*. Oxford: Oxford University Press.

Haugerud, Angelique. 2003. "The Disappearing Local: Rethinking Global-Local Connections." In *Localizing Knowledge in a Globalizing World: Recasting the Area Studies Debate*, ed. Ali Mirsepassi, Amrita Basu, and Frederick Weaver, 60–81. Syracuse: Syracuse University Press.

Held, David. 2006. *Models of Democracy*. 3rd ed. Cambridge: Cambridge University Press.

Herman, Edward S., and Noam Chomsky. 2002. *Manufacturing Consent: The Political Economy of the Mass Media*. New York: Pantheon.

Hermida, Alfred. 2010. "Twittering the News: The Emergence of Ambient Journalism." *Journalism Practice* 4 (3): 297–308. http://dx.doi.org/10.1080/17512781003640703.

Hill, Clara E., Sarah Knox, Barbara J. Thompson, Elizabeth N. Williams, Shirley A. Hess, and Nicholas Ladany. 2005. "Consensual Qualitative Research: An Update." *Journal of Counseling Psychology* 52 (2): 1–25. http://dx.doi.org/10.1037/0022-0167.52.2.196.

Hill, Clara E., Barbara J. Thompson, and Elizabeth N. Williams. 1997. "A Guide to Conducting Consensual Qualitative Research." *Counseling Psychologist* 25 (4): 517–72. http://dx.doi.org/10.1177/0011000097254001.

Hindley, Patricia, Gail M. Martin, and Jean McNulty. 1977. *The Tangled Net: Basic Issues in Canadian Communications*. Vancouver: Douglas and McIntyre.

Hintz, Arne. 2011. "From Media Niche to Policy Spotlight: Mapping Community Media Policy in Latin America." *Canadian Journal of Communication* 36 (1): 147–59.

Hintz, Arne. 2013. "Dimensions of Modern Freedom of Expression: WikiLeaks, Policy Hacking, and Digital Freedoms." In *Beyond WikiLeaks: Implications for the Future of Communications, Journalism and Society*, ed. Benedetta Brevini, Arne Hintz, and Patrick McCurdy, 145–65. Basingstoke: Palgrave. http://dx.doi.org/10.1057/9781137275745.0015.

Hintz, Arne, and Stefania Milan. 2009. "At the Margins of Internet Governance: Grassroots Tech Groups and Communication Policy." *International Journal of Media and Cultural Politics* 5 (1): 23–38. http://dx.doi.org/10.1386/macp.5.1-2.23_1.

Holstein, James A., and Jaber F. Gubrium, eds. 2008. *Handbook of Constructionist Research*. New York: Guilford.

Holston, James. 2008. *Insurgent Citizenship: Disjunctions of Democracy and Modernity in Brazil*. Princeton, NJ: Princeton University Press.

Hope, Chris. 2002. "Chasing Asper: The CRTC's Changing Stance on Convergence Through the Evolution of the Canadian Media Industry." http://www.friends.ca/pub/207.

Horkheimer, Max. 1972. *Critical Theory: Selected Essays*. New York: Continuum International.

Horkheimer, Max, and Theodor Adorno. 1972. *Dialectic of Enlightenment*. Trans. John Cumming. New York: Herder and Herder.

Hornmoen, Harald, and Steen Steensen. 2014. "Dialogue as a Journalistic Ideal." *Journalism Studies* 15 (5): 543–54. http://dx.doi.org/10.1080/1461670X.2014.894358.

Howe, Jeff. 2008. *Crowdsourcing: Why the Power of the Crowd Is Driving the Future of Business*. New York: Crown.

Howley, Kevin. 2005. *Community Media: People, Places, and Communication Technologies*. Cambridge: Cambridge University Press. http://dx.doi.org/10.1017/CBO9780511489020.

Howley, Kevin. 2010a. "Introduction." In *Understanding Community Media*, ed. Kevin Howley, 1–14. Los Angeles: Sage. http://dx.doi.org/10.4135/9781452275017.n1.

Howley, Kevin. 2010b. "Notes on a Theory of Community Radio." In *Understanding Community Media*, ed. Kevin Howley, 63–70. Los Angeles: Sage. http://dx.doi.org/10.4135/9781452275017.n6.

Hu, Yuheng, Shelly D. Farnham, and Andres Monroy-Hernández. 2013. "Whoo.ly: Facilitating Information Seeking for Hyperlocal Communities Using Social Media." Paper presented at the ACM Sig CHI Conference on Human Factors in Computing Systems, Paris, 29 Apr. – 2 May. http://dx.doi.org/10.1145/2470654.2466478.

Hutchins, Brett. 2004. "Castells, Regional News Media and the Information Age." *Continuum (Perth)* 18 (4): 577–90. http://dx.doi.org/10.1080/1030431 042000297680.

Icelandic Modern Media Initiative (IMMI). 2010. "IMMI Resolution." *International Modern Media Institute*. https://en.immi.is/immi-resolution.

Interactive Advertising Bureau Canada (IAB Canada). 2011. *Canadian Online Advertising Revenue Survey*. Toronto: IAB Canada.

International Modern Media Institute (IMMI). 2012. "IMMI Status Report." Apr. http://docslide.us/documents/2012-04-15-immi-status-report.html.

Iser, Wolfgang. 1974. *The Implied Reader: Patterns of Communication in Prose Fiction from Bunyan to Beckett*. Baltimore, MD: Johns Hopkins University Press.

Jackson, John, Greg Nielsen, and Yon Hsu. 2011. *Mediated Society: A Critical Sociology of Media*. Don Mills, ON: Oxford University Press.

Jackson, Sally. 2010. "NITV secures another $15 million in funding from Government." *Australian Business Review*, 19 Apr. http://www .theaustralian.com.au/business/media/nitv-secures-another-15m-in -funding-from-government/story-e6frg996-1225855312686.

Jakubowicz, Karol. 1999a. "Public Service Broadcasting: Proud Past, Interesting Future?" *Media Development* 46 (1): 32–6.

Jakubowicz, Karol. 1999b. "Public Service Broadcasting in the Information Society." *Media Development* 46 (2): 45–9.

Janowitz, Morris. 1952. *The Community Press in an Urban Setting*. Glencoe, IL: Free Press.

Java, Akshay, Tim Finin, Xiaodan Song, and Belle Tseng. 2007. "Why We Twitter: Understanding Microblogging Usage and Communities." *Proceedings of the 9th WebKDD and Ist SNA-KDD Workshop on Web Mining and Social Network Analysis*: 56–65. http://dx.doi.org/10.1145/ 1348549.1348556.

Jenkins, Henry. 2006a. *Confronting the Challenges of Participatory Culture*. Cambridge, MA: MIT Press.

Jenkins, Henry. 2006b. *Convergence Culture: Where Old and New Media Collide*. New York: New York University Press.

Johnson-Laird, Philip N. 1996. "Mental Models, Deductive Reasoning, and the Brain." In *The Cognitive Neurosciences*, ed. Michael S. Gazzaniga, 999–1008. Cambridge, MA: MIT Press.

Joint Economic Committee. 2009. *The Future of Newspapers: The Impact on the Economy and on Democracy*. http://www.gpo.gov/fdsys/pkg/CHRG -111shrg55622/html/CHRG-111shrg55622.htm.

Jones, Alex S. 2009. *Losing the News: The Future of the News That Feeds Democracy.* New York: Oxford University Press.

Jonsdottir, Birgitta. 2013. "Foreword." In *Beyond WikiLeaks: Implications for the Future of Communications, Journalism and Society,* ed. Benedetta Brevini, Arne Hintz, and Patrick McCurdy, xi–xviii. Basingstoke: Palgrave.

Joseph, Miranda. 2008. *Against the Romance of Community.* Minneapolis, MN: University of Minnesota Press.

Joss, Simon. 1995. "Evaluating Consensus Conferences: Necessity or Luxury?" In *Public Participation in Science: The Role of Consensus Conferences in Europe,* ed. Simon Joss and John Durant, 89–108. London: Science Museum.

Journalism Strategies Project. 2012. "Organizational Models Breakout Session." Unpublished raw data. 12 Apr.

Jurriens, Edwin. 2009. *From Monologue to Dialogue: Radio and Reform in Indonesia.* Leiden: KITLV Press. http://dx.doi.org/10.1163/9789004253834.

Kane, Laura. 2014. "CBC Lays Off Veteran Sportscasters Steve Armitage and Mark Lee." *Canadian Press,* 13 Aug. http://j-source.ca/article/cbc-lays-veteran-sportscasters-steve-armitage-and-mark-lee.

Kaniss, Phyllis. 1991. *Making Local News.* Chicago: University of Chicago Press.

Katz, Elihu. 1977. "Can Authentic Cultures Survive New Media?" *Journal of Communication* 27 (2): 113–21. http://dx.doi.org/10.1111/j.1460-2466.1977.tb01836.x.

Kaye, Jeff, and Stephen Quinn. 2010. *Funding Journalism in the Digital Age: Business Models, Strategies, Issues and Trends.* New York: Peter Lang.

Kellner, Douglas. 2003. *From 9/11 to Terror War: The Dangers of the Bush Legacy.* Lanham, MD: Rowman and Littlefield.

Kelly, John. 2009. "Red Kayaks and Hidden Gold: The Rise, Challenges and Values of Citizen Journalism." *Reuters Institute for the Study of Journalism,* Sept. http://reutersinstitute.politics.ox.ac.uk/sites/default/files/Red%20Kayaks%20and%20Hidden%20Gold%20The%20Rise%2C%20Challenges%20and%20Value%20of%20Citizen_0.pdf.

Kempf, Wilhelm. 2007. "Peace Journalism: A Tightrope Walk Between Advocacy Journalism and Constructive Conflict Coverage." *Conflict and Communication Online* 6, no. 2. http://www.cco.regener-online.de/2007_2/pdf/kempf.pdf.

Kent, Tom. 1992. "The Times and Significance of the Kent Commission." In *Seeing Ourselves: Media Power and Policy in Canada,* ed. Helen Holmes and David Taras, 38–9. Toronto: Harcourt Brace Jovanovich.

Khamis, Sahar, and Katherine Vaughn. 2011. "Cyberactivism in the Egyptian Revolution: How Civic Engagement and Citizen Journalism

Tilted the Balance." *Arab Media and Society* 14 (Summer). http://www
.arabmediasociety.com/?article=769.

Kidd, Dorothy, and Eloise Lee. 2011. "Digital Inclusion: Working Both Sides
of the Equation." In *Communications Research in Action: Scholar-Activist
Collaborations for a Democratic Public Sphere*, ed. Philip M. Napoli and Minna
Aslama, 11–27. New York: Fordham University Press.

Killebrew, Kenneth C. 2005. *Managing Media Convergence*. Oxford: Blackwell.

Kingdon, J.W. 1984. *Agendas, Alternatives, and Public Policy*. Boston: Little
Brown.

Knight Commission on the Information Needs of Communities in a
Democracy. 2009. *Informing Communities: Sustaining Democracy in the Digital
Age*. Washington, DC: Aspen Institute. http://www.knightcomm.org/wp
-content/uploads/2010/02/Informing_ Communities_Sustaining
_Democracy_in_the_Digital_Age.pdf.

Kondo, Dorine K. 1990. *Crafting Selves*. Chicago: University of Chicago Press.

Kovach, Bill, and Tom Rosenstiel. 2007. *The Elements of Journalism: What
Newspeople Should Know and the Public Should Expect*. New York: Random
House.

Kraeplin, Camille, and Carrie A. Criado. 2009. "The State of Convergence
Journalism Revisited: Newspapers Take the Lead." In *Understanding Media,
Convergence: The State of the Field*, ed. August Grant and Jeffrey Wilkinson,
18–30. Oxford: Oxford University Press.

Kraidy, Marwan. 2005. *Hybridity: Or the Cultural Logic of Globalization*.
Philadelphia: Temple University Press.

Kreimer, Seth F. 2006. "Censorship by Proxy: The First Amendment, Internet
Intermediaries, and the Problem of the Weakest Link." *University of
Pennsylvania Law Review* 155 (1): 11–101. http://dx.doi.org/10.2307/
40041302.

Krieg, Anthea S. 2006. "Aboriginal Incarceration: Health and Social Impacts."
Medical Journal of Australia 184 (10): 534–6. http://www.mja.com.au/
public/issues/184_10_150506/kri10234_fm.html.

Kurpius, David D., Emily T. Metzgar, and Karen M. Rowley. 2010. "Sustaining
Hyperlocal Media." *Journalism Studies* 11 (3): 359–76. http://dx.doi.org/
10.1080/14616700903429787.

Kymlicka, Will. 1998. *Finding Our Way: Rethinking Ethnocultural Relations in
Canada*. Don Mills, ON: Oxford University Press.

La Rochelle, Réal. 2009. *Le patrimoine sonore du Québec*. Montreal: Triptyque.

Laba, Martin. 1988. "Popular Culture as Local Culture: Regions, Limits and
Canadianism." In *Communication Canada: Issues in Broadcasting and New*

Technologies, ed. Rowland Lorimer and Donald Wilson, 82–101. Toronto: Kagan and Woo.

LaBelle, Brandon. 2007. *Background Noise: Perspectives on Sound Art*. New York: Continuum International.

Ladurantaye, Steve. 2012. "CRTC Spikes BCE-Astra Deal." *Globe and Mail*, 18 Oct. http://www.theglobeandmail.com/globe-investor/crtc-kills-bce -astral-deal-says-mega-company-impossible-to-police/article4621510/.

Ladurantaye, Steve. 2013a. "Torstar, Quebecor Paint Bleak Picture As Revenues, Profits Plunge." *Globe and Mail*, 8 May 8. http://www .theglobeandmail.com/report-on-business/torstar-quebecor-paint-bleak -picture-as-profits-plunge/article11778090/

Ladurantaye, Steve. 2013b. "Newspaper Revenue to Drop 20 Per Cent by 2017, Report Predicts." *Globe and Mail*, 5 June. http://www.theglobeandmail. com/report-on-business/newspaper-revenue-to-drop-20-per-cent-by-2017 -report-predicts/article12357351/.

Ladurantaye, Steve. 2013c. "Canadian Newspapers Saw Revenue Fall 13% in Last Five Years." *Globe and Mail*, 5 Dec. http://www.theglobeandmail.com/ report-on-business/canadian-newspapers-saw-revenue-fall-13-in-last-five -years/article15779886/.

Lambeth, Edmund, Philip E. Meyer, and Esther Thorson. 1998. *Assessing Public Journalism*. Columbia, MO: University of Missouri Press.

Langlois, Andrea, and Frédéric Dubois, eds. 2005. *Autonomous Media: Activating Resistance and Dissent*. Montreal: Cumulous.

Langton, Marcia. 1993. *'Well, I Heard It on the Radio and I Saw It on the Television': An Essay for the Australian Film Commission on the Politics and Aesthetics of Filmmaking by and about Aboriginal People and Things*. Sydney: Australian Film Commission.

Latham, Mark. 2012. *Experiments in Voter Funded Media*. Draft, 23 June 23. votermedia.org/publications. http://dx.doi.org/10.2139/ssrn.2098015.

Lazarsfeld, Paul F., and Robert K. Merton. 2008. "Mass Communication, Popular Taste, and Organized Social Action." In *Media Studies: A Reader*, ed. Paul Marris and Sue Thornham, 18–30. New York: New York University Press.

Leiserowitz, Anthony. 2005. "American Risk Perceptions: Is Climate Change Dangerous?" *Risk Analysis* 25 (6): 1433–42. http://dx.doi.org/10.1111/ j.1540-6261.2005.00690.x.

Livingston, Steven, and W. Lance Bennett. 2003. "Gatekeeping, Indexing and Live-Event News: Is Technology Altering the Construction of News?" *Political Communication* 20 (4): 363–80. http://dx.doi.org/10.1080/ 10584600390244121.

Livingstone, Sonia. 2005. "On the Relation Between Audiences and Publics." In *Audiences and Publics: When Cultural Engagement Matters for the Public Sphere*, ed. Sonia Livingstone, 17–42. Bristol: Intellect.

Livingstone, Sonia, and Peter Lunt. 2012. *Media Regulation: Governance and the Interests of Citizens and Consumers*. London: Sage.

Lorenzoni, Irene, and Nick F. Pidgeon. 2006. "Public Views on Climate Change: European and USA Perspectives." *Climatic Change* 77 (1–2): 73–95. http://dx.doi.org/10.1007/s10584-006-9072-z.

Lowe, Greg F., and Jo Bardoel, eds. 2009. *From Public Service Broadcasting to Public Service Media*. Goteborg: Nordicom.

Lowrey, Wilson. 2011. "The Challenge of Measuring Community Journalism." In *Foundations of Community Journalism*, ed. Bill Reader and John A. Hatcher, 88–104. Thousand Oaks, CA: Sage.

Lowrey, Wilson, Amanda Brozana, and Jenn B. Mackay. 2008. "Toward a Measure of Community Journalism." *Mass Communication & Society* 11 (3): 275–99. http://dx.doi.org/10.1080/15205430701668105.

Lynch, Jake. 2002. *Reporting the World*. Taplow Court, UK: Conflict and Peace Forums.

Lynch, Jake. 2008. *Debates in Peace Journalism*. Sydney: Sydney University Press.

Lynch, Jake, and Annabel McGoldrick. 2005. *Peace Journalism*. Stroud, UK: Hawthorn.

Magder, Jason. 2007. "'We Are Part of Society. We're Not Guests': New Solitudes." *Montreal Gazette*, 18 Aug., A4.

Mailhé, Chantal, Greg M. Nielsen, and Daniel Salée. 2013. *Revealing Democracy*. New York: Peter Lang.

Mandelzis, Lea. 2007. "Representations of Peace in News Discourse: Viewpoint and Opportunity for Peace Journalism." In *Peace Journalism: The State of the Art*, ed. Dov Shinar and Wilhelm Kempf, 97–110. Berlin: Irena Regener.

Marchessault, Janine. 2010. "Amateur Video and the Challenge for Change." In *Challenge for Change: Activist Documentary at the National Film Board of Canada*, ed. Thomas Waugh, Michael Brendan Baker, and Ezra Winton, 354–65. Montreal: McGill-Queen's University Press.

Marier, Jean-Sébastien. 2012. "Can Journalism Be a Profession?" *J-Source: The Canadian Journalism Project*, 17 Jan. http://j-source.ca/article/can-journalism-be-profession.

Marin, André. 2010. "Caught in the Act." *Ombudsman Ontario*, Dec. http://www.ombudsman.on.ca/Files/sitemedia/Documents/Investigations/SORT%20Investigations/G20final-EN-web.pdf.

Marlow, Iain. 2009. "Taking on Cable Giants." *Toronto Star*, 9 Oct., B01.

Marotte, Betrand. 2009. "Examiner Launches Canadian Website." *Globe and Mail*, 28 Oct., B11.

Martin, Robert. 1997. *Media Law*. Concord, ON: Irwin Law.

Marx, Karl. 1853. "Parliamentary Debates – The Clergy Against Socialism – Starvation." *New York Daily Tribune*, 15 Mar. http://www.marxists.org/archive/marx/works/subject/newspapers/new-york-tribune.htm.

Marx, Karl. 1861. "The American Question in England." *New York Daily Tribune*, 11 Octhttps://www.marxists.org/archive/marx/works/subject/newspapers/new-york-tribune.htm.

Marx, Karl, and Friedrich Engels. 1998 [1888]. *The Communist Manifesto*. London: Verso.

McChesney, Robert W. 1997. *Corporate Media and the Threat to Democracy*. New York: Seven Stories Press.

McChesney, Robert W. 2004. *The Problem of the Media*. New York: Monthly Review Press.

McChesney, Robert W. 2007. *Communications Revolution: Critical Junctures and the Future of Media*. New York: New Press.

McChesney, Robert W. 2011. "The Crisis of Journalism and the Internet." In *News Online: Transformation and Continuities*, ed. Graham Meikle and Guy Redden, 53–68. New York: Palgrave Macmillan.

McChesney, Robert W. 2012. "Farewell to Journalism: Time for a Rethinking?" *Journalism Practice* 6 (5–6): 614–26. http://dx.doi.org/10.1080/17512786.2012.683273.

McChesney, Robert W., and John Nichols. 2002. *Our Media, Not Theirs: The Democratic Struggle Against Corporate Media*. New York: Seven Stories Press.

McChesney, Robert W., and John Nichols. 2010. *The Death and Life of American Journalism*. Philadelphia: Nation Books / Perseus.

McChesney, Robert W., and Victor Pickard, eds. 2011. *Will the Last Reporter Please Turn Out the Lights: The Collapse of Journalism and What Can Be Done to Fix It*. New York: New Press.

McCombs, Maxwell E., and Donald L. Shaw. 1972. "The Agenda Setting Function of Mass Media." *Public Opinion Quarterly* 36 (2): 176–89. http://dx.doi.org/10.1086/267990.

McGuire, Jennifer. 2010. "Transitioning On-Line." Lecture presented at the Reader's Digest Annual Lecture Series, Concordia University, Montreal, 12 Mar.

McKercher, Catherine. 2002. *Newsworkers Unite*. Lanham, MD: Rowman and Littlefield.

McKibben, Bill. 2012. "Global Warming's Terrifying New Math." *Rolling Stone*, 19 July. http://www.rollingstone.com/politics/news/global-warmings-terrifying-new-math-20120719?link=mostpopular1.

McLeod, John. 2001. "Using Grounded Theory." In *Qualitative Research in Counseling and Psychotherapy*. London: Sage.

McQuail, Denis. 1992. *Media Performance: Mass Communication and the Public Interest*. London: Sage.

McQuail, Denis. 2010. *Mass Communication Theory*. London: Sage.

Meadows, Michael. 1988. "The Jewel in the Crown: The Coming of Television to the Torres Strait Could be as Significant as the Impact of Religion There, 117 Years Ago." *Australian Journalism Review* 10 (1–2): 162–9.

Meadows, Michael. 1993. "The Way People Want to Talk: Media Representation and Indigenous Media Responses in Australia and Canada." Doctoral dissertation, School of Humanities, Griffith University.

Meadows, Michael. 1994. "The Way People Want to Talk: Indigenous Media Production in Australia and Canada." *Media Information Australia* 73: 64–73.

Meadows, Michael. 1998. "Racism, Citizenship and Indigenous Media." *CQU Journal of Communication and Cultural Studies* 4: 52–69.

Meadows, Michael. 2000. "Deals and Victories: Newspaper Coverage of Native Title in Australia and Canada." *Australian Journalism Review* 22 (1): 81–105.

Meadows, Michael. 2001. *Voices in the Wilderness: Indigenous Australians and the News Media*. Westport, CN: Greenwood.

Meadows, Michael. 2005. "Journalism and Indigenous Public Spheres." *Pacific Journalism Review* 11 (1): 36–41.

Meadows, Michael. 2010. "Conducting Conversations: Exploring the Audience-Producer Relationship in Indigenous Media Research." *Observatorio* 4 (4): 307–24.

Meadows, Michael. 2012. "When the Stars Align: Indigenous Media Policy Formation 1998–2008." In *The Media and Indigenous Policy: How News Media Reporting and Mediatized Practice Impact on Indigenous Policy*, ed. Kerry McCallum, 23–32. Canberra: University of Canberra.

Meadows, Michael, Susan Forde, Jacqui Ewart, and Kerrie Foxwell. 2007. *Community Media Matters: An Audience Study of the Australian Community Broadcasting Sector*. Brisbane: Nathan Griffith Centre for Cultural Research.

Meadows, Michael, Susan Forde, Jacqui Ewart, and Kerrie Foxwell. 2009. "Making Good Sense: Transformative Processes in Community Journalism." *Journalism* 10 (2): 155–70. http://dx.doi.org/10.1177/1464884908100599.

Meadows, Michael, and Kerrie Foxwell. 2011. "Community Broadcasting and Mental Health: The Role of Local Radio and Television in Enhancing Emotional and Social Wellbeing." *Radio Journal* 9 (2): 89–106.

Mensing, Donica. 2010. "Rethinking [Again] the Future of Journalism Education." *Journalism Studies* 11 (4): 511–23. http://dx.doi.org/10.1080/14616701003638376.

Menzies, Peter. 2008. "Dissenting Opinion of Commissioner Peter Menzies." *Broadcasting Public Notice 2008-100.* Canadian Radio-television and Telecommunications Commission. http://www.crtc.gc.ca.

Mercer, Colin. 1989. "Antonio Gramsci: E-Laborare, or the Work and Government of Culture." Paper presented at the TASA conference, La Trobe University, Melbourne, Australia, Dec.

Merrill, John. 1974. *The Imperative of Freedom: A Philosophy of Journalistic Autonomy.* New York: Hastings House.

Merrill, John. 2006. *Media, Mission, and Morality: A Scholarly Milestone Essay in Mass Communication.* Spokane, WA: Marquette.

Merritt, Davis. 1998. *Public Journalism and Public Life: Why Telling the News Is Not Enough.* 2nd ed. Mahwah, NJ: Lawrence Erlbaum.

Merritt, Davis, Jay Rosen, and Lisa Austin, eds. 1997. *Public Journalism: Theory and Practice – Lessons from Experience.* Dayton, OH: Kettering Foundation.

Messina, Chris. 2010. "Hashtags Introduction." *Twitter Fan Wiki.* http://twitter.pbworks.com/w/page/1779812/Hashtags.

Metzgar, Emily T., David D. Kurpius, and Karen M. Rowley. 2011. "Defining Hyperlocal Media: Proposing a Framework for Discussion." *New Media & Society* 13 (5): 772–87. http://dx.doi.org/10.1177/1461444810385095.

Meyer, David S. 2005. "Social Movements and Public Policy: Eggs, Chicken, and Theory." In *Routing the Opposition: Social Movements, Public Policy, and Democracy,* ed. David S. Meyer, Valerie Jenness, and Helen Ingram, 1–26. Minneapolis: University of Minnesota Press.

Meyers, Oren. 2008. "Contextualizing Alternative Journalism." *Journalism Studies* 9 (3): 374–91. http://dx.doi.org/10.1080/14616700801999170.

Michaels, Eric. 1986. *Aboriginal Invention of Television Central Australia 1982–1985.* Canberra: Australian Institute of Aboriginal Studies.

Milan, Stefania. 2008. "What Makes You Happy? Insights into Feelings and Muses of Community Radio Practitioners." *Westminster Papers in Communication and Culture* 5 (1): 25–43.

Miller, Carolyn, Lee Rainie, Kristen Purcell, Amy Mitchell, and Tom Rosenstiel. 2012. "How People Get Local News and Information in Different Communities." *Pew Internet and American Life Project, Project for Excellence in Journalism, Knight Foundation,* 26 Sept. http://www.pewinternet.org/%7E/media//Files/Reports/2012/PIP_Local_News_and_Community_Types.pdf.

Miller, Hugo. 2014. "NSA Spying Sends Data Clients North of Border: Corporate Canada." *Bloomberg,* 9 Jan. http://www.bloomberg.com/news/articles/2014-01-09/nsa-spying-sends-data-clients-north-of-the-border.

Miller, John. 1998. *Yesterday's News.* Toronto: Fernwood.

Miller, Peter H. 2009. "The Business of Canadian OTA Television." *Canadian Radio-television and Telecommunications Commission*, 31 Aug. http://www.crtc.gc.ca/eng/publications/reports/miller09.htm.

Mitchelstein, Eugenia, and Pablo J. Boczkowski. 2009. "Between Tradition and Change: A Review of Recent Research on Online News Production." *Journalism* 10 (5): 562–86. http://dx.doi.org/10.1177/1464884909106533.

Molnar, Helen, and Michael Meadows. 2001. *Songlines to Satellites: Indigenous Communication in Australia, the South Pacific and Canada*. Annandale, Australia: Pluto.

Morison, Ora. 2012. "Consumers' Gain Is TV Stations' Loss as CRTC Cuts Local Programming Fund." *Globe and Mail*, 18 July. http://www.theglobeandmail.com/technology/tech-news/crtc-ruling-to-reduce-cable-satellite-bills/article4424958/.

Moser, Susanne C., and Lisa Dilling, eds. 2007. "Introduction." In *Creating a Climate for Change, Communicating Climate Change, and Facilitating Social Change*, 1–28. Cambridge: Cambridge University Press. http://dx.doi.org/10.1017/CBO9780511535871.003.

Mouffe, Chantal. 2000. *The Democratic Paradox*. New York: Verso.

Mouffe, Chantal. 2005. *On the Political*. New York: Routledge.

Muhlmann, Géraldine. 2004. *Du journalisme en démocratie*. Paris: Payot and Rivages.

Muhlmann, Géraldine. 2010. *Journalism for Democracy*. Trans. Jean Birrell. London: Polity.

Napoli, Philip M. 2000. "The Localism Principle Under Stress." *Info* 2 (6): 573–82. http://dx.doi.org/10.1108/14636690010801735.

Napoli, Philip M. 2001a. *Foundations of Communications Policy: Principles and Process in the Regulation of Electronic Media*. New York: Hampton.

Napoli, Philip M. 2001b. "The Localism Principle in Communications Policymaking and Policy Analysis: Ambiguity, Inconsistency, and Empirical Neglect." *Policy Studies Journal* 29 (3): 372–87. http://dx.doi.org/10.1111/j.1541-0072.2001.tb02099.x.

Napoli, Philip M., and Minna Aslama, eds. 2011. *Communications Research in Action: Scholar-Activist Collaborations for a Democratic Public Sphere*. New York: Fordham University Press.

Nerone, John. 2009. "To Rescue Journalism from the Media." *Cultural Studies* 23 (2): 243–58. http://dx.doi.org/10.1080/09502380802670406.

Newspapers Canada. 2015. "Ownership." http://www.newspaperscanada.ca/ownership.

Niblock, Sarah. 2008. "Features." In *Pulling Newspapers Apart: Analysing Print Journalism*, ed. Bob Franklin, 48–57. New York: Routledge.

Nichols, John, and Robert W. McChesney. 2005. *Tragedy and Farce: How the American Media Sell Wars, Spin Elections, and Destroy Democracy*. New York: New Press.

Nielsen, Greg. 2009. "Framing Dialogue on Immigration in the *New York Times*." *Aether: The Journal of Media Geography* IV (Spring): 37–57.

Nielsen, Greg, Brian Gabrial, Mike Gasher, Dominique Legros, and Lisa Lynch. 2009. *A New Ethics for Civic Journalism*. FQRSC Emergent Team Grant Proposal.

Nielsen, Rasmus K., and David A. Levy. 2010. "The Changing Business of Journalism and Its Implications for Democracy." In *The Changing Business of Journalism and Its Implications for Democracy*, ed. David A. Levy and Rasmus K. Nielsen, 3–15. Oxford: Reuters Institute for the Study of Journalism.

Nielsen, Rasmus K., and Geert Linnebank. 2011. *Public Support for the Media: A Six-Country Overview of Direct and Indirect Subsidies*. Oxford: Reuters Institute for the Study of Journalism.

Nip, Joyce. 2006. "Exploring the Second Phase of Public Journalism." *Journalism Studies* 7 (2): 212–36. http://dx.doi.org/10.1080/14616700500533528.

Nisbet, Matthew C. 2009. "Communicating Climate Change: Why Frames Matter for Public Engagement." *Environment: Science and Policy for Sustainable Development* (Mar.–Apr.). http://www.environmentmagazine.org/Archives/Back%20Issues/March-April%202009/Nisbet-full.html.

Nordicity. 2011. *Analysis of Government Support for Public Broadcasting and other Culture in Canada*. Apr. http://www.nordicity.com/media/20121112jzxkpxjc.pdf.

Norris, Pippa. 2000. *A Virtuous Circle: Political Communications in Postindustrial Societies*. Cambridge: Cambridge University Press. http://dx.doi.org/10.1017/CBO9780511609343.

O'Carroll, Lisa. 2012. "Paul Dacre Calls for New Certifying System for Journalists." *Guardian*, 6 Feb. http://www.theguardian.com/media/2012/feb/06/paul-dacre-leveson-certifying-journalists?CMP=EMCMEDEML665.

Office of Communication (Ofcom). 2009a. *Local and Regional Media in the UK*. http://stakeholders.ofcom.org.uk/market-data-research/other/tv-research/lrmuk/.

Office of Communication (Ofcom). 2009b. *Local and Regional Media in the UK: Nations and Regions Case Studies: Local and Regional Media in the UK: Annex 2*. http://stakeholders.ofcom.org.uk/binaries/research/tv-research/lrmannex2.pdf.

Ontario Community Newspaper Association (OCNA). 2011. *Ontario Community Newspaper Ownership and Title Statistics 1998–2011*. Burlington, ON: Ontario Community Newspaper Assocation.

Openly Local. 2015. "Hyperlocal Sites in UK and Ireland." http://localweblist.net/.

Open Net Initiative. 2012. "Global Internet Filtering in 2012 at a Glance." 3 Apr https://opennet.net/blog/2012/04/global-internet-filtering-2012-glance.

OpenMedia. 2014. "Government's Digital Strategy Leaves Canada Stuck in the Slow Lane." 4 Apr. https://openmedia.ca/news/government%E2%80%99s-digital-strategy-leaves-canada-stuck-slow-lane-fails-tackle-stark-digital-divide-and-na.

Overholser, Geneva. 2009. "What Is Journalism's Place in Social Media?" *Nieman Reports* (Fall). http://nieman.harvard.edu/reportsitem.aspx?id=101882.

Paulussen, Steve, and Evelien D'heer. 2013. "Using Citizens for Community Journalism: Findings from a Hyperlocal Media Project." *Journalism Practice* 7 (5): 588–603. http://dx.doi.org/10.1080/17512786.2012.756667.

Pavlik, John V. 2013. "Trends in New Media Research: A Critical Review of Recent Scholarship." *Sociology Compass* 7 (1): 1–12. http://dx.doi.org/10.1111/soc4.12004.

Pew Research Center, Project for Excellence in Journalism. 2014. *State of the News Media 2014: An Annual Report on American Journalism.* 26 Mar. http://www.journalism.org/2014/03/26/the-growth-in-digital-reporting/.

Phelps, Andrew. 2012. "MinnPost Ends 2011 in the Black." *Nieman Lab*, 26 Jan. http://www.niemanlab.org/2012/01/minnpost-ends-2011-in-the-black-adds-a-million-minnesotans/.

Pickard, Victor. 2011. "Can Government Support the Press? Historicizing and Internationalizing a Policy Approach to the Journalism Crisis." *Communication Review* 14 (2): 73–95. http://dx.doi.org/10.1080/10714421.2011.573430.

Pickard, Victor, Josh Stearns, and Craig Aaron. 2009. *Saving the News: Toward a National Journalism Strategy.* Washington, DC: Free Press.

Platon, Sara, and Mark Deuze. 2003. "Indymedia Journalism: A Radical Way of Making, Selecting, Sharing News?" *Journalism* 4 (3): 336–55. http://dx.doi.org/10.1177/14648849030043005.

Pollon, Christopher. 2012. "Great Bear Forest to Be Massive Carbon Offset Project." *Tyee*, 11 June. http://thetyee.ca/News/2012/06/11/Great-Bear-Carbon-Offset/.

Poster, Mark. 2001. *What's the Matter with the Internet?* Minneapolis: University of Minnesota Press.

Powell, Douglas. 2007. *Critical Regionalism: Connecting Politics and Culture in the American Landscape*. Chapel Hill, NC: University of North Carolina Press.

Preston, Julia. 2007. "Farmers Call Crackdown on Illegal Workers Unfair." *New York Times*, 11 Aug., A10.

Prévost, Hélène. 2012. "Le Navire 'Night.'" *Radio-Canada*, 15 Aug. http://ici .radio-canada.ca/radio/navire/.

Price, Monroe, and Peter Krug. 2000. *The Enabling Environment for Free and Independent Media*. Oxford: Programme in Comparative Media Law and Policy, Centre for Socio-Legal Studies, University of Oxford. http://papers. ssrn.com/sol3/papers.cfm?abstract_id=245494. http://dx.doi.org/10.2139/ ssrn.245494.

Public Values. 2012. "About Us." http://www.publicvalues.ca/AboutUs.cfm.

Puijk, Roel. 2008. "Ethnographic Media Production Research in a Digital Environment." In *Making Online News: The Ethnography of New Media Production*, ed. Chris Paterson and David Domingo, 29–44. New York: Peter Lang.

Putnam, Robert D. 1995. "Bowling Alone: America's Declining Social Capital." *Journal of Democracy* 6 (1): 65–78. http://dx.doi.org/10.1353/jod.1995.0002.

Quandt, Thorsten, and Jane B. Singer. 2009. "Convergence and Cross-Platform Content Production." In *Handbook of Journalism Studies*, ed. Karin Wahl-Jorgensen and Thomas Hanitzsch, 130–44. New York: Routledge.

Québec. 2003. Comité conseil sur la qualité et la diversité de l'information. *Les effets de la concentration des médias au Quebec: problématique, recerces et consultations*. Jan. http://www.mcc.gouv.qc.ca/publications/rapportst -jeantome_2.pdf.

Québec. 2010. Groupe de travail sur le journalisme et l'avenir de l'information au Québec. *L'information au Québec: un intérêt public*. (The Payette Report). Dec. Quebec: Groupe de travail sur le journalisme et l'avenir de l'information au Québec.

Quebecor. 2014. "Sale of Sun Media Corporation's English-Language Assets: Quebecor Reaches a $316 Million Agreement with Postmedia." Oct. http:// www.quebecor.com/en/comm/sale-sun-media-corporation%E2%80%99s -english-language-assets-quebecor-reaches-316-million-agreement-pos.

Quinn, Steven. 2005. *Convergent Journalism: The Fundamentals of Multimedia Reporting*. New York: Peter Lang.

Quinn, Steven. 2006. *Conversations on Convergence: Insiders' Views on News Production in the 21st Century*. New York: Peter Lang.

Raboy, Marc. 1990. *Missed Opportunities: The Story of Canada's Broadcasting Policy*. Montreal: McGill-Queen's University.

Raboy, Marc. 2006. "The 2005 Graham Spry Memorial Lecture, Making Media: Creating the Conditions for Communication in the Public Good." *Canadian Journal of Communication* 31 (2): 289–306.

Raboy, Marc, and Jeremy Shtern, eds. 2010. *Media Divides: Communication Rights and the Right to Communicate in Canada*. Vancouver: UBC Press.

Raboy, Marc, and David Taras. 2004. "The Politics of Neglect of Canadian Broadcasting Policy." *Policy Options* (Mar.): 63–8.

Radio-Canada. 2011. "Les grands chantiers de la métropole toujours perturbés." *Ici Radio-Canada*, 25 Oct. www.radio-canada.ca/regions/Montreal/2011/10/25/001-chantiers-situation-mardi.shtml.

Radio-Canada. 2014. "Restructuration de Radio-Canada: Une catastrophe, selon les syndicats." *Ici Radio-Canada*, 26 June. http://ici.radio-canada.ca/nouvelles/societe/2014/06/26/003-radio-canada-hubert-lacroix-reactions-alex-levasseur.shtml.

Rancière, Jacques. 1999. *Disagreement*. Minneapolis: University of Minnesota Press.

Rancière, Jacques. 2006. *The Hatred of Democracy*. London: Verso.

Rebillard, Franck. 2009. "Les évolutions du secteur des médias, vues de l'intérieur." *Les Cahiers du Journalisme* 20: 128–51.

Reese, Stephen D. 2010. "Journalism and Globalization." *Sociology Compass* 4 (6): 344–53. http://dx.doi.org/10.1111/j.1751-9020.2010.00282.x.

Reese, Stephen D., Lou Rutigliano, Kideuk Hyun, and Jaekwan Jeong. 2007. "Mapping the Blogosphere: Professional and Citizen-Based Media in the Global News Arena." *Journalism* 8 (3): 235–61. http://dx.doi.org/10.1177/1464884907076459.

Reimagine CBC. 2015. "ReimagineCBC." http://reimaginecbc.ca/share.

Rennie, Ellie. 2006. *Community Media: A Global Introduction*. Lanham, MD: Rowman and Littlefield.

Rennie, Ellie. 2007. ""Community Media in the Prosumer Era': 3CMedia." *Journal of Community, Citizen's and Third Sector Media* 3: 25–32.

Richards, Ian. 2013. "Beyond City Limits: Regional Journalism and Social Capital." *Journalism* 14 (5): 627–42. http://dx.doi.org/10.1177/1464884912453280.

Robertson, Grant. 2009. "A Week of Reckoning for Canadian TV." *Globe and Mail*, 31 Aug., B3.

Rochon, Thomas R. 1998. *Culture Moves*. Princeton, NJ: Princeton University Press.

Rodriguez, Clemencia. 2001. *Fissures in the Mediascape: An International Study of Citizens' Media*. Cresskill, NJ: Hampton.

Rodriguez, Clemencia. 2002. "Citizens' Media and the Voice of the Angel/ Poet." *Media International Australia* 103: 78–87.

Rodriguez, Clemencia, Dorothy Kidd, and Laura Stein, eds. 2009. *Making Our Media: Mapping Global Initiatives Toward a Democratic Public Sphere.* Cresskill, NJ: Hampton.

Romano, Angela. 2010. *International Journalism and Democracy: Civic Engagement Models from Around the World.* New York: Routledge.

Rosen, Jay. 1999. *What Are Journalists For?* New Haven, CT: Yale University Press.

Rosen, Jay. 2006. "The People Formerly Known as the Audience." *PressThink*, 27 June 27http://archive.pressthink.org/2006/06/27/ppl_frmr.html.

Rosenberry, Jack. 2011. "Key Works: Some Connections Between Journalism and Community." In *Foundations of Community Journalism*, ed. Bill Reader and John A. Hatcher, 25–42. Thousand Oaks, CA: Sage.

Roth, Lorna. 2005. *Something in the Air: The Story of First Peoples' Television Broadcasting in Canada.* Montreal: McGill-Queen's University Press.

Sabato, Larry. 1991. *Feeding Frenzy: How Attack Journalism Has Transformed American Politics.* New York: Free Press.

Salamon, Errol. 2012. "*Bridging Divides in Journalism Theory and Practice: A Case Study of the Journalism Strategies Conference.*" Roundtable conducted at the meeting of the Canadian Communication Association, Waterloo, ON, May–June.

Salter, Liora, and Rick Salter. 1997. "Displacing the Welfare State." In *Understanding Canada: Building on the New Canadian Political Economy*, ed. Wallace Clement, 311–37. Montreal: McGill-Queen's University Press.

Sauvageau, Florian. 2012. "The Uncertain Future of the News." In *How Canadians Communicate IV*, ed. David Taras and Christopher Waddell, 29–44. Edmonton, AB: University of Alberta Press.

Savage, Philip. 2008. "Gaps in Canadian Media Research: CMRC Findings." *Canadian Journal of Communication* 33 (2): 291–301.

Scammell, Margaret, and Holli A. Semetko. 2000. *The Media, Journalism, and Democracy.* Burlington, VT: Ashgate.

Schechter, Danny. 2009. "Credit Crisis: How Did We Miss It?" *British Journalism Review* 20 (1): 19–26. http://dx.doi.org/10.1177/095647 4809104199.

Scherer, Éric. 2011. *A-t-on encore besoin des journalistes?* Paris: Presses universitaires de France. http://dx.doi.org/10.3917/puf.hemi.2011.01.

Schiller, Dan. 1981. *Objectivity and the News.* Philadelphia: University of Pennsylvania Press.

Schudson, Michael. 2003. *The Sociology of News.* New York: W.W. Norton.

Schweizer, Sarah, Jessica L. Thompson, Tara Teel, and Brett Bruyere. 2009. "Strategies for Communicating About Climate Change Impacts on Public Lands." *Science Communication* 31 (2): 266–74. http://dx.doi .org/10.1177/1075547009352971.

Segnit, Nat, and Gill Ereaut. 2007. *Warm Words II: How the Climate Story Is Evolving and the Lessons We Can Learn / Or Encouraging Public Action.* London: Institute for Public Policy Research.

Shade, Leslie R. 2005. "Aspergate: Concentration, Convergence and Censorship in Canadian Media." In *Converging Media, Diverging Politics*, ed. David Skinner, James Compton, and Mike Gasher, 101–16. Lanham, MD: Lexington.

Shade, Leslie R, ed. 2009. *Mediascapes: New Patterns in Canadian Communication.* Toronto: Nelson Education.

Shade, Leslie R., and Michael Lithgow. 2010. "The Cultures of Democracy: How Ownership and Public Participation Shape Canada's Media System." In *Mediascapes: New Patterns in Canadian Communication*, 3rd ed., ed. Leslie R. Shade, 200–20. Toronto: Nelson Education.

Shirky, Clay. 2008. *Here Comes Everybody: The Power of Organizing Without Organizations.* New York: Penguin.

Shochat, Gil. 2010. "The Dark Country." *Walrus* (Jan.–Feb.). http://thewalrus. ca/the-dark-country/.

Shoemaker, Pamela J. 1996. "Media Gatekeeping." In *An Integrated Approach to Communication Theory and Research*, ed. Michael B. Salwen and Don W. Stacks, 79–92. Mahwah, NJ: Lawrence Erlbaum.

Shoemaker, Pamela J., and Tim J. Vos. 2009. *Gatekeeping Theory.* New York: Routledge.

Siles, Ignacio, and Pablo J. Boczkowski. 2012. "Making Sense of the Newspaper Crisis: A Critical Assessment of Existing Research and an Agenda for Future Work." *New Media & Society* 14 (8): 1375–94. http:// dx.doi.org/10.1177/1461444812455148.

Singer, Jane B. 2004. "More than Ink-Stained Wretches: The Resocialization of Print Journalists in Converged Newsrooms." *Journalism & Mass Communication Quarterly* 81 (4): 838–56. http://dx.doi.org/10.1177/ 107769900408100408.

Singer, Jane B. 2006. "Partnerships and Public Service: Normative Issues for Journalists in Converged Newsrooms." *Journal of Mass Media Ethics* 21 (1): 30–53. http://dx.doi.org/10.1207/s15327728jmme2101_3.

Skinner, David. 2012. "Sustaining Independent and Alternative Media." In *Alternative Media in Canada*, ed. Kirsten Kozolanka, Patricia Mazepa, and David Skinner, 25–45. Vancouver: UBC Press.

Skinner, David, James R. Compton, and Mike Gasher, eds. 2005. *Converging Media, Diverging Politics: A Political Economy of News Media in the United States and Canada*. Oxford: Lexington.

Skinner, David, and Mike Gasher. 2005. "So Much by So Few: Media Policy and Ownership in Canada." In *Converging Media, Diverging Politics*, ed. David Skinner, James Compton, and Mike Gasher, 51–76. Lanham, MD: Lexington.

Skoler, Michael. 2009. "Why the News Media Became Irrelevant – And How Social Media Can Help." *Neiman Reports* 63 (3): 38–40.

Soderlund, Walter C., Colette Brin, Lydia Miljan, and Kai Hildebrandt. 2012. *Cross-Media Ownership and Democratic Practice in Canada*. Edmonton, AB: University of Alberta Press.

Soffer, Oren. 2009. "The Competing Ideals of Objectivity and Dialogue in American Journalism." *Journalism* 10 (4): 473–91. http://dx.doi.org/10.1177/1464884909104950.

Soroka, Stuart N. 2007. "Agenda-Setting and Issue Definition." In *Critical Policy Studies*, ed. Michael Orsini and Miriam Smith, 185–210. Vancouver: UBC Press.

Sparks, Robert, Mary Lynn Young, and Simon Darnell. 2006. "Convergence, Corporate Restructuring, and Canadian Online News, 2000–2003." *Canadian Journal of Communication* 31 (2): 391–423.

Spry, Graham. 1965. "The Origins of Public Broadcasting in Canada: A Comment." *Canadian Historical Review* 46 (2): 134–41. http://dx.doi.org/10.3138/CHR-046-02-03.

Stamm, Keith R. 1985. *Newspaper Use and Community Ties: Toward a Dynamic Theory*. Norwood, NJ: Ablex.

Statistics Canada. 2011. *Service Bulletin: Newspaper Publishers 2010*. http://www.statcan.gc.ca/pub/63-241-x/63-241-x2012001-eng.htm.

Statistics Canada. 2013a. *Canadian Internet Use Survey, 2012*. http://www.statcan.gc.ca/daily-quotidien/131126/dq131126d-eng.htm.

Statistics Canada. 2013b. *Individual Internet Use and E-Commerce*. http://www.statcan.gc.ca/daily-quotidien/131028/dq131028a-eng.htm.

Stavitsky, Alan G. 1994. "The Changing Conception of Localism in U.S. Public Radio." *Journal of Broadcasting & Electronic Media* 38 (1): 19–33. http://dx.doi.org/10.1080/08838159409364243.

Straight Goods. n.d. "About Us." Accessed 28 May 2012. http://wwwstraightgoods.ca/Services/Masthead.cfm.

Streitmatter, Rodger. 2001. *Voices of Revolution: The Dissident Press in America*. New York: Columbia University Press.

Summerfield, Patti. 2006. "CHUM Swept by Layoffs amid News Overhaul." *Playback*, 24 July. http://playbackonline.ca/2006/07/24/layoffs-20060724/.

Taras, David. 2001. *Power and Betrayal in the Canadian Media*. 2nd ed. Toronto: Broadview.

Television, Maori. 2013. *Annual Report 2011*. http://www.maoritelevision.com/about/about-maori-television/official-publications.

Tellis, Winston. 1997. "Introduction to Case Study." *Qualitative Report* 3 (2). http://nsuworks.nova.edu/tqr/vol3/iss2/4

Terdiman, Daniel. 2010. "Photo of Hudson River Crash Downs Twitpic." *CNET News*, 15 Jan. www.cnet.com/news/photo-of-hudson-river-plane-crash-downs-twitpic/

Therborn, Göran. 2008. *From Marxism to Post-Marxism*. London: Verso.

Thomashow, Mitchell. 2002. *Bringing the Biosphere Home: Learning to Perceive Global Environmental Change*. Cambridge, MA: MIT Press.

Thompson, Jessica L., and Sarah E. Schweizer. 2008. "The Conventions of Climate Change Communication." Paper presented at the National Communication Association Convention, San Diego, CA, 20–4 Nov.

Thompson, John B. 1995. *The Media and Modernity: A Social Theory of the Media*. Stanford, CA: Stanford University Press.

Tinic, Serra. 2005. *On Location: Canada's Television Industry in a Global Market*. Toronto: University of Toronto Press.

Tinic, Serra. 2010. "The Global Economic Meltdown: A Crisotunity for Canada's Private Sector Broadcasters?" *Popular Communication* 8 (3): 193–7. http://dx.doi.org/10.1080/15405702.2010.493460.

Underwood, Doug. 1993. *When MBAs Rule the Newsroom: How the Marketers and Managers Are Reshaping Today's Media*. New York: Columbia University Press.

Ursell, Gillan. 2001. "Dumbing Down or Shaping Up?: New Technologies, New Media, New Journalism." *Journalism* 2 (2): 175–96. http://dx.doi.org/10.1177/146488490100200204.

Valaskakis, Gail G. 1993. "Parallel Voices: Indians and Others – Narratives of Cultural Struggle." *Canadian Journal of Communication* 18 (3). http://www.cjc-online.ca/index.php/journal/article/view/756/662.

Van Maanen, John. 1988. *Tales of the Field: On Writing Ethnography*. Chicago: University of Chicago Press.

Van Vuuren, Kitty. 2006. "Community Broadcasting and the Enclosure of the Public Sphere." *Media Culture & Society* 28 (3): 379–92. http://dx.doi.org/10.1177/0163443706062891.

Villeneuve, Nart. 2006. "The Filtering Matrix: Integrated Mechanisms of Information Control and the Demarcation of Borders in Cyberspace."

First Monday 11 (1–2). http://firstmonday.org/ojs/index.php/fm/article/view/1307/1227.

Villeneuve, Nart. 2012. "Fake Skype Encryption Service Cloaks DarkComet Trojan." *Trend Micro Inc.*, 20 Apr. http://blog.trendmicro.com/trendlabs-security-intelligence/fake-skype-encryption-software-cloaks-darkcomet-trojan/.

Vipond, Mary. 2011. *The Mass Media in Canada.* 4th ed. Toronto: James Lorimer.

von Finckenstein, K. 2007. Speech given at the annual Convention of the Canadian Association of Broadcasters, Ottawa, 5 Nov.

von Finckenstein, K. 2011. Speech given at the Banff World Media Festival. http://www.crtc.gc.ca/eng/com200/2011/s110613.htm.

Waddell, Christopher. 2009. "The Future for the Canadian Media." *Policy Options* 30 (6): 16–21.

Wahl-Jorgensen, Karin. 2008. "Op-Ed Pages." In *Pulling Newspapers Apart: Analysing Print Journalism,* ed. Bob Franklin, 70–8. New York: Routledge.

Waldman, Steven. 2011. *The Information Needs of Communities: The Changing Media Landscape in a Broadband Age.* Federal Communications Commission, July. www.fcc.gov/infoneedsreport.

Wallace, Kenyon. 2012. "Competitors Try to Block Bell Canada from Buying Astral Media." *Toronto Star,* 9 Sept. http://www.thestar.com/news/canada/2012/09/09/competitors_try_to_block_bell_canada_from_buying_astral_media.html.

Waltz, Mitzi. 2005. *Alternative and Activist Media.* Edinburgh: Edinburgh University Press.

Ward, Stephen J.A. 2004. *The Invention of Journalism Ethics: The Path to Objectivity and Beyond.* Montreal: McGill-Queen's University Press.

Washburn, Robert. 2010. "Hyperlocal News in Canada: A J-Source Project." *J-Source,* 3 Mar. http://www.projetj.info/article/hyperlocal-news-canada-j-source-project.

Washburn, Robert. 2011. "Hyperlocal News Is Not Dead Despite Rumours." *J-Source,* 26 Feb. http://jsource.ca/article/hyperlocal-news-not-dead-despite-rumours.

Waterman, Ellen. 2007. "Radio Bodies: Discourse, Performance, Resonance." In *Radio Territories,* ed. Erik G. Jensen and Brandon LaBelle, 118–34. Los Angeles: Errant Bodies.

Watershed Sentinel. n.d. "About the Watershed Sentinel." Accessed 30 May 2012. http://www.watershedsentinel.ca/content/about-watershed-sentinel.

Weinberg, Darin. 2008. "The Philosophical Foundations of Constructionist Research." In *Handbook of Constructionist Research,* ed. James A. Holstein and Jaber F. Gubrium, 13–40. New York: Guilford.

Wennersten, Marie. 2007. "To See with Each Other's Ears: SR c and Ambiguous Radio." In *Radio Territories*, ed. Erik G. Jensen and Brandon LaBelle, 84–9. Los Angeles: Errant Bodies.

Weston, Mary Ann. 1996. *Native Americans in the News: Images of Indians in the Twentieth Century Press*. Westport, CN: Greenwood.

Wiesner, Peter K. 2010. "Media for the People: The Canadian Experiments with Film and Video in Community Development." In *Challenge for Change: Activist Documentary at the National Film Board of Canada*, ed. Thomas Waugh, Michael Brendan Baker, and Ezra Winton, 73–102. Montreal: McGill-Queen's University Press.

Williams, Bruce A., and Michael X. Delli-Carpini. 2000. "Unchained Reaction: The Collapse of Media Gatekeeping and the Clinton-Lewinsky Scandal." *Journalism* 1 (1): 61–85. http://dx.doi.org/10.1177/146488490000100113.

Williams, Raymond. 1977. *Marxism and Literature*. London: Oxford University Press.

Wilson, Rob, and Wimal Dissanayake, eds. 1996a. *Global-Local: Cultural Production and the Transnational Imaginary*. Durham, NC: Duke University Press. http://dx.doi.org/10.1215/9780822381990.

Wilson, Rob, and Wimal Dissanayake. 1996b. "Introduction: Tracking the Global / Local." In *Global-Local: Cultural Production and the Transnational Imaginary*, ed. Rob Wilson and Wimal Dissanayake, 1–45. Durham, NC: Duke University Press. http://dx.doi.org/10.1215/9780822381990-001.

Winseck, Dwayne. 1998. *Reconvergence: A Political Economy of Telecommunications in Canada*. Cresskill, NJ: Hampton.

Winseck, Dwayne. 2010. "What Media Crisis?" *Mark*, 30 July. http://pioneers.themarknews.com/articles/1883-what-media-crisis/-. VVTdPUt3IvE.

Winseck, Dwayne. 2014. "Media and Internet Concentration in Canada, 1984–2013." 26 Nov. http://www.cmcrp.org/media-and-internet-concentration-1984-2013/.

Witschge, Tamara. 2013. "Transforming Journalistic Practice: A Profession Caught Between Change and Tradition." In *Rethinking Journalism: Trust and Participation in a Transformed News Landscape*, ed. Chris Peters and Marcel Broersma, 160–72. New York: Routledge.

Wong, Jan. 2013. "Canadian Media Guild Data Shows 10,000 Job Losses in Past Five Years." *J-Source*, 19 Nov. http://j-source.ca/article/canadian-media-guild-data-shows-10000-job-losses-past-five-years.

Wong, Tony. 2014. "CBC to Lose Up to 1,500 More Jobs." *Toronto Star*, 26 June 26.http://www.thestar.com/entertainment/television/2014/06/26/strategic_plan_cuts_hubert_lacroix.html<

World Association of Newspapers (WAN). 2008. *World Press Trends: Newspapers Are a Growth Business.* www.mynewsdesk.com/se/world _association_of_newspapers/pressreleases/world-press-trends -newspapers-are-a-growth-business-219757

Young, Iris Marion. 2000. *Inclusion and Democracy.* Oxford: Oxford University Press.

Zerbisias, Antonia. 2001. "Networks Balk at New Rules for Licenses." *Toronto Star*, 26 Apr., A31.

Contributors

Chris Albinati is a lawyer and graduate student at Osgoode Hall Law School at York University in Toronto where his research is generously supported by a Fellowship from the Law Foundation of British Columbia, his two kids, Theo and Uma, and his partner Carolyn. Chris works to support the Secwepemc people in their struggle to have their Territorial Authority acknowledged by researching Indigenous blockades as exercises of Indigenous law. Chris has been involved with campus and community radio projects and stations for more than ten years.

Christopher Ali is an assistant professor in the Department of Media Studies at the University of Virginia. With a Ph.D. from the Annenberg School for Communication at the University of Pennsylvania, he specializes in media policy, law, and regulation, particularly regarding local media, public media, and community media. His research interests include communication policy and regulation; localism; local media; public and community media; comparative media systems; critical political economy, normative theory; theories of the public and public sphere; and deliberative democracy. He is co-author of the book *Echoes of Gabriel Tarde* (2014) and is working on a new book entitled *Media Localism*, about local media politics in Canada, the United States, and the United Kingdom.

Colette Brin is a professor at Université Laval's Département d'information et de communication and director of the Centre d'études sur les médias. Her research and teaching focus on recent and ongoing changes in journalistic practice, through policy and organizational initiatives, as well as journalists' professional discourse. She is a member of the Chaire de journalisme scientifique and the Groupe de recherche en communication politique.

Kathleen Cross has held faculty positions in communication at Simon Fraser University, as well as Royal Roads and Capilano universities. Her research interests include democratic communication, news media analysis, gender in media, and political campaigns and elections. She was a director with Vancouver's Media Democracy Days from 2009 to 2013.

Christine Crowther was a broadcast journalist for fifteen years, primarily with the CBC. During that time she was based in Regina, Bangkok, Toronto, and London (UK). She is currently a Ph.D. candidate in the Department of Art History and Communication Studies at McGill University, and a lecturer in the Department of Journalism at Concordia University in Montreal.

Catherine Edwards has worked in film and television production since 1988. She is the president of TimeScape Productions and co-founded the Canadian Association of Community Television Users and Stations (CACTUS) in 2008. She has taught, consulted, and conducted research at community media centres worldwide, and is a committed advocate for citizen access to mainstream media.

Chantal Francoeur is a professor in the Department of Journalism at Université du Québec à Montréal. A former journalist with Radio-Canada, she is the author of *La transformation du service de l'information de Radio-Canada* (2013). Her research interests include the relationship between journalism and the public relations industry, public broadcasters, convergence, ethics, and new journalistic formats.

Mike Gasher is a professor and M.A. program director in the Department of Journalism at Concordia University in Montreal, and the director of the Concordia Centre for Broadcasting and Journalism Studies. A former newspaper reporter and editor, he is the principal investigator of the Geography of News Project and co-author of the textbook *Mass Communication in Canada* (2012, 2016).

Pinar Gurleyen is a Ph.D. candidate in the School of Communication at Simon Fraser University. Her research interests include alternative media and alternative journalism.

Robert A. Hackett is a professor of communication at Simon Fraser University, co-director of NewsWatch Canada, and co-founder of the Media Democracy Day project. His recent publications include *Expanding Peace Journalism: Comparative and Critical Approaches* (co-edited, 2011) and *Remaking Media: The Struggle to Democratize Public Communication* (co-authored, 2006). He has co-founded several community-oriented media advocacy and education initiatives, including NewsWatch Canada, Media Democracy Day, and OpenMedia.

Arne Hintz is a lecturer at the School of Journalism, Media and Cultural Studies at Cardiff University, and director of the School's M.A. program in Digital Media ad Society. His research connects communication policy, citizen media, and technological change. He is chair of the Community Communication Section, and vice-chair of the Global Media Policy Working Group of the International Association for Media and Communication Research (IAMCR). He has a practical background as a journalist, media activist, and communication rights advocate. His publications include *Civil Society Media and Global Governance* (2009) and the co-edited volume, *Beyond WikiLeaks: Implications for the Future of Communications, Journalism, and Society* (2013).

Gretchen King is a Ph.D. candidate in communication studies at McGill University. She conducted her dissertation fieldwork at Jordan's first community radio station, Radio al-Balad 92.4 FM. She approaches community radio stations as civic media institutions that facilitate political learning environments and thereby promote social change. Her research enjoys support from Media@McGill, McGill University's Faculty of Arts, the Social Sciences and Humanities Research Council of Canada, and the Fonds de recherche du Québec – Société et la culture. Previously news director at Montreal's community radio station CKUT 90.3 FM for ten years, Gretchen continues to work as a scholar-activist within community media movements and recently published on her experiences in *Islands of Resistance: Pirate Radio in Canada* (2010), *Free City Radio* (2014), *InCirculation* (2014), and *The Civic Media Reader* (2015).

Anabel Khoo is an artist, scholar, facilitator, and community organizer working on initiatives that bring together media production and collective healing through a visionary politics of liberation. She has recently completed an M.A. in communication and culture at York University in Toronto, focusing on two-spirit, queer and trans people of colour performance as social movement building.

Sneha Kulkarni is a brand marketing and public relations professional based in Oakville, Ontario. She works with clients in the manufacturing and retail rectors to create and execute marketing, communications, and business development programs. Prior to joining the marketing and PR field, Sneha gained ten years of experience as a television reporter, anchor, and producer for media outlets in British Columbia, Alberta, and Ontario. Her investigative reporting while with CTV Calgary earned an RTNDA award in 2011. Sneha holds a B.J. from Ryerson University and an M.A. in professional communication from Royal Roads University in Victoria, BC.

Michael Meadows is an adjunct professor of journalism in the School of Humanities at Griffith University in Brisbane, Australia. He worked as a journalist for ten years before moving into journalism education in the late 1980s. Since then, his research interests have included Indigenous and community media, journalism practices, the media representation of race relations and, more recently, media and images of landscape and the environment.

Candace Mooers earned a B.A. in history at the University of New Brunswick and studied in the Joint Graduate Program in Communication and Culture at York and Ryerson universities. She has been involved in community-based campus radio and other alternative media projects for over fifteen years in Fredericton, Halifax, Toronto, and Montreal. She is currently a co-producer of Prison Radio on CKUT 90.3 FM in Montreal.

Greg M. Nielsen is professor of sociology and research fellow with the Concordia Centre for Broadcasting and Journalism Studies at Concordia University in Montreal. He is author of *The Norms of Answerability: Social Theory between Habermas and Bakhtin* (2002) and *Le Canada de Radio-Canada* (1994). He is co-author of *Mediated Society: A Critical Sociology of Media* (2012) and co-editor of *Acts of Citizenship* (2008) and *Revealing Democracy* (2015). His current project at the CCBJS (in collaboration with Mike Gasher) includes a study of how mainstream journalism works to expand or reduce gaps between citizens and non-citizens that are reported on and the ideal audiences implied by the journalistic address.

Marc Raboy is a professor and Beaverbrook Chair in Ethics, Media, and Communications in the Department of Art History and Communication Studies at McGill University. A former journalist and an academic since 1980, he is the author or editor of numerous books, articles, and research reports on different aspects of media and communication policy. From 2006 to 2012, he was the founding director of Media@McGill, a research and public outreach unit on issues and controversies in media, technology, and culture.

Vincent Raynauld is assistant professor in the Department of Communication Studies and a research fellow in the Engagement Lab at Emerson College in Boston. He is a research associate in the Groupe de recherche en communication politique (GRCP) at Université Laval in Quebec, an academic adviser for the non-profit research organization Samara in Toronto, Canada, and he served a research consultant for the Senate of Canada between 2010 and 2012. His areas of research interest and publication include political communication, social media, research methods, e-politics and journalism.

Errol Salamon is a Ph.D. candidate in communication studies at McGill University. His research is focused on political economy, media workers, labour, activism, and policy. His work has been published on *J-Source* and *Rabble.ca*. He was a member of the Community News Collective of CKUT 90.3 FM in Montreal.

Florian Sauvageau is professor emeritus at Université Laval. He spent more than twenty years working in media before devoting himself full-time to teaching and research in the late 1980s. He helped establish Quebec's first journalism program at Laval in 1968.

David Skinner is an associate professor in the Department of Communication Studies at York University. His research centres on the critical analysis of media policy and production, alternative and independent media, and journalism studies. He is also actively engaged with issues of media reform. He is co-editor of *Alternative Media in Canada* (2013) and co-author of the textbook *Mass Communication in Canada* (2012, 2016).

Simon Thibault is an assistant professor in the Department of Political Science at Université de Montréal. He completed in 2015 a joint Ph.D.

degree in communication at Université Sorbonne Nouvelle – Paris III and Université Laval. His research is focused on policies implemented by international actors for reforming the media systems of post-conflict countries. He is the recipient of doctoral scholarships from the Joseph-Armand Bombardier Canada Graduate Scholarships Program (SSHRC) and the Trudeau Foundation.

Jacky Tuinstra Harrison is the general manager of CJRU: The Scope at Ryerson University, and has a background in not-for-profit management. She began her career reporting for *Egypt Today* magazine in Cairo, and freelanced for CBC Radio and the *Globe and Mail*. She is former program director for CKCU Community Radio in Ottawa, former news director of CHRY Radio, and former project coordinator for the National Campus and Community Radio Association.

Robert Washburn teaches in the Journalism: Online, Print and Broadcast program at Loyalist College in Belleville, Ontario, where he specializes in the use of new and emerging technologies in journalism. He is also a columnist at *Northumberland Today* and has worked as a journalist for nearly thirty years in newspapers, magazines, and radio.

Karen Wirsig is on staff at the Canadian Media Guild, coordinating outreach and mobilization efforts as well as policy analysis. A former municipal affairs reporter and community planner, she enjoys participating in projects to improve people's access to information, news, storytelling, and political action.

Index

Lightning Source UK Ltd.
Milton Keynes UK
UKOW02f1104131116

287527UK00003B/90/P